The China Incident

The China Incident
Igniting the Second Sino-Japanese War

G. WILLIAM WHITEHURST

McFarland & Company, Inc., Publishers
Jefferson, North Carolina

LIBRARY OF CONGRESS CATALOGUING-IN-PUBLICATION DATA

Names: Whitehurst, G. William, author.
Title: The China incident : igniting the second Sino-Japanese war / G. William Whitehurst.
Description: Jefferson, North Carolina : McFarland & Company, Inc., Publishers, 2021 | Includes bibliographical references and index.
Identifiers: LCCN 2020038063 | ISBN 9781476682334 (paperback : acid free paper) ∞
ISBN 9781476641355 (ebook)
Subjects: LCSH: Sino-Japanese War, 1937–1945. | China—Foreign relations—Japan. | China—Foreign relations—United States. | Japan—Foreign relations—China. | United States—Foreign relations—China.
Classification: LCC DS777.53 .W49 2021 | DDC 940.53—dc23
LC record available at https://lccn.loc.gov/2020038063

BRITISH LIBRARY CATALOGUING DATA ARE AVAILABLE

ISBN (print) 978-1-4766-8233-4
ISBN (ebook) 978-1-4766-4135-5

© 2021 G. William Whitehurst. All rights reserved

No part of this book may be reproduced or transmitted in any form or by any means, electronic or mechanical, including photocopying or recording, or by any information storage and retrieval system, without permission in writing from the publisher.

Front cover: Japanese soldiers atop the ruins of the City Wall of Nanking, China on December 13, 1937 (Everett Collection/Shutterstock)

Printed in the United States of America

*McFarland & Company, Inc., Publishers
Box 611, Jefferson, North Carolina 28640
www.mcfarlandpub.com*

In memory of
George M. Kaufman,
whose generous spirit
touched many

Acknowledgments

The author wishes to express his gratitude to the following persons whose help contributed to this book: John Magill, who utilized his position on Capitol Hill to secure much-needed research material; Justus P. White, for his unpublished doctoral manuscript notes; Gary Bonnewell, who gave the author access to the memorabilia of his grandfather, A.L. Zavilenski, a member of the crew of the USS *Augusta*; the National Archives, which made available the photographs referenced in this book; Dr. Tim Orr at Old Dominion University, who critiqued the first chapter and offered wise suggestions for changes; Helen E. Spore, for proofreading; my daughter, Frances W. Russell, who typed and edited my manuscript and communicated with the publisher; and finally, my late wife, Janie Whitehurst, who typed the original draft and was my first and best editor.

Table of Contents

Acknowledgments vi

Introduction 1

    I. An Empire and an Army Are Born   5

    II. The Army in Retreat   37

    III. The Struggle for Control   72

    IV. Triumph and Uncertainty   98

    V. The Marco Polo Bridge Incident   123

    VI. The China Incident   148

    VII. The Home Front   182

    VIII. North China and the Failure of Mediation   199

    IX. Quarantine the Aggressor   221

    X. Charade at Brussels   250

    XI. The Rape of Nanking   282

    XII. Aftermath   312

Chapter Notes 323

Bibliography 337

Index 343

Introduction

> What kind of a world do you think we live in? I call it a world where there is a struggle for power. Strong countries make it their business to conquer weak ones and constantly increase their territories. If life is a struggle, then our country must have adequate military strength to cope with reality. Without military strength, we cannot survive.... [Japan] is a country surrounded by seas. In naval warfare Japan is easy for the enemy to attack but hard for us to defend. Therefore, if we want to preserve Japan's independence permanently, we must possess territory on the continent. There are only two countries on the continent Japan can seize, China and Korea. Students talk about how barbaric and unprincipled this would be. Their talk about the superiority of Western civilization is in the same category. In the West, too, only the scholars, a bunch of empty-headed theorists, call for an end to wars of aggression. Politicians and businessmen are not so impractical. To strengthen Japan by war is to show loyalty to our country and to our sovereign. This should be our guiding principle.[1]

Taneomi Soejima wrote these prophetic words in 1885 when he was the Foreign Minister in the service of the Emperor Meiji. Years would pass before they were heeded, beginning with an apparently trifling episode involving the momentary disappearance of a Japanese soldier.

Where was Private Shimura? Captain Shimizu had summoned his company for a roll call when the first shells began to fall. Now, with his men huddled in the darkness on the bank of the Yungting River, one of his soldiers was missing. Shimizu recalled his apprehension earlier while he was eating his supper, that "something was going to happen that night."[2] Now his fears were confirmed. Calling off the maneuvers, he sent a messenger to his battalion commander to let him know about the missing soldier.

The report was quickly passed along to the regimental level. This was serious business: shooting from unknown sources and a Japanese soldier missing. Battalion Commander Itsuki's request to deploy his troops toward the scene of hostile fire was granted. More firing was heard. Was Private Shimura dead? Had the Chinese taken him prisoner? A search must be made, beginning at the walled town of Wanping. If the Chinese would not submit, the Japanese would use force.

This was an approach familiar to both sides. The Japanese had used it successfully since they had first gained a foothold on the Asian mainland, and the Chinese had all too often been their victims. The hunt for Private Shimura would lead not only to the breaching of the gates of an obscure village but to an assault on China itself.

That an event of such insignificance could precipitate a cataclysm of destruction and violence with the most profound consequences for both nations now seems incredible. Surely this was a calculated move hatched at the highest level of the military establishment, a provocation like the incident at Mukden nearly six years earlier that had led to the conquest of Manchuria. What followed seemed to give credence to the conspiracy theory. Many believed in it, especially Western observers who had been monitoring the Japanese penetration of North China. So did Chiang Kai-shek, who had wrapped himself in Sun Yat-sen's mantle as the unifier of his country.

But nothing could have been further from the truth, and this is what made the "China Incident" so disastrous. Each side, for its own reasons, preserved the fiction that they were not at war. Over months of conflict, a record of miscalculation, arrogance, blunder and stupidity would be compiled. The outcome of these failings would be appalling bloodshed, destruction, rape and pillage unparalleled in a decade of growing terror throughout the world.

Where indeed was Private Shimura? Some thought that perhaps he had left his comrades to enjoy the company of a prostitute, although that diversion seems unlikely given the brevity of his absence, since he turned up only twenty minutes after he had been reported missing. More likely, he had gone to relieve himself, as soldiers in the field often needed to do. On such trivialities, history often turns. As for his subsequent fate, he not only survived that summer night in 1937 but the China Incident as well. However, he did not survive the Great Pacific War. He was killed in action in Burma in 1943, a delayed casualty of the conflict he had unknowingly ignited.

The brief disappearance of a single Japanese soldier proved less significant than the action of his superior, Captain Shimizu. For reasons that will never be known, Shimizu delayed reporting Shimura's return for four hours. During that time there was an armed confrontation between Chinese and Japanese troops, the first breach in the fragile dike that had contained the peace in North China. It no longer mattered that a missing soldier was perfectly safe; when the Japanese insisted on searching Wanping, the Chinese garrison refused and opened fire. This should have been no more than a skirmish, but like the delayed report of the Japanese company commander, it led to escalation, each action in turn feeding on the one before. Saburo Matsukata, a Japanese journalist, was sent to North China afterward to present "the Japanese version." He was told by his patrons at the War Ministry that his propaganda mission would take no more than two weeks, since the army intended to resolve the matter quickly. Many years after the war, he recalled, "I was there for the next eight years."[3]

Under the circumstances, it is ironic that the name of the town, Wanping, meant "Obliging Peace." Yet although it was the scene of only an early battle, its name was not consigned to history. The Japanese referred to the clash as the "Incident at Lukouchiao," the name of an important railway junction nearby. The railroad from Peking to Hankow and Nanking in the south passed over the Yungting River and through Lukouchiao, with a shuttle connecting to the line to Tientsin on the coast. Significantly, this was the only remaining access to Peking that was not under Japan's control. For that reason, the Japanese coveted the area. They wanted to build a barracks and airfield there, and tried to pressure local landowners to sell their property. When rebuffed, they tried to intimidate the locals by holding military exercises on the land.[4]

Paralleling the railroad bridge was another span across the Yungting, a monument from the distant past when other invaders had been drawn to Lukouchiao because of its strategic position. A mutiny by troops of the last Ming emperor in 1215 had led to the capture of the city by Genghis Khan, followed by the fall of Peking and the overthrow of the Ming dynasty by the Mongols.

Later, during the reign of the great Khan, the Venetian traveler Marco Polo described his visit to the region: "When you leave the city of [Peking] and have ridden ten miles, you come to a very large river which is called Pulisgangkin and flows into the ocean, so that merchants with their merchandise ascend to it to the sea. Over this river there is a very fine stone bridge, so fine indeed that it has very few equals." Marco Polo went on to describe the ornate bridge in considerable detail, including the marble lions that graced it, never dreaming that a bridge completed in the last decade of the twelfth century by a Ming emperor would one day bear his name. Time and the elements forced the bridge to be rebuilt several times, but it would forever be known as the Marco Polo Bridge, and the fighting that began between Chinese and Japanese forces nearby at once became known as the "Marco Polo Bridge Incident."

This book reviews the events surrounding the Incident, including the birth of modern Japan and the Japanese Army itself, the Army's unique role in the life of the nation, and the escalation of the fighting that propelled Japan's military leaders on a mission to suppress all Chinese resistance by crushing the forces of Chiang Kai-shek. In doing so, they eventually aroused the ire of the United States, in particular its President, Franklin D. Roosevelt, who was influenced by his family's past. As America's interest in the conflict deepened, so did that of the League of Nations, to which China appealed. Frustrated in that quarter, China's last hope rested on a conference in Brussels of the parties to the Nine Power Treaty from the 1922 Washington Conference. Japan boycotted the conference in Brussels, and despite the attendance of American delegates, the Chinese were doomed to disappointment. Worse was to follow with the Rape of Nanking.

I

An Empire and an Army Are Born

Ficus Achates—faithful retainer. That was what the Emperor Meiji styled each soldier.[1] It was a calling that every soldier embraced. Its legacy had deep roots. For seven centuries, from 1185 to 1868, the Japanese feudal period, military clans held sway over the nation in the name of the Emperor.

In that long period of self-isolation, the real power was exercised not in Kyoto, where the Emperor first lived, but by the Shogun, the military commander. It was he who raised the army, the samurai, who over the years developed their own rules of conduct, the code of *bushido*, the way of the warrior, that would survive until 1945.

At the beginning of the seventeenth century, a single Shogun, Ieyasu Tokugawa, overcame the other warlords and brought all of Japan under his control. Leaving the Emperor in Kyoto, Ieyasu established his rule at Edo, the site of modern Tokyo. The Shogun was supported by 250 barons, each of whom was required to provide a force of samurai for the Shogun's army.[2] The Emperor remained a figurehead.

From that time until 1868, the samurai class enjoyed a privileged position. The Tokugawa system decreed that "the samurai are the masters of the four classes. Agriculturists, artisans, and merchants may not behave in a rude manner towards samurai." For their part, the samurai were to observe self-discipline and austerity, behaving as faithful vassals to their lords according to the *bushido* code.

Yet the samurai were more than bearers of arms. Since they were forbidden to engage in trade or the professions, they spent their free time writing poetry and practicing calligraphy. Thus they became an intellectual elite, and from their ranks would spring the leaders who toppled the Shogunate and brought about the restoration of the Emperor and the modernization of Japan.[3]

The modern Imperial Army would inherit the prestige of their samurai forebears, particularly after the stunning victories over China and Russia at the turn of the nineteenth century. Regrettably, other characteristics of samurai conduct were also transmitted. The arrogance of exclusivity generated brutality. In a nation where social customs had developed into an intricate web of manners and constraints, the samurai strutted among the lower classes, ever alert to any sign of disrespect. Woe be to the peasant or artisan who failed to bow when a samurai passed by. That oversight could cost him his head.[4] The samurai's most prized possession was his long sword, which he wielded with zest.

When the modern army came into being toward the end of the nineteenth century, the position of the samurai and the rigid social stratification of the feudal era provided the basis for the officer corps, and commoners filled the enlisted ranks. Indeed, when the modern army was established, a former samurai was almost always assured of a commission.[5] As they had led the nation in the feudal past, so would the samurai continue to provide the model for leadership, imparting the virtues of loyalty and discipline, the twin principles of an effective military force.

The European adventurers and empire-builders who commenced the subjugation of Asia did not fail to take notice of Japan. However, the Japanese resisted not only the religious overtures of the missionaries but European imperial aspirations as well. Successively, the Portuguese, Spanish, and Dutch endeavored to gain a foothold. None had lasting success. Christian propaganda was tolerated for a while, but ultimately the Shogun turned on the missionaries and their converts, expelling the one and massacring the other. A limited amount of trade was allowed along with sufficient contact with the world beyond to provide the Shogun with news of developments abroad. But foreigners were turned away or, if unfortunate enough to be shipwrecked, as occasional New England whaling men were, they met with a decidedly inhospitable reception. The Western code of aid to mariners in distress counted for nothing in a land where simply being marooned ashore put them in violation of Japanese law, for which they could be, and often were, summarily executed.

Inevitably, outrage over this barbarous behavior led to protests by American shipowners to the government in Washington. Although there had been numerous efforts by other nations to establish commercial contacts and seek a normal relationship, the Shogun's government had rejected them all. Yet there were elements within the nation that realized that Japan could not pursue its isolationist path much longer. Widespread poverty had affected even the samurai, some of whom were reduced to the status of *ronin*, masterless warriors. At the court there were some who felt that Japan would prosper if it lowered barriers to the West and permitted unfettered commerce.

I. An Empire and an Army Are Born

As it turned out, the Americans were the first through the door. In 1846, Commodore James Biddle appeared with two ships in Tokyo Bay, although a seemingly trivial incident caused his mission to fail. The Japanese sent a boat out to Biddle's ship, and when he boarded it, a Japanese sailor pushed and insulted him. From his perspective, Biddle did the honorable thing. He shrugged off the behavior instead of drawing his sword on the man or having him shot on the spot. In fact, the Japanese warned him to do the latter. Such a reaction would have instantly gained Biddle the desired respect of the Japanese. His failure to react to the insult left the impression that Americans were spineless. His overtures rejected, Biddle sailed away empty-handed.

In 1853 the Japanese encountered their toughest diplomatic challenge in the form of Matthew Perry (brother of Oliver Hazard Perry, the hero of the Battle of Lake Erie in the War of 1812). The U.S. government commissioned Perry to open relations with Japan and secure a profitable arrangement, which would include humane treatment of American castaways and the opening of one or two ports which would be available for trade and the supplying of coal for the California-Shanghai steamship route. The obliging Dutch had informed the Japanese of Perry's mission. Thus, when Perry's four ships arrived in Tokyo Bay on July 8, 1853, the Japanese were expecting him.

Perry also knew something about the Japanese. His principal interpreter was a missionary. From him and his contacts in Hong Kong and from the Dutch, Perry had learned about Japanese behavior patterns. Deciding to make a dry run which would send an unmistakable message to his reluctant hosts, he dropped anchor at Naha, the capital of Okinawa, the main island in the Ryukyu chain, which had been opened for trade. There he conducted himself like a visiting potentate. He obliged the Japanese to extend official recognition of his status, which included being entertained and having quarters for his crew ashore. So that the Japanese would see what was in store for them if they resisted, he conducted landing maneuvers with cannon and rifles in plain sight.

Word of this show of force reached the Shogunate as Perry knew it would. Perry's commission was officially expressed in a letter from the President of the United States. Ignoring the Japanese guard boats at the mouth of Tokyo Bay, Perry dropped anchor off the port of Uruga and informed the Japanese that he would give the President's letter to no one but the Shogun, the Emperor's first minister, in person.

This unprecedented action, a foreign officer demanding an audience at the highest level, threw the nation into confusion and set off strong anti-foreign protests. Yet Perry could hardly be evicted. The Shogun had only ten rounds for his puny coastal guns, which in any event would have been useless against Perry's heavily armed vessels. When the Japanese told Perry to leave, he simply moved his ships closer to Edo. Frightened and powerless, the Japanese sent emissaries for an exchange of gifts. Perry played his hand skillfully. He declared that he would return in one year for an answer to the President's letter, then sailed away.

Perry's action had shaken Japan to its core, and the death of Shogun Ieyoshi just eight days after Perry's departure was seen as punishment by the gods for his having submitted to the foreigners' demands. The public was now divided between those who favored rejecting and expelling all foreigners and those who saw that inevitably, Japan could no longer resist foreign overtures and would have to make concessions. Yet even those who favored concessions saw them as a stratagem to buy time for the nation to develop a Western-style army that would enable them to avoid the fate of China, which was slowly surrendering its sovereignty.

Even while Ieyoshi was alive there was growing pressure to restore the Emperor to imperial rule in the hope that it would bring economic revival. Ieyoshi was succeeded by Shogun Iesada, but the latter's leadership only added to the friction now building. Since he was childless, the two contending groups, those in favor of dealing with the Westerners and those opposed, began to compete for the shogunate itself, each side putting forth its candidates. The question of who would lead Japan was now intertwined with the more fundamental issue of whether to open the doors of the nation to the outside world for the first time in the country's history. In this environment, the movement to restore imperial rule began to accelerate. It was at this moment that Commodore Perry returned, not with four ships but with ten.

Perry had told the Japanese that he would be back in a year, but seeing that the French and the Russians were on the verge of cracking the Japanese shell, he decided to return sooner, arriving in Tokyo Bay on February 13, 1854. The dramatic increase in the number of ships in his naval squadron thoroughly cowed the Japanese, and when Perry bluffed that he had fifty more off their coast (which he did not), they decided that resistance was futile. Concessions could not be avoided. On March 31 the Treaty of Kanagawa was signed. Humane treatment of shipwrecked sailors was assured and two ports were opened and trade permitted, including a most-favored-nation provision. ("Most-favored-nation" means that both signatories agree that, if they subsequently grant commercial favors to other nations, those same favors will immediately be extended to each other.)

Other Western nations now followed America's lead. In October 1854, the British secured treaty rights with Japan. The Russians did the same in the following year, and then the Netherlands extracted two agreements.

Yet it was the Shogun with whom these treaties were made, not the Emperor. Imperial rule was still officially acknowledged, albeit not for much longer.

In August 1856, Townsend Harris arrived as the new American consul, with instructions to secure a commercial treaty. He took up residence at Shimoda but found his task challenging. The Japanese still felt strong antipathy toward foreigners and made it clear that they resented his presence. They restricted his movements, leaving him feeling more like a prisoner than an accredited diplomat. But Harris was not to be put off, and he persevered doggedly in his mission. A sticking point was extraterritoriality, an onerous and humiliating privilege that Westerners demanded in treaties with Asian governments. It stipulated that they could be tried only by their own judicial authority for offenses committed by them in the host country. It was a legacy of European colonialism, and Harris insisted on its inclusion in his treaty with Japan. Eventually the Japanese consented and Harris was received by the Shogun on December 7, 1857, at the palace in Edo, where he presented his credentials from the President of the United States.[6] It was a watershed for both nations.

Once again the Europeans followed in Harris's footsteps and secured treaties with similar rights and privileges. This concerted Western penetration only fueled the already strong anti-foreign sentiment. The Emperor, who refused to approve the Harris treaty, nevertheless found himself, with the rest of the country, swept along by events. Japan had been pried open. The question now was whether the Japanese would determine their own future or submit docilely to Western overlords.

There was never really any doubt about the course they would choose. Even before they stared down the barrels of Perry's cannons, they had known the power of Western arms. The Dutch had sold guns and mortars to the Tokugawa government since the seventeenth century, and a few officials had read books on Western military science. By 1849 two infantry companies had been trained in Western tactics, and in 1855 a warship had been purchased from Holland.[7] It was christened the *Kanko Maru*, and the Dutch sent naval instructors to teach the samurai crew how to operate it.[8] From this single vessel would grow Japan's Imperial Navy.

The Tokugawas also hired French officers to train infantry, artillery and cavalry units, while the powerful Tosa, Choshu and Satsuma clans organized rifle formations along Western lines. In what would be a portent of the future, the Choshu formed auxiliary rifle units among the peasants, with samurai officers. The traditional samurai scorned these developments, clinging to their swords as tangible symbols of their caste.[9] But like later generations who also stubbornly refused to adapt to new weaponry, they became the victims of their own pride and obstinacy. The contest over the imperial restoration, now only a few years away, would demonstrate once and for all the superiority of Western military technology.

Not only would the restoration of the Emperor rest on the shoulders of the clans that embraced military reform, but two of those clans would provide the basis for the modern army and navy. The Satsumas had a maritime tradition since they lived on the southern tip of Kyushu, where they carried on trade with nearby islands. The Choshu fiefs were located in the southwestern area of the main island of Honshu. They regarded themselves as the principal defenders against invaders from the Asian mainland. "Bred in these two traditions, it was natural that the deep concern of these two clans should center in the creation of a modern Navy and Army."[10] Eventually the Satsumas would dominate the Navy and the Choshu the Army; the seeds for their authority were to be sown in the conflict over imperial restoration.

Adopting the weapons of the foreigners was one thing, but welcoming them to the Japanese homeland was quite another. The Western aliens began to multiply with an insatiable thirst for tea, raw silk, and works of art. The demand outran the supply, which in turn led to high prices and profiteering.[11]

Harris must have been leading a charmed life, because Shogun Iyemochi was powerless to stem hostility against the foreigners. When the diplomats returned to Edo, another attack was made on the British legation and one of its members was wounded. Helpless, the Shogun could only send a personal letter to Queen Victoria pleading for the postponement of the opening of the ports.

All of these incidents were a prelude to the Richardson Affair, an affront so outrageous that no nation of principle would suffer it. In September 1862, a party of English merchants was riding from Yokohama toward Edo when they were approached by the procession of a Satsuma chief and eight hundred of his retainers. Whether in ignorance of protocol or for some other reason, the foreigners drew their horses to one side of the road but did not dismount as they were expected to when a great lord passed by. The infuriated samurai fell upon them, killing one, Charles Lennox Richardson, and wounding the others, who fled for their lives.

The British immediately demanded reparations, but the Shogun was unable to impose his will on a clan as strong as the Satsuma. Applying a method that they had exercised elsewhere in Asia, the British sent a squadron to the Satsuma capital of Kagoshima and bombarded the forts there. However, a typhoon swept in during the firing and forced the ships to leave, enabling the Japanese to claim victory, especially since they never gave up the assassins.[12]

Heady with "success," the elements around the Emperor at Kyoto set the date of June 1863 for the expulsion of all foreigners. On this occasion

I. An Empire and an Army Are Born

it was the Choshu who were determined to draw blood. They fired on the American vessel *Pembroke*, which was lying at anchor in the harbor of Shimonoseki. When other foreign ships were also attacked, retaliation was swift. In September 1864 a combined British, Dutch and American fleet bombarded Shimonoseki. But this time there was no providential typhoon.[13] The defending forts were crushed and resistance annihilated. The foreign powers demanded a three million dollar indemnity, which the Choshu refused to pay. The sum was certainly larger than any damages the attacking fleet had suffered, and the United States returned its share of $785,000.

From all of this the powerful Choshu and Satsuma clans had learned a lesson. Shimonoseki and Kobe were unmitigated defeats. Pushing the foreigners out was no longer possible. An accommodation would have to be made and the nation opened to the world. By knocking sense into the heads of the two strongest clans in Japan, the bombardments of Shimonoseki and Kobe proved therapeutic.[14] Japan was now on the brink of imperial rule.

In September 1866, Shogun Iyemochi died and was succeeded by the last of the Tokugawa line, Keiki, a young prince of the Mito family. He accepted the responsibility reluctantly. In the brief period of his authority he sent some of his countrymen abroad for instruction and began to bring in foreign military advisors. But the days of the Shogunate were numbered. On February 3, 1867, Emperor Komei, who had long resisted the foreign presence, died. His successor was fifteen-year-old Prince Mutsuhito, destined to become the renowned Emperor Meiji, who would preside over the regeneration of Japan. The new Emperor did not have long to wait. Even before his accession, two Satsuma vassals, Takamori Saigo and Toshimishi Okubo, were plotting to undermine the Shogunate. When Mutsuhito became Emperor, the feudal lords invited the Shogun to relinquish his authority to the Emperor. Keiki saw the handwriting on the wall and on November 3, 1867, sent a letter in which he reviewed the past but confessed his own shortcomings:

> Now that foreign intercourse has become more daily extensive, unless the government is directed from one central authority, the foundations of the state will fall to pieces. If, however, the old order of things be changed, and the administrative authority be restored to the Imperial Court, and if national deliberations be conducted on an extensive scale, and the Imperial decision be secured, and if then the Empire be supported by the efforts of the whole people, then the Empire will be able to maintain its rank and dignity among all the nations of the earth. I believe my highest duty to realize this ideal by giving up entirely my rule over this land.[15]

Nine days later, in a one-sentence reply, the Emperor accepted the mandate to rule Japan.

The significance of this transfer of power cannot be overstated. To unite the Japanese people, the new Meiji government advanced the concept of Emperor worship and Japan became a sacred country. It was revealed in a passage in the "Imperial Letter to Pacify the Multitude" of April 6, 1868.

> We hereby make an oath with all the government officials and the many lords to continue the great task bequeathed to us by Our ancestors. With no thought of the hardships or difficulties We must undergo, We will ourselves take charge of the administration and pacify the multitude. We wish to spread the national glory far beyond the seas and make the country secure like the towering Mount Fuji.[16]

Officially, anti-foreignism was abandoned, but only because it served the interest of the nation. Two months after the restoration, Tomoni Iwakura, a diplomat in the Meiji government, revealed his thoughts about diplomacy in a memorandum. Iwakura deplored the public misunderstanding of the new government's policy of friendship with foreign countries. He wrote:

> Although there was no alternative to establishing diplomatic relations with foreign countries, we must keep in mind that foreign countries are the national enemies of our imperial land. What is a national enemy? All countries strive for wealth and power by steadily developing their arts and technology. All try to become superior to others. A against B, B against A and C. Everywhere it is the same. And so I say that all foreign countries are the national enemies of our imperial land.[17]

This Machiavellian outlook reflected not only an ingrained xenophobia but also harbored an expansionist view that became the cornerstone of Japan's foreign policy.

At home the feudal system was quickly dismantled. The leaders of the four great clans, Satsuma, Choshu, Tosa and Hizen, led the way. All but 17 of the 272 *daimyo* (clan chiefs) voluntarily followed suit.[18] In an act of national unity unparalleled anywhere, the privileges of a thousand years were surrendered. The daimyos retired on an income one-tenth of their former revenues. Two million samurai were granted pensions, but these were so small that they were obliged to go to work to support themselves.[19] The Emperor, who took the name "Meiji," which meant "Enlighten-Government," set down his aspirations for the new nation: "Oh, how I wish to make this country inferior to none, adopting that which is good, and rejecting that which is bad."[20]

The capital was moved from Kyoto to Edo, which was then renamed Tokyo. Rapid modernization followed. The first daily newspaper was published in Yokohama in 1870. That same year, a telegraph line was opened between Tokyo and Yokohama. In 1872 an eighteen-mile railway between the two cities was completed. The postal service was in place by 1870, a mint was established, and lighthouses were erected along the coast.

The various clan divisions gave way to a new administrative system

I. An Empire and an Army Are Born

of prefectures with governors appointed by Tokyo. The rigid caste system of the Tokugawa days was abolished. No longer were there samurai, peasants, merchants and artisans. Instead, clan chiefs and court nobles became *kazoku* (peers); samurai became *shizoku* (gentry); and the rest of the population was lumped together as *heimen* (commoners). Later, in 1884, the peerage ranks of prince, marquis, count, viscount and baron were created.[21]

In concert with the transformation of the face of Japan, intensive military reform was undertaken. Railroads, telegraphs, and a revised administrative system were all well and good, but if the Japanese wished to preserve the nation's sovereignty and extend the frontiers of their empire, they needed a modern army to do so. Some of the clans had adopted Western arms and techniques in the late Tokugawa era, but when the Emperor Meiji came to power, he was without a national army. To preserve his authority, he relied upon loyal clans to provide him with a military force. Indeed, at the beginning of his reign, in January 1868, supporters of ex-Shogun Keiki, angry at their exclusion from positions in the new government, took up arms and marched on Kyoto. A force of about 1,500 Satsuma and Choshu men, using Western-style tactics and weapons, easily defeated the obsolete forces of Tokugawa. The early military reforms of the great clans were seen to have paid off. However, the Emperor exercised no command over Satsuma and Choshu troops. Once the opposition had been crushed, the soldiers followed their clan generals back to their home provinces, and the Emperor was powerless again, or nearly so. All he had was a personal guard of some 300 ronin and samurai which had been recruited from some of the minor clans.[22] This was intolerable. If the Emperor wished to execute the national will, he needed a military force. Otherwise, he would be a symbol of change but not the instrument of it. Easier said than done.

The battle with the former Shogun forces had been costly, and the government was constantly pressed for funds. Its only sources were contributions from imperial clans and compulsory loans from wealthy merchants. Only when the fiefs were abolished in 1871 and a national system of taxation was established could the central government rely on a steady source of income.

The man who earned the title of "father of the modern Japanese Army" was Masujiro Omura, a member of the Choshu clan. He had learned Dutch and English, and read widely in the fields of science, medicine and economics. More importantly, he devoted himself to military science, translating Dutch works on strategy derived from German theory. In the battles against the forces of the Shogunate, he commanded peasant armies trained in European tactics. His reputation earned him the post of Vice Minister of Military Affairs. Omura recognized that calling on the various bands of samurai to defend the nation was hopeless. They were neither reliable nor well trained. Put to the test, the peasant armies, property trained in the Western style, were far more effective soldiers.

The answer to Japan's national defense needs lay in yet another European institution, conscription. That meant the abolition of the samurai's exclusiveness as the bearer of arms. Thus, at a meeting of the Imperial Council in June 1869, Omura proposed that the fiefs and feudal armies and the special privileges of the samurai be terminated and a conscript army raised. In no other way would the government achieve independence and set the course of the nation. As it turned out, Omura was more bold than prudent, and in October of that same year he was assassinated by a band of impetuous samurai from his own clan. But Omura's seed took root, and his recommendations subsequently became the foundation of the Imperial Army.[23]

The feudal cadres had to be unified, but in the meantime the Council of State ordered the clans to organize their forces along Western lines. In a decree issued in October 1870, they were told that the navy was "to adopt the English system and the army the French system." The Japanese wished to model their respective services on those nations with the strongest military reputations. Britannia ruled the waves and the French army was thought to be the finest in the world. The armies of Napoleon III had routed those of Austria in 1858, and watching their prowess from afar, the Shogun opened negotiations in 1865 with the French minister in Edo. These resulted in a French military mission to Japan, composed of nine officers, eight noncommissioned officers, and eighteen soldiers, a small but eclectic lot with representatives from artillery, infantry and cavalry elements, and even some military musicians. A camp near Yokohama was set aside for instruction and an artillery range was planned.[24]

The French were careful to select for the mission only those men who would respect Japanese tradition and customs. Travel expenses were provided, and the personnel were to be paid their monthly salaries in the local currency. Although the training ground at Yokohama was too small, the instruction of the first group of Japanese officers and NCOs proceeded apace. Even after the Shogun fell from power, the training continued, only now it was moved to Tokyo, where larger facilities were provided. Barracks were built on European lines and a foundry at Yokosuka turned out the first rifles and cannon. The French provided sample uniforms and footwear. With a French school in Yokohama providing interpreters, the Japanese proved to be diligent students, and slowly all of the panoply of military organization and administration began to take shape.

The triumph of the Emperor over the Shogun placed the French mission in an awkward position, but that alone did not terminate it. The brief military challenge by the Shogun's followers had left the treasury short of funds, so the French departed after a stay of just over a year and a half. It was too short a time to effect lasting military reform, but the few soldiers who were trained fought well in the short civil war. Most important was the precedent set by the mission. It gave the French an initial advantage over any potential rivals in the development of the Japanese Army. The school at Yokohama taught French, so it was in this foreign language that the Japanese had the greatest fluency. Since there was a constant need for interpreters in the training of troops, the French had an edge. It was just easier to retain the French connection.

But there was competition in the wings. In 1868 the head of the Kishu clan ordered several thousand needle guns (Dreyse rifles) from Germany. A German noncommissioned officer, Sergeant Karl Köppen, asked to come along to teach the Japanese how to use the rifles. He did more. Sergeant Köppen's skill as a drillmaster soon provided the daimyo with 3,000 trained soldiers. Interestingly, no distinction in the ranks was made between samurai and peasant soldiers. It was a German army with an Asian face. The troops wore European uniforms and answered to German commands. The central government took note of the Kishu clan's forces, but with the abolition of the clans in 1871, Köppen's mission was at an end. His trainees were assimilated into the Emperor's Army.

For the time being, French influence remained paramount. For one thing, Aritomo Yamagata of the Choshu and Tsugimichi Saigo of the Satsuma clan had made a tour of Europe to study the military organizations of the leading powers. In August 1870 they returned and were put in charge of the Bureau of Naval and Military Affairs. It was their influence and guidance that led to the growth of the modern army. Yamagata's hand would be felt not only in the army's development in its early years but later in political circles when Yamagata won for the army an unchallenged claim on policy decisions at the highest level of the government. If he was Omura's acknowledged successor as "father of the Japanese Army," he must also be held responsible for the origins of its ultimate self-destruction. After victories over China and Russia, the army's paramount role in the success of the empire enabled it to insist on a decisive voice in determining the nation's future. In time, it would insist upon having the only voice.

Both Yamagata and Saigo determined that Japan needed the services of a foreign military mission to organize and train the new army, but there was disagreement over which one to select. Omura pushed for the recommendations cited in the Council of State decree, but it was Saigo's view that the French army should be their model. He was strongly influenced by his sojourn in France, and offered the opinion that the armies of Napoleon III would defeat the Prussians in the war then in progress. But Yamagata had traveled not only in France but elsewhere in Europe, and in studying the

English, French, Prussian and Russian military establishments, he had concluded that the French army, while formidable, was over-confident and lacked trained reserves. What impressed him most was the Prussian conscription system.

At length the French system was adopted. More clans were familiar with it, and their familiarity with the French language meant that the interpreter problem would be less difficult. Thus it was that on October 2, 1870, the government announced that the French military system would be used as a model, and negotiations were begun to bring a mission from France to Japan. Irony of ironies: the month before, Napoleon III and his army were defeated and he was a prisoner of Bismarck. Sedan, the scene of this historic event, was a disaster for the French. It was the end of the Second Empire and France would become a republic. The sun would set on the French military mission.

In the meantime, neither Yamagata nor Saigo wished to share the fate of Omura, but they were determined to raise a national army. To do that they had to proceed with caution. The three major clan military leaders were approached: Mori of Choshu, Itagaki of Tosa, and the "ranking military hero of the Restoration wars," Takamori Saigo of the powerful Satsuma. All were asked to transfer elements of their own armies to the Emperor. Thus Satsuma sent four battalions of infantry and two batteries of artillery; Choshu, three battalions of infantry; and Tosa, two battalions of infantry, two batteries of artillery and two companies of cavalry. Together they formed a division of 10,000 men.

Their origins might be Choshu, Toma and Satsuma, but their loyalty was now sworn to the Emperor. They were the *Goshimpei*, the Imperial Guard. The date was April 1871. In August, feudal autonomy was ended by order of the Emperor and all political, military and fiscal authority now reposed in the hands of the government. This coupling of military decisions with civil changes underscores the importance of the army's role in the Empire's infancy.[25] Competition for funds, so familiar to every Western nation, now beset the new government. This was not then seen as an omen of the future, but the triumph of the military in garnering a major portion of the national expenditures became a distant mirror over two generations later when the army seized the helm of the nation.

Universal military training was now made an order of the highest priority. On January 10, 1873, a conscription ordinance was decreed, based on the French model. Conscripts would serve seven years, of which three would be active duty and the remainder in the reserves. There were exemptions for criminals, hardship cases, and the physically disabled, as well as for heads of households, students, government bureaucrats, and teachers. But one could buy a substitute for 270 yen, a sum beyond the means of the average conscript. Who then was conscripted? The 1873 class comprised "second and third sons of impoverished farmers," but the army was small, numbering just 17,900, so relatively few men were drafted.[26]

The odds of being drafted depended upon the location of the potential inductee. In 1873, more than 85 percent of the men from the Tokyo and Osaka districts failed the physical examination, and 70 percent of those from the northeastern region also failed. Obviously, the rural areas provided healthier recruits. So, the chances of being drafted depended on where one lived. As late as 1934 the highest conscription rate was Shizouka Prefecture, whence 37 percent of those examined were inducted. Kagoshima had the lowest rate, barely 25 percent. (The people there were poor and backward.) Depending on the circumstances, men were assigned to various categories of reserve or militia service.[27] Not a few young men tried to beat the physical examination, just as draftees did in the United States in World War II. Both generations tried to do it by losing an excessive amount of weight. In Japan, drinking soy sauce could produce symptoms of heart trouble. But woe to the inductee if caught. That was a criminal offense.

Opposition to conscription was immediate in 1873. Thousands of peasants rioted in Okayama Prefecture, burning schools and the homes of the wealthy and murdering government officials and schoolteachers. Incredibly, they opposed not only conscription but also haircutting, and initially there were not enough troops to cope with the rioters.[28]

As time progressed, conscription was accepted as a natural extension of a young man's coming of age. By the 1930s, the army was producing a set of postcards showing what army life was like. They were sold to soldiers in the canteens for one sen, but they always showed soldiers in a group, and scenes with recruits performing for their comrades in the class above them were seen as a favor, although reality for recruits was radically different. The army regarded itself as an extension of the recruit's family, and postcards sent home attempted to reinforce this image. All of the traditional elements were there: respect for one's elders, and obedience.[29] The 1908 army handbook described the environment:

> The barracks is the soldiers' where together soldiers share hardships and joys, life and death.... A family means that the company is one household in the village of the regiment. The heads of the household are the father and mother. The company commander is a strict father, and NCO a loving mother. The lieutenants are relatives and in perfect accord with their company commander whom they loyally assist.[30]

Of course, this sort of thing would have been unthinkable in the American Army. No handbook was necessary to drive home to the G.I. what the pecking order was, beginning with the first sergeant. The Japanese family-like atmosphere created one of loyalty to superiors all the way to the Emperor, a distant figure, but one to whom all from the lowest private to the highest ranking general owed obeisance. Reinforcement came in the form of the Imperial Rescript to Soldiers and Sailors, which recruits studied daily, and on special occasions such as National Foundation Day on February 11 and Army Day, March 10, the Imperial Rescript was read to the troops. In addition, every morning they bowed toward the Imperial Palace, paying homage to the Emperor. Even the soldier's equipment carried the Emperor's imprint, the imperial crest, on his Type 38 rifle and other items, a visual reminder that everything issued to him came from the Emperor, all the more reason to take care of it. If that was not enough, any flaw reflecting on improper care was sure to bring a thrashing by the sergeant. Discipline was severe and certain.

The young recruit moved into a rigorously controlled barracks. He was forbidden to read newspapers, magazines or books unless his commander gave prior permission. The barracks became the place where the recruit would sleep, eat, stand inspection, stand guard, and cultivate self-discipline. He awoke to the bugle, stood morning inspection in rank in the aisle between two rows of beds left free, ate by the third bugle, and ultimately turned out the lights with the final bugle. A bugle call normally announced reveille, inspection, meals, reports, sick call, sentry duty, roundup of horses and lights out. The bugle started daily life and chased time in the new rhythm of military life.

With some exceptions, the bugle routine would be familiar to any American soldier or sailor from the Second World War, the various calls well known to him.

Petty harassment, present in every army and navy, was an annoyance, but in the Japanese Army, physical abuse was singular. Face slapping was so common that it was accepted as routine, but for the recruit, it went beyond that to sadistic. Beatings by second-year men at night after lights out were worse, and many recruits had bruised and swollen faces from the hands of their superiors. Whatever consolation they might have was the knowledge that the following year, they could dish out similar treatment to new recruits.

A recruit's family received 30 sen a day in military relief pay, and death benefits prompted one father to write to his son to get killed in action because the family would get a death benefit of 150 yen.

Training was in four month cycles and as they progressed, competition between regiments was encouraged. The fall maneuvers were conducted in the presence of the Emperor and observed by townspeople or villagers in a carnival-like atmosphere. For the recruits, these maneuvers must have been welcome, relieving them of the terrors or boredom of the barracks and finally enabling them to see themselves as soldiers.

I. An Empire and an Army Are Born

Harsh as it was, this kind of training imbued the Japanese soldier with a sense of martial spirit and self-confidence second to none. Later, however, when he was challenged in combat by an adversary equally inspired but better armed, he would lose his belief in his invincibility. Such was the case in the battle at Khalkin Gol in Siberia in May 1939. Outmaneuvered by the then General Zhukov, confronted by a superior foe that possessed more aircraft and artillery and was well trained, the Japanese soldier not only paid a heavy price for his ardor, but lost confidence in his leaders and his own sense of indestructibility. Admittedly the Japanese Twenty-third Infantry Division at Khalkin Gol was filled with first-year troops, not a seasoned unit by any measure, but the results would have been the same regardless. Believing in an inevitable triumph, decimated on the battlefield with 70 percent casualties, the survivors lost discipline and units their cohesion.[31] That would have been the fate of soldiers in any army, but it was singular for the Japanese soldier, whose training was unlike any other soldier elsewhere. When the Yamato spirit failed, what was left?

Officer training commenced in 1875, when a single military academy was founded. The most outstanding students received further education abroad, and by 1880 there were 44 officers studying in Europe. This was followed by the establishment of the War College in 1883 under the jurisdiction of the Chief of the General Staff. Regimental commanders recommended their most promising candidates, and those who passed preliminary examinations in subjects such as tactics, weapons, topography, communications and military organization were eligible for the final examination at the General Staff College. Of those who passed, 50 were selected to attend the College each year. Like their counterparts in the West, the graduates of the War College were on the fast track to the highest ranks. Through this competition and the army promotion system, intellectual potential as well as actual performance received major consideration leading to advancement.

In the years following the Meiji Restoration the military organization underwent a continuing metamorphosis. The Army and Navy Affairs Section became the Office of Military Defense, subsequently the Department of Military Affairs. In August 1869 it changed again, to the War Department, only to be divided three years later into separate army and navy departments. Under German influence the Staff Bureau of the War Ministry, which had been responsible for planning and operations, became General Staff Headquarters, independent and more prestigious because it was no longer subordinate to the Ministry. The political consequences of this change were profound, because the Chief of Staff became the principal adviser on military policy to the Emperor, and thus superior to the War Minister. More importantly, it meant that now the cabinet would be unable to impose political restraints on the Chief of Staff, a deficiency that would have serious consequences in the tumultuous decade of the 1930s. The Chief of Staff was given this free hand, making him responsible to the Emperor alone, due to a desire to keep civil authority from interfering in matters of national defense and strategy. As subsequent events proved, the Emperor would have been far better served had the civil government been able to put the brakes on the General Staff.

It has never been easy to carry water on both shoulders. For the Japanese War Minister, the military bureaucracy was an almost impossible burden. Consider his dilemma: the Chief of Staff was not answerable to him, and the civil authority was divorced from matters of national security. He was first and foremost a soldier and thus bound to represent the army's view in the cabinet of which he was a member. But if he failed to persuade his cabinet colleagues, he was then obliged either to adopt the decision of the majority and risk opposition from his brother officers, or to resign from the cabinet, which would bring it down. Finally, if as less frequently happened, he favored policies at odds with those of the Chief of Staff, he ran the risk of reducing his authority over the army. He was between a rock and a hard place.

It was impossible to separate civil and military authority in spite of regulations that expressly forbade military personnel from participating in the political process. The Imperial Rescript of 1882 specifically warned soldiers to "neither be led astray by current opinions nor meddle in politics, but with a single heart fulfill your essential duty to loyalty." Such admonitions turned out to be meaningless. The line between what was exclusively political or military was often blurred. Political acts could be justified by military necessity. Since the military establishment was responsible to the Emperor alone and not to the civil authority, the army did not hesitate to intrude into political matters, justifying its actions in the name of the Emperor, particularly if its actions could be characterized as a matter of national security.

The army's ability to paralyze the civil government, as it would in the 1930s, and thereby bend it to its will, was made possible by having only active generals and admirals as service ministers in the cabinet. In 1913, the active-duty requirement was dropped and reserve or retired officers were allowed to serve, but in 1936, at the insistence of the military, it was reinstated. As a result, if a cabinet policy was introduced that the army regarded as inimical to their interests, they had only to withhold the appointment of a war minister or have him resign, and the cabinet could not function. If in office, the prime minister and his cabinet would also have to resign, and if a new government was formed, the offensive policy or point of contention would have to be resolved on the army's terms before a war minister could be named. The same would be true in the case of the navy, although in the 1930s the army was the more recalcitrant branch. The Mukden Incident in 1931 made it clear that the Japanese army could not be controlled. What civilian government could function when civilians had no voice in military affairs?

From the time that the cabinet system was initiated in 1885, it was dominated by generals and admirals, a situation that lasted until Japan's defeat in 1945. Over this period, half of the thirty prime ministers were military leaders, of whom nine were generals and six admirals. In addition to the military posts which by law were held by army or navy officers, one-fourth of the civilian posts in that period were occupied by generals and admirals. In eleven of the forty-three cabinets in those years, a military officer was named Home Minister, and in fourteen, Foreign Minister. The only department that was never administered by a military officer was the Finance Ministry, which was not surprising. That was one task the military were happy to leave in the hands of civilians. In the early Meiji period the military dominated the successive cabinets. Not until 1898 did civilians gain a majority, but with the wave of assassinations and attempted coups that marked the 1930s, the civilian cabinet officers who did serve became little more than pawns as the army gained ascendancy.

Only in the years between 1912 and 1930 did the power of the military wane. Force levels were reduced and civilian rule established on Formosa and Korea. During this same period, reserve or retired officers were allowed to hold the posts of service ministers, and men in that category, especially retirees, were subject to far less pressure from their peers than those on active duty. The brief flirtation with Wilsonian idealism in the post–World War I years resulted in reductions and limitations to the armed forces, particularly the navy, as Japan committed itself to the provisions of the Washington Conference and the London Naval Conference. The concessions made in London in 1930 were to be the last. Thereafter the army and navy reasserted their independence, and the decade that followed brought about the demise of civilian control and the triumph of the military oligarchy. Control of the government was not brought about by a carefully conceived coup. Disparate elements within both the army and the navy had their own agendas which were often independent of or contrary to the aims of their senior officers. Their often bloody attempts to seize the throttle impelled the army down a path of military dictatorship at home and dangerous adventurism abroad. Such a possibility could hardly have been imagined at the dawn of the Meiji era. The revolutionary changes in the national defense structure, however, were almost bound to set off a reaction. It came in the form of the Satsuma Rebellion, in effect the last gasp of the old order, a final act of defiance by the samurai who refused to accept their demise. As is often the case, a seemingly trivial matter triggered the crisis.

Japan was already moving to establish a foothold on the Asian mainland, and when a Korean court rejected a Japanese request to open diplomatic relations, it was regarded as a major challenge to the central government. A belligerent faction insisted that grounds for war existed, but many believed that the army was not ready to undertake a foreign military campaign. In the debate that followed, this view prevailed, but that was not the end of it. Five ministers resigned in protest and many of the samurai, already smoldering with resentment over military reforms, added their chorus of dissent. A brief flare-up was put down by a nervous government, which then, to dissipate the appetite for a campaign, launched an expedition to Formosa against a native tribe that had generated unrest. If nothing else, the operation exposed the unpreparedness of Japan's forces—combined units of army troops, marines and some samurai volunteers, hampered by poor discipline and disorganization. Had the Japanese confronted a modern foe, the result would have been a disaster.

Yet samurai unrest continued. Isolated uprisings tormented the government in 1876, portending the last and most serious challenge that the imperial government would face from the samurai class. Ironically, the man who raised the standard of revolt in the winter of 1877 had been the Emperor's most popular and effective general in the war of the Restoration, Takamori Saigo. Heaped with honors and made commander-in-chief of the Imperial Army, Saigo was a dejected and resentful hero. He shared the concern of many of his class, a bitter hostility toward the Westernization of his country which would spell the end of the values and virtues he held dear. When the government failed to react with samurai courage to the insult of the Korean court in 1873, he resigned his post and returned to his home in Kagoshima on the island of Kyushu. There he spent his time with young samurai at a school he had established to preserve their class and traditions.[32]

When the samurai were disestablished as a class in 1876, Saigo was driven to the precipice. The following year the government ordered the military authorities in Satsuma Prefecture to transfer guns and ammunition to a safer district because of growing fears of a rebellion. With that, Saigo raised the standard of revolt, gathered an army of 15,000 men, and commenced a march on Tokyo.[33] But the sun of the samurai had already set. Although they made the government forces pay a terrible price for victory, their ancient muskets and swords were no match for a conscript army with modern weapons. Despite heavy losses and the forced commitment of its entire peacetime force of 32,000, and reserves of more than 10,000 men, the central government managed to crush Saigo's followers. The ending had all of the character of a classic Japanese stage tragedy. Seeing the inevitable, Saigo retreated to a cave near Shiroyama just north of Kagoshima and committed *hara-kiri*.³⁴ It had been a costly victory.

Shaken by the ordeal, with the finances of the nation drained, the Meiji government now determined upon a thoroughgoing reorganization of the military system. That the army had prevailed was due less to planning than to the individual courage manifested by the Emperor's soldiers. All of the logistical elements that permit a military force to take the field and operate smoothly were missing. The French military mission which had been brought in to advise and shape the army command structure had to shoulder much of the blame. The Germans were superior in organizational ability, and the Japanese took note. The French still kept a presence and remained until 1880. Believing that Japan needed to start from the bottom, they emphasized tactics rather than strategy. But the Japanese were impatient and, after the Satsuma Rebellion, in which the army had proven itself, its leader no longer saw the need to preserve a student-teacher relationship with the French. However, the Japanese were not about to abandon their ties with Europe in developing and modernizing their army. Technology had revolutionized warfare in the middle and last half of the nineteenth century. Improvements in rifles and artillery increased their accuracy and killing power. It was inevitable that tactics would be changed to meet this evolution.³⁵

The link between Japan and developments two continents away came in the person of Klemens Jacob Meckel, a Rhinelander who found his way into the Prussian army in 1860. Subsequently commissioned, Meckel was to have a distinguished career, graduating from the War Academy and participating in the war with Austria in 1866 as well as in the conflict with France in 1870–1871. In the years that followed, Meckel wrote a series of books on tactics which established his credentials as an authority on infantry warfare and led to his promotion to the rank of major.

Meckel believed that the fundamental principle that held an army together was obedience. On the battlefield, it ensured that leadership would be unquestioned, and a disciplined soldier performed best under orders. We cannot measure the degree to which this emphasis on unflinching obedience was influenced by Meckel's own experience as an adviser to the Japanese army. Its attitude toward suffering and death was far different from that of Western soldiers. Meckel's influence on the German army was minimal. He made his reputation in Japan.

Yet there were pro–French officers in the Japanese military leadership who were reluctant to sever their ties with France. Ultimately, a token group of two infantry officers and two noncommissioned officers was employed to teach at the War Academy and lesser schools. A German officer would go to the recently established Army Staff College, thus ensuring the permanent influence of Germany military ideas on the Japanese army.

A Japanese military mission led by General Iaawo Oyama, the Army Minister, traveled to Europe in 1884, arriving in Berlin in July. When the Japanese asked for a German staff officer to be assigned to the Japanese army, Major Meckel's name came up. The Japanese knew about him. Meckel must have been flattered by his invitation to Japan, but his reaction was mixed. He asked for permission to delay his decision for twenty-four hours, and only then did he consent. Meckel was something of a character. When asked the next day by the taciturn Chief of Staff, Helmuth von Moltke, why he hesitated over his decision, Meckel replied, "To tell the truth, I cannot live without Mosel wine. If I do not have it with dinner I cannot sleep at night. So I inquired whether it could be shipped to Japan." Even Moltke could not contain his laughter.

The Japanese military mission made superficial visits to Vienna and St. Petersburg, but it was the Germany army system that interested them and now absorbed them for most of their European stay. Finally, they returned home by way of the United States, arriving back in Japan in January 1885. Two months later Meckel landed and began teaching at the Army Staff College.

Not surprisingly, there was considerable rivalry between the small French mission and the lone German during their respective tours in Japan. At the army training school at Toyama, the French toiled away with their students, instructing subalterns and noncommissioned officers in marksmanship, fencing and gymnastics. There were also lessons for a fledgling band, which Meckel criticized for being out of tune when he heard it. For his part, Captain Henri Berthaut, the French infantry officer engaged by the Japanese, "filled his reports with carping comments about Meckel's lectures."[36] In particular, he resented Meckel's attempt to become the spokesman for all foreign officers in Japan. He told General Miura, the commandant of the Academy, that "he did not concern himself with the Staff College and that Meckel should not interfere with the Academy's work."

The French underestimated the ability of the Japanese to learn Western military technique, and Captain Berthaut had a habit of over-simplifying his lectures, which might have stemmed from the false beliefs in the inferiority of non-white intelligence that many Occidentals held. It was an error that Meckel avoided. His lectures were not only enlightening but stimulating to the imagination of the Japanese officers. The Japanese were not slow to compare the two men, and French influence waned further.

German dominance in the Japanese military camp accelerated in the decade following 1884. The Staff College was now the prestigious institution, not the Military Academy, and French officers continued in the classroom except when they went into the field with their students. Still, when Berthaut's contract came up for renewal, the Japanese pressed for it. Promoted to major, Berthaut attempted to poach on Meckel's territory by offering an advanced course in strategy and tactics to the Japanese faculty at the Academy and to the officers of the Tokyo garrison and Imperial Guard. He no longer had contact with his students and believed that he was not competing with his German counterpart. Why did the Japanese retain his services? Perhaps because the Japanese preferred to continue having the benefit of French views, but more likely it was the lingering pro–French element in Japanese military circles that prompted the action.

In any event, Berthaut and his countrymen were waging a losing battle. Unquestionably the scars of the Franco-Prussian War were still painful for the French mission, but the Japanese recognized a winner and overhauled the Military Academy, which had been modeled on St. Cyr. In June 1887 it now "bore all the marks of a German coup." Essentially the reforms ordered by the Army Ministry stripped away much of the "academic" character of the school, obliging all cadets to have one year in the army unless they had graduated from the preparatory school, in which case six months would suffice. The first-year course, which included general studies, was eliminated entirely and the entire program was cut from three years to eighteen months. Graduates entered the army as adjutants and six months later would be commissioned as second lieutenants. Berthaut was told by two Japanese generals that the initiative to make the change had come from the Germans. There is no reason to believe otherwise. As for Meckel, the bright morning of a rising sun beckoned.

Jacob Meckel was 43 when he came to Japan, and he looked the image of a Prussian officer. The Japanese liked him in spite of his being a harsh taskmaster, or perhaps because he was. Away from his duties, he was affable and cheerful. Unlike the French officers, who wore their uniforms all the time and thus offended Japanese national feelings, Meckel wore his uniform only on official occasions. His sensitivity did not go unnoticed by his hosts. Meckel did not lack for comfort. A German-style red brick cottage was built for him and a horse provided. Later Meckel's house, erected between the Army Ministry and his staff office, was used by the Chief of the General Staff. When the Emperor Meiji visited the Staff College, Meckel was presented to him. The German recognized that a special honor had been conferred on him.

German ascendance in Japan was reflected in other ways as well. Besides looking to Germany for military guidance, the Japanese invited a German nobleman, Ottmar von Mohl, to the Imperial court as chamberlain to reorganize protocol. German furnishings were ordered for the

Emperor's new palace and other ministries received German advisers, all of which prompted the English to say that "Japan had a bad case of German measles."

Meckel lectured in German, assisted by a translator. The dearth of knowledge of tactics and logistics among Japanese trained in Europe prompted Meckel to stress these areas in his lectures, along with military history and the development of the General Staff. He brought with him maps and battle plans of the Prussian campaign against Metz in the war with France. His views on military command emphasized its importance in communications and supply. In field exercises, Meckel elevated planning to division-size units and "spoke in terms of future operations on the Asian continent." Small wonder that his pupils became enthusiastic. The conflict with Russia was barely twenty years away, but Meckel had begun to alert Japanese generals to the basic requirements of modern warfare. Now officers from the Army Ministry, the General Staff, the Imperial Guard, and other departments and units began to attend his lectures. What especially appealed to the Japanese was his use of military history to teach the lessons of the battlefield. The Japanese saw in Meckel's "practical examples and illustrations ... a 'scientific and logical strategy' which made more sense than theory."

In the field, Meckel was tireless in his instruction, forcing his students to learn how to maneuver an army in open country with all of the attendant problems of supply, bridge construction and topographical barriers. His criticisms were open, without rancor and more importantly, incisive and intelligent.

While Meckel's contributions to the development of the Japanese army were the most significant made by a foreigner, not only his lectures but also his writing, which was translated into Japanese and published, the modernization could not have gone forward without the initiatives of the army's own leaders, men like Generals Katsura, Kawakami and Kodama. It was their efforts that brought the army to the level of professional standards and competence prevalent in the West. The division became the principal formation of the Japanese army, and the command structure that emerged comprised the Army Ministry, General Staff and Inspectorate General. Meckel could not have foreseen the serious political implications of this arrangement, in which each was independent of the other and answerable only to the Emperor, but it had its origins in two reports based on his recommendations: "Major Meckel's Opinion and Organization According to Meckel's Proposal."

In light of Japan's war in the twentieth century being fought beyond its home islands' shores, it is somewhat surprising that it was initially focused on repelling invaders. In the absence of a powerful navy that would take time to build and train, the army would have to bear the burden of defense. Meckel worked on the problem with his charges. The Prussians had used railroads in the wars against Austria in 1866 and the French in 1870. Meckel proposed that the Japanese construct a railway that avoided the coastal routes then being planned. However, it was one thing to recommend and another to follow through. The truth was that Japanese railroads were utterly incapable of moving military forces no matter where they were located. Yet Meckel persevered. He pushed to reform the conscription law which had been the handiwork of the French. In spite of the changes that had been made, many men, especially from the upper class, succeeded in avoiding military service A new law following Meckel's guidelines was adopted in January 1880 and ended most exemptions.

In March 1888, Meckel's service ended, and he departed for home, where he resumed his career in his own army. In his remaining years of active service, Meckel rose to the rank of major general and served a tour as Quartermaster General of the General Staff. Before that, he taught at the War Academy, where he counted among his students several officers whose influence and fame would far exceed his own, including Wilhelm Groener, Erich Ludendorff and Hans von Seeckt. Ordered to take command of an infantry brigade in 1896, Meckel duly reported and then requested retirement. He went to live at Gross-Lichterfeld, a Berlin suburb, spending his time raising dogs and composing music. He died in 1906 at the age of 64.

Back in Japan, the French position continued to decline as that of the Germans rose. Yet neither the French nor the German military mission was slated to last long. The Japanese army was ready to walk on its own legs. That it had learned its lessons from both sides was made evident in March and April 1890, at large-scale maneuvers conducted near Nagoya. All foreign representatives were invited to attend, including the French and Germany military advisers. The exercise was an expansion of one developed by Meckel. The scenario involved an invasion of Japan by a foreign army, opposed by a Japanese army supported by naval units. The war game was impressive: it included 31,000 men, 88 pieces of artillery, 4,500 horses, and 23 warships. All of the foreign observers were impressed, even if some strategic weaknesses were exposed. It was a far cry from the semi-feudal force that had struggled to put down the Satsuma Rebellion. The American representative commended upon the "French appearance" of the soldiers: "[T]he dress and equipment of the Japanese army are strongly marked by earlier French influence. The troops dress much like the French soldiers dress.... The foot soldiers seen walking along the streets of Tokyo ... pass fairly well in Paris."

The army might have looked French, but it fought German. The Japanese assured the French that the two military missions would terminate simultaneously. This was not entirely true. The Army Staff College still felt the need for German tutelage and once more engaged an officer for that purpose, Major Baron von Grutschreiber. Like Meckel, he served a three year term "to complete the conversion of the army to the German system." When Grutschreiber's contract ended in July 1894, he left for home and from then on the army managed its own affairs. Only in 1918 did they again seek European guidance, and that was to establish an army aviation corps. Then a French military mission was again summoned, the Germans having lost the war just ended.

Despite the undeniable personal impact made by Major Meckel, and the incorporation of German organization into the army's structure, it was the French who laid the foundation, giving the army its first officers, establishing its schools, and providing its training. In these and other ways, French influence persisted. The Japanese learned their lessons well from both nations, and in their first test of arms against China, and later against Russian, they confirmed their ability to fight and win a modern war.

The first conflict did not involve extensive forces. When Japan went to war with China in 1894, it was confronting a power already weakened by its capitulation to successive Western demands for commercial privileges. With only limited quantities of Western arms, China was no match for the small but well organized Japanese military forces.

However, there was sporadic disaffection about the war. In Gifu Prefecture in 1894, for example, there was no standing army, and fears for their safety led several soldiers from the 5th Division at Hiroshima to flee. Four of them were shot as deserters, but that was not all. A soldier in an infantry regiment at Toyohashi in adjacent Aichi Prefecture tried to shoot his sergeant while he was sleeping. The bullet ricocheted off the sergeant's armor and pierced the chest of another sergeant. The soldier then shot and killed himself.[37]

For the most part, discipline prevailed, but back in Germany the General Staff, which had dispatched Major Meckel to instruct the Japanese in warfare nine years earlier, had little confidence that Japan could defeat China, but the utter inability of the Chinese to fight a modern war quickly became evident. The Chinese were ill-officered; the Japanese were led by professionals. The Chinese soldiers suffered from poor morale; the Japanese were inspired. The Chinese wasted their ammunition in shooting sprees marred by undisciplined and poorly aimed firing; the Japanese had long since learned to appreciate the accuracy of well-aimed fire.

Meckel's emphasis on leadership was manifested in the behavior of Japanese officers, who were found at the head of their troops, exhorting by example and, given their penchant for frontal assault, taking a heavy proportion of the casualties. But Meckel's strategic training—men attacking across open ground and throwing themselves down before moving forward again—brought success. Cohesiveness and obedience to command were preserved. The main target of Japan's invasion of the Asian mainland, Port Arthur, at the end of the Liaotung Peninsula, was captured in a single day on November 21. By February 1895 Japan held all of Korea and the Liaotung Peninsula. China was defeated. "The Japanese had won their first modern war and they knew who to thank for it."[38]

For the first time, the Japanese public got a visual reporting of the war with China. The press, of course, gave it a large spread, but a new medium, the magic lantern, was introduced. The war scenes could now be shown via glass plates through which a light was passed and the images projected into a screen. This meant that even people in the hinterland could actually see what they had never before witnessed. In one county, the locality bought several hundred slides and charged admission fees benefiting the families of men on active service.[39]

Thoroughly beaten, the Chinese accepted Japanese peace overtures and Viceroy Li Hung-Chang came from China to Shiminoseki to negotiate. Already in control of Korea, the Japanese made claim to Shanhaikwan, the gateway through the Great Wall to Mongolia, as well as Tientsin and Tangku. But before they could impose these terms on China, they were embarrassed by an incident that caused them great humiliation. A Japanese assassin attempted to kill Viceroy Li. It was an affront so egregious that the Emperor sent his personal physician to visit the Chinese envoy and the prime minister proffered a personal apology. In the eyes of the world Japan was shamed, and the peace terms were softened in atonement.

They might have "lost face" by this untoward event, but the Japanese still came out of the peace conference as candidates for membership in the imperial club. China was forced to cede Taiwan (renamed Formosa), the Pescadores Islands and Liaotung Peninsula, and all of Manchuria. China promised to pay an indemnity of 360 million yen, which was three times the national budget of 1894. The Japanese were also granted trade privileges at Weiheiwei on the northern shore of the Shantung Peninsula, and the Chinese renounced all claims to Korea, putting the "Hermit Kingdom" in the Japanese sphere.[40] The cost of the war had been 200 million yen, which was recouped by the indemnity that China had to pay, plus interest.[41]

The war with China spawned aggressive and imperialist tendencies in Japan. Encouraged by organizations like the Black Ocean, "it showed the Japanese bourgeoisie to be a good ally of the Samurai caste." They would join the generals in their eagerness for conquest, "as a means of increasing the rate of primitive capitalist accumulation, which was hindered by the small capacity of the internal markets of Japan."[42]

The Chinese could not reconcile themselves to a Japanese presence on the Liaotung Peninsula. Having lost in a trial of arms, China opted for the only other course open to it, great-power intervention that would force Japan to rescind that clause of the treaty. Accordingly, China appealed to Russia, which viewed with alarm the Japanese success and acquisitions. The Czar's ministers reacted favorably to China's request, but first sought support from the other major Western powers with Far Eastern interests. The British found a Japanese presence in Manchuria less disturbing than a Russian one and turned a cold shoulder to the Russian overture. But France and Germany were more amenable, the French because of loyalty to a new ally and the Germans because it would earn them Russian gratitude at no cost. The three now pressured Japan to restore Port Arthur and the Liaotung Peninsula to China.

Of the actions by the two powers that had helped Japan's army, the Japanese least understood that of the Germans, and this sowed suspicions that ultimately drove them apart. The rift was compounded by the anti–Japanese attitude of the new German Minister to Japan, Baron von Gutschmid.

The Russian note which "advised" Japan to relinquish Port Arthur prompted the Emperor Meiji to call an Imperial Conference. The objection of only the foreign minister, Munemitsu Mutsu, was heard. Everyone else knew that Japan was not prepared to confront the Russians, much less a combination of the great powers. The nation would have to endure the humiliation, but it did not do so silently. A wave of anti-foreign sentiment swept the country. What had happened was a direct challenge to Japan's destiny. Why indeed should not Korea and Manchuria be annexed, asked Japanese newspapers? The consolidation by the European powers of their own territorial holdings in China only rubbed salt into an open wound. Japan had forced its way to the imperial table only to be told that there was no room. In their attempt to exclude it, the other powers only intensified Japanese nationalistic feelings.

The Russians moved promptly to replace Japanese hegemony in Manchuria. Railroad construction and mining development under Russian control and management followed large loans to the Chinese government. Port Arthur, which the Japanese had fought for, became the principal base of the Russian Pacific fleet. In March 1898 the Germans pressured the Chinese into granting them a 99-year lease on Kiaochow Bay. The best the Japanese could do was consolidate their position in Korea, but even there the Russians showed their intent to poach on Japanese interests by a timber-cutting concession on the Yalu River in northern Korea. It was clear in Tokyo that there must be an accounting with Russia if Japan was to secure a toehold on the Asian continent.

The government at once redoubled its efforts to increase its military strength. The indemnity from China helped, but the nation dipped into its

I. An Empire and an Army Are Born 31

own treasury to build up the army and navy. Forty-three percent of the annual budget in 1896–1897 was devoted to military spending, and the following year it reached 51 percent. A force of 400,000 men was organized into twelve divisions, double the size it had been when Meckel was present. Nor did the Japanese lose touch with their old mentor. Japanese officers were sent to Germany in the 1890s for instruction, some of them becoming pupils of Meckel again at the War Academy.[43]

Meanwhile the Japanese government tried to seek an accommodation with Russia while at the same time preparing for an armed confrontation. These twin policies reflected the political division in Japan that marked the years between 1895 and 1904. Two factions of the Choshu clan vied for control of the nation. One was led by General Yamagata, who believed that the military should rule through the Emperor, while Prince Ito held that civil power should prevail, though also through the throne. Yamagata had the support of the Kenseito Party, and Ito formed the Seiyukai Party in opposition. Toward Russia, Yamagata sought a military solution while Ito favored a diplomatic one.

When Ito's government fell in 1901, General Taro Katsura, a protégé of General Yamagata and a former student of Meckel's, became the new prime minister. He at once began preparations for war before the Russians completed the Trans-Siberian Railway. Simultaneously, the former prime minister, Prince Ito, traveled to St. Petersburg in a vain attempt to secure an agreement whereby Japan would promise not to interfere with Russian designs in Manchuria in return for a Russian promise to recognize Korea as an exclusive area of Japanese interest.[44]

Russian policy in China entered a new and more aggressive phase in 1901. Following the Boxer Rebellion, an uprising in China aimed at overthrowing foreign domination, the various powers that withdrew most of their troops when the Boxers had been suppressed left the Russians, who stayed on in Manchuria.

None of the other powers was unmindful of Russian aims in North China. The French, who were busy carving out their own area of influence in South China, could not object to Russian ambition in the north. Nor would the Germans object so long as they could be assured of concessions, but Great Britain and Japan looked askance at Russian behavior. Britain had more extensive investments in China than anyone else. Any violation of the territorial integrity of China would be inimical to her interests. Japan had already been thwarted in its attempt to acquire Port Arthur and the Liaotung Peninsula, and there was no confidence now that even Korea would be safe from Russian encroachment.

The coinciding of British and Japanese interests produced the Anglo-Japanese Alliance of 1902. Each of the signatories agreed to remain neutral if the other was involved in a war with a third power, but if the third power was aided by a fourth, the remaining signatory was obliged to come to the aid of its partner with armed force. For Japan, the Alliance ensured that Russia would be deprived of any help in the forthcoming war with Japan. Britain was now an ally, the most formidable naval power on earth. Who among the European powers would be willing to come to the aid of Russia in a Far Eastern war? The leaders in Tokyo knew the answer to that question: Russian would be isolated.

Yet even at that stage, war was not inevitable. The Russians knew that the Anglo-Japanese Alliance was aimed at them and that they could expect no help from anyone in the event of a conflict. Accordingly, the government in St. Petersburg agreed to withdraw from Manchuria in three stages by October 1903. If the Russians had honored that pledge and avoided meddling in Korea, war with Japan might have been averted. But Czar Nicholas II seemed to make a career of accepting bad advice and ignored his foreign office. Instead he followed the intemperate counsel of Vyacheslav Plehve, his scheming Minister of Interior, and Alexander Bezobrazov, an expansionist adviser, and failed to carry out the second stage of evacuation that had been scheduled for April 1903. Not only were the Russians in Manchuria ordered to remain, but the Czar allowed continued timber exploitation along the Yalu. More ominously in the eyes of the Japanese, the Czar approved the infiltration of disguised Russian troops in northern Korea.[45] The Russians turned a deaf ear to Prince Ito's offer. Japan now decided that war was inevitable.

Although the Japanese army and navy were at full strength, their leaders were under no illusions about the task that confronted them. Most of the world would have given Japan little hope of defeating a nation whose standing army of a million men was twice as large as the Japanese army, even including its reserves. The Western world also continued to harbor convictions of racial superiority. Japan's only war had been with a weak fellow Asian country. Against a European power, the outcome would be different. Such thinking, as events proved, was folly. The Trans-Siberian had been completed, but it was a single-track railway and there was a gap in it at Lake Baikal, which meant Russian troops would have to cross the 40-mile expanse of the frozen lake with their supplies before being able to reboard the train. At best, it was a tenuous connection to carry a multitude of supplies and reserves from European Russian to the Far East. Japan's military leaders counted on this great distance to balance their numerical inferiority in Asia where the war would be fought.[46]

Critical to Japanese success was control of the seas, so they began the war with a surprise attack on the Russian fleet at Port Arthur, bottling it up there and rendering it immobile. The other Russian fleet at Vladivostok was similarly defeated, and Japan enjoyed unfettered control of communications with the mainland. At the outset of the war, the Russians sneered at the Japanese, referring to them as "macaques" (monkeys). The Japanese would soon teach them a lesson.

Hostilities had begun with the attack on Port Arthur on February 8, 1904. By the end of March, 100,000 Japanese troops had landed in Korea. The peninsula was quickly cleared by a 40,000-man army under General Kuroki, which drove a much smaller Russian force out of the Yalu region. This victory was not without heavy losses, though, and it called into question the revered tactics of the army's German mentor, Major Meckel. The massed infantry assaults, so earnestly studied, might have prevailed against the untrained marksmanship of the ill-led legions of China, but the Japanese recognized what the Western powers were to spend four years of futile carnage ignoring, that waves of infantry are helpless against an entrenched foe armed with repeating rifles, machine guns and rapid-fire artillery. Where the Russians had field fortifications, they inflicted severe losses on their enemy.

The Japanese forces eventually adjusted to the new conditions of warfare, but the changes were not uniform throughout the army. Massed infantry attacks were the order of the day against Port Arthur, but the capture of the city, in January 1905, had cost six months of heavy fighting and the lives of 51,800 men, more than a third of the besieging forces. The Japanese employed looser formations in the battle for Mukden, the capital of Manchuria, and the casualties were not so one-sided. Indeed, Russian losses exceeded those of the Japanese by a ratio of three to two. Nevertheless, the casualty rate among Japanese officers continued to be high. A French observer attributed this to two factors: first, the concept of *bushido*, the code of the warrior; and second, Meckel's tactical doctrines. If "the spirit of self-sacrifice, so prominent in *bushido*, and the ruthless tactics preached by the Prussian had found it easy to join hands," nevertheless automatic weapons were the great equalizer on the battlefield, and in the face of them, it would take more to achieve victory "than aggressive tactics and a willingness to die." The war was indeed costly. Of 1.1 million men under arms, 80,000 were killed and more than 300,000 wounded.[47]

Yet Meckel lived long enough to see the triumph of his pupils, many of whom acknowledged their debt to him, which filled him with understandable pride. Their terrible losses notwithstanding, the Japanese paid homage to him after his death in July 1906. When news of it reached Tokyo, a memorial service was arranged by General Kodama, a former pupil who addressed Meckel following the battle at the Yalu with the respectful term "younger brother." Before the service could be conducted, Kodama himself died, but the ceremony he had planned for his old teacher went forward. Ernst Presseisen wrote a sentimental account of the farewell:

In contrast to the unnoticed funeral in Berlin, the ceremony in Tokyo was enormous. The auditorium of the Army Staff College was completely filled with officers, including Generals Kuroki and Nogi, the Army Minister, the new Chief of Staff and many diplomats. Kodama's oration—his last—was read by an officer, and Shinto priests performed religious rites. Every guest received a picture of the general; a telegram of condolence had been sent to Frau Meckel; in short, nothing was neglected to indicate Japan's gratitude and regret. One gesture could still be made. In 1909, a bust of Meckel, set on a shaft of stone, was unveiled in front of the Army Staff College, where it remained until 1945. His work lasted as long.[48]

The Russo-Japanese War ended in a dramatic sea battle. The defeat of both naval squadrons at Port Arthur and Vladivostok prompted the Russians to amass their Baltic Sea Fleet and send it on a herculean voyage to the Far East. Forced to recoal at sea because the British denied them the use of coaling stations along the way, the Russian fleet took seven months to reach its destination. With the fall of Port Arthur, a decision was made to sail for Vladivostok. Most of the ships never got there. In the Tsushima Strait, separating Japan and Korea, a Japanese fleet commanded by Admiral Heihachiro Togo, administered a crushing defeat.

From the beginning the Japanese looked to Great Britain for the creation of their navy and the training of naval officers. Having learned English at school in Yokohama, Togo joined twelve midshipmen at the Thames Nautical Training School in England and then went to sea in the training ship *Hampshire*. By the time he returned to Japan, he was thoroughly versed in British seamanship and tactics. As the Japanese navy expanded, Togo rose in rank, distinguishing himself in the war with China and leading the attack on Port Arthur at the outset of the war in 1904. He would crown his success as a naval strategist with his triumph in the Battle of Tsushima. Aboard his flagship, "*Mikasa*," Togo and his swift ships succeeded in crossing the Russian battle line, bringing his main batteries to bear, a tactic known as "crossing the T." All but four small Russian ships were either captured or sunk, and the Russians lost 4,830 of their sailors, while the Japanese lost only 110 men.

(*NOTE: The *Mikasa* has an interesting history. As Togo's flagship in the stunning victory at Tsushima, it acquired a reputation that can best be compared to the American battleship *Missouri*, on which the Japanese surrender was signed in 1945. When the *Mikasa* became obsolete the Japanese could not bring themselves to scrap it, so they moved it to a parade ground at the Yokosuka naval base where it served as a shrine to Japan's naval success in 1905. On July 18, 1945, an American Navy air group struck the base at Yokosuka, its target the battleship *Nagato*, one of the last remaining Japanese capital ships. The *Nagato* was in a slip, and torpedo bombers from the carrier *Yorktown* were armed with 1,500-pound bombs with special fuses to sink her. The aircraft would dive at a forty-five degree angle, a technique known as "glide bombing." The author of this book was there on that day, manning a .30 caliber machine gun behind the bomb bay in one of the attacking planes. Peeling off at 10,000 feet amidst heavy anti-aircraft fire, nine bombers dove on the target. The procedure called for the aircraft to pull out at 3,000 feet, and when he did not feel the "G's"—that is, the sensation of pulling out of the dive—he looked over his shoulder and saw the altimeter needle drop past 3,000 and 2,000, and finally stop at 1,000 feet. Alarmed, he called the pilot on the intercom and was told to take a look at the left wing, where a 40-millimeter shell had hit the leading edge, opening a large hole. The pilot had made a long shallow dive to save pressure on the wing. He said that we had been hit at 6,000 feet and he had jettisoned the bomb, knowing that it would have been fatal to complete the dive with it. And where did the errant bomb fall? Perhaps you have guessed. The *Mikasa* was about a hundred yards from the *Nagato* and suffered a direct hit. For a 1905 ship that was devastating. The Japanese could never understand why the Americans would want to bomb an old ship that was on land, and refused to believe that it was a mistake. The Yokosuka naval base is now occupied by the American Navy and the *Mikasa*, long since restored, is still in her old location, for which our Navy can take partial credit. Admiral Chester Nimitz, who commanded U.S. naval forces in the Pacific in World War II, contributed to the restoration of the *Mikasa* and in 2009, crew members from the carrier USS *Nimitz* painted the *Mikasa*. Admiral Togo would probably be pleased that a former enemy of his country has honored his memory.)

The Japanese asked Theodore Roosevelt to mediate between them and the Russians, and at his invitation, both powers sent emissaries to Portsmouth, New Hampshire, to negotiate peace. Although instructed to make no territorial concessions or promises to pay indemnity, the Russian representatives found themselves forced to compromise, as did the Japanese, who wanted indemnity and made extensive territorial claims. In the Treaty of Portsmouth, signed on September 5, 1905, Russia forfeited all interest in Korea and accepted it as a Japanese protectorate. The Japanese got back their lost gains in China. Russia ceded its rights to the Liaotung Peninsula and Port Arthur, and to the South Manchurian Railway from Port Arthur to Changchun. Finally, Russia gave up the southern half of the island of Sakhalin, which the Japanese renamed Karafuto. But the Russians did not have to pay indemnity, a concession for which the Japanese bitterly blamed the United States. The ill feeling generated by this disappointment fed on an earlier confrontation in Hawaii, with profound consequences for both nations. The Japanese, before their showdown with the Russians, had been alarmed by American expansion in the Pacific. Sensitive about the rights of Japanese nationals in Hawaii, who comprised roughly forty percent of the population, ten times that of whites, the Japanese government dispatched the battle cruiser *Naniwa* to Honolulu, commanded by none other than the future hero of Tsushima, Captain Heihachiro Togo, "as a demonstration to protect the rights of Japanese citizens."[49] This demonstration backfired when American expansionists pushed back with a demand that America take the islands.

It now seems portentous that the first confrontation between Japan and America took place over Hawaii. Coupled with what later happened in Portsmouth, Japan no longer saw America as a benign ally but as a growing adversary and in time, the principal barrier to Japanese ambitions in Asia.

II

The Army in Retreat

> Truly we are a small island, completely isolated in the Eastern Sea. One false step and our nation will again fall into the desperate state of crisis—dilemmas at home and abroad—that marked the period before and after the Meiji Restoration.
> —Ikki Kita, "An Outline Plan for the Reorganization of Japan"

On the morning of July 30, 1912, the forty-five-year reign of the Emperor Meiji came to an end. After a brief illness, Mutsuhito, who had presided over the rebirth of his nation, expired. By his example he had laid the foundation for the adoration of his station as a god. His devotion to his people was manifest in all his acts. In his Spartan lifestyle, he reflected the virtue of strength through hardship and identity with those he ruled. His interest in the arts and his skill in composing Japanese verse were evidence of his civilized nature. The national period of mourning that followed was genuine. On the day of his funeral, his most illustrious general in the war with Russia, Maresuki Nogi, and his wife resorted to the ancient custom of *junshi*, of following their ruler in death by committing *hara-kiri*. The Japanese people reacted to the suicide of General Nogi and his wife with bittersweet emotion. It was an act that reminded the nation of its samurai heritage and was the ultimate expression of loyalty, the most important virtue of all.

Mutsuhito was succeeded by his third son, Yoshihito Harunomiya, the issue of one of his concubines. While he was still a boy, Yoshihito was stricken with meningitis, an illness that would stalk him the rest of his life. He became increasingly unstable mentally, with periods of sanity and derangement alternating unpredictably. Yet preparations went forward for his coronation. An imperial rescript announced that Yoshihito's reign name would be Taisho, which meant "great rectification, reform." The name and its definition were not chosen by happenstance. They conveyed the message that the revolutionary changes wrought in Japanese society and institutions during the Meiji era were in place. All that was needed now was "adjustment."[1]

So, Yoshihito became the Emperor Taisho in an elaborate Shinto ceremony in November 1915. Had the new Emperor been in full control of his faculties, the "adjustments" called for in the imperial rescript might have turned out to be nearly as revolutionary as the changes of the past. There were calls for sweeping aside the old political leaders and developing a new political consciousness. One writer declared

> In antiquity the people stood outside the orbit of politics. Those who filled the ranks of the Restoration movement were recruited from the lower samurai class but the enterprise of Taisho must add to it ordinary peasants and merchants ... we must open up a politics of democratism which is founded on the idea of the Emperor.[2]

There would be a shift in political patterns and even a brief parliamentary interlude, but the Emperor Taisho was not the architect of these developments. He had scarcely taken the throne when he again began to exhibit the eccentric behavior that betrayed his instability. He fell off his horse at parades and occasionally whipped the soldiers he was inspecting. It was clear to court advisors that the Emperor would have to be retired to private life. Any remaining doubts about the state of his mental health were removed when he rolled up the speech that he was supposed to read to the members of the Diet (parliament) and put it to his eye like a telescope to observe them. Following this antic, he was confined to his beach palace at Hayama, where the Empress indulged his idiosyncrasies until his death on Christmas Day 1926.[3] For the last ten years of his life, his son, the Prince Imperial Hirohito, became the focus of his attention and Hirohito's accession was patiently awaited.

The political pot had begun to boil in Tokyo even as Taisho prepared to succeed his father; the Army General Staff was responsible. They wanted two new divisions funded, but Prince Kinmochi Saionji, the Prime Minister, backed by a majority of his cabinet, resisted. In fact, the finances of the country would not permit it. The Minister of War then resorted to a tactic that would be repeated over and over in years to come. General Uehara, who filled this position, submitted his resignation directly to the Emperor without informing Saionji. While the Constitution allowed Uehara to do this, his action nevertheless precipitated a government crisis. The Saionji cabinet could not survive without a Minister of War and was obliged to resign as well. General Katsura, who had served twice before as Prime Minister, was now asked to form a government. The appointment was made in December 1912, prior to the meeting of the Diet. When it did convene, opposition to Katsura was raised at once. The general was viewed as a martinet and his leadership thoroughly resented. Nor did the navy want

Katsura. Besides the natural rivalry of a sister service, the old clan rivalry between the Satsuma and Choshu reasserted itself. Finally, the press was hostile to Katsura, and while only three million people were entitled to vote in 1913, the newspapers acted as a catalyst for the electorate and the public at large.[4]

The Diet members perceived that the real issue was whether Japan was going to have representative government or suffer clan politics. A prominent member of the parliament, Yukio Ozaki, made a vigorous attack on Katsura and his colleagues, setting off a dispute that spilled out of the Diet into the rest of the country. Riots in Tokyo and other major cities resulted in loss of life and necessitated the summoning of military forces to aid the police.

Japanese Emperor Hirohito, who reigned between the 1920s and 1950s (Library of Congress).

Ultimately, Katsura bowed to the opposition and resigned, yet it was not a victory for parliamentary democracy but a triumph for the Satsuma clan, with whom the Seiyukai, the majority party of the Lower House, had made an alliance. Proof of this was the appointment of the new Prime Minister, Admiral Gombei Yamamoto, a Satsuma man. Having the navy at the helm did not result in calmer waters, however. A few months after Yamamoto was sworn in, a number of high-ranking officials were exposed as having accepted bribes from the Siemens-Schuckert Company for assistance in their bid to obtain the contract to build a Japanese warship. Although no cabinet minister was involved in the scandal, the Yamamoto government could not survive the public outrage that followed.[5]

After more political jockeying, Count Okuma, the founder of Waseda

University, formed a new government in April 1914. In doing so, he had the cooperation of a new party, the Doshikai. He named Baron Takaaki Kato, the leader of the Doshikai, as the new Foreign Minister. The Great War was only four months away. When it broke out, Japan would take advantage of it and attempt to extend her imperial domain.

The Anglo-Japanese Alliance had been renewed in 1911 for another decade, with an alteration in its terms to ensure that it would not apply if either power became involved in a dispute with the United States. Nothing was said about a war with Germany, yet when the war began Great Britain did not expect Japan to be an active belligerent. What the British did expect was cooperation from Japan in dealing with German commercial raiders in the Far East. Beyond that, a Japanese declaration of war would have far more serious consequences for China than it would for Germany. If Japan entered the war against Germany, the immediate objective would be the German base at Tsingtao, followed by an attempt to gain control of Shantung Province. There were also fears in Australia, New Zealand and the Netherlands that Japan would take the German-owned islands in Micronesia and establish permanent bases in the Marshalls and Carolines. Such a prospect created similar worries in the United States.[6]

Kinmochi Saionji, Japanese elder statesman, the "genro" who advised the emperor (*The Imperial Pictorial*, vol. 2, Tokyo: Fuzanbo Publishing Co.).

If the government in Tokyo was aware of these concerns, it didn't discuss them. The Japanese saw the European conflict as a providential opportunity to seize what they could from the beleaguered Germans, to whom they now sent an ultimatum. It gave Japan intense satisfaction to craft the language in the very terms that she had been given at the time of the Triple Intervention, the demands by Russia, France and Germany that she give up a major share of the spoils exacted from China in the Treaty of Shimonoseki. Now Japan paid the Germans back in kind, "advising" them to remove or disarm their naval vessels and other ships in the Far East. Additionally, she "advised" the Germans to surrender Tsingtao and the Kiaochow leased territories, adding mendaciously that these possessions would eventually be restored to China. An expiration date of August 23, 1914, was given; in the absence of a reply, Japan declared war.

Since most declarations of war are designed for home consumption, the imperial edict in this case can be partly excused for its hypocrisy. "It is with profound regret, that We, in spite of Our ardent devotion to the cause of peace, are thus compelled to declare war, especially at this early period of Our reign an while We are still in mourning for Our lamented mother."[7] (The latter reference was a technical error. The widow of the Emperor Meiji had died in the spring of 1914. She was not the mother of Taisho, but in a larger sense was revered as the mother of the nation.)

In the beginning there was a division of opinion within the Japanese military about the outcome of the war. Not surprisingly, the army thought that the Germans would win, while the navy favored the British. Each service reflected its training model. What confirmed the army observers in their bias was the performance of a small British expeditionary force comprising a Welsh battalion and a half-battalion of Sikhs. This little contingent shared the siege of Tsingtao with a larger Japanese force. The Japanese were unimpressed by the fighting qualities of their ally, particularly the British officers, who the Japanese felt came from wealthy families and were soft. As for the Germans, they put up a spirited defense for several weeks before surrendering in early November.[8]

The early British reverses at sea in the war also tarnished the reputation of British prowess. The cautiousness of the British Admiralty in prosecuting the war with Germany appeared in sharp contrast to the aggressiveness that the Japanese had shown in attacking Port Arthur. All these developments certainly made Japan feel less of a junior partner in its alliance with Great Britain.

As for the German possessions in Micronesia, the Australians and New Zealanders had only themselves to blame for not moving expeditiously to seize them. They had opened hostilities with Germany three weeks before Japan and had ample opportunity to take them first. The Australians especially showed their naiveté by quickly taking German New Guinea and Samoa, and then assuming that this gave them a claim to the German islands to the north. They should have known better. Even before the siege of Tsingtao ended, the Japanese fleet had captured the largest of the Marshall Islands, on October 6, and Yap the day after. By October 20 all the Marshalls, Ladrones and Carolines were in Japanese hands. All would be retained as mandates after the war and would be used as anchorages and forward bases in military operations a generation later.

Now in possession of Tsingtao, the Japanese wasted no time in trying to turn a comparatively small gain into a much larger one. In the course of doing so they overplayed their hand and exposed a rapaciousness that was to cost them the good will of China and the Western world as well. The Rising Sun had hardly been raised over the former German territories when the infamous Twenty-One Demands were hatched.

The Japanese outlook toward China revealed a Kiplingesque parody of "The White Man's Burden." Just as the Europeans justified their imperialism on the basis of duty to bring the benefits of "civilization to Asians and Africans," so did the Japanese try to justify theirs on the basis of their self-perceived superiority and uniqueness. In 1881, Yukichi Fukuwaza boasted in his essay, "A Critique of the Times," that none of the other Asian countries could match Japan in assimilation of Western learning and technology. Since Japan alone possessed this ability, he claimed, it bore the responsibility of protecting all of East Asia.

> Some Japanese believe that it is proper to take measures for their own independence, but useless to protect others. This is not so. For example, suppose we have a stone house. If there are wooden buildings in the neighborhood, we must still worry about fires. In fire prevention, we have to think about the whole neighborhood and not only our own house. If there is an emergency, we give aid, of course. But it is a serious matter to enter a neighbor's house on an ordinary day and demand that he construct it of stone, like ours.
>
> The neighbor will do as he pleases and may or may not build a new house. In an unusual case, we might have to force our way in and build this house ourselves, not for the sake of the neighbor but to stop the fire from spreading. The way in which Western countries are now expanding their influence in Asia is analogous to the spreading of fire.
>
> Neighboring Korea and China, which have no equal in foolishness, are like wooden houses unable to survive a fire. So Japan must "give them military protection" and be their "cultural inspiration," not for their sake but ours. If necessary, "we must threaten to use force if they don't make progress" and allow no opposition. Although it is commonly said that we have a "lips and teeth" relationship with them as equals, to think that there could be any cooperation between us and China in its present state is the height of stupidity.[9]

By 1915 the Japanese had imposed their "stone house" on Korea. Now they would try to do the same with China.

Since it had waged war on the Manchus, China had become a republic, but it was even more disorganized than before. The Japanese viewed China with a mixture of scorn and satisfaction. With the European powers preoccupied with their self-induced slaughter half a world away, Japan could now assert itself in China without interference. Had Baron Kato displayed less avarice and more reason, he might have consolidated substantial territorial gains for his country. It was a failure to be repeated by his successors twenty-two years later. The Foreign Minister simply overplayed his hand.

The Twenty-One Demands covered a plethora of Japanese interests in China. The military attaché in Peking made some of the recommendations, but the principal work was done by a bureau chief in the Foreign Ministry in Tokyo. Nevertheless, it was Kato who aggressively pushed for their acceptance by the Okuma Cabinet and insisted that they be served on the Chinese government in Peking. Normally, important questions of foreign policy were referred to the *Genro*, a small body of elder statesmen who had made their reputation in the building of the Meiji state. This peculiarly Japanese institution had served the nation well. Until 1901 they had provided nearly all of the Prime Ministers, and thereafter they played a behind-the-scenes role, manipulating cabinet appointments and generally serving as "guardians of the administration."[10] Kato was so strong-willed that he broke with custom and ignored the *Genro* in adopting the Twenty-One Demands. In so doing he incurred the wrath of the redoubtable Aritomo Yamagata, the powerful prince of the Choshu clan, a former Prime Minister and still the army's principal mentor. Yamagata was the leading *Genro* and Kato would come to rue his omission.[11]

Essentially, the Twenty-One Demands would have put China under the administrative and economic control of Japan. The first four groups of the Demands would have obliged China to recognize the Japanese seizure of German rights in Shantung; extend Japan's lease on Port Arthur and Dairen to 99 years; acknowledge trade, land-owning, rail and various industrial concessions in Manchuria, Inner Mongolia and the Yangtze Valley; and agree not to negotiate loans or agreements with any other power without Japanese consent. All of these were onerous enough, but it was a fifth group that aroused the bitterest controversy. Had the Chinese agreed to them, they would have forfeited their sovereignty. Under this group of demands, there would be joint Japanese control of arsenals and police, and the Japanese would have the right to own land on which they could build hospitals, temples and schools.

In January 1915, the Japanese Minister in Peking presented the demands to President Yuan Shih-kai with instructions to observe the strictest secrecy. For the luckless Yuan the Japanese claims could not have come at a worse time. He was preparing to restore the monarchy by declaring himself Emperor, a dubious prospect in any event, and now he was confronted by a militant neighbor bent on subverting his country. He protested and procrastinated, knowing that little help would be forthcoming from the West. For six months he fended off the Japanese, but in the meantime, word of the demands leaked out. As a result, there was an outbreak of violent anti–Japanese sentiment in China, accompanied by a boycott of Japanese goods. Kato soon found himself besieged. He had served as Ambassador to Great Britain before the war and in 1913 had held discussions with the British Foreign Secretary, Sir Edward Grey, expressing an interest in expanding

Japan's sphere of control in China. While the record of these meetings is incomplete, it is certain that Grey never agreed to anything beyond Japanese hegemony in South Manchuria. Kato assumed otherwise and compounded his error by omitting all reference to the shameless fifth group, the so-called "desire," when he communicated Japanese intentions to Grey in 1915. At first the British raised no objection, but when the full story became known in London, the Japanese were told bluntly that Group V was inconsistent with the terms of the Anglo-Japanese Alliance.

In Peking the crafty Yuan played his last card, turning the tables on Kato at home. Through a Japanese emissary, he appealed to Yamagata, who had been incensed from the outset by Kato's highhanded behavior. In May, Yamagata and his *Genro* colleagues met with the entire Cabinet and prevailed upon them to drop the invidious "desires" of the fifth group. Yamagata claimed later that if Japan had insisted upon them it would have disgraced its honor, but there was no reluctance about forcing Yuan to accede to the rest.

Whatever Japan gained in the short term it lost in the long. Unwittingly the Japanese had nourished Chinese nationalism, which now expressed itself in unremitting suspicion, fear and hatred of Japan. It would, however, take more than shared national animosity to unite China. Yuan's imperial aspirations came to naught. He declared himself Emperor three months after the Twenty-One Demands, but instead of rallying the people to his side, he divided them. Too late, he cancelled his decree as the nation began to fracture. When he died two months later, China was already on the path to an inglorious period of predatory rule by adventurers whose self-aggrandizement mocked the rump government in Peking and left the nation less able than ever to resist foreign domination. The northern warlords from the provinces of Anhwei and Fukien controlled the so-called "Government" in Peking, which suited the Japanese and Western powers. The latter were content to recognize it, while the Japanese funneled loans to the provincial masters who preserved the sham regime's fictional legitimacy.[12]

In the south, Sun Yat-Sen, who had led the revolution that overthrew the Manchu Dynasty in 1911, reestablished his Kuomintang government in Canton. But his claim to be the only constitutional authority in China fell on deaf ears. None of the foreign powers cared to change the status quo. A strong, unified China would represent a threat to their interests. A divided China served them best—so long as no one of their number tried to gain an edge over the others.

Despite Kato's setback in failing to meet all of the Twenty-One Demands, Japan continued to press its advantage. General Terauchi, whose military background gave hope to the caste from which he came, proved to be even less effective in his China strategy, which added "to the burden of Japanese discredit."[13] replaced Okumo as Prime Minister in 1916 and switched from the mailed fist policy of his predecessor to that of the velvet glove, using loans and bribes to control China. But he had no intention of relinquishing Japan's hold on Shantung and the other German possessions in the Pacific. Accordingly, in 1917, the Japanese generated the rumor that unless they were confirmed in their holdings, they might change sides in the war. The tactic succeeded. Secret agreements were made with Britain, France and Italy to support Japan's claims at the peace conference. When the United States entered the war that year, the Japanese sought to bring the Americans into the understanding. The result was the Lansing-Ishii Agreement, signed that fall in Washington. The Chinese were dismayed to learn that the Americans, who had sponsored the "Open Door" policy of equal access for all in commercial relations and a pledge to respect the territorial integrity of China, had signed an agreement which acknowledged that because of her "territorial propinquity," Japan "had special interests in China, particularly in the part to which her possessions are contiguous." In spite of the fact that the Chinese had agreed with these provisions in signing the Twenty-One Demands, they had expected better of the United States. In Washington, the agreement was looked upon as a wartime necessity. No one wanted to alienate Japan.[14]

By now, the Chinese too were looking beyond the war to the peace table. Believing that they could earn a place there and thus protect themselves from further encroachment, both the Peking and Canton regimes declared war on Germany in August 1917. The Allies welcomed Chinese participation. Chinese labor battalions would be helpful, and Chinese belligerency offered the chance to eliminate the German presence from the Orient. If the Chinese wanted to believe that they might win concessions, then let them.

The war in Europe paid other dividends for Japan besides those in Asia. Like the growing industrial giant on the other side of the Pacific, Japan's economy received an enormous stimulus from the war. This came at a propitious time. Japan's population had grown from under forty million in 1890 to nearly fifty million by 1910. During these same years, the nation made great strides in industrialization. No longer did Japan have to rely on foreign yards to build her warships. She now had the capacity herself. Yet despite her progress in metallurgy, and her production of machinery and tools, ceramics and glassware, lumber and wood products, Japan continued to suffer an imbalance of trade. The addition of ten million more mouths to feed obliged Japan to import food, including rice. Had the Japanese not exploited Korean production, they would have been even worse off in their balance of payments and reliance on foreign food sources.

With the advent of the war in 1914 there was an immediate need for Japanese goods, textiles being in particular demand by the belligerents. Now Japan, like America, switched from being a debtor to a creditor nation. The government paid off its foreign loans, wiped out the national debt, and increased its gold reserves to one billion dollars. Most of the war-generated wealth flowed into the hands of the *Zaibatsu* (money groups), which were composed principally of the four giants of Japanese finance and industry—the houses of Mitsui, Mitsubishi, Sumitomo and Yasuda. Although Yasuda was primarily concerned with banking interests, all four groups were engaged in business activities that often overlapped. The largest of them was Mitsui, which was involved in banking, manufacturing, mining, railways and department stores. It even ran a newspaper, the Osaka *Mainichi*, one of the most influential in Japan. Both capital funds and business experience were concentrated in the hands of a few families, and the state had no choice but to make use of them.[15]

These conditions led to considerable war profiteering and an extravagance which caused deep resentment among the growing middle class and workers toward a minority who had made their wealth overnight on profits as high as 200 percent.[16] Wages failed to keep pace with inflation, and trade unions, almost unknown before 1916, began to assert themselves. Industrial strikes in 1917 and 1918 were a prelude to "rice riots" in Kobe in August 1918, which led to the downfall of the Terauchi Ministry. The riots were an interesting phenomenon, since they spread spontaneously from Kobe across the country without organization or leadership. The army finally had to be called out to quell the violence. Terauchi was succeeded by the first commoner to head a Japanese ministry, Takashi Hara, a leader of the Seiyukai, the majority political party. Although the Hara government went along with the army's intervention policy in Siberia, there were nevertheless hopes for more democratic rule at home. The surviving *Genro* began to decline in influence, and the call now was for *ninsei*, *ninken* and *jiyu*, popular government, popular rights and liberty.[17] The 1920s seemed to fulfill such expectations, but the decade would prove to be a false dawn. The Asian mainland was still an irresistible magnet.

When the war in Europe shuddered to an end in the fall of 1918, Japan stood ready to reap the benefits of it. The conflict had enabled her to improve her position in China, and as a result of the Bolshevik Revolution in Russia, an unexpected bonus seemed to be in the offing in Siberia. In Paris, Japan would rely on her diplomats to confirm her gains in China and the Pacific. The army would try its luck in Siberia. The diplomats would face obstacles, but these were nothing compared to what the army confronted.

Japan sent her leading statesmen to the peace conference, men who had made their reputations in the Meiji era and enjoyed widespread

II. The Army in Retreat 47

confidence. Heading the delegation was Marquis (later Prince) Saionji, who would survive as the last of the *Genro*, Baron (later Viscount) Makino, Viscount (later Count) Chinda, Mr. (later Baron) Matsui, and Mr. (later Baron) Ijuin.[18] The Japanese had two objectives at the conference, one that appealed to the altruism of the other delegates and the other to what they felt was a fair distribution of the spoils. Altruism and fairness are not characteristics for which the Paris peace conference is remembered, and the Japanese had a right to react with indignation when their proposal to make equality of all nations a basic principle of the new League of Nations was rejected. They had originally sought the inclusion of the phrase "racial equality," but the British yielded to the opposition of the Commonwealth delegates, led by Australian Prime Minister William M. Hughes,[19] and offered the compromise language "equality of all nations." The League commission accepted this by a vote of eleven to five, but President Wilson, under strong British pressure, used his influence as chairman to defeat it by ruling that a resolution on a matter of principle needed a unanimous vote.[20] When word of Wilson's action reached Japan, there was understandable outrage. The press labeled him a "hypocrite" and a "transformed Kaiser."[21]

The Japanese were more successful in winning assent to their territorial claims. The United States was wary of Japanese expansion into the Pacific Ocean and would have preferred to place the former German possessions under Australian administration, but Great Britain, in deference to her ally, upheld Japan's claims. Under the mandate granted, the islands north of the Equator, including the Carolines, Palau, the Ladrones and Marshalls, plus the island of Yap, were placed under Japanese administration. All the islands to the south were put under the control of New Zealand and Australia.

Disposing of the German possessions was one matter; the Germans had been an enemy. But China was an ally, and prying territory from her would not be easy. Both the "official government" in Peking and the rival Kuomintang regime from Canton were present at the peace conference and joined ranks against the Japanese claim to Shantung. Dr. Wellington Koo, who would speak for China in world councils a generation later, presented the Chinese case and won the sympathy of President Wilson. But the Japanese held a strong hand. Baron Makino revealed that the Chinese Prime Minister had signed a covert agreement recognizing Japan's Shantung claim in 1915. Moreover, in exchange for a railway loan in September 1918, the Peking government had secretly agreed to the arrangement. When these tactics failed to persuade the Americans, the Japanese disclosed the terms of the secret treaties that they had signed with Britain, France, Italy and Russia in 1917, in which those nations had pledged to support Japanese claims to Shantung and the German islands in the Pacific. They then clinched their case by informing Wilson that if China's objections prevailed, Japan would withdraw from the peace conference and would not join the League of Nations.[22]

Wilson was on the horns of a dilemma. There were thirty million Chinese in Shantung. What would become of the noble principle of self-determination that Wilson had extolled when he proposed the Fourteen Points of peace? And yet, if Japan bolted from the peace conference and failed to become a member of the League, Wilson's most cherished goal, long-term peace, might be imperiled. Orlando of Italy had already left the conference table because of the denial of his country's claim to the city of Fiume, now part of the newly created nation of Yugoslavia. If the Japanese left too, the blow to Wilson's hopes might be fatal. So, Wilson capitulated to a face-saving compromise: Japan would keep the economic holdings of the Germans in Shantung, but the peninsula itself would be restored to China, an agreement that the Japanese honored in 1923. Wilson won few points with this bargain. When he brought home the Versailles Treaty in 1919, it was the Shantung settlement that fueled opposition in the United States Senate. In Paris, Clemenceau was prompted to sneer, "Wilson talked like Jesus Christ, but acted like Lloyd George."[23]

The Japanese had played their hand well, but they left the conference with a sour taste in their mouths. Although Wilson had finally agreed to a satisfactory settlement with regard to Shantung, they would not forget how his Secretary of State, Robert Lansing, had behaved. Lansing had taken a strong pro–Chinese stance at Paris, which seemed to them to be a betrayal of the understanding that he had made with Viscount Ishii when they penned their agreement in Washington in 1917. The Americans might say that Shantung did not fall within the terms of that agreement, that Shantung was not "contiguous" with Japanese possessions, but the Japanese felt that it was, under the definition of the word "propinquity." Kato thought that he and Grey had had an understanding in their London talks. Ishii believed that he and Lansing had one with respect to Shantung. The misunderstanding led to recriminations on both sides.[24] In America the press railed against "the crime of Shantung" and called Japan "the possessor of stolen goods."[25] In Japan, America was seen as a citadel of hypocrisy, a nation that gave lip service to the principle "all men are created equal" but in reality practiced the opposite at home and abroad, and whose agreements were not to be trusted, so filled were they with cunning and guile.

The Siberian adventure proved to be a costly failure. In this respect Japan had company. The British, French and Americans all committed military forces to Russia following the Bolshevik Revolution, and all were ultimately to withdraw them under pressure. But Japan had made a far heavier investment, which exacerbated the disillusionment with the army when they were finally forced to pull out.

Japan's leaders were never interested in becoming embroiled in Europe's war except for the opportunities presented to them in their own part of the world. However, when the Czar's government was replaced by a republic in March 1917, the Japanese began to stir, particularly when they received reports that fall that the new Russian government had agreed to allow American investment in the Siberian provinces.[26] When Lenin's Bolsheviks overthrew Kerensky's provisional government in November, all of the Western allies had cause for deep concern. Kerensky had stayed the course in the war with Germany. Lenin was determined to take Russia out of it.

The Allied powers could not force the new revolutionary government to honor the old one's commitment, but they could keep the enormous stock of military supplies that they had shipped to Russia from falling into German hands. Accordingly, two Allied expeditions landed in North Russia in 1918, but the most important intervention occurred in eastern Siberia. Besides the need to secure the military stores at Vladivostok, the action was rationalized by a bizarre episode that briefly took center stage and caught the attention of the Allies; indeed, it captured the admiration of the Western world. Word came of a force of 50,000 Czechoslovaks who were fighting their way across Siberia toward the Pacific. It was thought that these brave men might be in danger from German and Austrian prisoners of war. That was a specious argument for sending troops to Siberia, yet it was precisely the one given by Secretary of State Lansing when the United States invited Japan to participate in a joint expedition in July 1918. In fact, the German and Austrian prisoners were never a threat to anyone. The Czechs were strung out along the Trans-Siberian Railroad, and the only fighting they were doing was with the Bolsheviks.[27]

The fate of 50,000 Czechs was hardly of any concern to Japan, but the birth of a Marxist state adjacent to the Japanese Empire was. Everything about that alien philosophy was antithetical to the imperial mind. Yet despite their fears about the threat of Communism or possible American economic penetration in the region, the Japanese hesitated to dispatch soldiers into the eastern provinces of Siberia. The military leadership in this instance was more cautious about taking up the American invitation than was the civilian. Nevertheless, once they did so they did so with more ardor than Washington expected or wished. The Americans sent 9,000 of their own men to Siberia and asked the Japanese to commit 7,000. The Japanese ultimately sent 72,000 troops and the French and British token contingents. The appearance of this Japanese army raised suspicion in the United States that Japan had a lot more in mind than simply protecting the far-from-embattled Czechs. President Wilson had acted without Congressional approval in sending American troops to Vladivostok and Archangel, but he was strongly anti–Bolshevist and wished to encourage the counter-revolutionary forces battling the Red Army. Now, in the Far East, he hoped that the American presence would discourage Japan from taking the Pacific portions of the old Russian empire and adding them to its own.

Friction soon developed between the principal interventionists, and the Japanese sparred with General William S. Graves, who headed the American contingent. The Japanese armed and gave limited financial support to Cossack and other anti–Bolshevist elements. They also occupied the Trans-Siberian Railway between Vladivostok and Lake Baikal. These operations brought them into conflict with partisan groups who were resisting the depredations of the White Russian forces of Admiral Kolchak, and when Kolchak's armies were drive back in 1919, the Siberian partisans intensified their attacks on the Japanese, Czechs and Cossacks along the Trans-Siberian. As the fighting spread eastward, more Americans were killed, sapping support for the enterprise in the United States. Washington was fast coming to the same conclusion reached by the British and French, that the forces of revolution that Lenin had unleashed in Russia were beyond their control. The last American soldiers embarked for home in 1920. As they boarded their ships, a Japanese band played Stephen Foster's "Hard Times, Come Again No More."[28] The musical salute of good riddance might have summed up the feelings of the Japanese commanders, but the prolonged campaign in Siberia proved no more popular in Japan than it had in the United States.

Unlike previous wars in which the population spontaneously supported the army, the Siberian expedition drew no crowds on the railway platforms when the troops departed. Over a thousand young men dodged the draft in one year, a figure unheard-of in the history of the army. The operation could not be sustained, and a face-saving way out of it was sought. When a Far Eastern Republic was declared in Siberia, complete with an American-style constitution, the Japanese negotiated a withdrawal with the new regime and pulled out the last of their soldiers in October 1922.[29] They had stayed for more than three years and had committed eleven divisions, of which 1,475 officers and men were killed and about 10,000 wounded. The cost of the expedition was over $700 million, and there was nothing to show for this sacrifice of blood and treasure.[30] Perhaps the army leaders had had a sixth sense in their initial reluctance to get involved. If so, they should have heeded it. As for the Far Eastern Republic, it was short-lived. Once the Japanese were gone, it became a part of the Soviet Union. The only other territory of which Japan had gained temporary control was the northern

II. The Army in Retreat

half of the island of Sakhalin, but in 1925 they gave up this last spoil as well. Altogether it was an unhappy chapter in the empire's history.

Simultaneously with the pulling back of their military forces in Siberia, the Japanese entered a new era of understanding with the West and their neighbor China. It is significant that the treaties that followed were negotiated following the stewardship of Takashi Hara, the first commoner Prime Minister of Japan. In some respects, Hara was contradictory in his views. He was not necessarily all things to all people, but his policies and statements sometimes seemed inconsistent. At times he could be very critical of the military, yet he seldom differed with his Minister of War, General Terauchi. He was hostile to the budding labor movement and hardly a devotee of Western democratic ideals, yet he was a highly effective politician and managed to gain the reputation of being "the most able in the history of the Diet."[31] Hara knew whom to cultivate in order to survive in the challenging arena of government. He made a point of getting along with the aged patriarch, Yamagata, the most powerful of the *Genro*. Yamagata never reconciled himself to party government, but Hara managed to retain his favor "with a skilful blend of deference and charm." Had Hara survived, the roots of parliamentary government might have grown deeper, for Hara certainly managed to develop the strength of his party, the Seiyukai, while balancing the *Genro*, the army and the bureaucracy. But it was not to be. Hara was assassinated in November 1921, stabbed to death by a young fanatic. His premature death came just three months before the passing of Yamagata, which marked the demise of the old era and was an ominous portent of the new. Nevertheless, a new climate had been ushered in and Japan would embark on a series of agreements that seemed to signal the dawn of international harmony.

These events occurred against the backdrop of the first successful arms reduction conference of the twentieth century, the Washington Conference of the winter of 1921–1922. Out of this conference came a major agreement placing sharp restrictions on naval tonnage of the principal maritime powers; a comprehensive treaty pledging respect for China's territorial and administrative integrity; and a pact among Britain, France, Japan and the United States in which they promised to consult one another in the event of future disputes or if their rights were threatened by another power. The Four Power Pacific Pact did something more. It specifically terminated the Anglo-Japanese Alliance, relieving Great Britain of an obligation that had become an encumbrance in a changing world. The Japanese acceded to all the terms of the various covenants, but not without misgivings.

The environment which had engendered the Anglo-Japanese Alliance had long since changed. Russia was no longer a threat to the Asian concerns of either Britain or Japan. The Bolsheviks were too engrossed in consolidating their revolution to disrupt Western or Japanese interests in the Orient. True, the partners had renewed their agreement in 1911, but it was already starting to fray. The provision regarding the Americans would make the alliance meaningless should either have a dispute with the United States. But there was more. Despite the exclusionary clause, Washington was unhappy about *any* Anglo-Japanese security arrangement, a fact of which London was well aware. Proponents of a large American navy openly pointed to the Anglo-Japanese Alliance as a threat to U.S. maritime interests. The First World War had made America a Great Power for the first time. Given the post-war unrest in Ireland and India, Britain could ill afford the enmity of its powerful wartime ally. Nor were the Japanese unanimous in their attachment to the alliance. The army was not enamored of it, and Japanese businessmen were frequently critical of the British; there were periodic attacks in the press, further signs that strains were beginning to increase.[32]

Still, neither side openly indicated an intent to terminate the alliance. Indeed, in the spring of 1921, Crown Prince Hirohito visited England on a Grand European Tour. It was a momentous event; there was no precedent for such a journey in the 2,500-year history of Japan. In all respects Hirohito's trip was a success, although Japanese sensibilities were severely tested at Buckingham Palace when King George V burst into the suite of the Crown Prince at breakfast time. Half dressed, wearing trousers and suspenders, carpet slippers and an open shirt, the King walked directly to Hirohito and slapped him on the back.

> "I hope, me boy," he said, "that everyone is giving you everything you want while you are here. If there is anything you need, just ask. I'll never forget how your grandfather treated me and me brother when we were in Yokohama. I've always wanted to repay his kindness." He chuckled. "No geishas here, though, I'm afraid. Her Majesty would never allow it."[33]

This episode and a few others notwithstanding, Hirohito was warmly greeted by the English people; the news was received with pride and gratitude at home. The British too were heartened by the visit, and Prime Minister Lloyd George told his associates "he hoped nobody would contemplate 'dropping' Japan."[34] Yet when the glow of the Imperial visit had faded, that is precisely what happened.

The origin of the Washington Conference lay in the aftermath of the defeat of the League of Nations by the United States Senate. Having killed it following a bitter fight with the now-crippled Woodrow Wilson, the Republicans felt obliged to make an effort towards arms reduction and international security. With the election of Warren Harding in the fall of 1920, the way was paved for a Republican administration to make its mark.

A Senate initiative by Senator William Borah, who ironically had been one of the League's principal opponents, moved the new Secretary of State, Charles Evans Hughes, to send informal inquiries to London, Paris, Rome and Tokyo. The British suggested that not only arms but Pacific and Far Eastern issues be taken up as well. That meant inviting Belgium, China, Portugal and the Netherlands. All accepted, but the Japanese delayed their reply, suspecting that they would be the losers whatever transpired at the proposed conference.

They had good reason to be dubious. In the summer of 1921, a meeting of British Empire leaders had taken place in London, at which the Anglo-Japanese Alliance was debated. The British found themselves pulled in opposite directions by Canada and Australia. The Canadians were aware of American opposition to the alliance and had no desire to be at odds with their neighbor. The Australians were just as insistent that the agreement be renewed. They knew that a war between Britain and Japan would put them at the mercy of the Japanese navy, and American help was far away. The Japanese watched this debate from the sidelines, not fully realizing that a fundamental change in their relationship with Great Britain was imminent.

It is an old axiom that nations act out of self-interest. The concerns of Britain's dominions were always important, but London was moved by other factors as well. America might have withdrawn to the wings of the world stage following Wilson's failure to win approval of the League at home, but the power of the United States was undeniable. Whatever empire worries she might have, Great Britain at heart knew the necessity of retaining American friendship, an amity that would be a basis for cooperation and thereby strengthen Britain's own position and welfare in the world. Despite Lloyd George's admonition about preserving the Japanese alliance, after the Imperial Conference it was just a matter of time before Japan would be dumped. The only question was how to manage this. The answer was found in the Four Power Pacific Pact, signed in Washington on December 13, 1921.

Simply put, the Japanese grudgingly allowed the bilateral treaty, which had been a cornerstone of their foreign policy, to be merged into a larger pact that was far less categorical in its guarantees than the old one. A pledge to respect one another's rights and confer in the event of a dispute moved one Japanese diplomat to complain, "We have discarded whiskey and accepted water."[35] The British and Americans might have congratulated themselves on removing this impediment to their relations, but it left the Japanese with a lingering feeling of having been jilted. When Japan commenced its military campaign in China in the 1930s, there were numerous incidents in which British subjects in China were insulted or humiliated.

The Japanese seemed to take a perverse pleasure in these. It was not hard to see why.

The Washington Conference skyrocketed with the opening address by Secretary Hughes, who shocked the delegates by recommending deep and specific cuts in their respective navies. What Hughes proposed was that Britain, the United States and Japan accept a ratio of 5-5-3 for capital ships and vessels (not including aircraft carriers) exceeding 10,000 tons or armed with guns in excess of 8-inch caliber. The United States, Hughes said, would scrap 30 ships, while Great Britain and Japan should scrap 19 and 17 respectively. Since the British were willing to accept American naval parity, and both countries were under strong domestic pressure to cut defense spending, the reductions were a popular move. Even a glance at the numbers told the Japanese that they were a junior partner. That alone was enough to make them unhappy, but the ceiling itself was galling. There were massed protest meetings throughout the country, as well as scathing newspaper editorials decrying the proportions. They were willing to settle for less, but they wanted something more on the order of 10-10-7. That would enable them to fulfill their defense goals. In the end, however, the Japanese accepted the Hughes figures. They might not have done so had the wishes of Vice Admiral Kanji Kato prevailed. There were two Katos (not related) at the conference. The senior one was Admiral Baron Tomosaburo Kato, and Vice Admiral Kanji Kato was his advisor. The latter strongly believed in a large fleet and found the 5-5-3 ratio anathema. As it turned out, illness obliged him to leave for home before the conference ended. That was not the last of him, though. In 1930, at the London Naval Conference, he reappeared, truculent as ever, and created a storm of controversy.[36]

The 5-5-3 ratio was made more palatable by an agreement not to construct or further fortify any bases west of Hawaii or north of Singapore. This gave Japan the guarantees she needed. Without adequate bases in the Philippines, Guam, Wake and the Aleutians, there was no way that the American navy could challenge Japan in her home waters. France and Italy were added to the naval agreement, each receiving 1.7 on the 5-5-3 scale, although Gallic pride very nearly sabotaged it. At length ruffled feelings were soothed and all parties signed the treaty on February 6, 1922. It was to be effective until 1936, when any of the parties might terminate its obligations with two years' notice.

There was one last piece of business. The cloud of Shantung would not go away, and China's future had to be settled. Baron Kijuro Shidehara, the principal Japanese delegate, declared that Japan would withdraw from Shantung. A bilateral agreement was worked out, with Japan retaining economic benefits and receiving compensation for the Kiaochow-Tsinan Railway, which had been built at Japanese expense. Chinese sovereignty and its administrative and territorial integrity were then guaranteed by all of the nine powers in attendance in the Nine Power Treaty. The "Open Door" of equal commercial opportunity for all in China was reaffirmed. China was far from unified, but at least it was to be left alone. When Baron Shidehara became Foreign Minister, he continued the policy of friendship and non-interference with China, but there were elements in Japan that chafed over the abandonment of the imperial dream.

Throughout much of the 1920s, the nation seemed uncertain of its destiny. Outwardly it appeared that Japan was on a steady road to parliamentary democracy. The hand of the military lay less heavily on the government, and the army itself had undergone significant changes following Yamagata's death. However, there were the traditionalists on the other side who viewed the new trends with alarm. It appeared to them that Japan was surrendering her birthrights, as liberal elements prevailed with their policy of accommodation with China and the Western powers. Chauvinist societies began to proliferate, often bearing allegorical names that belied their violent intentions.

On the surface the political party system looked healthy and vibrant. To be sure, the Japanese Diet did not exercise the kind of powers that its parliamentary counterparts in the West did. It passed laws, could amend the constitution, and generally controlled the purse strings, but the legislative branch seldom restrained the executive branch. The latter could dissolve the House of Representatives (the lower house) at its pleasure and introduced all important bills, and because certain areas of appropriations were outside the purview of the Diet, it could raise revenues through emergency and deficiency appropriations or simply re-execute the previous year's budget. It could also issue ordinances at will and thereby ignore the elected body whenever it wished.[37]

The upper house of the Diet, the House of Peers, was not an elected body and was filled by men of wealth or drawn from the ranks of the nobility. It was so conservative that it served as an additional instrument of the ruling oligarchy or, as one writer put it, was "an enlarged edition of the Privy Council."[38]

The two principal parties were the Seiyukai (Party of Friends of Constitutional Government) and the Minseito (Democratic Party), formerly the Kenseikai until its name was changed in the 1920s. The Minseito was generally regarded as the more liberal of the two and the more internationalist in outlook, while the Seiyukai, dominated for years by the Choshu clan and subservient to the Mitsuis, was more conservative. It was not surprising, then, that the Seiyukai drew most of its strength from the rural areas and the Minseito from the cities.

To the Western eye the party system in Japan appeared to be a mirror image of the conservative-liberal factions found in Washington, London or Paris. But like other layers of Western veneer that overlay an ancient culture, it was a thin crust. The Meiji elite from the very beginning had been hostile to political parties and tried to ignore them. They made certain when the Constitution was framed that the Throne, through appointed leaders, would hold most of the power. Party politicians discovered that if they "wished to share in the material rewards, such as offices, government contracts, expenditures for public works, subsidies, and so on, it was incumbent on them to cultivate good relations with the government."[39]

Japanese political parties were also different in that they began as small rural societies which were generally recognized by one or two local leaders. As they developed, the parties were transformed into loose federations and never acquired the firm structure of their Western counterparts. Over the years party leaders consolidated power in their hands, a pattern that was reinforced as the franchise was extended and party candidates were forced to raise large sums of money for their campaigns. Only the party leaders had access to the bankers and industrialists who would open their purses for political contributions. In this respect Japanese politicians discovered a universal principle: money is power and access to it brings almost unlimited influence and leverage.

Only men voted in the Meiji era, and not many of them had the privilege. Direct tax requirements sharply limited the number of adult males who were granted suffrage. As time passed, however, property qualifications were eased, and the number of voters increased from one and a half million in 1912 to over three million in 1920. In 1925 the Minseito pushed a universal suffrage bill through the Diet, granting all males over the age of twenty-five the right to vote. By 1928 the number of voters had leaped to almost twelve and a half million, and by 1936 it was over fourteen million.

Despite this participation in the political process, rank-and-file Japanese voters never really trusted the parliamentary system, and did not understand that since the reins of power were withheld from elected representatives, the latter could never develop a responsible, cohesive institution. During those brief periods when there were strong political leaders and outside circumstances permitted, both the Diet members and the executive branch fell into line and parliamentary rule appeared robust. But these interludes only proved that it was the strength of the individual that counted, not the collective dynamism of a healthy party structure. In the absence of strong leaders the parties degenerated into factionalism and self-interest. At those times the Diet appeared more than ever to be an alien body, thoroughly un–Japanese in character. Decision-making in the villages was traditionally achieved through discussion and consensus, "without open debate or a visible split between majority and minority. To the

II. The Army in Retreat

public generally, the principle of majority rule as used in the Diet seemed strange and even outlandish." By the time of the Second World War, the military grip on Japan was so tight that the political parties had become totally superfluous and had lost their identity, becoming merged into a single organization called the Imperial Rule Assistance Association.

The expansion of the electorate in the 1920s, however, seemed to offer broad participation in the government. Some of the small labor parties gained strength, but the conservatives remained firmly in control. The Communists were banned altogether, and in 1928 Prime Minister Tanaka persuaded the Emperor to sign an ordinance punishing by death anyone who joined an organization or group that was opposed to the existing political or economic order.[40] A Peace Preservation Law was passed by the Diet delegating broad powers to the police to arrest anyone harboring "dangerous thoughts."[41] With these enactments the possibility of radical inroads was quashed. Any threat to the existing system would come from the right, not the left.

The executive branch of the government was composed of the Cabinet, the Privy Council, the Ministry of the Imperial Household, and the *Genro*, with the Emperor at the top. Under the Meiji Constitution, the Emperor enjoyed unlimited power; all branches and agencies of the government were subservient to him. Every law, every ordinance, every treaty, and all executive appointments were made in his name. He commanded the armed forces, received foreign envoys, and conferred with the Privy Council. No other twentieth century ruler enjoyed so completely the prerogatives and prestige embodied in the term "Divine Right" as the Emperor of Japan. He was "the immutable symbol of national unity, and his person sacred and inviolable."[42]

There was no reference to a Cabinet in the Constitution and only a brief mention of Ministers of State, who were charged with giving advice to the Emperor and counter-signing imperial ordinances and rescripts, but over the years the Cabinet evolved into a powerful executive body. When the Diet was not in session, the Cabinet ruled by decree, including issuing financial ordinances when needed. It was true that the Diet could override these measures when it reconvened, but this never happened. The Diet was not reduced to the status of a debating society, but neither was it allowed to steer the ship of state. Later, when the war in China made increasing demands on the treasury, the militarists took advantage of this executive power by securing the necessary appropriations through Cabinet action. We have already seen how within the Cabinet it was possible for the military to force their views on the government by resigning or threatening to do so. This gave the army and navy a free hand to maintain exclusive control not only over their own affairs, but also over the nation's foreign policy.

Instead of the armed forces' being employed to carry out a freely developed foreign policy, the militarists in the 1930s initiated their own strategy of expansionism and adventurism, and the Foreign Office was obliged to follow in their wake. The end result was that "while the War and Navy Offices were allowed to interfere in foreign policy decisions, the Foreign Office was not permitted to share the least of military secrets." Occasionally the Prime Minister could bridge this gap, but so long as the War or Navy Minister remained independent of him, he too was held hostage to their whims.

The Emperor's highest body of constitutional advisors was the Privy Council, composed of twenty-five men who had distinguished themselves in the Emperor's service. Its approval was required for all important laws, treaties and ordinances, and since it was a conservative group, it tended to give a strict interpretation of the Constitution. Finally, there was the Imperial Household Ministry. Its two most important figures were the Lord Keeper of the Privy Seal and the Lord Chamberlain. The Emperor relied upon them for advice and counsel in making decisions; only the *Genro* had greater influence on him.[43] Cabinet Ministers could sit in the Privy Council and vote, but in spite of the powers delegated to the Council, it had no administrative authority and did not even have the right to review decisions of the Supreme Command of the armed services. The military enjoyed direct access to the Emperor, which made their independence complete.

That left the *Genro*, a dying legacy of the Meiji era, to put a brake on the military or warn against any unwise course the government might be tempted to embark upon. The term *Genro* can be translated either collectively as the Council of Elder Statesmen, which they were, or as a single person. They were a holdover from the days of the clans when no major decision was made without their consent. The Emperor Meiji had relied upon them to settle disputes between the Cabinet and the Supreme Command, but more than anything else, for "maintaining the unity and solidarity of the nation."[44] Yamagata had been the principal *Genro* before his death in 1922. Now the only one left was Prince Saionji. Although his influence waned, he was still consulted, often against his will. Saionji trusted the new path of constitutionalism and parliamentary democracy. He felt that the time of the *Genro* was over. The Emperor should rely upon his constitutional officers, not a relic from the past. Yet Saionji continued to recommend candidates for the office of Prime Minister into the 1930s. Only after the militarists had gotten the upper hand did he finally decline to give advice. By then he had come to despair of Japan's leadership and the suicidal course being taken.

The Emperor was at the apex of a complex pyramid which, depending on the circumstances, could be seen as resting on its base or balancing precariously on its point. The Emperor Meiji had managed well. Few men could have so skillfully brought a nation from the feudal era into the twentieth century. When he died, the throne had come to symbolize the nation's unity and its success in overcoming social and economic challenges at home and winning an empire abroad. All had been done in the name of the Emperor. To contain and channel the diverse currents that swirled around the throne in the 1920s and the decade beyond would have required a ruler of indomitable will. Standing in the wings, however, was a biologist, not another Meiji.

When Taisho died at the end of 1926, the nation hailed its new monarch, who took as the title of his reign *Showa*, which meant "enlightened peace." When Hirohito died in 1989 many Japanese recalled those words. Those with long memories did so sardonically. Yet no one could have doubted the sincerity of the young Emperor when he ascended the throne. Hirohito's reliance upon the aged Saionji seemed to be a good omen. There was no reason to believe that the new era of *Showa* would not live up to its name.[45]

Indeed, even with the pitfalls inherent in the Constitution, Japan seemed to be on the road to responsible parliamentary government. The Seiyukai had strong leaders in men like Korekiyo Takahashi, the brilliant Finance Minister of those years; Yuko Hamaguchi of the Minseito, who served as Prime Minister between 1929 and 1930 until a would-be assassin incapacitated him; Reijiro Wakatsuki, who succeeded Hamaguchi as Prime Minister; and Baron Shidehara, architect of the policy of cooperation with the Western powers and the benign exploitation of China. All of these men dominated the parliamentary scene, and all believed in parliamentary government.[46] No body of lawmakers has ever been without its complement of thieves, however, and what hurt the efforts of the statesmen who endeavored to bring parliamentary democracy to maturity was the rampant graft that seemed to go hand-in-hand with civilian-controlled government. The scandals that ensued served to confirm the widely held belief that the two major parties were in the hands of the most powerful business interests, the Minseito in the clutches of Mitsubishi, and the Seiyukai of Mitsui.[47] Although the army and navy had their own scandals involving secret service funds, they were generally perceived as virtuous and unsullied, a reputation that was cultivated among the younger officers who chafed at their shrinking role in the nation's life and affairs.

Yet if the nation was experiencing democratic growing pains, the military could hardly be said to be passing through a period of tranquility. Until the end of the First World War the army, under Yamagata's eye, had not only preserved its primacy on the political scene but possessed a spirit of unity, forged from its unbroken record of victories on the battlefield. Only when the Great War ended were there signs of dissent. Karl Marx once wrote that "Wars are the express trains of history." In light of the political and social upheavals of 1917–1918, that was certainly true, but the war had also brought rapid technological change on the battlefield. The Japanese officers who had been to France recognized when they returned home that the strategy and tactics that had won the war against Russia in 1905 would no longer prevail. Few professionals are more averse to change than old generals and admirals. Yamagata's generation was unimpressed by the reports of the younger officers, and the old war horse himself remained adamant about preserving the status quo. That was not all.

For years, preference was given to the Choshu Clan for promotion to the higher ranks. Conservative officers, particularly those with Choshu origins, were favored. The younger officers, impatient with a system that was both biased and outdated, resented this favoritism and pressed for change.[48] The end of the long Choshu domination of the army came with the death of their leader, Prince Yamagata, in February 1922. Once can truly appreciate the iron hold that he had had on the army when one sees the sweeping changes that occurred in the five years following his death. Reorganization went forward on a scale not seen since the days of Major Meckel, with changes in personnel, framework, size and technical equipment. At the same time the stranglehold of the Choshu Clan was broken, and a new breed of leadership emerged. Among them were men like Issei Ugaki, who had samurai roots in a lesser clan but nevertheless had ties to the Choshu. Another was Sadao Araki, the son of a poor priest, a firebrand who was to become a favorite of the fanatical Young Officers group. The two men would rise to the top but emerge as opponents from contending cliques. When the power of the Choshu was shattered, the descendants of samurai from the smaller clans took control. It was in one way more of a bane than a blessing. With Yamagata gone the army was rudderless, and a bitter struggle for leadership began.

The other major change in personnel was the increased number of young officers who came from the former "merchant class." Not only had the Choshu lost their influence, the samurai heritage itself was now challenged. The number of officers without samurai forebears was limited before the First World War, but with the reorganization of the army in the early Twenties, they began to increase. In 1927 the Volunteers Act was passed, opening the officer corps to anyone who met the requirements, which entailed passing the necessary examinations. Thus, a democratic base was established. If a man was ambitious and able, no matter what his station in life had been, he could now make a success of himself in the army. General Araki had begun his life as an apprentice in a pickle factory, and General Sugiyama, who became War Minister in the 1930s, was the son of a country schoolmaster.[49]

Far more than in the structured civilian world outside, in the army one could move upward fairly quickly; by the 1930s a Japanese officer could anticipate reaching the rank of major by the time he was forty and lieutenant colonel at forty-five. Three years later he could expect to retire at the rank of colonel with a monthly pension of about ¥100 ($50). For those years, that was not a bad base income, and the retired officer could generally supplement it with post-service employment. A Japanese writer of that era estimated that of the 800 cadets who entered the Military Academy annually, one would become a general, thirty lieutenant generals, and fifty major generals. The rest of the class would retire before reaching the age of fifty. The lower middle class, the small shopkeepers and the petty landowners, now provided a willing pool of officer candidates for the army, so much so that by 1927 it was estimated that thirty percent of the officer corps were drawn from this class.[50] By the end of the 1920s, then, the officer corps was divided into three distinct groups: the remnant of the Choshu leaders, field grade officers below them who came from the lesser clans but were now moving to the top, and junior officers with plebeian origins. Of the three, the last were closest to the peasant conscripts who comprised the bulk of the army. This bond was forged not just because they saw their own men at daily musters, but because their own petty bourgeoisie background made them sensitive to the social and economic problems that befell Japan after the Great Depression.

With the Shidehara line dominating abroad and assertive party leadership in the saddle at home, military spending was cut. General Ugaki, the War Minister, disbanded four divisions, but part of the savings was plowed back into modernization. Armor and motor transport were introduced. Since the officers of the four divisions could not be retained on active service, they were assigned as instructors for military drill in the middle and high schools. This move was resented by both the military and the students. Furthermore, the army was still smarting from the failure of the Siberian

Hajime Sugiyama, Japanese field marshal, later minister of war (*Rekishi-Shasin Kai*, August 1938).

venture and with the prevailing liberal spirit, soldiers and soldiering were less than popular. Soldiers found it prudent to go in mufti when off duty. Many of them complained that it was difficult to find suitable marriage partners, and there were frequent incidents of revolt and discourtesy by students toward military instructors.[51] The army's sudden descent in public esteem has to be seen against the backdrop of post-war idealism that was almost universal in those years. Despite their disappointment with Wilson's decision to kill the "equality of nations" clause in the League Covenant, the Japanese were swept up with the rest of the world by his concept of a Brave New World. The Washington Conference embodied this doctrine; it reached its zenith in the Kellogg-Briand Pact of 1928 in which war "was outlawed as an instrument of national policy." Japan was a signatory along with nearly every other country in the world. This Indian summer of progressivism, however, could not last. Developments both within Japan and without were at work that would undo the labors of Shidehara and his democratic colleagues.

A severe banking crisis in the spring of 1927 shook the nation, and the ensuing financial panic was followed by a recession. Silk and cotton production fell. The markets for paper, coal, cement and ceramics shrank. In the face of these economic conditions, medium- and smaller-sized firms were absorbed by the Zaibatsu or went out of business. Financial institutions also suffered. In 1926 there had been 1,420 ordinary commercial banks; three years later there were only 881.[52] The man in the street viewed these developments with dismay and anger. When the dust had settled, Mitsui controlled forty percent of the nation's imports and thirty-two percent of its retail business. The three giants, Mitsui, Mitsubishi and Sumitomo, controlled twenty-five percent of Japan's wealth. More than fifty percent of Japan's assets were now owned by eight families.[53] Disgust with politicians went hand-in-hand with indignation over the influence exercised over them by the great business houses. There was a saying that "the only difference between the Seiyukai and the Minseito is the difference between Mitsui and Mitsubishi." The Minseito Cabinet of 1924 was commonly called the "Mitsubishi Cabinet." Four members of it had direct connections with the company, and others had interests related to Mitsubishi. Baron Shidehara was married to the sister of Baron Iwasaki, head of the House of Mitsubishi, and the Finance Minister in the Minseito Cabinet which was in power in 1931–1932, Junnosuke Inouye, was Iwasaki's brother-in-law. While the behavior of these men was above reproach, the same could not be said of rank-and-file members of the Diet. Not only did they receive large sums of money for their campaigns, they were also given lucrative memberships on industrial directorates, which was a gross conflict of interest and incompatible with their positions as lawmakers. At least it can be said that they fulfilled the dictum of Simon Cameron that "an honest politician is one who, when he is bought, stays bought." The Diet members voted large subsidies to businesses, drew tariff schedules that favored them, and insofar as was possible, made the government a willing partner to the interests of the Zaibatsu.

The army in particular chafed at the Minseito Party's policy of cutting its budget. By 1927 the military's share of government spending was only twenty-seven percent, compared to forty-two percent five years earlier.[54] Shidehara's China policy of conciliation was cause for further aggravation. It was not hard for the army to make a connection between Shidehara's peaceful diplomacy and the extensive commercial interests that Mitsubishi had in China. In the past the Chinese had retaliated against unpopular Japanese actions with a boycott of Japanese goods. Keeping China friendly served Mitsubishi's interests.[55]

The financial crisis ultimately worked to the army's benefit because it brought to power General Baron Giichi Tanaka. He not only took over as Prime Minister but also received the portfolio of Foreign Minister, holding both offices during his premiership from April 1927 to July 1929. Tanaka was a remarkable person. He was raised in Choshu province, the homeland of the great military clan whose leader, Prince Yamagata, had left his imprint on the modern army. Tanaka was one of the last of Yamagata's protégés, but he possessed in his own right the martial virtues of a rigorous upbringing. It was said that when Tanaka was a boy he was expelled from primary school, at which point his father told him that he should commit *hara-kiri*. Only the intervention of his mother prevented Tanaka from doing so.[56]

As Tanaka grew to manhood, he was seen as a "jovial figure, driven by his emotions, but gifted with organizing ability and a strong, if primitive, intelligence." He enjoyed a successful military career and then entered politics, becoming president of the conservative Seiyukai Party. He had a leading role in the creation of the Imperial Military Reserve Association, which was to play an influential part in the 1930s in promoting the army's policies at home and abroad. More than anything else, Tanaka sought to prevent the spread of communist or other subversive ideas. During his tenure as Premier, thousands of Marxists and their sympathizers were arrested, and many received stiff prison sentences under the Peace Preservation Law.

Events in China, however, became a principal focus of concern. As long as China was divided, Shidehara's policy of benign exploitation left Japanese interests relatively secure, but the growth of Chinese nationalism in the last half of the 1920s admitted of no exploitation, benign or otherwise. Following the death of Sun Yat-sen in 1925, his successor Chiang Kai-shek moved swiftly to complete the unification of China. As his

Nationalist Army moved north, the Japanese as well as the Western colonial powers could see the handwriting on the wall. The warlords were no match for Chiang's army; Changsha, Nanchang, Hanchow, Shanghai and Nanking fell. The British, French, Americans and Japanese nervously reinforced their garrisons in Shanghai, but Chiang was not ready to challenge them yet. To consolidate power within his own ranks, he broke with the Communists who had been his allies, and in a sudden murderous purge executed thousands of them in Shanghai, which had been a Red stronghold. Simultaneously he expelled his Russian advisers and severed relations with the Soviet Union. In his turn to the right, he allied himself with the great financial interests in Shanghai, symbolically consummating the union by marrying Meiling Soong, who came from a wealth Shanghai Christian family. Meiling's brother was T.V. Soong, who had extensive financial holdings, and her sister was the widow of the famed Sun Yat-sen. Chiang had initially proposed marriage to Mme. Sun through an intermediary but was rejected. He then turned his attention to her sister. To win Meiling's hand he had to divorce two earlier wives and convert to Christianity, a small price in Chiang's eyes to bring the powerful Soongs and their friends to his side.[57]

In 1928 Chiang moved his capital to Nanking and in May of that year his army advanced on Tsinan, the capital of Shantung. Tanaka at once authorized the landing of 7,000 troops at Tsingtao, 200 of whom were moved up the railway line to Tsinan to protect Japanese nationals. A number of clashes with Chinese soldiers occurred, with casualties on both sides. At this point the Japanese occupied all of Shantung. Chiang's route to the north was temporarily blocked, and faced with a Japanese demand to withdraw, he turned back to Peking, leaving Shantung in Japanese hands.

Chiang Kai-Shek, Chinese nationalist leader during the 1930s through World War II.

II. The Army in Retreat 65

Chiang regarded this as a momentary setback. He entered Peking on July 3, and then the richest prize of all lay just beyond: Manchuria. Its warlord was Chang Tso-lin, known as the "Old Marshal." In a curious way, the paths of Tanaka and Chang had crossed years before, during the Russo-Japanese War. Then a colonel in the Japanese army, Tanaka captured a group of Chinese guerrillas who were fighting on the Russian side. Chang Tso-lin was among the prisoners. Tanaka could have executed him, but Chang's bearing impressed him. He spared Chang and thereafter referred to his as his "younger brother."[58] At one time Chang had harbored the same ambition as Chiang Kai-shek, of unifying all of China, and while he had received support from the Japanese-owned South Manchurian Railway, he did not regard himself as their puppet. Yet he was not strong enough to challenge the approaching Nationalist army. The Japanese also had no desire to see fighting spread to Manchuria. They warned both sides that if hostilities broke out in the Peking-Tientsin region they would take whatever action was necessary to protect South Manchuria. To that end, they persuaded Chang to return to Mukden, the Manchurian capital, thereby denying Chiang Kai-shek an excuse to invade the province. What followed was a harbinger of things to come, an overt act taken without the authority or knowledge of the government in Tokyo by an officer with the Japanese garrison forces in Manchuria, the Kwantung Army.

The distance between Mukden and Tokyo is a thousand miles, but it might as well have been ten thousand given the independence manifested by the army in Manchuria. Its officers fed upon their isolation and came to regard themselves as guardians of the nation's destiny. Poised on the frontier of the empire, the Kwantung Army saw its role not just as the defender of the Emperor's domain but as an instrument to direct the nation on the path to imperial greatness. Rather than allowing the conflict between Chiang Kai-shek and Chang Tso-lin to resolve itself, the officers of the Kwantung Army decided to take advantage of it by disarming Chiang's forces and then extending their occupation over all of Manchuria. Chang was to be sacrificed to effect their scheme. They would assassinate him, believing that his death would create unrest and thus give them a pretext to carry out their plan under the guise of "restoring order." On June 4, 1928, the deed was done. Chang was returning from Mukden to Peking when his train passed under an overhead bridge of the South Manchurian Railway, where an explosion killed the Old Marshal. Since the South Manchurian Railway was under the protection of the Kwantung Army, it was immediately assumed that the Railway was responsible. (The plot to kill Chang Tso-lin was hatched by Colonel Kawamoto, a staff officer of the Kwantung Army, but this was not revealed until after the Second World War.[59])

Tanaka and the Japanese military authorities denied all culpability, and it is certain that Tanaka had no personal inkling of the plan. Indeed, he insisted privately that the perpetrators should be punished, but he was overruled by the Army Chief of Staff and others. To discipline these men, they said, would have an adverse effect on the entire army. What they were really saying was the "the officers of the Kwantung Headquarters ... were out of control and ... must be given their own way."[60]

In any event, the plot did not produce the desired result. The violence expected by the Kwantung officers never materialized, depriving them of any excuse for making their move. Chang Tso-lin's son, Chang Hsueh-liang, succeeded his father as warlord and shortly afterward ordered that the Nationalist flag be raised over all Manchuria. In doing so, the younger Chang extended the unification of China to its northernmost limit, and since he also publicized a plan to build an independent rail and harbor system in competition with Japanese holdings, it was clear that the region would soon be firmly under the control of Chiang Kai-shek.[61]

Tanaka viewed these developments as a *fait accompli*. He withdrew the troops that had been sent to Shantung, thereby admitting the failure of his interventionist policy, and he recognized the Nationalist government as China's legitimate authority. It was a sharp reversal for the military, and they blamed Tanaka for being weak-kneed in the face of events. The loss of confidence forced Tanaka to resign in early July 1929. It had been a bitter experience for all parties. The clumsy attempt to thwart China's drive toward unification had earned nothing but resentment and opposition in China, along with condemnation abroad of the heavy-handed tactics of the Japanese army during its campaign in Shantung. During their bombardment of Tsinan, the Japanese had killed an estimated 3,600 Chinese. The Chinese reaction to this was an intensified boycott of Japanese goods, while the rest of the world denounced Japan for its brutal conduct.[62]

Tanaka's resignation brought another brief respite for the forces of democracy and internationalism. Yuko Hamaguchi, the president of the Minseito, now became Prime Minister. Confronted by ailing finances at home and opprobrium overseas, Hamaguchi moved to retrenchment and reform to repair the former, and a return to the spirit of the Washington Conference to address the latter. To this end he appointed Junnosuke Inoue, the former head of the Bank of Japan, to be his Finance Minister and brought back Shidehara as Foreign Minister. His two service ministers, Ugaki of the army and Admiral Takarabe of the navy, were both moderates.

Had the world not sunk into financial depression, Hamaguchi's administration might have been a success. The Tanaka Cabinet had abandoned the gold standard in 1927 in order to stimulate the economy. Japan prospered for a brief period. Rice rose to $4 a bushel and raw silk to $690 a bale, but the good times did not last long. Hamaguchi proposed budget reductions including a ten percent cut in pay for civilian and military leaders. The pay cuts were rejected and the Prime Minister, in an effort to bolster the value of the yen and halt inflation, returned Japan to the gold standard and lifted the embargo on gold that had been in place since 1917. However, the stock market crash in America was the final blow to Japan's recovery. Silk goods were luxury items in the United States, and no longer in demand. By May 1932 silk had fallen to $150 a bale, and rice was selling at $1.50 a bushel. All of Japan suffered, but farmers were hardest hit. Poverty was the lot of most of them, particularly in the north. Four years of bumper rice crops, along with competition from Korea and Taiwan, had undermined prices. Between 1925 and 1931, the price of rice fell by fifty-five percent, the price of raw silk by sixty-seven percent, and the price of cocoons by more than two-thirds. Rice and cocoons had been the two principal sources of income for farmers, and a substantial loss of income from these two staples had catastrophic consequences. Many went into debt and lost their lands, becoming tenant farmers. Desperate to keep their property, or just to survive, many farm families sold their daughters to agents who toured the countryside on behalf of teahouses, cafes, and brothels. In one village in northern Japan, 110 of the 467 girls between the ages of 15 and 24 were sold, most of them to become prostitutes, and the rest factory workers.[63]

It is easy to see why the officers in the Imperial Army reacted as they did to these appalling conditions. Most of their soldiers came from the peasantry, and many of the officers themselves were from medium-sized and small landowning families. The northern prefectures, where circumstances were harshest, had the reputation of providing the best soldiers. Company and platoon commanders could not help but feel anguish for their brothers and sisters condemned to a life of humiliation.[64] They burned with anger and frustration, particularly at rich Zaibatsu and venal politicians whose greed and selfishness were an affront to every decent Japanese. Believing that the government would be forced to abandon the gold standard again, wealthy financiers led by the Mitsui interests bought up American dollars, thus aggravating the flight of gold from the country. When the news of this speculation reached the public, there was an outcry against "selfish, unpatriotic traitors who had 'sabotaged the nation to enrich themselves.'" The right-wing societies that sprang up in the early 1930s found willing recruits among young officers who saw parliamentary government as a refuge for corrupt politicians who permitted and indeed abetted the debasement of the nation. It was unconscionable that they should wallow in luxury and decadence while their friends and relatives were starving to death in the countryside.[65]

On the international scene the Hamaguchi government found itself in troubled waters. By 1930 it was time for the signatories of the Five Power Naval Treaty to confer on an extension of their earlier agreement and also try to find an acceptable formula for warships other than battleships. A harmonious settlement would not be easy to reach. Even within the Japanese navy there was anything but harmony.

There is a remarkable parallel between the army and the navy in Japan during the 1920s. We have already seen how the post–Yamagata years were marked by friction among several contending groups for army leadership in the officer corps. The navy experienced similar dissension. This surfaced at the Washington Conference in the "battle between the two Katos." Admiral Tomosaburo Kato was the Navy Minister and head of the Japanese naval delegation. He accepted the sixty percent ratio in capital ships because he recognized that Japan could not afford to engage in a naval race with the United States. He regarded the Japanese navy as "an instrument of deterrence, not of war." His chief naval aide, Vice Admiral Kanji Kato, insisted that Japan could not meet its strategic requirements with less than a seventy percent ratio, but he was overruled. So long as the elder Kato lived, he was able to prevail, but his sudden death in 1923 broke the dam on "navy orthodoxy" and released the militant elements that eventually gained control of the Imperial Navy.

While this factionalism was fueled by the discussions at the London Naval Conference in 1930, its origins were to be found in the rivalry between the Navy Ministry and the Navy General Staff. The former was in the hands of officers noted for their "politico-administrative ability" while the latter was dominated by officers of the "warrior type." Since the officers at the Ministry customarily served as spokesmen for the Imperial Navy and received most of the publicity, the General Staff officers came to resent them as prima donnas. Had this been the only difference between the two groups, the distinction would have been superficial. What really set them apart was their respective attitudes toward the United States. At the London Conference, Admiral Kanji Kato was present in his capacity of Chief of the Navy General Staff, and he demanded that the ratio for cruisers and other surface warships be set at 10-10-7 and that Japanese submarine tonnage, which totaled 78,000, be retained. Supported by his Vice Chief, Admiral Nobumasa Suetsugu, Kato declared that Japan could accept nothing less, even if it meant wrecking the conference.[66] Try as they might, Kato and Suetsugu could not budge the Americans, who insisted on a 10-10-6 ratio in heavy cruisers, although they were willing to allow a 10-10-7 ratio in destroyers and parity in submarines. To Reijiro Wakatsuki, the ex-Prime Minister who headed the delegation, and Admiral Takarabe, the Navy Minister, the compromise seemed equitable. Moreover, the Hamaguchi Cabinet endorsed the agreement, believing that it left Japan's security intact while bringing the bonuses of international goodwill and relief for the budget.[67] Walking out on the conference, as Kato was willing to do, was out of the question. But if Hamaguchi was strong-willed, so was Admiral Kato. When the recalcitrant mariner returned to Japan, he exercised his right of direct access to the throne and appealed to the Emperor, first denouncing the treaty and then resigning his post. (In 1924, Admiral Kato was appointed Commodore of the Yokosuka Navy Yard and attended the ceremony installing the *Mikasa* as a form of naval museum. He had served as Chief Gunner aboard her at Tsushima.[68]) Hamaguchi was also criticized by two members of the Privy Council, Miyoji Ito and Kiichiro Hiranuma, but Hamaguchi had a strong ally in the old *Genro*, Prince Saionji, and more importantly, had a Minseito majority in the Diet. The treaty was ratified.[69]

As for the navy, it now found itself divided into a "treaty faction" and a "fleet faction." Although not all of the officers of the Combined Fleet opposed the treaty, the names stuck. As for Kato, his resignation in no way diminished his influence. In 1932 he had a protégé, Admiral Sankichi Takahashi, appointed Vice Chief of the Navy General Staff and the next year Admiral Suetsugu became Commander-in-Chief of the Combined Fleet. Important though these assignments were, the seeds that Kato had sown much earlier bore the richest fruit. Between 1911 and 1913 Kato had been vice president of the Naval Academy. Seven years later he had a term as president of the Navy War College. The young officers who served under him idolized him, especially when he boasted that Japan could easily defeat a combined Anglo-American fleet.

Kato's hostility toward the United States and Great Britain was matched by a tilt toward Germany, particularly after the termination of the Anglo-Japanese Alliance. In 1920 he made an inspection tour of Europe and was especially impressed by German technology in submarine and optical equipment. In his reports home he recommended the introduction of German weaponry. As the decade drew to a close, Japan's German connection became stronger. Japan sent more naval architects to Germany to study than to Britain or America. After Hitler came to power and German-Japanese geopolitical goals began to coincide, the ties became even closer. Following the signing of the anti–Comintern Pact in 1936, the number of Japanese naval officers posted to Berlin was invariably more than the number of those serving in Washington or London.

Kato was not content with imposing his views on his own branch of the military. As the 1930s opened, the Kato-Suetsugu group moved to assert the navy's equality with the army. They did this by installing Prince Hiroyasu Fushimi, a member of the royal family, as Chief of the Navy General Staff. Getting parity with the army wasn't easy. The navy's officer corps had always been less than a fifth of that of the army, and following the restrictions imposed by the Washington Treaty there was a sharp cut in enrollment at the Naval Academy. Not until 1937 did the numbers again reach pre-1921 levels. So the appointment of Prince Fushimi was a shrewd move. The navy would thus have a member of the royal family in a high-level defense position just like the army, which had installed Prince Kanin as Chief of the General Staff. Moreover, Fushimi had shown his partiality to the views of the Kato-Suetsugu group at the London Naval Conference, making him their perfect candidate. Both Admiral Okada, the senior naval officer, and Saionji, the *Genro*, feared that Fushimi would become a tool of the militants. Their alarm was justified by subsequent events. Prince Fushimi served as Chief of the Navy General Staff from January 1932 to March 1941. Throughout that period his vice chiefs constantly used him to enhance their power, invoking his royal status when necessary to bend the Navy Minister or even the Prime Minister to their will. To compound the problem, as a member of the imperial family, Prince Fushimi could not be held accountable for his mistakes. That made policy decisions in the navy farcical.

Depression and military discontent now combined to make a witches' brew that would prove fatal to parliamentary government. First the army and then the navy had been manipulated by the politicians and senior officers from their own ranks who submitted to Cabinet rule. The despicable Diet had become the tool of unscrupulous profit-seekers while the mass of the people endured unspeakable hardships. Elections were meaningless because they served merely as a revolving door for scoundrels. Cabinet governments followed one another in futile succession. Military and right-wing extremists argued that, by its own acquiescence, Japan had relegated itself to an inferior rank as a military power and seemed ready to relinquish its rightful role as the paramount nation in East Asia. They were convinced that there was no reforming the hated political system. Only direct action would suffice to save Japan from those who would betray it. In the past, assassination, while frequent enough, had still been an aberration. Now it was to become the accepted means of shaping the future as well as rectifying the present. Those individuals who were seen as part of the problem were to be targets. They could be military or civilian leaders, nobles or commoners; it didn't matter. Only the Emperor was inviolable, although ironically, the crimes were often committed in his name. In time the assassinations or attempted slayings became group affairs, a purge of selected officials who had earned the enmity of a band of militants, but individual acts of violence did not abate.

It was bloody but effective. In less than five years parliamentary government in Japan had become a fiction, the civilian leaders thoroughly cowed and submissive. The military oligarchy went through the motions

II. The Army in Retreat

of constitutional practice, but this was a sham. The change began with an attempt on the life of the Prime Minister himself. Yuko Hamaguchi was shot and seriously wounded by a right-wing fanatic in November 1930 on the platform of Shimbashi Station. It was nine years nearly to the day since Prime Minister Hara had been shot in the same Tokyo station.

III

The Struggle for Control

> It is true that we military men should not be influenced by public opinion and should not participate in politics. On the other hand, we bear responsibility for national defense. If national defense policy is imperfect, our nation will be in danger. This being so, our discussion of national defense issues should not be regarded as meddling in politics.
> —A communication to army and divisional commanders from Army Minister Ugaki in January 1931.[1]

The twenty-five army officers who met in late September 1930 did not adopt a name for their organization right away, but in a few months, they began to speak of it as the *Sakurakai*, the "Society of the Cherry Blossom." Like the chrysanthemum, the national symbol of Japan, the cherry blossom was prized for its image. The chrysanthemum, with its many petals, appears to be a fragile bloom, but in reality, it is a survivor in nature's hostile world. What could be more appropriate for a nation that combined beauty and strength in its character? Let the Americans have their eagle and the British their lion. The Japanese were too subtle for such overt expressions of self-esteem. In the eyes of the true samurai, the cherry blossom embodied all that was noble. The petals flourished briefly and then fell, like the samurai, glorious in his calling and ready to die at a moment's notice, if need be.[2]

There was no mistaking the purpose of the Cherry Blossom Society. It was dedicated to the overthrow of the parliamentary system of government and the substitution of one controlled by the military. The initial members included three lieutenant colonels: Kingoro Hashimoto from the General Staff Headquarters; Yoshiro Sakata from the Ministry of War; and Kiichiro Higuchi from the headquarters of the Guards Division. At its height, it had just over one hundred members. Membership was restricted to "army officers on the active duty list, of the rank of lieutenant colonel and below, having a deep concern for national reorganization and no private axe to grind." The men came from various military commands and units in the Tokyo area; twenty-nine from the General Staff Headquarters, nine from the War

III. The Struggle for Control

Ministry, forty were instructors or students at various military academies or specialized technical schools, and the remainder were part of the Kempei (military police) headquarters or belonged to Guards and infantry regiments. Although he was not a member by reason of his rank, Major General Yoshitsugu Tatekawa, who headed the Second Division of General Staff Headquarters, was the driving force behind the founding of the society. His immediate subordinates were Hashimoto and Lieutenant Colonel Nemoto, who were in charge of the Russian and Chinese sections respectively. No other division of the General Staff was more important than the Second. It was responsible for the planning of military operations and significantly, in 1930, was devoting itself to "problems relating to Manchuria and Mongolia."

The limited membership of the Cherry Blossom Society in no way diminished its importance nor the dimension of the nationalist movement. Between 1880 and 1922 there were only nineteen radical right-wing societies. In 1923 the number increased by another ten, and thereafter the groups proliferated, reaching an all-time high in 1932, when 196 new "patriotic" societies were established. By then, 494 nationalist organizations had been formed, over half of them in the last two years, and by 1936 their membership had doubled, from 300,000 to over 600,000.[3]

In addition to the Cherry Blossom Society, there were others that received the army's support or cooperation. Among them were the Black Dragon Society, known for urging "direct actions" to achieve nationalist goals, and the Country Foundation Association, which dated back to the early Meiji era and was known for its promotion of patriotism and opposition to foreign influence. Among its members were Generals Araki, Mazaki, Hata and Matsui, all of whom would make their reputations in Manchuria and China. The Ocean-Ocean Society drew appropriately from admirals as well as generals in the reserves. The Imperial League of Young Officers included in its ranks cadets and officers of junior grade, all disciples of General Araki, who inspired them with chauvinist lectures.[4] He was known as a man of action, early on calling for the army to move into Manchuria. Finally, there was the One Evening Society, which was organized in 1929 and whose membership included Daisaku Komoto, Tetsuzan Nagata, Hideki Tojo, Tomoyuki Yamashita, Kenji Doihara, Taisuke Itagaki, and Ishi Kanji, all of whom would be involved in Japan's march to conquest.[5]

Out of these and the myriad of other disaffected groups that sprang from the officer ranks, two principal groups emerged. First were the *Kodoha*, or Imperial Way Group. The group's name came from a speech made by General Sadao Araki in June 1933, when he said that the path of the Japanese people to follow was the "Way of the Emperor." He declared that the army of Japan was the Emperor's army, and its mission was to spread the "Imperial Way." The phrase came to be identified with the Araki faction of the army.⁶ The group comprised younger officers, many of whom came from rural areas where the conditions were wretched. They vehemently opposed the capitalist regime and were bent on overthrowing it. Poorly organized, because of their hostility to centralized rule, they often acted impulsively, striking suddenly and violently at their foes in waves of assassinations and coup attempts. They were inspired by Generals Araki and Mazaki, two officers who preached the Yamato spirit as the conquering factor on the battlefield.

In the 1920s, Araki as the head of the *Kodogikai* called for military training at home and expansion abroad.

With his chiseled features and handlebar moustache, Araki looked the part of the Prussian militarist. But appearances were deceptive. He was a highly intelligent and sophisticated man, with an "unusually attractive" personality and a taste for philosophical discussion—no mindless fanatic, but one of the army's intellectual elite. His advocacy of *Kodo* was functional—a spur to military sacrifice and a shield against Communist infiltration. Araki never forgot his service in Russia during the Bolshevik revolution; he perfectly understood the fatal attraction of communism for the poor and starving.⁷

Araki was convinced that the growing strength of the Soviet Union was a menace, would lead to war with Japan no later than 1936, and called for immediate rearmament.

The other faction was the *Toseiha*, or Control Group, composed of senior officers, many of whom served in the War Ministry. Recognizing that in the twentieth century, returning Japan to its early centralized government was impossible, the Control Group sought to merge existing political parties into a single-party system under the thumbs of the *Zaibatsu* and Court officials. They would achieve control, not by violence but by gradual pressure, using the terms of the Constitution that held Cabinet policy hostage to the army's participation. If the Group didn't follow the bloody path of the *Kodoha*, they nevertheless found the tactic of assassination useful since it rid them of troublesome foes.⁸

While the young officers in the army comprised the body of the Imperial Way, its leaders came from the anti–Choshu faction. General Ugaki became an outspoken critic of the defense policy. He remembered when he was a division commander, when his soldiers in their maneuvers had to practice with paper models of airplanes stuck on bamboo poles and rattle sticks to imitate machine guns. He remembered his soldiers' shabby clothing and their carrying out bayonet exercises barefoot in order to save their boots. He remembered the shortages of food and fuel and the vermin-infested barracks. Finally, he remembered the plight of officers, so ill-paid that they lived in near poverty.⁹

Araki sympathized with the young officers, and while he wanted to acquire modern implements of war, he retained his faith in the indomitable spirit of the Japanese soldier as the key to victory on the battlefield. He was most influential among the General Staff, where many officers shared his views, but the Imperial Way possessed a dynamism of its own.

Opposing the Imperial Way was the *Toseiha*, or "Control Faction" as they were called by the Kodo officers, although they did not so identify themselves.[10] The Kodo, however, prepared for war, Araki being convinced that war with Russia was inevitable. To create a martial spirit, Araki "personally revived the ancient craft of sword-making, which had virtually died out in the nineteenth century when Yamagata decided on mass-produced swords for the new army." Critical metals were now imported for weapons production: zinc, lead, nickel, and aluminum from London, and from the French colony in New Caledonia, three shiploads of chrome. Germany and Belgium sent barbed wire, England sent tank engines, and Sweden sent enough ball bearings "to equip six hundred aircraft engines and fifty tanks per month.... [I]n September 1932, the Japanese warned Ford and General Motors that their factories in Japan might be requisitioned and taken over 'at any moment.'"

The military found sympathetic allies among right-wing groups. One of the most important spokesmen of the ultranationalists was Ikki Kita, who in his "General Outline for the Reconstruction of Japan" said that the Emperor should abolish the Constitution and the Diet and turn the government over to a junta of officers elected by the reserve army officers. All property above a fixed value should be expropriated, and Manchuria and Siberia should be seized to provide Japan with necessary natural resources. Kita believed that any use of force by a "have-not" nation against a "have" nation to correct international injustice should never be considered an act of aggression. Indeed, he felt that it was right for any nation to make war on another which was monopolizing large areas of land in defiance of the natural law of human existence.[11]

Like ultranationalists everywhere, Kita and others believed in the uniqueness of Japanese character and its superiority to all others. The divine Emperor was the fount of all values, and through him they felt that they possessed spiritual qualities that set them apart from all other people on earth. In that belief they found justification for their proclaimed role as the guardians of all Asians. Shumei Okawa, a radical like Kita, declared, "It is my belief that Heaven has chosen Japan as the champion of the East."[12]

The assault of so many dissident groups was not long in coming. Each plot by itself was a failure, but collectively and in time they achieved their purpose by destroying parliamentary government in Japan. The Cherry Blossom Society made the first move. In January 1931, a committee of eleven met to plan a coup d'état. Since they wished to form a militaristic government, they tentatively chose General Ugaki to be its head. For his part, Ugaki had sent word that he was willing to assume the leadership once the present government resigned, a condition that was anticipated with the death of Prime Minister Hamaguchi, who was dying from wounds inflicted by an assassin. The problem for the plotters was that Ugaki was not willing to be party to a coup. As Minister of War he had become a skilled politician in his own right. He certainly was ambitious, setting himself the goal of being another soldier-premier like General Tanaka, but he would have rather have dealt with the Seiyukai politicians than with Cherry Blossom zealots. He let them know that he was opposed to any military initiative.[13]

The Emperor was certainly not in sympathy with nationalist hotheads, but he was not like his grandfather, who set his own course and didn't blow with the winds. Nor were his advisers at the Court bold, at least not those who believed that Japan should follow a constitutional path. Hamaguchi's assassination had cowed the politicians, whose ranks were already short of inspired and determined leaders. It was already early August when the venerable Prince Saionji learned of the March conspiracy, as it came to be called. He urged the Lord Keeper of the Privy Seal, Count Makino, to say that he was opposed to any military initiative.[14]

Time ran out in September 1931. The blow was struck in Manchuria, not Tokyo, but given its effect on the civilian government, the result was the same. In manufacturing the incident at Mukden and seizing all of Manchuria, the army radicals demonstrated conclusively that they could carry out their designs. For the civilian leadership it was the ultimate humiliation. They would not be killed or forced out. They would simply be ignored.

The Manchurian operation was not hastily conceived. As early as the winter of 1930–1931, the General Staff had made plans to seize the province. Several factors drove it to conclusion: the Cherry Blossom conspirators had hoped that after they reorganized the government on their terms they could begin to fulfill their imperial dreams abroad. When Ugaki frustrated their coup, the Cherry Blossoms and other ultranationalist groups moved to conquer Manchuria on their own. They were aided by several incidents that year. A clash over water rights between Koreans and Japanese in Wanpaoshan, northwest of Changchun, in the late spring of 1931 obliged the Japanese police in Manchuria to intervene. In June, the Chinese shot two Japanese agents who were caught in a restricted zone in Manchuria. The latter incident aroused strong anti–Chinese sentiment in Japan, and Shidehara's conciliatory course toward China came under heavy criticism.[15]

What did the army hope to gain by seizing Manchuria? Was it simply a grab for more territory to extend the boundaries of the empire and exploit the region for Japan's economic gain? The army's goal extended beyond

III. The Struggle for Control

these obvious ends. A Japanese Manchuria would demonstrate the army's ability to administer and develop a segment of the empire on their own terms and present it to their countrymen as a model in contrast with the fumbling, venal leadership at home. Whatever followed, in the beginning they "saw Manchuria as a steppingstone not to control China but reform Japan." With these imperial, economic and ideological foundations as a basis for action, the army made its first move at a table where each hand was played with ever-increasing risks and the ante raised until the nation itself was staked on the outcome. In the end all was lost, but the first hand was won so easily that the army came to believe itself invulnerable, the fatal failing of gamblers.

There can be no doubt that Japan feared the rise of the Nationalist regime in China. The warlords had been systemically subdued, and the Kuomintang regime now dominated central and north China. As for Manchuria, the warlord Chang Hsueh-liang proved a faithful ally of Chiang Kai-shek, who at the time was no friend of the Soviet Union. In 1929, Soviet citizens were arrested, and Soviet consulates closed. Chiang seized the Chinese Eastern Railway, the telegraph system, and Soviet shipping on the Sungari River.[16] Moscow withdrew all of its personnel from Manchuria, protesting Chiang's action, and Chiang saw the danger that he had brought on himself and now sought support from the West. That still did not dissuade Moscow from taking military action in response. In November 1929, a single Soviet division scattered the forces of Chang Hsueh-liang and penetrated 150 miles into Manchuria. This was enough to prompt a settlement, so the Soviets got their way and the status quo was restored.

The Japanese drew their own conclusions from this episode. First, they recognized the strength and resolution of the Soviet Union. The Chinese in Manchuria were soft and there would be no interference from outside powers. Conditions now seemed ripe for the ambitions of the Kwantung Army in Manchuria. China was weak and would be unable to interfere with the Kwantung Army when it made its move. A protest might be made to the League in Geneva, but that organization was toothless. Manchuria was an important source of food and significant mineral deposits and could be an outlet for a population at home. The Kwantung Army conspirators were sure that the War Office back in Tokyo would not interfere, and that their plot would be welcomed by officers at the rank of lieutenant colonel and above.

Kanji Ishiwara and Seishiro Itagaki, a pair of Kwantung Army officers, masterminded the plot. On September 18, 1931, a bomb would be set off to derail a South Manchurian Railway train, and the Chinese would be blamed. Lieutenant Suemori Kawamoto and a handful of soldiers under his command detonated it on the railway line three miles north of Mukden.[17]

The charge was set off beneath the southbound express, which was due in at 10:30 p.m., but the damage was so slight that the train's momentum carried it over the broken rail and it arrived in Mukden on time. The intended sabotage had misfired, but that did not stop the conspirators from executing the rest of their plan. The bombing was blamed on the Chinese and attacks were immediately launched on the Chinese garrison in Mukden.

Not everyone in Tokyo was in on the ruse. At dawn, on September 19, Lieutenant Colonel Hitoshi Imamura, the operations section chief in the Army General Staff headquarters, was jarred from a sound sleep by a telephone call from Colonel Yoshiro Umezu. "The railway near Mukden was blown up last night and the Kwantung Army seems to have marched. I'm going to my office to confirm the cable. I'll send a car to your place; come as quickly as possible."[18] Telegrams flooded in, but no one was allowed to interfere. Morito Morishima, a diplomat attached to the consulate in Mukden, tried to persuade Colonel Itagaki to confirm the policy of the Foreign Office and reach a peaceful settlement. In his memoirs many years later, he recalled Itagaki's reply: "This has already been decided by the Supreme Command. Is it the intention of the General Consulate to ignore the Supreme Command?" A young staff officer, Major Tadashi, drew his sword menacingly, saying, "I'll allow no one, no matter who, to interfere with the Supreme Command."

While the army in Manchuria proceeded with its conquest of the entire province, the government of Prime Minister Wakatsuki in Tokyo suffered embarrassment and frustration. Foreign Minister Shidehara and Finance Minister Junnosuke Inoue pressed to have the incident localized and settled peacefully, but the General Staff declared that the Cabinet decision could not be binding because of the "independence of the Supreme Command." On the mainland the Kwantung Army requested reinforcements from General Senjuro Hayashi, the commander of Japanese forces in Korea. Hayashi complied, even though it meant violating the rule which prohibited field commanders from sending troops outside their jurisdiction without imperial consent. Shidehara failed to have Hayashi censured, but the army promised to negotiate a new treaty with Chiang Kai-shek's regime to guarantee Japanese rights and interests in Manchuria, a superfluous act since the Kwantung Army was rapidly occupying the entire region.

The forces of Chang Hsueh-liang were incapable of putting up any effective resistance and the Nationalist Government of Chiang Kai-shek was similarly ill-prepared for a military confrontation because of its own civil war with the Communists. The only recourse for the Chinese was the League of Nations, to which they now appealed for help. Given their record with past international forums, the Japanese tried to delay the League's involvement by giving assurances regarding their intentions. That bought them several weeks' respite, but when the Kwantung Army continued its occupation of the province, the League Council reconvened and passed a resolution calling for the withdrawal of Japanese troops by November 16, 1931. But that same month, the Japanese contacted Henry Pu Yi, the last Manchu emperor, who had been living in the Japanese concession in Tientsin following a physical assault by Peking's warlord in 1924, and persuaded him to come to Manchuria. After Manchuria declared its independence in February 1932 and Manchukuo proclaimed it a state in March, Henry Pu Yi was installed as emperor.[19]

Because of the independent relationship that the army had with the civilian government, the outside world saw the contradiction between the government's assurances and the military action as gross deceit. In reality, Wakatsuki and Shidehara were sincere in their desire to effect a peaceful reconciliation with China, but public opinion swiftly endorsed the army's action, and Shidehara found himself besieged. Patriotic fervor was fanned by members of the Military Reserve Association. Within the Cabinet, Kerzon Adachi, the Minister of Home Affairs, boycotted the meetings in protest against Shidehara's settlement policy. Even Saionji, the peace-loving *Genro*, advised Shidehara "the entire national opinion called it mistaken and wrong."[20] Shidehara gave in, and on December 12 the Wakatsuki government resigned. His successor was seventy-five-year-old Tsuyoshi Inukai of the Seiyukai Party. Inukai temporarily retained the post of Foreign Minister as well as the premiership, and he tapped General Araki to be Minister of War. The Cabinet Secretary was Kaku Mori, who favored a Seiyukai-army dictatorship. The omens were not favorable for Inukai. The Emperor was concerned about the army's intrusion into domestic and foreign affairs and told Inukai that he wanted it to stop. The luckless Prime Minister, who had been warned by a right-wing friend, Mitsuru Toyama, not to take the office because doing so would put his life in jeopardy, felt bound to carry out the Emperor's wishes. Six months later, he would pay for his loyalty with his life. Even in his brief tenure he might have succeeded had he been quick enough to take the one action that might have brought the army to heel. If he had petitioned the Emperor to issue a rescript ordering the army to stop its operations in Manchuria, the military authorities would have had to either comply or defy the Emperor. It's possible that Inukai was not sure that Hirohito would have been obeyed, and rather than risk the prestige of the throne, he tried unsuccessfully to hold the army in check on his own.[21]

Although he had been one of Shidehara's harshest critics, Inukai now decided to send a close friend on a secret mission to China to try to open negotiations that would lead to peace. He arranged for his friend to communicate by a secret code that was unknown to the army. Inukai's son said later that his father really did intend to have the Emperor issue the imperial rescript to end army operations in Manchuria. Perhaps, but he should have kept the decision to himself. Instead, he foolishly confided in Kaku Mori, who in turn informed the ultranationalists, thereby sealing Inukai's death warrant.[22]

The occupation of Manchuria rekindled anti–Japanese feeling in China, particularly in Shanghai, the center of Chinese xenophobia. Under Communist influence, Chinese workers confronted Japanese industry with large-scale strikes. The situation was made more precarious by the presence in Shanghai of the 19th Route Army, which was not under firm control by the government in Nanking. As tensions increased, the Japanese Ambassador to China, Mamoru Shigemitsu, counseled Japanese business owners to remain calm, but emboldened by their army's success in Manchuria they began to demand a firmer policy in dealing with anti–Japanese agitation and urged that Shigemitsu be recalled. At his own request, Shigemitsu returned to Japan in January 1932, seeking to confer with the new Foreign Minister, Kenkichi Yoshizawa, but despite his urgent pleas he was put off.[23] While Shigemitsu was absent in China, the master intriguer Itagaki saw an opportunity to fan jingoistic flames, and bribed some Chinese to incite a riot against Japanese residents in Shanghai.[24] As he hoped, Japanese marines landed and battle was joined with the 19th Route Army. Shigemitsu returned immediately and saw at once that the landing force was inadequate to protect the lives of the Japanese residents. He requested reinforcements, and four divisions in addition to more naval units were committed before the 19th Route Army was finally driven out. During the bloody weeks of fighting, the Japanese used navy aircraft to bomb densely populated Chapei in Shanghai, inflicting heavy casualties. As a military tactic, the bombing was questionable; politically it was an absolute blunder. Not only did it harden Chinese resistance, it turned world opinion decisively against Japan.

By early March, the Japanese had control of Shanghai, and Shigemitsu arranged a cease-fire. The truce was nearly derailed by a Korean nationalist who threw a bomb at Japanese dignitaries attending a celebration of the Emperor's birthday on April 29. Shigemitsu was seriously wounded but persisted in the negotiations, and an agreement was signed on May 5, 1932. He then had his leg amputated.[25]

As the world's attitude hardened toward Japan for its brutal reprisal in Shanghai and its aggression in Manchuria, the nation reacted with recalcitrance. Inukai, like Shidehara before him, found himself facing a tide of nationalist sentiment that would inundate any path toward peace on the mainland. In January 1932, Secretary of State Henry Stimson declared that the United States would not accept any violation of the 1928 Pact of Paris.

III. The Struggle for Control

The League Council appointed a commission headed by Lord Lytton to investigate the Japanese action in Manchuria. The Kwantung Army officers were not deterred. On the contrary, they were buoyed up by a wave of chauvinism in Japan and proceeded to establish a separate state in Manchuria. It was at that point that Henry Pu Yi was invited to be the titular head of the new state of Manchukuo.

The Inukai government withheld formal recognition of the new state. Not until September 1932, when the Saito government had succeeded the by-then-assassinated Inukai, did Tokyo extend legitimacy to Manchukuo. With the exception of Japan's later allies, Germany and Italy, few other nations recognized Manchukuo as anything but what it was: a puppet regime controlled by the Kwantung Army, Japanese officials, and the South Manchurian Railway.[26] Henry Pu Yi, the pathetic pretender dreaming of monarchy, accepted the title of emperor, but by the close of his reign, even he recognized it for the fiction it was. His dreams ended with the invasion of Soviet forces in August 1945, and Henry Pu Yi suffered the final indignity of a prolonged "reeducation" at the hands of the Chinese Communists.

The Lytton Commission completed its report in the fall of 1932, one year after the incident at Mukden. The report pulled no punches. It held that the Japanese actions on the night of September 18–19 did not constitute self-defense, nor was the new state in any way an expression of Manchurian self-determination as the Japanese alleged. Having disposed of Japan's claims, the Commission recommended that an autonomous regime under Chinese sovereignty be created, that all Chinese and Japanese troops be withdrawn, and that Japanese rights and interests be guaranteed by a new Sino-Japanese treaty that would allow Japan to share in the economic development of Manchuria. This might have satisfied Shidehara, but it found no favor with the army of the Saito government. Japan responded in February 1933, when the League Assembly adopted a report reflecting the Commission's findings. As the cameras rolled, revealing for posterity the League's impotence, Yosuke Matsuoka, the diminutive Japanese delegate, disdainfully dismissed the League's decision and left the podium. Walking up the aisle, he jerked his thumb at the Japanese delegation, which obediently rose and followed him out of the hall. The gesture was an unmistakable declaration of Japan's intentions. Her formal withdrawal from the League on March 17, 1933, seemed almost superfluous.

Throughout these months, while the Kwantung Army was working independently to bring Manchuria into the imperial orbit, the ultranationalists renewed their plot to destroy constitutional rule in Japan. Two more abortive revolutions in the fall of 1931 followed the March attempt. Ugaki's disciples, who had sought to elevate him in the spring, initiated another plot in October. They called it the "Revolution of the Imperial Flag." Less than a month later, the followers of General Araki, then Inspector General of Military Education, planned to install him as head of a new revolutionary government. The conspirators included members of the *Kokuhonsha*, the Country Foundation Association. They hoped that their coup would draw support from the Azabu Regiment, the Imperial Guard, and thousands of reservists.[27] Both plots were uncovered by the police and quashed. Neither general was a party to these conspiracies, nor were any senior officers involved.

Civilian extremists now stepped up where the military had failed. They formed the *Ketsumeidan*, or Blood Brotherhood League. Although they had ties to the military, they planned a campaign of assassination rather than an organized coup to overthrow the government. Nissho Inoue, a fanatic nationalist Buddhist monk, inspired the young men who were drawn to the *Ketsumeidan*. They met in his temple in Mito, north of Tokyo, a community that in the words of the British Ambassador had "bred more patriotic assassins and political gangsters than any other town in Japan."[28]

That statement contrasted sharply with one made by comedian Charlie Chaplin, who had landed at the port of Kobe on May 14, 1932, proclaiming, "The Japanese are the hardest working people in the world and I respect them for it."[29] They might have been the hardest working people, but the British Ambassador was closer to the mark in view of what followed. May 14 was a Sunday, and Prime Minister Inukai was relaxing at his official residence in downtown Tokyo. Late that afternoon, two taxis pulled up and out piled a group of naval officers and army cadets. Forcing their way inside, they headed straight for the Prime Minister's room. Hyoe Murakami described what happened next.

The Prime Minister sat behind a table, surrounded by military men. Riveting his eyes upon them, he opened the lid of a cigarette box and offered it around without a word. Not one of the officers put out a hand. Inukai then addressed the intruders: "Won't you at least remove your boots?"

"You needn't worry about our boots. You know what's happening," shouted the leader, Lieutenant Mikami Taku, in an excited voice, aiming his pistol. "If you have any last words, let's have it quick."

Inukai calmly retorted, "There's no need to get excited. If we talk this over, we can come to an understanding."

His tranquility made a strong impression on Lieutenant Mikami and he lowered his pistol, but another lieutenant shouted angrily, "No discussion, shoot, shoot!"

The Prime Minister raised his hand as though to calm the attacker. At this point a young Second Lieutenant who had just burst into the room suddenly pulled the trigger. Lieutenant Mikami also fired a shot. The Prime Minister collapsed face down on the table.[30]

III. The Struggle for Control 83

Inukai died that night and as he breathed his last, he kept repeating the words, "If only we could have talked."[31] The bloodbath included not only Inukai but also his predecessor Wakatsuki; Junnosuke Inouye, who had opposed the army budget in the Minseito Cabinet; and Baron Takum Dan, the director of Mitsui. To the Blood Brotherhood, these men represented a cancer in the breast of the nation that had to be excised, along with Saionji, the meddlesome *Genro*; Wakatsuki and Inukai, enemies of the nationalist cause; and Baron Dan, who personified the corrupt influence of the *Zaibatsu*. Wakatsuki escaped death, as did Saionji, but Inouye and Dan were killed.

When the full story of the so-called "May 15 Incident" became known, it was revealed that the arms had been provided by the ever-cooperative Hashimoto, who in turn procured them from his friends in the Kwantung Army.[32] The Blood Brotherhood was less successful in carrying out the bomb attacks that were its part of the mission. Most of the bombs failed to explode, and those that did go off caused little damage. The conspirators had not made firm plans beyond their initial acts of violence. They hoped that the disruption would bring about martial law, to be followed by the establishment of a military dictatorship. Pending that outcome, they surrendered to the police. The hoped-for coup never materialized. General Mazaki, the Vice Chief of Staff, was confronted by a group of officers who demanded that General Araki be put in charge of a new government, but Mazaki refused. Once he was able to escape, he had them arrested and the coup was over. Unfortunately, so was civilian control of Japan.

The trials of the conspirators provided them with a podium from which to lecture the public on their patriotic virtues. Even the Minister of War was feeble in his response:

> The crime was indeed committed in violation of national law, and therefore must be punished without mercy, but they acted neither for the sake of fame nor gain nor treason. They acted upon the genuine belief that this was for the interest of the Imperial country. The case should not be dealt with in a narrow-minded way.[33]

Nor was it. The trials of the accused were divided between military and civilian courts, depending on the status of the defendants. The judges in both courts not only had to put up with the patriotic demagoguery of the defendants but faced outside pressure as well. The press, which covered the trials in detail, were sympathetic to the accused and quoted their statements at length. Petitions for the release of the young assassins, signed by over a million Japanese, flooded the court and cabinet offices. Many of these were signed in blood, and others were accompanied by severed fingers, a digital expression of *hara-kiri* by petitioners to prove their sincerity and show how far they were willing to go should the judges not show mercy. The *Meirinkai*, the retired officers association, also issued a warning to the judges.[34] Even the murdered Inukai's family came to the defense of his killers. The defendants became national heroes and generally received light sentences. Not a single death penalty was imposed in the cases involving assassinations, and most of those who went to jail served short terms, reduced in many cases for good behavior.

The army now stepped in and declared that there could be no more party cabinets. In the future, cabinets were to be "national" in character; that meant the exclusion of party politicians except in subordinate roles.

Admiral Viscount Makato Saito was chosen to be the next Prime Minister. His cabinet and the succeeding ones were dominated by the military and the bureaucracy. Party ministers who received cabinet appointments got them either because the military wanted to ensure the party's cooperation with the cabinet, or because the appointment was conditional on the person's resigning from his party or putting aside party views. At first, Saito appeared willing to seek cooperation with the principal parties and consult with their leaders, but the military and bureaucracy objected, and Saito backed off. The demise of party influence became final when Saito established the Five Ministers Conference in 1933. This was composed of the Prime Minister, Foreign Minister, Finance Minister, Army Minister and Navy Minister, and its job was to formulate diplomatic, fiscal and national defense policy.[35] It excluded the parties completely. Saito's Army Minister, the arch-nationalist Sadao Araki, made it clear that there was no room for party involvement in developing defense policy. The Conference, having rejected political party involvement, now took up the development of Manchukuo, the strengthening of national defense, and the execution of various administrative reforms.[36] The Seiyukai and Minseito members were unhappy about their exclusion and made a half-hearted effort to united to preserve parliamentary government, but dissension between the factions and within their ranks foiled any chance of success.

Finally, the members of the Diet knew that the government could dissolve it at whim. Few incumbents relish elections, so the Diet preferred submission to challenge. In fact, the Diet's capitulation was underscored by the self-imposed restriction on its members from making "improper statements." The Seiyukai, which held a majority under the Saito cabinet, sought to muzzle its own members by forbidding them to speak on sensitive political subjects. Not everyone could be silenced, and Kunimatsu Hamada, an outspoken Seiyukai member, confronted Army Minister Terauchi during the term of the Hayashi Cabinet. This was referred to as the "hara-kiri exchange" and Hamada clearly got the better of Terauchi. However, when Hamada later sought permission to speak in defense of his earlier statements, the Seiyukai and Interparty Council refused his request.[37]

III. The Struggle for Control

The Meiji Constitution required that the government's annual budget be approved by both houses of the Diet. In theory it should have enabled the parliamentarians to rein in the military, but in fact it did not. Shinosuke Abe, a political critic of the day, attended the session of the 68th Diet during the administration of Koki Hirota and wrote a derogatory description of the proceedings:

> What strikes me about the Diet is its resemblance to a cageful of monkeys. Excluding those who are too few to count, the rest all support the government. Yet one can clearly see that beneath the surface they go along with the idea of "national unity" reluctantly contrary to their true feelings.[38]

The military's contempt for the Diet was expressed by General Terauchi in 1936. Pointing to the new Diet Building which had just been completed, he scoffed, "Wouldn't the money have been better spent on two divisions?"[39] Ironically, the Diet Building proved more durable than the Army. It was one of the few public structures to survive the war intact.

In any event, Terauchi need not have begrudged the Diet its new building. The military got its own share of the budget and then some. In 1931, the military's portion was ¥450 million; by 1934 it had grown to ¥940 million and it continued to swell, to ¥1.05 billion in 1936 and ¥1.4 billion in 1937. By 1935, military spending comprised fifty percent of the total annual budget, and that was two years before war began in China.[40] Kireikyo Takahashi, Saito's Finance Minister, who had once espoused financial prudence, now submitted to military pressure and resorted to internal loans to balance the government's books. Even that was not enough. Araki would harangue the Diet, insisting that all the resources of the state should be mobilized for what he termed the international crisis that Japan would face in 1936. Yet when questioned about the nature of the pending crisis, he was never able to provide a satisfactory explanation.[41] Still, from 1933 to 1941 the Diet willingly fed the military's insatiable appetite and never once rejected or amended the budget that was presented to them.

Now, in addition to their budget demands, the military sought total dominance over the government. In 1936, when Hirota became Prime Minister, they won it. The requirement that only active duty officers could fill the posts of service ministers was revived. In the fight over increasing the Army's strength by two divisions back in 1913, the parties had been successful in abolishing the active duty requirement on constitutional grounds. For twenty-three years, retired officers, who were not bound by service pressure, had held the ministerial positions. Now, the Diet and the four Seiyukai and Minseito ministers in the Cabinet meekly submitted to the military's demands. The Japanese public knew nothing of the move until it was accomplished. Succeeding cabinets would now be held hostage by the Army and Navy, either of which could prevent the formation of a government by refusing to name a representative.⁴² Not content with bending the Cabinet to its will, the military often had the premiership itself. From May 1932 until August 1945 four admirals and four generals headed the government, and only three civilians. Ironically, the admirals tended to be moderate, and the civilians conservative servants of the chauvinistic generals.

Unencumbered now by either world opinion or the government in Tokyo, the Kwantung Army advanced into Jehol Province in Inner Mongolia, driving Chinese forces south of the Great Wall. If the government felt helpless, the Emperor did not, and in mid–April voiced his disapproval. He told General Shigeru Honjo, who had commanded the Kwantung Army at the time of the Mukden Incident and was now his aide-de-camp, that he was concerned that Japan's integrity was being undermined by the advance of Japanese troops toward Peking and Tientsin. The government had promised the foreign powers that its forces would not move into China proper. Honjo reacted with alacrity, relaying the Emperor's concern to the General Staff, which ordered the Army to withdraw to the Great Wall.

Kohki Hirota: Japanese prime minister in 1937, supported the invasion of China (*Rekidai Shusho tou Shashin*).

Then the Emperor compromised himself by adding that circumstances might have arisen which would excuse the advance, although the action was still a violation by the Chief of Staff and "from the standpoint of the preservation of discipline and authority and [the integrity] of the supreme command" was not "a trifling matter." Honjo caught the nuance of the objection at once. Henceforth, if there were changed circumstances on the battlefield, the Chief of Staff should first advise the Emperor and secure his approval before altering plans. In his diary, Honjo delineated the Emperor's role as Commander-in-Chief. "His Majesty does not necessarily intend to place restrictions on military strategy, but he will not condone infractions against the principles of supreme command."⁴³ If that was the case,

III. The Struggle for Control

Hirohito would be no more of a deterrent to aggression in China than the Diet. All the army had to do was keep Hirohito apprised of its plans in a timely manner. Beyond that, the throne would not be an obstacle.

In North China, the Kwantung Army finally paused. It negotiated the Tangku Truce with the Chinese in May 1933. Under its terms, Jehol Province was annexed to Manchuria and the Japanese gained control of the Shanhaikwan Pass. A demilitarized zone was established north of Tientsin and Peking, under the nominal control of the Nationalists but with growing Japanese economic and political penetration. Had Chiang Kai-shek not had his hands full trying to suppress the Communists, he might have offered more resistance.

The extension of the empire's frontiers on the mainland and its defiance at Geneva combined to nurture a growing chauvinism in Japan. This was expressed in a memorandum prepared by the Kwantung Army just before the Mukden Incident: "If we win this war, it should not matter what the world thinks of us."[44]

In April 1934 a Foreign Office official issued the "Amau Statement," a declaration comparable to the Monroe Doctrine, claiming that Japan must preserve peace in the Far East and warning other powers to refrain from involvement in China. China was Japan's responsibility and the Chinese were not to look to the Western powers for economic or any other assistance. The Amau Statement was premature and embarrassing. Hirota, as Foreign Minister, disavowed it and reprimanded Amau, but he did not remove him from office. Hirota knew his own limitations.

In Japan itself, jingoism smothered all ideological opposition. A campaign to rid the nation of "dangerous thoughts" was mounted, and many of the Communists who had been arrested and imprisoned now renounced their Marxist views and became converts to the Imperial Way. Communism was not alone in crumbling under attacks by the right. All of the other Western-inspired concepts of liberalism, pacifism and internationalism fell out of favor and their adherents came under fire. The universities, which had historically been citadels of free thought, were subjected to a purge. Communist professors had already been expelled, but in 1933, Yukitori Takigawa, a law professor at Kyoto University, was dismissed on orders of Ichiro Hatoyama, the Minister of Education. He charged that Takigawa had written law books critical of existing social and legal practices.[45]

In July 1934 Saito resigned when it was revealed that certain officials had received bribes from a rayon company.[46] Once more Prince Saionji was consulted about a successor. The venerable *Genro* was now eighty-four years old. He had twice served terms of his own as Prime Minister over the course of the century. Since 1912, when the Emperor appointed him, Saionji had been a member of the exclusive circle that advised the Throne on national and international affairs. Only nine men had received the coveted Imperial Command. Saionji was the last. As the sole survivor, throughout the period following the First World War, he had been consulted on foreign policy and was a force for moderation whenever possible, but his principal role was that of adviser in choosing a new Prime Minister.[47] As the militarists consolidated their power after 1933, however, Saionji came to see his position as an exercise in futility. He continued for a while but finally gave up. He knew that he was no longer a player.

To choose a successor to Saito, Saionji decided to call a conference of all the senior statesmen and consult with all of the former Prime Ministers, the Lord Keeper of the Privy Seal, and the President of the Privy Council. By doing so, he probably felt that he could win a broad base of support for his choice, Admiral Keisuke Okada, a moderate. This was a shrewd move. Okada was approved and preserved the moderate makeup of the previous government by retaining the incumbent army, navy and foreign ministers.

But friction developed in the navy and intensified after the signing of the London Naval Treaty of 1930. Admiral Suetsugu scorned the U.S. Navy, believing that Japan would win a great naval battle that would take place between the two fleets. He said the American fleet would be cut by thirty percent by repeated Japanese submarine attacks as it made its way westward for a showdown in Japanese waters with the Combined Fleet. In retrospect, his arguments appear ludicrous, given the misdeployment and general ineffectiveness of Japanese submarines in the Second World War, and the Japanese navy's dismissal of an American submarine threat.

Just as they believed that they could fight better at night than the Americans, the Japanese also believed that American sailors could not stand prolonged submarine duty. They felt that two weeks was the limit of American endurance. Meanwhile, in America, the same smug opinion was widely held with regard to Japanese fighting abilities. Of course, in both cases, these beliefs were founded on racial bias. In spite of the decisive defeat that Japan had inflicted on Russia, most Americans had little respect for Japan as a potential adversary. Three and a half years of bitter fighting between 1941 and 1945 cured both sides of their misconceptions.

Obviously, not all Japanese naval officers shared Suetsugu's views. Admiral Isoroku Yamamato, Japan's brilliant strategist during World War II, saw America as a formidable foe and regarded Suetsugu's submarine—main fleet scenario as antiquated. Like so many admirals and generals, Suetsugu was given to fighting the last war over again. Air power was the wave of the future, said Yamamoto, not battleships. He had become a convert following an inspection tour in 1923–24 and later as naval attaché in 1925–27. He was present when General "Billy" Mitchell was court-martialed, but he knew that Mitchell was right, and that bombers would prevail over battleships.

Yamamoto's interest became so keen that when he returned from the London Naval Conference in 1930, he asked to be appointed chief of the Technical Division of Naval Aviation. In 1935–36 he supervised the Naval Aviation Headquarters; by then, he was a strong advocate for air power. Even more outspoken was Admiral Inoue, who headed Naval HQ in 1940–41. In a memorandum to the Navy Minister, Inoue declared that it was pointless for Japan to worry about naval ratios, calling this "ratio hypnosis." Spending money on battleships, he said, was a waste of money since they would be exposed to land-based aircraft; the Americans would hardly conduct an offensive in the Western Pacific so long as Japan had control of the air. Japan should therefore look to occupy and build air bases on the islands of the South Pacific if it wanted air superiority. Any future war with the United States, he predicted, "would revolve around a conflict for those islands."

A similar struggle was being waged against battleship adherents in the American Navy. The coming war would settle the argument. Admiral Inoue would repeatedly prove to be foresighted as the Americans bloodily wrested one island after another from Japan in their sweep across the Pacific. Air power indeed decided the outcome of the war.

The split between Admirals Kato and Suetsugu, the battleship supporters, and Admirals Yamamoto and Inoue reflected more than just a dispute over battleships versus air power. The former seethed with rage and resentment and their belief in "will" and the "Yamato spirit," but they also advocated a more aggressive foreign policy and confrontation with the Western powers in Asia. They sought closer ties with Nazi Germany as the latter grew in power in Europe. The two nations were hardly racially compatible, but their foreign policies were aimed at the same enemy.

Yamamoto and Inoue were also loyal subjects of the Emperor, but they knew that it would take more than equality in battleships or the "Yamato spirit" to prevail in a war with the United States. The nation's defense would best be served by reallocating its resources into a strong and well-trained air force, both naval and land-based. This could be achieved at far less cost than constructing sea-going behemoths that would be defenseless against hostile aircraft. Abrogating the naval agreements with the Americans and British would not make Japan more secure, but would have the opposite effect, because it would set off a naval race that Japan could not afford and risk a war that Japan could not win. Yamamoto contrasted the "Yamato spirit" with the "Yankee spirit." The former, he observed, was too often one of "blind deviltry" while the latter was based on science and technology. Yamamoto had traveled across America and its vast resources had impressed him. "Anyone who has seen the auto factories in Detroit and the oil fields in Texas," he said, "knows that Japan lacks the national power for a naval race with America." As far as the Washington Treaty was concerned, Yamamoto declared, "The 5-5-3 ratio works just fine for us; it is a treaty to <u>restrict</u> the other parties [the United States and Britain]." So it was the fate of a man who wished to avoid war with the United States to develop the plans that enabled Japan to deliver the most punishing blow ever dealt the U.S. Navy. The attack on Pearl Harbor justified Yamamoto's boldness, but his prediction that the industrial might of America would ultimately be decisive was ultimately confirmed.

Even though the government had accepted the limitations imposed by the London Naval Conference in 1930, the navy pushed to have its budget increased. Its demands were endorsed in a document presented by the Supreme War Council in July 1930, which stated that when the London Treaty expired at the end of 1936, "the empire should complete its naval defense by whatever means it deems best." Obviously, the treaty was not going to be renewed without significant revisions if at all. A supplemental building program was launched to span the years 1931–36; by 1933 Japan's overall fleet strength was approaching eighty percent of that of the United States, which had failed to build up to the limits permitted by the Washington and London agreements.

The Manchurian Incident fueled the navy's demands for a budget increase, especially when the American Navy, following its summer maneuvers, kept the Scouting Force on the Pacific coast rather than returning the Force to its Eastern home ports. Naval expansionists in Japan cited this as proof of the U.S. Navy's "war-like preparations." With Japan's withdrawal from the League of Nations in March 1933, there was an increased American naval buildup and the potential for intervention by the United States and Great Britain in the Far East. Japanese naval leaders concluded that they could no longer abide the inferior position allotted to them by the Washington and London naval treaties. Either they would get parity at the next conference or they would walk out.

Admiral Kato declared that if the "cancer" of the Washington Naval Treaty was removed, "the morale and self-confidence of our navy would be so bolstered that we could count on certain victory over our hypothetical enemy, no matter how overwhelming the physical odds against us." Since Germany had withdrawn from the European disarmament conference under the pretext of equality, the navy felt that it had grounds to insist on whatever level it felt necessary. At a Five Ministers Conference in October 1933, Mineo Osumi stated, "If the United States should take a strong stand in opposition to our fundamental policy, we must resolutely repel it, and with this in view we must proceed to complete our [naval] preparedness." Achieving this, he said, required "freeing ourselves of the disadvantageous restrictions imposed by the existing naval treaties."

From the army's point of view, it would be better for the navy to seek an accommodation at the forthcoming talks in London rather than hold out for terms that would cause the conference to collapse. The army tried in vain to dissuade the navy from its course. Now it became a Cabinet issue. Osumi told Prime Minister Okada that he would resign as Navy Minister if the navy's demand for parity was rejected. He said that the navy's position was laid out in a private communication presented to the Emperor by Prince Fushimi, the Chief of the Navy General Staff. The document stated, "There is no other choice but to discard the existing system of [discriminatory] rations and vigorously pursue a policy of equality [of armaments]; otherwise the navy will not be able to control its officers." The Emperor was bothered by the presumptuousness of the document and upbraided Fushimi for submitting it.

That availed Okada little, but he did his best. At a meeting of the Five Ministers on July 24, 1934, he said that notice of the abrogation of the Washington Naval Treaty should be temporarily delayed pending preliminary talks in London. All except the Navy Minister supported him. Knowing the financial difficulty that would arise from a naval arms race, they warned Osumi that Japan could face bankruptcy within a couple of years. Moreover, Japan's China policy might be jeopardized should the United States and Britain collaborate. Osumi was unmoved, saying that naval circles "could hardly be pacified by such an explanation."[48]

What Osumi was referring to was the behind-the-scenes machinations of Admirals Kato and Suetsugu, who rallied support among the commanders of the Combined Fleet. At a meeting of senior naval officers, Kato warned that if the Cabinet did not agree to parity, "the navy would no longer be able to maintain control over its restless young officers." Having stirred them up in the first place, Kato now claimed that they could not be controlled unless his demands were met. It was hypocrisy of the worst kind, but Okada was powerless. He considered replacing Osumi with the moderate Admiral Kobayashi, but ruled out that option, fearing that such a move would only heighten tensions and bring on a bloody coup attempt on a worse scale than the May 15 Incident. On September 7, Okada and the Cabinet capitulated and decided that by the end of the year the required two years' notice would be given, abrogating the Washington Naval Treaty.

As Commander-in-Chief, the Emperor was entitled to know what was going on. He was fully aware of Suetsugu's bellicosity and knew the kind of influence he had. Suetsugu's reputation was obviously known outside the fleet. What most disturbed Hirohito was the naval race he feared would be forthcoming with the nullification of the Washington Treaty and the heavy burden this would place on the people. Fushimi dissembled in response. He said that if the existing Washington Treaty remained in effect for eight years after 1937, the government would have to spend ¥230 million to replace the old warships. But if there was no treaty and Japan then could decide what type of warships would be most useful for national defense and build what was necessary for that purpose, an average of only ¥210 million would be needed for the same period. Thus, "the absence of a treaty would not result in an inordinate increase in national expenditures."[49] It is unfortunate that Hirohito did not recognize that it would have been the first time in history that killing an agreement limiting naval tonnage would result in less money being spent on warships.

Fushimi's implausible argument notwithstanding, the Emperor was not happy about breaching the Washington Treaty, nor was he keen on the suggestion that he meet with his marshals and fleet admirals to discuss national defense issues. Hirohito seemed to suspect that he was being manipulated by Fushimi and the Kato-Suetsugu group to give his blessing to the termination of the naval treaty and thereby strengthen their cause. The Emperor feared that any action he took that hastened the end of the Washington Treaty would also diminish whatever chance there was of reaching an understanding in London. On October 31, 1934, the group met at the palace but not in the Emperor's presence. Hirohito received their report from the two chiefs of staff. In his reply, the best he could do was to urge that the matter be deliberated further by the government. When Okada met with him two days later, the Prime Minister assured him that while the treaty would be abrogated, the government would continue with its "deliberations." This was nothing more than lip service. The navy had no intention of making concessions to the Western powers in London, and it seemed that withdrawal from the Washington Treaty would render the London Conference moot.

Not only did Kato and Suetsugu prevail in ridding themselves of the hated Washington Treaty, they succeeded in ramming through their outmoded battleship construction program on a scale unmatched by any other navy in the world. They were determined to build the mightiest warships afloat. Thus were born *Yamato* and *Musashi*, the plans for which were developed in the fall of 1934. No nation had ever built warships of this size. The two vessels would each displace over 70,000 tons and carry 18-inch guns, the largest caliber ever mounted at sea. Construction was kept secret; the Japanese knew that the ships would be handicapped by not being able to transit the Panama Canal. But one battleship enthusiast crowed that *Yamato* and *Musashi* would "at one bound raise our [capital ship] strength to a position of absolute supremacy." That might well have been true as far as battleship competition was concerned, but in terms of raw naval power it was not. At enormous cost, the monster ships were built and put to sea, joining the Combined Fleet shortly after the attack on Pearl Harbor. They became twin monuments to the misjudgment and obstinacy of Kato and Suetsugu. Not a single 18-inch shell was ever fired in a battleship exchange with the U.S. Navy, and both fell victim to aerial torpedo attacks. The *Musashi*, part of a Japanese armada aimed at Leyte Gulf and the American invasion force there, was sunk in the Sibuyan Sea on October 24, 1944. The *Yamato* met its end on April 7, 1945, during a desperate suicide sortie to Okinawa, then under American amphibious assault.

While the blueprints for these dinosaurs were being prepared in 1934, preliminary debate in London failed predictably. Parity, as expected, was the shoal on which it foundered. Admiral Yamamoto had the unpleasant task of representing Japan at the conference. Even as he went through the motions of carrying out his instructions, he reported to the Throne that "there was no appearance whatsoever of the two powers [the United States and Great Britain] combining to oppose the third [Japan] at these talks."[50] His superiors were not pleased with his observations. Once or twice he asked for instructions from the Navy Ministry in the hope that a compromise could be reached but Kato and Suetsugu's group held fast. There could be no compromise, and the London Conference fell apart. On December 20, 1934, the American delegation left for home, and in late January Yamamoto and his civilian counterpart, Ambassador Matsudaira, did the same.

While Admirals Kato and Suetsugu were having their way in the Navy, the Army as usual was in crisis mode. The fiery Araki, who had pushed rearmament in preparation for the expected clash with the Soviet Union, could not get Cabinet support for his budget and was at odds with General Tetuzan Nagata, chief of the War Ministry's second department in charge of mobilization and ordnance. While he was able to get Nagata transferred from the Tokyo headquarters, he was still unable to gain Cabinet support for his budget. His primary ally was General Jinsaburo Mazaki. Both had agitated for war with the Soviet Union, which Nagata knew to be foolhardy. A chasm now opened. Nagata joined with General Hideki Tojo to form what would become known as the "control faction" which promoted a "national mobilization state that would modernize the army."[51]

The officer class was divided by the split. Since June 1933, General Mazaki had assumed the post of inspector general of military education. There, he stirred up support among junior officers who were opposed to Nagata's policies. Finally, the Supreme Military Council reassigned him to a ceremonial position on its board of Supreme military councilors, but he fired up his young officers by leaking to them an account of what had happened. They in turn released inflammatory pamphlets blaming Nagata, thereby sealing his fate. The unbalanced Lieutenant Colonel Saburo Aizawa went to Nagata's office at the War Ministry on August 12, 1935, and drawing his sword hacked him to death. Aizawa's trial, not surprisingly, created a "media spectacle and a state for imperial way propaganda."

The Young Officers had had enough and now determined upon a coup d'état. In a "Manifesto" they "proclaimed that this special polity had been fully expressed in the Meiji Restoration but now, because of the encroachments of 'evil and selfish people' on the Emperor's authority, it required to be 'strengthened and expanded.... Therefore ... we have risen to smash the traitors and save Japan.'"[52] They were convinced of the justice of their cause.

The coup began on February 26, 1936. Tokyo lay under a heavy snowfall from the day before. Early that morning, 1,400 troops led by twenty-two of the Young Officers occupied the government district, including the Prime Minister's official residence and the War Ministry.

Like previous insurrections, this one involved assassinations. Several prominent leaders were singled out: Prime Minister Okada, Finance Minister Takahashi, Prince Saionji, the Inspector General of Military Education General Watanabe, Lord Keeper of the Privy Seal Makato Saito, Grand Chamberlain Baron Kantaro Suzuki, and Count Nobuaki Makino. Watanabe was the only military name on the list. Asaichi Isobe and Koji Muranaka, two officers who had been discharged from active service for their part in a previous conspiracy, led the attack. Muranaka said afterward, "We intended to punish traitors with a minimum loss of human lives."[53] A second list of victims who would be executed later included General Hayashi and Colonel Ishiwara, one of the Mukden plotters, who was initially thought to be a supporter of the rebels. In any event, the murder of Prince Saionji was cancelled. Although the Young Officers saw him as their enemy, they recognized the unique position that he occupied. As *Genro*, Saionji nominated the Prime Minister; he could be used. Once Okada was killed, they would have Saionji to recommend General Mazaki to succeed him.[54]

The picked band of assassins set about their work. They managed to kill three of the victims on their list and seriously wounded another. The rest escaped, but Saito, Takahashi and Watanabe did not. They were cut down in cold blood.

The night before, Viscount Saito had been honored by Ambassador Joseph Grew at a diplomatic dinner at the American Embassy. A special postprandial treat was arranged for the Lord Keeper of the Privy Seal: a showing of the film "Naughty Marietta," starring Nelson Eddy and Jeanette MacDonald. It was the first "talkie" that Saito had ever seen. Grew reserved a comfortable chair for Saito in case he wanted to doze during the movie, but the old man was intrigued by the novelty and stayed until nearly midnight. Five hours later he was dead, his body riddled by thirty-six bullets.[55]

Suzuki also received several bullet wounds, but he survived and ultimately returned to serve as Prime Minister in the closing months of the Second World War. Of the others who survived, Okada had the strangest escape. The assassins stormed his official residence but mistook Colonel Matsuo, Okada's brother-in-law, for the Prime Minister. The facial resemblance cost him his life. The soldiers announced Okada's death, but Okada's servants had hidden him. Two days later he made his escape by posing as one of the mourners at his own funeral. The admiral may have con-

Ambassador Joseph Grew, U.S. Ambassador to Japan, 1931–1941 (Library of Congress).

gratulated himself on his good fortune, but the British Ambassador said later that many Japanese felt it was bad form on the admiral's part and that "he had no business being alive after the Emperor had been notified of his death."

Although groups of soldiers seized the War Office, the Police Headquarters and the buildings in the neighborhood of the Imperial Palace, the operation lacked a single military commander. The twenty-one officers who led it, including Isobe and Muranaka, who donned their uniforms for the occasion, acted jointly. The ninety non-commissioned officers who obeyed orders issued to them were willing participants. Other NCOs who were offered the opportunity were allowed to decline. The 1,350 soldiers in the ranks were another matter. They were not given a choice and followed the orders given to them, some more enthusiastically than others. Half were recruits who had joined the First Division the previous month, but all were well disciplined and treated the civilian population respectfully.[56]

When the wave of assassinations was over and the heart of Tokyo under their control, the rebels issued a manifesto. It contained the justification for the murders that had taken place and an indictment of the by-now-familiar villains: senior statesmen, politicians, bureaucrats and misguided military leaders. The rebels called upon the Minister of War to take over and implement the Showa Restoration and make General Araki commander of the Kwantung Army. General Ugaki and other opponents were to be arrested.[57] In this respect, the February 26 Incident was like previous rebellions. The Young Officers' scenario was incomplete. They never proceeded beyond the first act of the play, hoping that sympathetic superiors would finish it. In light of the encouragement they had received, they had every reason to expect that Isobe's officers would do so. Unfortunately, the generals were uncertain about what to do next. Kawashima sympathized with the rebels, but he lacked the backbone to see the matter through. Mazaki and Araki firmly supported the insurgents, and Mazaki tried to convince Kawashima to persuade the Emperor to accede to their demands. Had Ishiwara been Minister of War and on the side of the rebels, the Showa Restoration might have had a chance of success. But the man who carried through the Mukden Incident was now on the other side. Ishiwara, supported by the offices of the General Staff, ordered an army division from outlying districts of Tokyo into the city. The navy also remained loyal, especially after learning that three officers on the assassins' hit list were admirals. Warships anchored off Tokyo trained their guns on the mutineers.

In the end, it was the Emperor who decided the outcome of the rebellion. Hirohito was outraged by it and acted with a decisiveness that he had not often shown in his reign. On February 27, the entire Cabinet resigned, including the waffling Kawashima, whom the Emperor rightly suspected of having failed in responsibility. Hirohito then ordered the commander of the Imperial Guard Division to disarm the rebel troops, by force if necessary although he left that to the commander's discretion. This opened the path toward ending the affair without military fratricide. The same day, the Emperor's aide-de-camp, General Honjo, tried to downplay the conduct of the rebel officers and thereby betrayed sympathy for them. He told the Emperor that while it was true that they had violated the supreme command, "from the standpoint of the spirit that moved them to action, because they were thinking of the good of the nation, they should not necessarily be condemned." It was Aizawa's defense all over again. The Emperor was unmoved. "[Not to] condemn these criminally brutal officers who killed my aged subjects whom I trusted the most is akin to gently strangling me with floss-silk." Hirohito said that if the army authorities did not promptly suppress the rebels he would "personally lead the Imperial Guard Division and subdue them."[58] It was this resolution that carried the day. The acting Prime Minister, Fumio Goto, declared martial law on February 27. As additional military forces were brought to bear against the insurgents, the latter turned in desperation to General Mazaki. Whatever hopes Mazaki might had had about becoming Prime Minister were dashed by the Emperor's command that the troops return to their barracks. Surrounded by superior forces, their dreams of a "Showa Restoration" shattered, the Young Officers yielded, and their soldiers were ordered to return to their First Division compound. Two of the officers committed suicide. They rest of them decided to surrender and stand trial, then use the courtroom as a forum for their views as Aizawa and others had done. They never got the chance. The conspirators were tried swiftly and secretly. Nineteen of them were executed, including Isobe, Muranaka, Kita and Nishida. As is often the case, justice was not evenly applied. Kita, for example, knew of the plot, but while he was an inspiration to the Young Officers he had not actually participated in the planning or execution of it. Nonetheless, because he had stirred the conspirators to action and had been influential in shaping their ideas, the army decided to be rid of him once and for all.

Although Kita was a civilian, he was tried by a military court along with the others. He went before a firing squad on a sultry summer day. Hyoke Murakami described the scene: "A certain Lieutenant Nishida Nitsugu who, along with Kita, sat blindfolded against a stake, turned to Kita and said, 'Let's give three cheers for the Emperor.' Pausing for a moment, Kita replied, 'I'd rather not.'" Almost immediately after this exchange, shots rang out.[59]

Nor did Aizawa escape punishment. A second trial was held, and he was executed. Among the rebels, no one over the rank of captain was shot, though all knew the roles Mazaki and other senior officers had played. Mazaki was tried but acquitted. Nevertheless, he and Araki were placed on the inactive list. Others were transferred from key posts. The purge was directed by Juichi Terauchi, the new Minister of War, and his Vice Chief Yoshijiro Umezu.[60] Their triumph over the rebels brought the army closer to absolute power. Not only did they clamp down on their own dissidents, they rendered civilian authorities impotent. From the spring of 1937 onward, the army steadily tightened its grip on the government and the nation.

IV

Triumph and Uncertainty

> But in the Army, particularly among those connected with the administration and with China questions, more importance was attached to a disposal of the problem of China as a whole. And they were blindly followed by those of the senior staff of officers that had already had a hand in Chinese affairs. The desire for honor and glory over a second Manchukuo had a great deal to do with this.
> —Mamoru Shigemitsu, *Japan and Her Destiny*

"The Hirota Cabinet was little more than the tool of the military. But since it was not made to order but merely a makeshift, it never worked satisfactorily."[1] That was the judgment of Mamoru Shigemitsu, whose fate it was to sign the instrument of surrender in 1945, ending the ruinous conflict that had begun in China nearly a decade before. Shigemitsu was a survivor; an assassin had crippled him, and he suffered four years of imprisonment at the hands of the victors. But if Shigemitsu was a faithful servant of the Emperor, he was not a willing pawn of the military oligarchy. Years ago, the author asked Ambassador Joseph Grew if Koki Hirota deserved the death penalty that was imposed on him by the International War Crimes Tribunal. "Absolutely not," was the reply. And then he paused and added sardonically, "Maybe he should have been given ten years for keeping bad company."[2] However, Hirota acquiesced in the aggressive acts of Japan's military masters. For that he was hanged in Sugamo Prison in December 1948, the only civilian to die of the seven major war criminals who went to the gallows.

Koki Hirota's career might have taken a different turn if he had shown a better mastery of English during his years at Tokyo Imperial University. Following his graduation, he applied for a post in the American Embassy as a clerk to the military attaché. Hirota got the job but was fired after three days because his English was not satisfactory. His boss was an officer who would build a reputation based on uncompromising standards as he rose through the ranks of the U.S. Army. At the time, he was just a captain; his name was John J. Pershing. When the story was revealed many years later, Hirota had become Foreign Minister of Japan. A highly amused Ambassador Grew told him that he intended to write to General Pershing and tell him whom he had fired. Hirota got the joke and replied that he should tell Pershing that he was still not very good at English.³

Whatever his proficiency in English, Hirota was destined for a career in the Japanese Foreign Office and followed the traditional route of foreign postings interspersed with duty at home. By 1915 he had made enough progress to be involved in the drafting of the Twenty-One Demands, although he strongly opposed the ulti-

Mamoru Shigemitsu, Japanese diplomat and politician, encouraged efforts to negotiate with the U.S.

matum that followed. As the years passed, Hirota continued to climb the ranks and broaden his horizons. He foresaw Britain's renunciation of the alliance with Japan and warned against it. He worked for a rapprochement with the Soviet Union, particularly after the treaty with Great Britain was abrogated. Not surprisingly, he served a tour in Moscow as Japan's Ambassador.⁴ In September 1933 he was appointed Foreign Minister for the first time. From then on, he would be keeping the company of men whose views did not always coincide with his own but with whom he felt bound to cooperate. Hirota publicly defended the events which the Foreign Office had been powerless to prevent: the conquest of Manchuria and the subjugation of Jehol. He spoke of his desire to preserve the arrangement that kept North China administered under the terms of the Tangku Truce Agreement. But these actions were all after the fact. The Foreign Office was a distant caboose attached to an army-driven train. Hirota's role seemed to be primarily one of trying to persuade Japan's neighbors and the world of the reasonableness and sincerity of her policies. This meant, of course, accepting a premise that was the foundation of Japanese imperial policy. Hirota embraced it as ardently as the ultranationalists and he spoke for them and for himself when he told the Diet, "We should not forget for a moment that Japan, serving as the cornerstone for the edifice of the peace of East Asia, bears the entire burden of responsibility. It is this important position and these vast responsibilities in which Japan's diplomacy and national defense are rooted."[5]

Hirota had been a member of the *Genyosha*, the Black Currant Society, one of the many patriotic organizations previously mentioned. Yet despite his affiliation with a group of this kind and his undeniable nationalist outlook, Hirota was uncomfortable with the army activists. Nevertheless, he felt it necessary to accommodate himself to their policy. As Shigemitsu said, "He himself would never stir himself to set things in motion. He seemed rather to study what was happening around him and to act accordingly."[6] If he had had his way, Hirota would have steered a safer course for the nation, preserving the status quo and reestablishing friendly relations abroad. It was for this reason that Saionji tapped him to succeed to the premiership in the wake of the February 26 Incident. Hirota was not the *Genro*'s first choice. He had first asked Prince Konoe, the president of the House of Peers, but Konoe declined on the grounds of ill health, though the time would come when he could not refuse the summons. So Hirota got the nod and immediately exposed his impotence by submitting to the army. General Masatake Terauchi, whom he chose as his Minister of War, demanded that the army have the right of veto over other Cabinet appointments, and Hirota gave in. Four men initially selected were summarily rejected and two others were moved to different posts. The army would tolerate no critics in the Cabinet. Their influence was strengthened further by the appointment of Baron Kiichiro Hiranuma as President of the Privy Council. He was a leader of the *Kokuhonsha*, the right-wing Country Foundation Association.

Military domination of the Cabinet was enough of a problem, but it was compounded by continued friction between the two services. Once Manchuria had been conquered and Japanese control pushed south to the Great Wall, the army, particularly the *Kodoha*, the Imperial Way faction, focused their attention on the Soviet Union. Neighboring Soviet Siberia presented both a challenge and an opportunity. Indeed, General Araki, who had inspired the Imperial Way, predicted war with Russia in 1936. The *Kodoha* were opposed to any further advance into China or interference in Chinese affairs. Had the *Kodoha* prevailed over the *Toseiha* faction and the February 26 revolt succeeded, it is possible that events in the Far East might have taken a different turn. That was certainly the view of Prince Fumimaro Konoe, who served as Prime Minister during the critical years of 1937–1939 and again from 1940 to 1941. He cited the triumph of the Control Faction over the Imperial Way as a major factor in the decision to advance toward the south rather than to the north. In the closing months of World War II, with defeat imminent, Konoe looked back on the February 26 Incident as a turning point for Japan:

> The ideology of the Kodo generals was exclusively concerned with the Soviet Union. They were, for example, completely opposed to Japan's interference in China or to the advance into Southeast Asia.... Consequently, when these officers were removed in the aftermath of the February rebellion, it furnished the Control Faction with an opportunity to alter Japan's foreign policy, a change which later caused the China Incident and the present war.[7]

Hindsight lends credibility to Konoe's thesis, but there were undoubtedly also Control Faction officers who shared a genuine concern about a Soviet threat to Manchukuo and saw no future in further adventures in China. Araki's warnings about a conflict with the Soviet Union were not entirely groundless. In March 1936, Moscow concluded a mutual assistance pact with the Mongolian People's Republic, thwarting the Kwantung Army's goal of a Japanese-controlled pan–Mongolian state. A boundary dispute between Manchukuo and Soviet Siberia also remained unresolved.

Fumimaro Konoe, Japanese Prime minister off and on during the 1930s through 1941, approved the invasion of China.

The alarm in Tokyo over these developments led to the conclusion of a new relationship with Berlin. It began in the fall of 1935 when the Japanese military attaché in Germany, General Hitoshi Oshima, received overtures from Joachim von Ribbentrop with regard to an anti–Soviet agreement. Ribbentrop suggested a passive one. If either Germany or Japan became involved in a war with Soviet Russia, the other would not aid that power. The idea appealed to the Japanese military, and a representative from the Army General Staff was dispatched to Berlin to pursue the proposal with Ribbentrop and General von Blomberg, the German Minister of Defense. Out of those talks came the framework of the Anti–Comintern Pact.

The Japanese Foreign Ministry believed that the agreement might be widened to include Great Britain and some of the other Western European powers. The army opposed British involvement, but the Foreign Ministry declared that it could not support a purely German-Japanese pact. The army grudgingly gave in, and Shigeru Yoshida, Japan's new Ambassador to Great Britain, approached the London Foreign Office. The Germans welcomed this move; Ribbentrop was about to represent his own country in England and hoped to bring about an Anglo-German understanding. Nothing came of either overture, and Ribbentrop's record as an ambassador was a failure.

The Netherlands were also approached and at first seemed interested, hoping that a cooperative arrangement would lead to the monitoring of Communist activities in Asia that were causing anti-colonial disturbances in the Dutch East Indies. But the Dutch wanted no part of an agreement that would draw them into a German-Soviet conflict. The upshot was a German-Japanese pact. Whatever objections the Foreign Ministry had were swept aside; the military wanted a hedge if they had an armed conflict with the Soviets in Asia. The Anti-Comintern Pact was signed on November 25, 1936, toward the end of Hirota's tenure, but he had practically nothing to do with it. Like so many of the treaties that bound international partners, this one had secret as well as public provisions. To the world, the Anti-Comintern Pact announced a cooperative effort to combat the subversive activities of the Communist International. Privately, the two signatories agreed not to give aid to the Soviet Union or take any measure that would assist it if that power launched an unprovoked attack or made an unprovoked threat against either of them. Moreover, they agreed that, for the five years the pact was in force, neither would conclude any other treaties with the Soviets.

At the International Military Tribunal following Japan's defeat, Kensuke Horinouchi, who at the time of the Anti-Comintern Pact had been Vice Minister of Foreign Affairs, told the court that the secret clauses were so designated at the request of the Japanese government because of its concern about a Soviet reaction. Russian agents, however, intercepted the terms and the Soviet government rejected the specious Japanese claim that the pact was aimed at the subversive Third International and not at the Soviet Union itself. Moscow just as mendaciously denied that it had any control over the Third International, but it recognized the concealed danger and broke off negotiations for a new fisheries treaty with Japan.

Admittedly the agreement with Nazi Germany did not commit Japan to a military alliance but it placed her in the Axis camp, not just in the eyes of the Soviet Union but in those of the Western world. The octogenarian *Genro*, Prince Saionji, privately denounced the Anti-Comintern Pact, telling Baron Harada, his private secretary, that it benefited only Germany and was of no conceivable value to Japan:

> The Japan-German pact is 100% to Germany's benefit and can be nothing but a loss to Japan. So far, pro–German feelings have been confined to the habatsu and the feelings of the mass of the people are pro–Anglo-American rather than pro–German…. Geographically, we are much better off keeping close relations with England and America. If Japan were in the position of Turkey, or one of the Baltic states, then the current methods might be valid, but in terms of geography, we are very different…. Whichever way one looks at it, the Japan-German pact has diminished Japan.⁸

Saionji suspected that the agreement was related to the desire of the army and the Hirota government to strengthen Japan's position in China. This worried him even more.

> What do they really intend with China? They know nothing, any of them. Manchuria is a land with a long history, and she has suffered considerably in her relations with Japan. Well, there is no good crying over that now; but does the future hold any happiness for the children of Manchuria or will it bring only continued despair? I am consumed with worry at the various things which are being done in North China.

Had the *Genro* fully realized what the navy was up to, he would have been even more worried. By the summer of 1936 the navy was proposing to extend the Japanese Empire beyond North China to the South Pacific.

This ambitious design was the brainchild of the Fleet Faction, which conceived it as a counter to the perceived Anglo-American naval threat. In their paranoia they believed that the United States was drawing a noose around Japan with its bases in Hawaii, the Philippines and the Aleutians, and suspected that the British were collaborating with the Americans by fortifying Singapore. By aiding China and recognizing the Soviet Union, the Americans were clearly trying to hem in the Japanese Empire. In 1936 a Japanese observer returned from an inspection tour of Southeast Asia and reported that a "military-political-economic ABCD encirclement" of Japan was well under way.⁹ This preposterous claim fed the irrational convictions of the expansionists who insisted that the nation's defense should be concentrated against the United States.

Which way to go, then, north or south? The question was resolved on August 7, 1936, at a Five Ministers Conference. A statement was drafted, the "Fundamentals of National Policy," a document with far-reaching consequences. "Foreign policy and national defense must be correlated in order to guarantee the Empire's footing on the continent in East Asia as well as to expand in the direction of the South Seas."¹⁰

The national policy statement declared that Manchukuo should be secured against the menace from the Soviet Union, and in order to "provide against trouble from Britain and the U.S.," close economic ties should be developed between Japan, Manchukuo and China. It called for "racial and economic development in the South Seas" by peaceful means, if possible, but to ensure the achievement of its goals, the army was to be strengthened so that it would be more than a match for Soviet Far Eastern forces and the navy to a level that would "guarantee supremacy in the West Pacific against the American Fleet." This grandiose scheme was to be assisted by vigorous diplomacy (including the Anti-Comintern Pact), changes in domestic administration and an enormous increase in defense spending.

So the navy's policy of "defend the north, advance to the south" prevailed. Both services would reap a harvest of armaments from the expanded defense budget, but the navy had set the geopolitical goals. Nearly four months before the fateful Five Ministers Conference, a navy policy paper had addressed the southern strategy in far more aggressive terms. It noted that Japan must "as a matter of course anticipate obstruction and coercion by the United States, Great Britain, and the Netherlands, etc., and must therefore provide for the worst by completing preparations for a resort to force."[11] This was the first time that Great Britain had been included with the United States as a potential enemy. It is interesting to note that this contentious outlook was not shared by Japanese naval officers and attachés stationed in China. The commander-in-chief of the Third Fleet cautioned that the Soviet Union constituted the principal threat, not the United States, with which war should be avoided. But the Navy General Staff, intoxicated by the dream of unchallenged mastery of the Pacific, spurned this advice. Furthermore, if the navy could not justify its ambitious shipbuilding program, the army would walk away with the lion's share of defense funding.

Shortly after the Fundamentals of National Policy were adopted, the navy found a pretext for making the first move south. A series of anti-Japanese incidents occurred in southern and central China, beginning on August 24, 1936, at Chengtu, the capital of Szechuan Province and then spreading rapidly to Peihai on the Kwantung coast bordering the Gulf of Tonkin. By September 23, disturbances had broken out at Hankow and Shanghai. These seemed heaven-sent opportunities for the navy. The Navy General Staff recommended a retaliatory attack on the Chinese coast, the creation of a joint army-navy security zone around Shanghai and Tientsin, and a blockade of southern and central Chinese ports.[12] The real prize, however, was the large island of Hainan, which would provide a major stepping stone in the march southward. Expecting that this could well lead to hostilities with England and possibly the United States, the Operations Section drafted a preliminary fleet mobilization plan to prepare for war against not only China but also Britain and America. The army would not hear of such a move. With the exception of the Intelligence Division, the Army General Staff rejected the overture, advising the navy to leave settlement of the problem to the Foreign Office and its representatives in Nanking. Kanji Ishiwara, now a general in command of the Operations Section of the General Staff and no longer the firebrand who had planned the Mukden Incident, told his navy counterpart that "the army has no interest in an all-out war with China." That was the end of that; without army support the navy had to back off. However, it was not the end of machinations by less restrained army elements in north China. Ishiwara might have become moderate as he rose in rank and pursued his career at army headquarters back in Tokyo, but his former comrades in the Kwantung Army were as restless as ever. The army leadership would find it far easier to check the ambitions of the navy than to impose its will on its own officers on the mainland.

As for Hirota, he did not realize that he had signed his own death warrant when he presided over the Five Ministers Conference that drew up the Fundamentals of National Policy. The International Military Tribunal, which tried Hirota after the Second World War, convicted him on the charge that the Fundamentals of National Policy was the "blueprint for imperialism" that caused the Pacific War.[13] Hirota certainly did not regard the Fundamentals as a ticket to war. While they staked out the essential boundaries of what would eventually be described as the "Co-Prosperity Sphere," Hirota believed that policy could be managed without resort to arms. In February 1935, during his tenure as Foreign Minister, he was the object of a scathing article in the Japanese press for his perceived weakness in dealing with China. He was called an "'aged boatman' willing to drift ashore without rowing."[14] Later, following the outbreak of fighting in the summer of 1937, Hirota took a more military stance. Konoe was Prime Minister and Hirota was back in the more familiar post of Foreign Minister. He threw in his lot with the army, supporting the extension of the war in China, and turned his back on appeals from his own ministry, which opposed further escalation and called for scaling down the forces being sent to China. This shift in behavior coincided with Shigemitsu's assessment of the man. He said that Hirota's character "was that of one that had mastered the secrets of Zen philosophy ... a Buddhist sect that taught that knowledge came not from reason but from inspiration [enlightenment]."[15]

In 1936, Hirota found little solace in Zen. The army was pressing him to surrender further control of the government to them. That fall he met with War Minister Terauchi at Sapporo to discuss a military plan for administrative reform which included, among other things, the establishment of a nebulous vice premier for reform and the joining of the Foreign Ministry with the Overseas Affairs Ministry. Additionally, the army proposed to totally subjugate the political parties by cutting the powers of the Diet. Hirota and the other Cabinet members resisted, which only increased the determination of the generals and admirals to have their own way. When rumors of Terauchi's plans leaked out, the political parties, in a final burst of independence, staged a series of anti–Cabinet rallies. They correctly foresaw that the last shred of Diet power would disappear if Terauchi's "reforms" were adopted. A Diet System Enquiry Commission was formed and cross-examined Hirota at his official residence. He spent most of the hearing struggling to allay its concerns. His problem was obvious: he was in the delicate position of trying to appease them without offending Terauchi. In December, the Cabinet approved a new budget and sent it to the Diet. It called for expenditures of over three billion yen, of which the army's share was ¥720 million and the navy's ¥680 million. That amounted to forty-six percent of the entire budget and caused an uproar in the Diet.

The following month a member of the Seiyukai, Kunimatsu Hamada, took the army to task for its actions, charging that it was dominated by elements who wanted to impose a military dictatorship. The testy Terauchi lashed back at Hamada, accusing him of insulting the army. Hamada was undaunted and said that he would review his statement and if he found that he had insulted the army he would commit *hara-kiri*. Terauchi was beside himself with indignation, and when Hirota refused to dissolve the Diet the War Minister resigned, bringing down the Cabinet. Nothing could have demonstrated more graphically the vulnerability of the Cabinet than this petulant display of pride by the army's representative.

What followed was further proof of the army's supremacy. Once more the aging *Genro* was called upon to recommend a Prime Minister and the Lord Keeper of the Privy Seal, Baron Kuruhei Yuasa, took a train to Saionji's home in Okitsu to confer with him. Saionji's first choice was General Ugaki, whose record made him acceptable to the public and the financial community. But in the eyes of the army and navy, Ugaki carried too much baggage. Not only had he supported arms reduction when he was Minister of War, he had vacillated during the March Incident of 1931, and they were suspicious of his ties with party politicians. Ugaki was aware of the opposition but doggedly tried to form a Cabinet. When the army refused to nominate a War Minister, he realized the futility of his efforts and gave up the attempt. The army wanted General Hayashi, and for the last time the *Genro* played his part, submitting to the army's will and giving them their man. Four days after Hayashi was sworn in, Saionji advised the Lord Keeper of the Privy Seal that he wished to be relieved of the responsibility of nominating the Prime Minister. He said that he was too old, too ill, and "out of touch with the personnel of politics." He asked to resign as *Genro*. The Court was dismayed by his request. Saionji was told that he was too essential as a bridge between the various factions, so he agreed to stay on but only on condition that in the future the Lord Privy Seal would recommend

Prime Ministers. Saionji, however, was not allowed to retire altogether, and the Court still sought his advice, even to the approval of Hayashi's successor, Prince Konoe, and Konoe's Foreign Minister.

Senjuro Hayashi was born in 1876 and enjoyed a successful military career. He was already a captain in the army when the Russo-Japanese War broke out and fought in the battle at Port Arthur. He served a term as President of the Military Academy and commanded the garrison in Korea at the time of the conquest of Manchuria. In May 1932, he was elevated to one of the "big three" posts as Inspector General of Military Education, and less than three years later he succeeded General Araki as Minister of War. But whatever his achievements in the army, as Prime Minister he was a disaster. His administration lasted four months. He failed to appoint a single political party member to his Cabinet, demonstrating his contempt for the Diet. He also damaged his relationship with the army in the same way. Despite successfully securing passage of his budget, Hayashi was dissatisfied, and he dissolved the Diet when its session ended. The angry Seiyukai and Minseito members united in opposition and in the election that followed, Hayashi found himself facing a hostile Diet. The small ultranationalist party that had supported him lost seats and the other parties increased in strength. Hayashi submitted to the inevitable and resigned. The military still controlled the government, but the Prime Minister could not ignore the Diet, at least not yet.

The man who succeeded Hayashi was something of an enigma all his life, but Sir Robert Craigie, the British Ambassador during those years, achieved what many Japanese could not: he peeled away the inscrutable and drew a marvelous portrait of Prince Fumimaro Konoe:

> For a Japanese he is large in stature. Though not strong in health, he has the easy gait of the athlete. His expression denotes neither energy nor determination, but rather a sense of philosophic doubt. Calm and unruffled in all circumstances, he is by disposition phlegmatic. His eyes are his best feature, denoting intelligence and political acumen, combined with a touch of laziness. The profile is disappointing and does not bear out the promise of the striking full face. These facial contrasts fit in with his enigmatic character. There were moments when his actions showed a touch of genius. Time and again one was impressed by acts of statesmanship, only to be irritated just as often by his apparent lack of firmness in leadership and his failure at times of crisis to use his strong personal position to curb the extremists. His Japanese friends were completely baffled by many of his actions, wondering whether he really stood for what he was supposed to represent—a moderating influence—or whether, unknown to his more responsible friends and followers, he was a totalitarian at heart and rather enjoyed giving the Army its long rope.[16]

Fumimaro Konoe was born in 1891, but he traced his family lineage back to the "Age of the Gods." He was a descendant of the Fujiwara line; his father, Atsumaro Konoe, had served as President of the House of Peers from 1896 to 1903, a position that Fumimaro would assume thirty years later. By the time of the First World War, the young prince had graduated from the law school at Kyoto Imperial University and was already taking part in affairs of state. Along the way he had acquired strong nationalistic views, which he expressed in an article entitled "Reject the Anglo-American Peace." In it he paid lip service to the ideals of democracy and humanitarianism but charged the Americans and British with interpreting those values to suit themselves in exploiting the "less civilized" areas of the world. Konoe warned his countrymen not to be taken in by "flowery Anglo-American proclamations" and he insisted that economic imperialism and the discriminatory treatment of Asian people must end. At the subsequent peace conference, he said:

> We must require all the powers to open the doors of the colonies to others, so that all nations will have equal access to the markets and natural resources of the colonial areas. It is also imperative that Japan insist on the eradication of racial discrimination. At the coming peace conference we must demand this in the name of justice and humanity.... Japan must not blindly submit to an Anglo-American-centered peace; it must struggle for the fulfillment of its own demands, which are grounded in justice and humanity.[17]

These comments caused some embarrassment to Prince Saionji, who headed the Japanese delegation to the Paris Peace Conference. Konoe had persuaded the *Genro* to allow him to join the delegation. Saionji was an internationalist and placed great stock in Japan's preservation of her friendship with Britain, France and the United States. He took Konoe to task for his remarks, but that was not the end of his troubles with Konoe. When they were about to land at Marseilles, the *Genro* was shocked to overhear Konoe tell the other young men in the delegation how to evade the questions of French customs officials. Later in Paris, Konoe posed as a reporter in order to attend a conference from which aides were specifically barred. Saionji warned him that this kind of behavior could result in his dismissal from the delegation.

Konoe's conduct may have improved, but what happened at the peace conference reinforced the views that he had expressed before he came. In another article, "My Impressions of the Paris Peace Conference," he stated that the great powers had revealed their true intentions. There was no hope for justice and humanity, he said. Instead of embracing the principle of racial equality, the League Covenant had rejected it and sanctioned the Monroe Doctrine. Japan had proposed that that principle be included in the document but had been outvoted because she was a small power, while the Doctrine was included because the United States, a large power, had insisted on it. Konoe returned to Japan with an understandably jaundiced outlook.

In the decade that followed the Paris Peace Conference, Konoe became an increasingly important player in the political arena. This was partly because Prince Saionji perceived Konoe's intelligence and charm and sought to prepare him for a leadership role, but as a Court noble, Konoe also had his own entree into the highest government circles, and his keen interest in statecraft gave him a significant opportunity. However, Konoe viewed the military's growing influence with ambivalence. Unlike Saionji, who feared the consequences of its activism and sought to blunt it, Konoe knew that it could not be pushed aside or ignored. He felt that he must work with the military and that by doing so he could achieve a cooperative arrangement that would restrain the more radical forces within its ranks.

It is curious that Konoe acquired a reputation as a liberal. He was certainly not enamored with American democracy and often criticized it, but his willingness to listen to all sides of an issue helped to win him this reputation. He vexed Saionji, his mentor, who resented Konoe's capitulation to the militarists after he became Prime Minister. Yet the *Genro* himself had endorsed him for the position, in the vain hope that Konoe might rise to the occasion and resist the slide toward military autocracy. Konoe did not see himself as the army's puppet. After he became Prime Minister he was asked by an acquaintance for a sample of his calligraphy and responded with his brush, "I am a man of the Land of the Rising Sun. The time has come for me to perform my duty as a man of the Land of the Rising Sun." At heart he was a nationalist, and he came to believe that Japan would find salvation in neither fascism nor parliamentary government as it currently existed. He favored the adoption of a program of internal reform and the establishment of a "national unity Cabinet" to include reform elements and the military, united under the Emperor. This amorphous concept bore a strong resemblance to the views of those who espoused the Imperial Way.

Konoe's first call to leadership came after the February 26 Incident. As noted earlier, Konoe declined on grounds of ill health. Saionji reminded Konoe of his popularity with the disparate groups in the Diet and the military, but Konoe disingenuously replied that this simply showed he had no real support anywhere. The *Genro* treated him like a spoiled child and told him that he was going to submit his name to the Emperor anyway, but Konoe avoided the mandate, pleading with Hirohito for time to reconsider. In the end the Emperor gave in to his wishes and Hirota was appointed instead.

In the ensuing months Konoe continued to be a source of irritation and disappointment to Saionji. Throughout 1936 the young Peer issued statements that reflected close ties with the far right and hard-core military. The *Genro* told Baron Harada, "I deplore a man of his ability and birth acting as he does. If only we could somehow bring him back to a reasonable course." Harada replied, "Konoe would understand if they spoke to him about his behavior but that he lacked courage and worried too much about his popularity."[18]

With the collapse of the Hayashi government, Konoe found himself again in the spotlight. This time he could not avoid the summons, although he tried desperately to do so, joining Hayashi and others in recommending General Sugiyama, who had been Hayashi's Minister of War. When Saionji's counsel was sought, he put aside his misgivings and declared that only Konoe would do. He was the *Genro*'s last hope of putting a brake on the military.

Thus, at the age of forty-five, Prince Fumimaro Konoe became Japan's newest Prime Minister, entering the office on a wave of popularity and goodwill not enjoyed by any of his recent predecessors. Yoshitake Oka, his biographer, wrote:

> His ancient lineage and noble birth, his tall, imposing stature, and his nonchalant manner, all worked to give him an enchanting aura of elegance. He was known to have superior intellectual ability, and so his never-failing courtesy and lack of arrogance were all the more appealing. He appeared as a democratic presence, in sharp contrast to the profound aristocratic pride hidden within him. Konoe's popularity was generated to a large extent by the popular tendency to adore the powerful, but his congenial deportment projected an air of intimacy and only made the people push him higher up on his pedestal.[19]

He might have added what Shigemitsu said about Konoe, that "here was a Court noble who passed his life swimming with the tide."[20] That perhaps more than anything else sums up the life and career of Fumimaro Konoe. His problems developed after the Empire was washed away in 1945. Konoe had clung to the now-discredited military; the people felt that he had betrayed them, and his popularity evaporated. He briefly tried to serve the conquerors but they soon saw him as a liability. Barely four months after Japan surrendered, he was put on trial for war crimes. Konoe could not bear the shame; he was a prince of the realm and would not submit to the humiliation of a trial. Early on the morning of the day he was to report to Sugamo prison, he killed himself with potassium cyanide.

Shortly before Konoe committed suicide, he spent an evening with a close friend contemplating his life and career. Looking back on past events and his role in them, Konoe passed judgment on himself:

> Before the war I was ridiculed for being indecisive, during the war rebuked as an escapist peace-seeker, and after the war accused as a war criminal. I am a child of fate. A man's life cannot be judged before his death. It will be decades, even centuries, after my death before the historian finally judges my career objectively.... All kinds of people have come and gone within my circle of associates. I have been surrounded by rightists and leftists and those in between ... no, I have allowed them to surround me, and that is what brought this fate upon me. It is my own fault, but it is also a tragic reality.[21]

In this sentimental self-assessment, Konoe came to terms with himself, but it has not taken centuries to judge him. His contemporaries saw his failings in his lifetime. That was the tragic reality.

Konoe got off to a mixed start as Prime Minister. Before he announced his Cabinet appointments the army gave him a list of its own. Hirota was brought back into the Cabinet as Minister of Foreign Affairs; General Hajime Sugiyama was retained as Minister of War; Mitsumasa Yonai, a moderate admiral who would play an important role in Japan's decision to surrender in 1945, was appointed Navy Minister. But Konoe rejected the army's demand that Eichi Baba be made Minister of Finance. Baba had followed a pro-military policy as Finance Minister in the Hirota Cabinet, and the swollen military budget had alienated the business community. Instead, Konoe appointed Okinori Kaya as Finance Minister and put Baba in charge of Home Affairs. That move was opposed by the powerful *Tokyo Asahi*, which published an editorial critical of Baba's appointment to a post that was said to be almost the equivalent of Vice Premier. The editor reminded readers of Baba's past unpopular financial policy and asked for assurance that the Cabinet was going to be a Konoe Cabinet and not a Baba Cabinet. The editor's fears were misplaced; it was going to be an army Cabinet, no matter who was in it.

Nevertheless, the Emperor was pleased to have Konoe as his Prime Minister. The fact that Konoe and Hirohito were both of noble blood undoubtedly put their relationship on an intimate basis. That was certainly the case as far as Konoe was concerned and it bothered some Court officials who observed Konoe's informality when he was in the Emperor's presence. A chamberlain complained that while other senior officials stood while reporting to the Emperor, Konoe would take a seat, cross his legs, and ask the Emperor familiarly, "How are you? It's been quite a while, hasn't it?"[22] Moreover, Konoe mixed affairs of state with a variety of other subjects, misleading the Emperor about what was official and what was not. If Saionji heard about this deportment, he must have shaken his head in dismay; it was the same kind of behavior he had witnessed nearly twenty years earlier.

On June 4, 1937, the Konoe Cabinet took up its duties. With all the hopes reposed in it and the popular Prime Minister, no one would have guessed that in just five weeks the nation would enter a protracted struggle that would consume its energies, blind its leaders, and ultimately lead to a larger war and disaster. While the China Incident was unplanned, the environment in which it occurred had been created long ago.

As was his custom, the American Ambassador to Japan, Joseph C. Grew, sent to Washington at the beginning of each year a survey of the circumstances that confronted Japan. Toward the end of February 1937, Grew dispatched his report. It was remarkably prescient.

> The failure of Japan's diplomacy and consequent loss of face in China arise from the fact that save in a few instances where local incidents have been settled through minor concessions, few if any of [its] general demands have been met. Protracted conferences have taken place in Nanking and official announcements have frequently been made in Tokyo to the effect that the negotiations were proceeding, but so far as the Embassy is aware, they have led nowhere. Their failure has been ascribed to China's "insincerity," a somewhat overworked expression habitually used by the Japanese to characterize those foreign governments which fail to concede Japan's desiderata by signing on the dotted line.
>
> While this Embassy is not informed of the specific results of the Nanking conversations, it would seem that the astuteness rather than the insincerity of the Chinese government has succeeded in playing the Japanese negotiations along without surrendering Chinese sovereign rights. Moreover, serious military involvement in China has been avoided by the Japanese Army because of the markedly improved morale and military forces of China and the changed situation in Siberia—a very different Eastern Asia from 1932.
>
> It does not appear necessary, for the purpose of this report, to deal extensively or in detail with Japan's diplomacy and activities in China during the past year. Suffice it to say that the overt intention and efforts of the Japanese military to detach the five northern provinces from the jurisdiction of Nanking largely miscarried....
>
> The Japanese nation seems to be somewhat thunderstruck by the sudden and unexpected determination of China to yield no more to Japanese pressure. The nation is, figuratively, scratching its head and wondering what it should do next. There has been some discussion in the newspapers of a reorientation of policy toward China, but there has been no indication as yet of the direction which that reorientation will take. It is strange but true that Japan appears to have been the last to appreciate the changed conditions in China. Now that Japan realizes that its bluff of military pressure no longer works, some other aggressive method of dominating North China may be tried.[23]

Ambassador Grew put his finger on Japan's dilemma: the conditions that had been so favorable to the expansionists in 1931–1932 had changed. On the one hand there had been a significant buildup of Soviet military strength along the Manchurian border. The political overtures made by Moscow to Outer Mongolia threatened Japanese influence in Inner Mongolia and jeopardized Japanese plans for a pan–Mongolian state. But this development was not nearly so troublesome as the consolidation of power in China by the Nationalist regime of Chiang Kai-shek. The Kwantung Army and the Ministry of War faction back in Tokyo saw themselves in a race for control of China's five northern provinces, which they felt to be essential to the protection of Manchukuo and possession of the region's rich economic resources.

It was a glittering prize; the provinces comprised 600,000 square miles and encompassed 170 million Chinese. Although he eventually reversed his thinking, Kanji Ishiwara, when he was still a field-grade officer in Manchuria, expressed the expansionist view when he wrote, "In order to prepare for world conflict, the Japanese people will also eventually have to obtain coal from Shansi, the iron of Hopei, and the cotton of Honan and Shantung."[24] The Chief of Staff of the Kwantung Army, General Seishiro Itagaki, said much the same thing to a visitor in the spring of 1935: "Though we have obtained Manchuria, the natural resources there are nothing compared to North China." Itagaki went on to say that unless the Japanese moved quickly to get North China in their hands, Britain or America might preempt them and take over the iron and coal supplies in Shansi. If Itagaki really believed this, he was living in the distant past. The time had come and gone when the Western powers might be able to engage in the unrestricted exploitation of China's riches. The justification for aggression was an old one: Japan had to be self-sufficient and needed living space for an expanding population. The military ultimately won control of North China, but the fabled raw materials of the area contributed little to the Japanese economy and very few Japanese migrated there. Foresight was in short supply among the military expansionists. If the Empire was to be secure and prosper, they felt that North China had to be brought under Japanese domination.

What they did not realize was that the more they intrigued to achieve their goal, the more they fanned the flames of Chinese nationalism and stiffened Chinese resistance. China was still torn by the bitter struggle between the Nationalists and Communists. While Chiang Kai-shek appeared to have gotten the upper hand in his campaign to exterminate the Reds, the contest was by no means settled. Mao led his ragged and mauled survivors on the "Long March" to the remote region of northern Shensi Province in 1935 and the fight continued. But the heavy-handed Japanese subversion in North China aroused the Chinese people, who demanded that Chiang and the Communists set aside their differences and unite against the invaders.

The record of the years between 1933, when the Tangku Truce was signed, and 1937, when the China Incident began, is one of increasing diplomatic and military pressure on the part of the Japanese and caution mixed with determination to resist on the Chinese side. The Truce, concluded between the Kwantung Army and the Chinese forces in North China on May 31, 1933, created a demilitarized zone south of the Great Wall, thereby arresting Japan's advance into the five northern provinces of Hopei, Chahar, Suiyuan, Shantung and Shansi. For the next two years, the Japanese consolidated their hold on their new creation, Manchukuo, while contemplating their next move. Clues to Japanese intentions were to be found in the foreign policy promoted by Prime Minister Hirota. At a Cabinet meeting that fall he outlined his program of peace for the region. A "triangular relationship" was to be established that would foster cooperation among Japan, Manchukuo and China. The end result would be a "Pax Japonica, the imposition of Japan's hegemony on East Asia."[25]

Given his continuing conflict with the Communists and his own internal problems Chiang Kai-shek deemed it unwise to challenge Hirota. Instead he sought a temporary accommodation and early in 1935 dispatched Wang Chung-hui, the Chinese representative to the Permanent Court of International Justice, to Tokyo. What followed was a sparring match. Wang told Hirota that friendly relations could be preserved on the basis of three principles: first, there should be mutual respect for the other's territorial integrity and absolute independence; second, genuine friendship should be demonstrated by reciprocal measures, such as China's suppression of anti-Japanese activities and Japan's cessation of assistance to "regional governments" in China; and third, the peaceful settlement of disputes should be handled through the normal channels of diplomacy. As a first step toward the restoration of friendly relations, Wang recommended an exchange of ambassadors.

Hirota neither accepted nor rejected the Chinese proposals, but that May the two governments formally recognized each other. In the meantime, the Nanking government put its best foot forward by suppressing the publication of anti-Japanese speeches and replacing its propaganda minister, who had previously been orchestrating the anti-Japanese campaign. The exchange of ambassadors gave the Chinese an advantage that they had not had before. Now they could behave like equals, which they promptly did, insisting that the issues between the two countries be resolved. Hirota was in a bind. If he agreed to Wang's three principles, Japan's position in China would be weakened and the army would take umbrage. So, in October, he countered with three principles of his own: China would cease all anti-Japanese activities, would grant de facto recognition of Manchukuo, and would cooperate with the Japanese in suppressing the Communists. The army was certainly behind Hirota's proposals, although there were elements within the General Staff Headquarters and in the Kwantung Army who felt the terms to be too lenient. That was hardly the reaction in Nanking. The Chinese were dissatisfied and relations cooled.

The expansionists were unwilling to await the outcome of diplomatic exchanges between Nanking and Tokyo. As early as 1934 the Kwantung Army asserted its independence by encroaching in Chahar Province. General Kenji Doihara, chief of the Mukden Special Service Organ, launched a campaign to stir up anti-Chinese feelings among Mongolian leaders in Chahar. His object was the creation of an autonomous Mongolian state to be known as "Mengukuo," a sister state to its sound-alike, Manchukuo. Military preparations were made and in January 1935 Manchurian troops, supported by Japanese aircraft, overran the northeastern part of Chahar. The Chinese defenders were no match for the invaders and quickly signed an agreement along the lines of the Tangku Truce. The demilitarized zone was extended deep into Chahar, increasing Japan's strategic advantage.

IV. Triumph and Uncertainty

To Doihara goes the credit (or blame) for being the principal architect of the plan to attack North China. Like Hirota, Doihara met his end on the gallows at Sugamo Prison. His culpability as a war criminal, however, was far greater.

At first Doihara's moves seemed to pay off. Through a combination of pressure and incidents, the Nationalist armies and Kuomintang elements were forced out of the provinces of Hopei and Chahar. Alarmed at the developing trend, the Nanking government in September offered to recognize Manchukuo if Japan would support the Kuomintang in North China. For a moment it seemed that a long-term accommodation might be reached. The Foreign Ministry in Tokyo thought so, but the military felt otherwise. Public attacks on Chiang Kai-shek by expansionists and continued subversive actions snuffed out the faint hope of a settlement.

In the meantime, Doihara intensified his efforts to put together an autonomous committee of Chinese. At length he persuaded Sung Che-yuan, the former governor of Chahar Province and commander of the Chinese garrison forces in the Peking-Tientsin area, along with Han Fu-chu, the governor of Shantung, and Shang Chen, the governor of Hopei, to serve. Never hesitating to use intimidation when it served his purpose, Doihara deployed two squadrons of army planes near the North China border to show he meant business. In this way the three governors and some of the lesser officials were brought into line, albeit reluctantly. Most of them were members of the Kuomintang and were not comfortable trying to serve two masters. Sung sent a message to Nanking describing his plight and asking for instructions.

The impatient Doihara tried to expedite Nanking's response by telling a group of reporters on the afternoon of November 19 that "the Chinese plans for the autonomy of North China" were already at hand and a formal announcement could be expected soon. Doihara's ploy failed. Following a speech to the Kuomintang Fifth Party Congress in which he declared that China was determined to preserve her territorial integrity no matter what the cost, Chiang Kai-shek sent telegrams to all of North China's leaders advising them to cease negotiations with Doihara "since the problem of North China was being taken up in Nanking between the Chinese Foreign Ministry and the Japanese Ambassador."[26]

This rebuff put Doihara's scheme in limbo. More importantly, it brought in the Japanese government as a direct participant. Doihara had acted recklessly. The Foreign, War, and Navy Ministries consulted and issued their own statement, postponing the move to autonomy. The significance of the event was not lost on either Nanking or Peking. Chiang Kai-shek had played his hand well in bringing Tokyo to the table and making the fate of North China a government-to-government issue instead of a regional issue to be settled by surrogates. In Peking, where warlord politics had long prevailed and procrastination and obfuscation were a way of life, Sung and his associates must have congratulated themselves on avoiding Doihara's snare while retaining the semi-autonomous power of their fiefdoms. The collapse of his plans not only earned Doihara repudiation from his superiors in Tokyo but incurred the anger of his brother officers in Tientsin. The commander of the Japanese garrison was Lieutenant General Hayao Tada, who had his own ideas about how North China should be managed. Officially, Doihara had been designated as Tada's assistant, but to the latter's chagrin, Doihara behaved as if their roles were reversed.

Doihara was undaunted. Not for nothing was he called "the Lawrence of Manchuria," a sobriquet acquired as a result of his clandestine operations there.[27] He was never one to give up a quest nor to brook delay. Immediately reapplying himself, he sought out Yin Ju-keng, a local administrative commissioner who was married to a Japanese and known for his pro–Japanese sympathies. On November 25, the two announced the formation of the East Hopei Anti-Communist Autonomous Council, a name that was designed to "distract the Chinese Nationalists and … be used as a pretext to suppress the anti–Japanese movement of the Chinese people."[28] Other North China leaders were invited to join, but no one was fooled by what was obviously a Japanese front. It was greeted by an outburst of patriotic protests and hostile signals from Nanking and as a result, Yin's council attracted few adherents.

Disappointed but still determined, Doihara refused to give up and turned his attention once more to the redoubtable Sung, who soon found himself in another tug-of-war between Doihara and Nanking. After considerable maneuvering, the Hopei-Chahar Political Council was set up on December 6, 1935, with Sung as chairman. In this instance the Nanking government concluded that cooperation was the better part of wisdom and concurred, appointing seventeen members to it in the hope of preserving control over North China. This was not exactly what Doihara had in mind, because the Council was dominated by the Kuomintang. Doihara's frustration was compounded by continued friction with General Tada in Tientsin, a quarrel that finally led to Doihara's departure from North China. In the spring of 1936 he was recalled to Tokyo and attached to the headquarters of the 12th Division. Doihara had spent six months relentlessly pursuing his goal and at several points appeared to be on the verge of success. That he was outmaneuvered by Chinese like Sung, the very individuals he had sought to subvert, was less a sign of ineptitude than evidence of prevalent anti–Japanese feelings and the effectiveness of the Nanking government in keeping North China officials in line. For the next year and a half, the Hopei-Chahar Political Council continued to meet as did its rival, the

Japanese-controlled East Hopei Anti-Communist Autonomous Government, as it had come to be named. North China was firmly neither in Nanking's nor Japan's orbit. Still, Japanese penetration was clear for all to see. A bevy of Japanese businessmen swarmed into the region bringing cheap Japanese goods. A thriving drug traffic and silver smuggling operations prospered under Japanese military commanders.[29] Doihara had returned to Japan, but Japanese designs on North China had not subsided. At some point in the near future, there was sure to be a showdown.

It was against this backdrop that there occurred the "Sian Incident," an extraordinary expression of determination to form a unified Chinese front against Japan. Its instrument was the "Young Marshal," Chang Hsueh-liang, who had been forced out of first Manchuria and later Peking and had finally taken refuge in Shensi Province, where Mao Tse-tung and his Communist remnants had established themselves. Chang and Mao joined forces, and while the Communists were still too weak to mount much of a military effort, they had great success in recruiting converts in the countryside. Throughout North China their slogan, "Liberation of the Chinese People," was taken up by a populace seething with hatred for Japan.

In December 1936 Chiang Kai-shek came to Sian for the opening of his sixth anti–Communist offensive. While he was there he stopped for a visit with Chang Hsueh-liang. The Young Marshal begged him to abandon his fight with the Communists and instead unite with them in a common front against Japan. Chiang told him that it was impossible for him to fight Japan until he had first dealt with his internal threat. To Chiang's shock and dismay, his host placed him under arrest. That he was not killed, a fate that he expected, was due to a combination of factors, some as bizarre as the arrest itself. Everyone suddenly realized that he was indispensable in the struggle against Japan. No one else in China enjoyed the stature that Chiang did; Chiang alone had the power to stop the civil war, an essential step toward creating a united front. Ironically his mortal enemies, the Communists, played a key role in his survival, primarily at Stalin's insistence. If Chiang were executed, there would be chaos in China from which Japan alone would benefit. The Soviet Union would be far better served if Chiang's leadership was preserved. A united China would drain Japan's resources and energies and keep their attentions directed southward rather than north toward the Soviet maritime provinces.

Chiang Kai-shek put up a bold front but made enough concessions to gain his freedom on Christmas Day. He cancelled the sixth extermination campaign and agreed to a temporary alliance with the Communists, who in turn agreed to place their troops under Nationalist command. In fact, little came of the union, since neither side trusted the other. Chiang suspected that the Communists wanted to draw him into a protracted war with Japan that would sap his strength and enhance their cause. Chiang, while unwilling to give Japan a free hand in North China, hoped to avoid a conflict until the Western powers became involved. Then he would have enough support to expel Japan and turn his attention again to the Communists. Once they were eliminated China would be his. Despite the war that was forced upon him and the reverses that he suffered throughout, he never wavered from that plan.

The hardening of Chinese resolve and the dangers inherent in a costly conflict with China were not lost on everyone in the Japanese military hierarchy. Kanji Ishiwara, who had been in the vanguard of the Kwantung Army's radical element, subsequently returned to Japan, and following a regimental command at Sendai became chief of the Operations Section of the General Staff. Five years had passed since Ishiwara had connived with his brother officers in the Mukden Incident and the creation of Manchukuo. In that time he had undergone a transformation in his thinking, a reversal of view that was influenced by the growth of nationalism in China and the consolidation of power by the Kuomintang. This in turn fed another concern, the belief that war with the Soviet Union was inevitable and would come in 1941. Whether or not Ishiwara was correct in expecting war with Russia, he was absolutely right when he concluded that Japan could not prepare for such a conflict with a hostile China to its rear.

Like Yamamoto and Inoue in the navy, Ishiwara was not intoxicated by the bombast of the super patriots who claimed that the indomitable Japanese fighting spirit could conquer all. Ishiwara had spent several years as a young officer in Europe, as both a student and an attaché, and he had not forgotten the lessons he had learned there. Wars were won by marshaling all of a nation's economic resources and producing an abundance of weapons. Spirit was fine but it would not bring victory. To defeat the Soviet Union would test Japan's endurance to the limit just as it had in 1905. If there were war with Russia, China's friendship would be vital.

Ishiwara was originally somewhat ambivalent, and it took about a year for him to finalize his opinions about Japan's relations with China. For example, in June 1935 he had already come to believe that the Soviet Union was the main threat and Manchukuo, not North China, should be the focus of development. "Japan should stick to consolidating Manchukuo," he wrote. "If Manchukuo is managed creditably, North China will follow suit [since] it can be influenced by virtuous example.... It is stupid, therefore, to carry on petty plots in North China and to stick our fingers in the Mongolian pot."[30] In spite of these reservations, Ishiwara reluctantly went along with the plan for expansion into North China, chiefly because he felt that the region's raw materials were vital for the five-year defense plan.

By the spring of 1936, however, Ishiwara no longer attached such importance to North China's resources. Moreover, his professional eye now saw Chinese military power in a new light. With German military advisers, Chiang's armies were a far cry from the ragtag formations of the warlords. A successful Japanese military operation on the mainland would, in his judgment, require at least nine divisions. It followed that if Japan was to prepare for war with the Soviet Union, conflict with China must be avoided. A geopolitical grand plan now began to take shape in Ishiwara's mind. Not only should Japan avoid war with China, China should become its partner in a step-by-step plan to expel all of the white races from East Asia, commencing with Russia. Ishiwara set down these ideas in mid-summer 1936 in a proposal entitled "Outline of State Policy for National Defense." He followed it in September with another paper, "Examination of China Policy," in which he challenged assumptions long held by the expansionists. Ishiwara argued that they "confused the national character of the Chinese people with the semi-legal nature of the Nanking government." He went on to say that in singling out Chiang Kai-shek as her main foe, Japan had lost sight of the fact that it was the white nations behind Chiang who supported and encouraged anti–Japanese policies. If Japan was to wean China from its dependence on the West, she had to abandon her harsh tactics in North China and behave as a good neighbor. "The West's greatest fear is a Japanese policy of 'benevolence' towards China; its greatest hope is that through Japanese policy that promotes feelings of oppression in China there will be racial conflict between the two."[31] If Japan persisted in her present course of attempting to subvert North China and separate it, he warned, war with the Nationalist government was inevitable. Ishiwara reminded his military colleagues of the consequences of such a conflict, citing the fate of Napoleon's armies wasted in a debilitating guerrilla campaign in Spain. Prophetically he said Japan risked coming to the same end.

The expansionists interpreted Chiang's kidnapping and subsequent release as proof of a Sino-Soviet threat to Japan. They argued that the Chinese Communists were acting under the direction of Moscow, and with the Kuomintang-Communist alliance, China and Russia represented a joint menace. Ishiwara scoffed at this notion. Early in 1937 he wrote that China's hostility was the fault not of the Soviet Union but of Japan. "The issue was whether Japan would 'discard its past imperial policy of imperialist aggression and thereby display the sincerity of the true Japan.'"[32] He concluded by urging that Japan give up its scheme of trying to separate the five northern provinces and recognize the region as an integral part of China, subject to the jurisdiction of the government in Nanking.

Apparently Ishiwara's argument persuaded enough of his colleagues on the General Staff of the wisdom of acting with greater caution, because when the navy put forth its plan for military retaliation following the incidents at Chengtu and Peihai in the late summer of 1936, the Army General Staff rejected it out of hand. Ishiwara had less success with his old outfit, the Kwantung Army, which continued to agitate and scheme in North China. That fall Ishiwara traveled to the mainland, passing through Hopei Province. There he learned that a plot was under way to create the same kind of puppet state in Inner Mongolia that had been formed in Manchuria. The young officers he talked to laughed at his warnings, and shortly afterward a Mongolian force supported by Kwantung Army weapons and aircraft invaded Suiyuan Province. Ishiwara, who had flown to Dairen, was furious and swore, "The next time I visit the Kwantung Army I'm going to piss on the floor of the commanding officer." Ishiwara's embarrassment at the flouting of the General Staff's authority must have been aggravated by the memory of his own role in this same army five years earlier. In a sense his successors had taken their cue from him.

What followed was an even greater embarrassment for the plotters. The invasion was a disaster. The warlord of Suiyuan Province was Yen Hsi-shan, a Kuomintang supporter, whose forces inflicted a bloody defeat on the invaders, foiling the separatist plot so carefully orchestrated by the Kwantung Army. Across China, news of the victory caused jubilation but also a serious error in judgment. Chiang's forces were led to believe that Yen's forces had defeated Kwantung Army troops, a far more formidable host than their Mongolian surrogates. This false report emboldened the Nationalists in their determination to resist further encroachment.

The implications of these developments were not lost on General Ishiwara. In January 1937 he issued several memoranda to the General Staff, setting forth grounds for a fundamental shift in Japanese policy toward China. Summarizing the lessons to be learned from the Sian Incident, he wrote, "The mounting revulsion [in China] at the sight of Chinese fighting Chinese [has created an] intense desire among all Chinese for national unification." The Chinese people, victimized by years of foreign exploitation, he said, were now gripped by a national consciousness that would no longer tolerate it. In an extraordinary admission of guilt for past sins, Ishiwara acknowledged that the Manchuria Affair and Japanese machinations in North China had contributed greatly to China's hostility. It was, however, not too late to change course. He proposed a list of actions that Japan should take to win China's friendship, including abandoning the separatist movement in North China, adopting fairer trade practices by not trying to dump cheap textiles in the Chinese market, and respecting Chinese sensibilities by not insisting on the presence of Japanese political and military advisers in North China.

Ishiwara's propositions would have found favor in China had they been a solid basis for improving relations with the Nanking government, but his concept of an East Asian league to merge the economic interests of Japan, Manchukuo and China was unrealistic. In trying to refute the expansionists, Ishiwara felt it necessary to propose a more attractive alternative, one that carried fewer risks and offered a better payoff. He believed that China could be drawn into a partnership established on a foundation of equality and racial cooperation. Perhaps because Manchukuo was his own handiwork, Ishiwara saw it as a successful experiment rather than a Japanese protectorate. If Manchukuo was to be the "essential bridge" between Japan and China then China, as a precondition of the new association, must formally recognize it. Until the Nanking government did so, Ishiwara was willing to see East Hopei held hostage "'in a laboratory for the construction of a new China'—until such time as the two nations permitted its return to the Nationalists."

Ishiwara had been led to believe that the Hayashi government would act positively on his recommendations, but relations were allowed to drift. In one respect, however, Ishiwara had made progress. The General Staff agreed that the resources of North China were not vital to Japan's war planning. The radicals, however, refused to consider a retreat. To do so would result in a loss of face and only encourage the growing recalcitrance of the Chinese. Those who shared Ishiwara's views were a small minority, while the expansionists dominated the General Staff, particularly the Intelligence Division, which was in the control of "old China hands," officers whose knowledge of China was based on their narrow field service and not on a study of its culture, civilization and history.

Peattie has pointed out that Japanese officers at the time were generally mediocre. At least until the 1930s, the cream of the officer corps sought assignments in Europe and America. China was seen as a backwater and extended service there was not felt to be helpful to a professional military career. With a few exceptions, the "China group" were seen to be "men of limited vision and understanding, and the China Section maintained too long as a dumping ground for second-rate talent." They were to a large degree a product of their experience. China was viewed as a place of scheming with cliques and warlords, elements unworthy of respect, and Chiang Kai-shek was no different from the rest nor considered to be an obstacle to Japanese domination in North China. Chinese military forces were held in contempt:

> Chankoro ["chinks"] they called them, who would surrender at the first show of force. Ishiwara had no patience with this kind of thinking. "You people are completely worthless!" he told a meeting of the China Section one day. "NCOs would do better in your place. You don't do any real work; you just sit around on your tails and theorize."[33]

Needless to say, Ishiwara was not very welcome around the China Section.

In retrospect, it is obvious why the Japanese Army was unprepared for the challenges of a long campaign in China. But its lack of preparedness was also due to the fixation of the General Staff on an expected war with Russia. Practically all of the Staff's planning was directed toward that end and only the sketchiest plans were made for military operations in China. The greatest irony of the incident that sparked the conflict in China was that the Japanese soldiers engaged in night maneuvers near the Marco Polo Bridge on July 7, 1937, were training for war with the Soviet Union, not China.

But China was very much on the mind of the Kwantung Army zealots, who were still chagrined over the debacle in Suiyuan. Ishiwara had made enemies by his opposition to it, and the China Group within the Intelligence Division sneered at his persistent calls for a new direction in China as weak capitulation. Ishiwara's position and influence suffered in the spring of 1937 as new faces appeared in the General Staff and his friends and allies retired or were sent elsewhere. Ishiwara was Chief of the Operations Division, but the number two man was Colonel Akiro Muto, a hard-liner who believed that North China could be detached and brought under Japanese control. The other division and section heads were either indifferent or opposed to Ishiwara's views. When the fighting began near Peking that summer, Ishiwara found himself very much alone in his efforts to contain the conflict. In the Ministry of War conditions were much the same. He could expect no help from General Sugiyama, the War Minister, and the Vice Minister, Yoshijiro Umezu, was an active hard-liner.

Ishiwara's diminishing influence in the General Staff was compounded by a personal shortcoming that damaged his efforts to set Japan on a different course in China. In the face of opposition at meetings of the General Staff divisions, Ishiwara would yield rather than fight his critics, making the excuse that he had no choice. This set a poor example for subordinates who shared his views on China and "took the heart out of their struggle to limit operations once the fighting had begun [and] also made a mockery out of Ishiwara's ringing declaration a month before the China War: 'I shall never send a single soldier to China as long as I live.'"

Thus, the officer whose scheming had set the army on the path to conquest in North China now labored in vain to bring it to a halt. Once the fighting began, Ishiwara's dilemma became more and more painful. He could not avoid his responsibility as a soldier, yet he saw clearly where the escalation would lead. Three months after the incident near the Marco Polo Bridge, Ishiwara's career was over. By then the military commitment had gone too far and there was no place in the councils of war for a general who desperately wanted to make peace.

V

The Marco Polo Bridge Incident

> An old saying has it that there is nothing more uncontrollable than a woman. China is like an unchaste woman. She is a sycophant before the stronger and a braggart before the weaker. In dealing with such a nation, it is necessary for Japan to strike her first and then caress and coddle her.
> —From a speech by Koichiro Ishiwara[1]

On June 28, 1937, Hallett Abend, the Far Eastern correspondent for *The New York Times*, flew from Shanghai to Kiutang, where Chiang Kai-shek was vacationing. Abend told the Generalissimo that he feared Japan was planning a full-scale invasion of North China that summer. Abend's fears were based on the news of Konoe's appointment as Prime Minister. He regarded it as a signal that the military were planning to move. Konoe, he said, was not the liberal that many believed him to be but instead represented the military's choice as one who would cooperate with their schemes. Abend later wrote that he did not probe Chiang but knew "from his grim determination that this time he would not yield again to Japanese pressure but would fight to the finish."[2] Chiang did tell his visitor that he wished he had more time to prepare, particularly to enlarge China's air force. However, he confessed that if he submitted to a Japanese occupation of North China without a fight, he would lose the support of the Chinese people and that of many of his generals.

Abend's concerns were without foundation. Konoe's role as Prime Minister had nothing to do with what eventually happened in North China. Nevertheless Abend was not the only person who suspected that trouble was brewing there. Back in Tokyo, General Ishiwara at General Staff headquarters received a report that elements of the China Garrison Army were planning an "incident" near Peking similar to the one carried out at Mukden in 1931. Knowing that zealots on the mainland had a penchant for mischief, Ishiwara asked the Ministry of War to dispatch Colonel Kiyotami Okamoto of the Military Administration Section to North China to investigate & put the area commanders on notice that Tokyo was opposed to any provocative action. With assurances in hand, Okamoto returned to headquarters on June 27 and reported that all was well. Not everyone shared Okamoto's optimism. The Japanese Assistant Military Attaché in Peking, Major Takeo Imai, told Okamoto that conditions were very tense and a clash was likely, yet Okamoto failed to mention this conversation in his report, an omission that prompted Ishiwara to say later that he wished he had gone to China to see the situation for himself. It would be interesting to know whether Ishiwara ever saw the June 9 message sent by General Hideki Tojo, Chief of Staff and the Vice Minister of War. If he had, he would certainly have had cause for alarm. In a telegram marked "urgent" and "top secret," Tojo addressed the current operational capabilities of the Kwantung Army against the Soviet Union. It was Tojo's opinion that a blow against the Nanking government would remove the "menace" that threatened Japan's rear.[3] Tojo took note of anti–Japanese sentiment in China and cited both the declared hostility of the Chinese Communist forces and popular antagonism in the Peking-Tientsin region. Under these circumstances, the Kwantung Army would rest easier if preemptive action was taken to stabilize North China.

Naturally, when shooting broke out on July 7, suspicion arose that the incident was premeditated. Baron Harada wrote in his memoirs on July 14 that the War Minister had been worried "the young officers overseas might start something before the August promotions and transfers."[4] Harada wondered if the failed Suiyuan operation might have been a factor, or even the Mazaki trial then in progress. Chinese and Western circles were convinced that the affair had long been planned. Not until after Japan's defeat in 1945 and the subsequent war crimes trials got under way was it determined that the spark was spontaneous. The tinder, however, had long been piled up. It was not a question of whether but of when. Rumors filled the air in Peking during the first week of July. Over lunch and dinner tables and in the hotels and private clubs, there was speculation about when the Japanese were "going to strike."[5] Western correspondents quizzed their sources but could get no confirmation. There was just a "feeling" that something was going to happen. A story in the *Peiping* [Peking] *Chronicle* on July 1 fueled the tension:

> Precautionary measures have been strengthened by the local defense authorities during the last two days as the result of rumors that the plainclothesmen have smuggled themselves into the city for the purpose of creating disturbances. Semi-martial law was enforced on Monday and Tuesday nights when pedestrians were subject to search. The continuance of field exercises by Japanese troops at Marco Polo Bridge and vicinity has given rise to considerable anxiety in Chinese circles. It is stated that at first the Chinese authorities were given to understand that these exercises would last only one day, but they have since continued for three days.[6]

V. The Marco Polo Bridge Incident

Those field exercises, of course, were the source of the incident. They and the Japanese military presence in the Peking area had their origin in the Protocol that had been signed following the suppression of the Boxer Rebellion in 1900. At that time China had conceded the right of foreign powers with interests in China to guarantee the security of their nationals by stationing troops at certain points between the capital and the sea. The Chinese Nationalist government, however, made the legal point that since 1928 Nanking had become China's capital and that the Protocol arrangements concerning Peking were obsolete. Nevertheless, given the limited power that the Nationalists exercised in North China, no effort was made to oust foreign field forces. The British, French, Americans and Italians continued to maintain contingents in Tientsin and Peking, but these were hardly more than token forces. The United States 15th Infantry Regiment had been based at Tientsin and over the years acquired a colorful reputation as the "Can Do" outfit. Like the "Old China Hands" in the navy, many enlisted men spent most of their careers in China, retiring there and taking Chinese, Korean, German or White Russian wives. The Marine counterpart was the 4th Marine Regiment. While they marched under the same flag, the soldiers and Marines engaged each other in battle more than foreign enemies. The most memorable of these was a brawl in Tientsin in summer 1928. A bar fight soon involved several thousand soldiers and Marines in the streets. Store windows were shattered and there was considerable property damage. The Marine commander, General Smedley Butler, a colorful character in his own right, ended the fight by promising his men that he would "take up their grievances with the colonel commanding the 15th and that if the matter were not settled, I myself will lead you to clean up on the 15th Infantry."[7] A number of officers who were to make their reputations as senior commanders in World War II spent their junior years in China.

July 7, 1937, was an evening to savor and Colonel and Mrs. Joseph Stilwell and their daughter Nancy joined Ambassador and Mrs. Nelson T. Johonson, Colonel John Marston, commander of the Marine Embassy Guard, his wife, and Stilwell's friend, John Goette, for a barge excursion on the Per Hai Lake in the Imperial City. With lanterns swaying gently, Ambassador Johonson took out his guitar and played "Down That Weary Road," his favorite song. The reflection of the lanterns and the moon on the lake's surface and the "softly gleaming white marble tower of the Dagba [that] rose out of the darkness like the vision of a Buddhist Grail" produced an idyllic setting.[8] The mood was broken by the passing of a boat carrying a group of Japanese officers. Colonel Marston commented that as a senior officer of the foreign units in Peking he had been advised by the Japanese that their troops would be conducting maneuvers that night at the railroad bridge at Lukouchiao, twelve miles to the west on the Peking-Hankow line.

The tranquility of the evening was about to be broken by gunfire, an unnecessary outbreak of shooting that should never have occurred. Mamoru Shigemitsu, whose wisdom was often ignored, observed that if Japan had displayed patience and prudence "she should never have stirred beyond Manchuria. [It was] the spark of a conflagration that brought the Japan of the *Showa* era to the brink of destruction."[9]

Captain Shimizu finally got around to reporting the temporarily missing Private Shimura, but it was already too late to prevent the confrontation at Wanping. Eight trucks filled with soldiers were dispatched to demand restitution for the "kidnapping" of their comrade. Wanping drew in not only the Japanese; the peasants living in open villages nearby had been trying to escape the Japanese and sought refuge within its walls. The commander of the Chinese garrison, meanwhile, had closed the gates and barred all entry until the Japanese returned to their compounds in Peking and Tientsin. The plight of the peasants huddled outside notwithstanding, the Chinese garrison was under specific orders from General Sun Che-yuan of the Chinese 29th Army to avoid a confrontation with the Japanese.

While sporadic fighting continued, the two sides tried to contain the dispute. The next day the assistant American military attaché, Major David D. Barrett, took his office touring car, a 1929 Dodge, and drove to Wanping to investigate. There he witnessed a curious sight. The Japanese and Chinese were shouting at each other from the roads and parapets. The garrison commander would not open the gate, but he agreed to a parley and was lowered unceremoniously to the ground in a wooden armchair tied to a couple of ropes. From the sullen looks he got from both sides, Barrett realized that he wasn't welcome and got back into his car. As he drove away he saw a dead Japanese soldier on the ground, "surrounded by a grim platoon of guards."[10] The shaky truce that Major Barrett had observed did not last long.

The Chinese opened fire and fighting became general. Then Colonel Stilwell drove out on July 9 to talk to the commander at Wanping. He found himself in the middle of heavy rifle and machine gun fire and prudently returned to Peking. Two days later, with the arrival of reinforcements, the Japanese renewed their assault and Wanping fell.

There was now a lull as both sides considered their next moves. The Japanese command began to move troops into the Peking-Tientsin district. The Sakai and Suzuki Brigades from the Kwantung Army were sent through the Great Wall into Hopei Province, while trucks carrying men from the 5th and 20th Divisions clogged the roads into Tientsin. Western newsmen reported that martial law had been declared in Peking and the gates of the city were closed to thousands of refugees clamoring for admittance. Both sides charged each other with shooting first. The Hopei Chahar Political

Council sent a message to the Nationalist authorities blaming the Japanese and promising to offer "formidable resistance." Most Chinese saw the action as a preliminary move by the Japanese to expand their control over the Peking-Tientsin area. Journals of the patriotic societies called for a formal declaration of war. This was heady talk for a nation as ill-prepared for war as was China.

The first reports of the skirmish at the Marco Polo Bridge reached Tokyo in the early hours of July 8 but did not seem to be cause for alarm. Nevertheless, the high command was anxious that the fighting go no further. The Chief of Staff, Prince Kanin, at General Ishiwara's urging, sent a message to the China Garrison Army commander, instructing him to "avoid further use of force so as to prevent extension of the conflict."[11] There can be no doubt that the military leadership first sought to contain the incident but Tokyo wanted to be sure that whatever happened, it would be in control and not the Kwantung Army hotheads. Accordingly, the China Garrison Army was informed that if additional troops were needed, the government would provide them. Orders were then issued to the divisions west of Tokyo not to discharge any soldiers scheduled for separation on July 9.

Hardliners in the General Staff, however, saw an opportunity to strengthen Japan's position in North China by presenting terms to the Hopei-Chahar Political Council that would further weaken Chinese control. Pressed by this faction, the General Staff on July 9 issued an "Outline for the Solution of Problems in North China." The Garrison Army was told "to avoid involvement in political issues at this time" but to submit to the Hopei-Chahar Political Council the following terms for a settlement: "Withdrawal of Chinese troops from the vicinity of the Marco Polo Bridge and from the left bank of the Yungting River. Guarantees against any recurrence of the incident in the future. Punishment of those responsible for the incident. A Chinese apology for the incident."[12]

Given the differences of opinion within the General Staff and the Army Ministry, it is not surprising that there was no unanimity over these terms. While Ishiwara advised Prince Kanin to send a message to the China Garrison Army to seek a local settlement of the incident, Colonel Akira Muto, Chief of the Operational Section, and Colonel Shinichi Tanaka, Chief of the Military Section of the Army Ministry, wanted to go much further and make Hopei Province "a second Manchukuo."[13] When they heard that the Nanking government was dispatching four divisions to North China, they began to urge that three Japanese divisions be mobilized. Ishiwara was opposed. He and General Torashiro Kawabe, the War Guidance Chief, who shared his view, said that if the decision to mobilize went forward, the use of the divisions should be strictly limited. A tug of war now ensued. Muto objected that "neither Ishiwara nor Kawabe knew how to deal with the Chinese," and did his best to sabotage Ishiwara's position.[14] On one occasion, when Ishiwara made a long-distance call to field unit commanders in China to urge restraint, he heard the voices of War Ministry officers cut in to tell the field commanders to administer a crushing blow to the enemy.

Whether the outcome of the Marco Polo Bridge Incident might have been different if Ishiwara had not acceded to the militants is impossible to say. His instincts were correct, but he found himself not only under intense pressure from Muto and Tanaka but misled by faulty intelligence. The Japanese Military Attaché in Nanking sent word that the Chinese were sending strong reinforcements to North China, and a Japanese news agency dispatch from Hankow on July 11 seemed to confirm this. Four divisions of the Chinese First Army were reported headed up the Peking-Hankow Railway. German-trained, the First Army was reputed to be the finest unit of the Chinese army and was known as Chiang Kai-shek's Own. Ishiwara's fears for the safety of 12,000 Japanese civilians in North China and his comrades-in-arms who would be overrun by a far more numerous foe prompted him to reverse himself and advise the War Ministry to mobilize the three divisions. The more cool-headed Kawabe went to Ishiwara's office and protested the decision, accusing him of giving in to Muto. Smarting from the charge, Ishiwara strode to the China theater map on the wall and reminded Kawabe that his own brother was in command of the North China Brigade that would be imperiled unless reinforcements were sent. Kawabe questioned the accuracy of the report of Chinese troop movements, but Ishiwara refused to listen to him. As it turned out Kawabe was right. The massive Chinese forces that Ishiwara feared would encircle Kawabe's brother's brigade did not materialize. Furthermore, word soon reached the high command that a local settlement had been reached in Peking between the Chinese commander and General Gun Hashimoto, the acting commander of the Chinese Garrison Army.

While the moderates and radicals were facing off in the General Staff and Army Ministry, a special Cabinet meeting was called on the morning of July 9. General Sugiyama, the Army Minister, asked that three divisions be sent to China, but he qualified his recommendation by saying that he sought only Cabinet authorization to act as the situation required, that the "actual order to dispatch troops would be issued only when appropriate."[15] Both Foreign Minister Hirota and Navy Minister Yonai opposed the motion. Yonai rightly feared that sending troops could lead to an all-out war, insisting that the government would be overreacting by sending three divisions to China. Hirota agreed, and the other ministers fell into line. Debate was cut short when a message arrived that a local agreement had been reached. The fact that Sugiyama had been so quick on the draw, however, attests to the influence of hardliners on the War Minister and through him, on the Cabinet itself.

What followed was a pattern of mismanagement that almost defies belief. The Japanese military authorities in North China and those in Tokyo reacted to each other as though they were in different worlds. Having ordered the China Garrison Army to seek a local settlement, which it did, the military command at home, through the Army Minister, then impulsively seized the initiative by ordering more divisions to the mainland. What could have been a footnote to Sino-Japanese relations in the mid–1930s was turned into a multi-volume life-and-death struggle for both nations.

On the morning of July 9, a local agreement was reached in the Peking area between Colonel Matsui, representing Japanese forces, and Chin Te-chun, deputy commander of the Chinese 29th Army. The Chinese agreed to withdraw their troops to the right bank of the Yungting River and replace the garrison soldiers in Wanping with members of the paramilitary Peace Preservation Corps. But before the terms took effect, there was more fighting. That evening, General Hashimoto went to Peking to negotiate with representatives of the Hopei-Chahar Political Council, taking with him the "Guidelines" sent to him by the General Staff. The Chinese balked at the General Staff's insistence that they withdraw their troops and a brief deadlock ensued, but by the evening of the 11th a truce had been arranged under which both sides agreed to pull back. The Japanese pretty much got what they wanted, although no apology was tendered nor was anyone punished. It was decided to leave these matters in the hands of the chairman of the Council, Sung Che-yuan. Captain Shimizu, whose lapse had triggered Japanese hostilities at Lukouchiao, thought "it was almost too lenient in suggesting that first of all, Japanese troops would withdraw voluntarily" from the Marco Polo Bridge area.[16]

Captain Shimizu need not have worried that the terms were too generous. Before his superiors had even heard about them, they decided to send reinforcements on specious grounds advanced by Ishiwara, that the China Garrison Army and Japanese citizens were "in danger of being heavily encircled by superior Chinese forces."[17] A division of the Kwantung Army, one from the Korean Army, and three divisions from Japan were earmarked for service in China. On the morning of July 11 Sugiyama sought and got approval from the Cabinet for mobilization plans. Of the five divisions in question, three would go to North China and the other two to the Shanghai and Tsingtao areas. Theater operations would be restricted to the Peking-Tientsin area, while "as a matter of principle, force [would] not be resorted to in Central and South China."[18] The Cabinet then composed a memorial to the Emperor summarizing its policy:

> In dispatching troops to North China, we aim, through demonstration of our power, to make the Chinese forces apologize to us and to have them assume responsibility for future eventualities.
>
> Our attack against Chinese forces will commence only when it becomes clear that they will not accept our demands.
>
> The principle of localizing the incident and settling it through negotiations by field commanders will be observed to the last.
>
> If it is proved that the newly militarized troops need not be dispatched, the projected dispatch will be abandoned.[19]

When the Cabinet meeting was over, Prime Minister Konoe held a press conference in which he announced the decision to mobilize five divisions and asked for public support. In his statement he blamed China, which he said was guilty of aggression. "The Chinese authorities must apologize to us for the illegal anti–Japanese actions and properly guarantee to refrain from repeating such actions in the future."[20] Following his announcement to the press, Konoe invited representatives from both houses of the Diet, the press, and the business community to meet with him at his official residence, where he made a plea for their support. He was not to be disappointed. The press outdid itself in calling for decisive action against China. Only the *Japan Weekly Chronicle*, an English-language journal, cautioned against overconfidence and warned against "dazzling visions of swift military success."[21]

The Cabinet memorial contradicted itself. The government declared itself in favor of settling the issue locally, but at the same time ignored the successful arrangement worked out with the Chinese governing body of North China by its own local military commander. By authorizing the sending of five divisions to China, it sent the message to Nanking that Japan would not shrink from using force to have its way. More ominously, the dispatching of such a large force was a strong indication that Japan wanted more from China than an apology for a minor skirmish. Coupled with Konoe's press conference demagoguery, the Cabinet's memorial constituted a serious and unwarranted escalation of tension.

The question now was, what would China do? In his report of mid-July 1937, Stilwell declared that the Japanese would not have rushed a division of troops inside the Great Wall unless they meant "to get something."

> Chiang Kai-shek has ... [declared] that China will stand no further aggression from Japan. The aggression has come; what is China going to do? No indications of any definite plans to resist by force have as yet been reliably reported. No Central Government troops have moved up the Tientsin-Pukow line through Suchow, Kiangsu, nor any have moved north from Hangchow. There are vague reports of movements through the Lunghai Railway and talk of Central Government forces and airplanes being sent toward Paoting in Hopei. It will take much more than this to stop the Japanese war machine now in action around Tientsin and Peiping. "Distant water cannot put out a near fire."

V. The Marco Polo Bridge Incident

> If Chiang Kai-shek means to fight in this crisis, his troops should be moving now. ... This office ... maintains that Chiang ... will not fight Japan, certainly not in North China. After all, North China brings little money, and [money] is a fair measure with which to predict the amount of resistance which [the Chinese] will put up to prevent the loss of territory.[22]

Stilwell misjudged Chiang's determination to resist. In this, one may detect Stilwell's own bias. He was not a fan of the Generalissimo and as the war in China expanded, Stilwell's opinion hardened. In World War II, when Stilwell was the senior American commander in China, he tried in vain to prod Chiang into taking the offensive against the Japanese, but Chiang refused, husbanding his forces and his mounting pile of American arms for a post-war showdown with the Communists. As friction between the two men grew, Stilwell saw his own position eroding and his recall inevitable. In his diary, he called Chiang "the Peanut" and he relished the few times he could cause him to lose face.

Stilwell was mistaken in believing that Chiang would be willing to write off North China. The day after Stilwell filed his report, the Generalissimo summoned China's leaders, including the Communists, to an unprecedented meeting at his summer headquarters in Lushan. In a toughly worded speech, Chiang reminded his audience that six years had passed since Manchuria had been stolen, and now they confronted a challenge at Lukouchiao at the gates of Peking. He drew a parallel between the two events. If Lukouchiao fell, Peking would become a second Mukden and ultimately Nanking would suffer the same fate. Therefore, China's destiny hinged on resolving the Lukouchiao incident. Chiang warned that even on the brink of annihilation, the Chinese would fight, no matter what the sacrifice. He said that although China was a weak power, the people would protect their country and carry out the responsibility their ancestors had bestowed upon them.

Although the speech was published in Japan, it was dismissed there as a bluff by hardliners, but not by General Ishiwara. Having panicked at false reports of massive Chinese movements, Ishiwara now read Chiang's speech as the signal for a long and difficult struggle. He went to the War Ministry and presented two drastic proposals: the army should withdraw all its troops in North China to Manchukuo, and Prime Minister Konoe should fly to Nanking to negotiate a settlement with Chiang. Military necessity, he said, drove these two motions. Japan had thirty divisions available for mobilization, but nineteen were needed against the Soviet Union. That left eleven, of which six were required for a central reserve. Therefore, only five would be available for operations in China, an insufficient number for an all-out war. Japan, he warned could find itself in a situation like that which brought disaster to Napoleon in Spain, a slow sinking into the deepest bog.

General Sugiyama and his Vice Minister, General Umezu, scoffed at Ishiwara's concerns. Umezu asked him if he was speaking for himself or for the General Staff and if he had really thought about what he was suggesting.

Did Ishiwara know Konoe's own views on a meeting with Chiang Kai-shek or whether the Prime Minister had any confidence in a negotiating position? Was Ishiwara prepared to throw away Japan's vested rights and interests accumulated over the decades in North China by withdrawing the very military force that maintained them there?[23]

Ishiwara agreed that withdrawing troops might place Japanese interests in jeopardy but said that Konoe could resolve that issue in negotiations with Chiang. Sugiyama dismissed this argument, saying that Chiang would hardly agree to any Japanese proposal that was made from a position of weakness and that he would "become a laughing-stock if he took Ishiwara's proposals to Konoe."

Ishiwara refused to accept Sugiyama's rebuff. He telephoned Konoe's chief secretary, Akira Kazami, and put the plan to him. When Konoe was told about Ishiwara's call, he voiced his approval and Kazami ordered a plane made ready. But the radicals soon learned what Ishiwara and the Prime Minister were doing and raised a howl of protest. Sugiyama then called Konoe to tell him that Ishiwara was speaking for a small minority within the army and recommended that the trip be cancelled. Both Foreign Minister Hirota and Kazami also counseled Konoe not to go, telling him that whatever he accomplished in Peking would be sabotaged by hardliners in both China and Japan. Reluctantly Konoe gave up the plan. When Ishiwara later called Kazami for an update, he was told that Konoe had decided against the trip. Ishiwara lost his temper and said, "Tell the Prime Minister than in two thousand years of our history no man will have done more than he by his indecisiveness in this crisis."

But Konoe did want to act and now decided to try his own approach, which was to send a surrogate who would represent him on a mission to Nanking. Not long afterward, he asked Ryusuke Miyazaki to undertake the journey, but Miyazaki never made it. When the Chinese Ambassador in Tokyo was told that Miyazaki was to be sent as a secret envoy of Konoe, he prepared a coded message informing his government and sent it off. The army, however, intercepted and deciphered the telegram and detained Miyazaki in Kobe as he was preparing to leave. When Konoe heard about this, he advised Miyazaki to postpone the mission, but in the meantime, Miyazaki had been arrested by the Kempei-tai, the secret police, probably at the army's request.

As the crisis grew in North China, Konoe felt increasingly isolated. He complained to Baron Harada that the other Cabinet ministers would not stray beyond their own bailiwicks to share responsibility for a China

V. The Marco Polo Bridge Incident

policy. Harada wrote in his journal that Konoe "felt forlorn and helpless as he explained his situation to me," and when he reported the conversation to Saionji, the old *Genro* expressed his sympathy, acknowledging that the Prime Minister was in a lonely situation.[24] As for the nation's course, Saionji said:

> Even among the Chinese, there are some who are more clever than the Japanese. Not only that but there are people of the other countries besides China who have seen through the intentions of Japan. Therefore, extreme caution is necessary. If Japan does not watch her step, she will be made a fool of by other countries.[25]

The peripatetic Harada then consulted the Foreign Minister, asking him if he had any hope of a diplomatic solution, but Hirota's experience as Prime Minister had convinced him that it would be difficult to act without the cooperation of the army. He told Harada that he would like to find a "non-expanding settlement" of the incident without regard to the army's feelings but found that path nearly impossible given the instability within the army itself. Apparently, it never occurred to Hirota to work through the Navy Minister and try to gain leverage through him. Konoe came up with the most bizarre scheme of all. He contemplated sending Mitsuru Toyama, the Black Dragon leader, on a mission to Nanking. In spite of his strong nationalism, Toyama was a long-time friend of Chiang Kai-shek. Konoe reasoned that if someone with Toyama's credentials acted as his agent, he would be able to "fight poison with poison."

Nothing came of these plans, probably because fighting broke out in Shanghai in August and by then neither side was in a mood to negotiate. But in these maneuvers by Hirota and Konoe, we see once more the quandary that ensnared civilian ministers in an army-controlled government. In the early stages of the China Incident, the tentative peace moves had no chance of success so long as the army was held hostage by radicals. Hirota was right about that, and Konoe stopped short of direct confrontation, probably because Saionji and others had told him that he was the only man who could control the military. He told his confidants that if he tried to block the army, Sugiyama would resign, and the Cabinet would fall. Anyone replacing the Prime Minister would face the same dilemma, so Konoe felt that he had no choice but to act as he did. His delicate peace probes were like those of a surgeon trying to operate on a minotaur. He knew that the moment he touched a nerve the monster would turn on him.

As the war expanded, Konoe continued to hope that an opportunity for peace would present itself. In August, when fighting had become general in the Peking-Tientsin area, Konoe met with Yukei Nashimoto, a China expert who had recently returned from the battlefront. Konoe told him that reinforcements had been sent; China would see Japan's resolve and would yield. Nashimoto replied that Konoe was mistaken, and that China regarded the struggle as one of life and death and would not "play with tactics." Konoe then said that he had spoken with a staff officer stationed in China who had said that if Japan seemed to hesitate the Chinese would take that as a sign of weakness. This was essentially the pattern of escalation throughout the war. Each side waited for the other to blink and neither did.

The Japanese army's thirty divisions were a potent military force. They were well-equipped and well-trained. Most of the officers were competent and dedicated. Behind the main army were 1.5 million trained reserves and a replacement pool of almost 2.5 million partly-trained men. A Japanese infantry division at full strength comprised 21,945 men and 5,849 horse. It was organized into two brigades of two regiments each, an artillery regiment, a quartermaster regiment, a tank company, and miscellaneous headquarters personnel.

The Chinese army had 182 infantry divisions, few of which were ever at full strength, and which were smaller than their Japanese counterparts. In theory, they could muster forty-six separate brigades, nine cavalry divisions, and twenty-eight artillery regiments, but these elements were mostly on paper. There were no trained reserves, and although there was a vast reservoir of peasants that could be drawn on, their worth as soldiers was mainly as cannon fodder. Unlike Japan, where the army had developed over a period of decades, first under Western tutelage and later by their own professionals, the Chinese had only the beginnings of a modern army. Chiang Kai-shek had just ten divisions that approached Western standards, although German officers had tried to bring them the lessons and skills that Major Meckel had brought to the Japanese two generations earlier. If they had had more time and Chiang had been able to acquire more modern equipment, the Nationalist armies might have been a match for their foes. Unfortunately, the bulk of the Chinese army had received little or no training and its arms were a decidedly mixed bag. Not only was ammunition scarce but unit commanders, knowing that it was in short supply, tended to hoard it. Ill-fed soldiers pulled the bullets out of their casings and ate the gunpowder for its salt content. Worse yet, Chiang was able to exercise direct control over no more than a fourth of his armies, albeit the best fourth. Another quarter was in the hands of warlords who were nominally loyal to Nanking but used their forces as they saw fit. The remaining half was commanded by regional leaders with whom Chiang was obliged to make deals in order to have the services of their troops. To the trained professional eye the Chinese army was a motley array. One American officer referred to it as a "goddam medieval mob."[26]

Given their own professional standards, the scorn that the Japanese had for the Chinese army is understandable. Yet they failed to subdue their enemy. This was due to several factors. The most obvious was China's size; the distances were vast and the terrain often difficult. The almost inexhaustible supply of manpower was another. China could fight a war of attrition, a strategy that Mao advocated from the outset and Chiang ultimately adopted because he could use no other. Japan did not expect to fight that kind of war, nor did they think it would be necessary to do so. They had conquered Manchuria with ease and had defeated the Chinese at Shanghai in 1932. The army expansionists relied on striking fast and securing key areas; the navy would be responsible for sea transport and communication and would also provide air and gunnery support where practicable. The Chinese, they felt, would be sufficiently intimidated by the superiority of Japanese arms to surrender.

This was a false assumption, as Mao pointed out in a series of lectures that he delivered in Yenan during the late spring of 1938. In "On Protracted War," Mao cited five fundamental Japanese errors in the field: "piecemeal reinforcement, absence of a main direction of attack, lack of strategic coordination, failure to grasp strategic opportunities, and failure to annihilate Chinese forces after their encirclement."[27] Mao said that the Japanese had only themselves to blame for their failures, because their strategic and field commands were incompetent. Moreover, they had not only underestimated Chinese capabilities but suffered from shortages in their own troop strength.

On this last point Mao could have rested his case. The General Staff of the Japanese army never expected that it would be necessary to commit more than eleven divisions to China, or fifteen at most if reserves were called up. Ishiwara's warnings had been prescient. By the end of 1937, less than six months after the onset of fighting at the Marco Polo Bridge, Japan had been forced to send sixteen divisions to China. Two years later, Japanese forces in China totaled twenty-three divisions and twenty-eight brigades, which were the equivalent of another fourteen divisions, plus an air division, for a total of 850,000 men, a figure that would have been called unbelievable in the summer of 1937. By the end of the Pacific War in 1945, the Japanese Army in China numbered 1,050,000, which was nineteen percent of the entire Japanese army of 5,550,000. Arrayed against them were three million Chinese Nationalist troops and 500,000 Chinese Communists. By then most of the fighting was occurring elsewhere, but China was still unconquered.

Meanwhile, the diversion of troops to operations in China left the Japanese army weakened in the of face its principal enemy, the Soviet Union. All the Kwantung Army had to defend Manchukuo was six regular ground divisions and five air groups. The Russians were in far better shape. By the end of 1937 they had an estimated strength of twenty rifle divisions, four or five cavalry divisions, 1,500 tanks and 1,500 aircraft. Total Russian manpower in Siberia comprised 370,000 officers and enlisted men. The Japanese were made painfully aware of this military power in 1938 and 1939 when they engaged the Soviets in several bloody border disputes. The Japanese were not only outnumbered but suffered from a shortage of ammunition. The Russians won the test of arms, leaving the Japanese to wonder what the outcome might have been had they not been entangled in the conflict to the south.

Ishiwara, who by then had been removed from the center of operations in Tokyo and assigned to minor posts until his retirement in 1941, refused to shut up. "China is like an earthworm," he said. "Cut it in two and it will keep wriggling." He was most angered by those in the ruling hierarchy who continue to boast that China could be defeated by a single blow, and he was infuriated when officials tried to deceive the Japanese people about the progress of the war. "Those who excite the public by claims of victory, just because the army has captured some-out-of-the-way little area, do so only to conceal their own incompetence as they squander the nation's power in an unjustifiable war."[28]

Meanwhile, skirmishing around Peking continued. With the distant rumble of artillery echoing inside the walls, the Chinese garrison began to dig trenches and fill sandbags in preparation for the defense of the city. A spokesman for the Hopei-Chahar Political Council bravely announced: "If the Japanese army carries its acts of provocation to [Peking's] gates, we intend to resist with all the resources and manpower at our command. We will not surrender but are fully prepared to withstand a siege until help comes."

"Until help comes." That was a phrase that worried the new Japanese commander, General Katsuki, who arrived on the scene on July 20 and began to deploy his troops in the Wanping area. The movement was hardly begun when there was another clash. A group of Japanese soldiers left their train at Langfang, between Peking and Tientsin, and entered the Chinese barracks there, demanding to use the military telephone. When the Chinese asked them to leave their weapons outside, the Japanese forced their way in, took control of the exchange, and then attacked the barracks itself. The Chinese retaliated with a surprise assault on a Japanese signal unit repairing the telephone lines along the Peking-Lunghai railway near Langfang. Katsuki then sent an ultimatum to General Sung, demanding that Chinese forces be withdrawn from the Wanping area within twenty-four hours. Sung had was not about to accede to this demand and immediately cabled Nanking of his intentions. "The continued dispatch of Japanese troops and repeated provocations have left no alternative to the Chinese troops but to defend the country to the best of their ability and resources."[29]

V. The Marco Polo Bridge Incident

Sung's soldiers were spoiling for a fight. The Japanese ultimatum was ignored, and the conflict now spread to Peking itself. About 7:00 p.m. on July 26, a detachment of Japanese troops tried to enter the city. There was an argument about their admission at the Southwest Gate, but it was finally opened, and truckloads of soldiers began to pass through. What they entered was a Chinese ambush. When part of the formation was inside, the Chinese closed the gate and began to drop hand grenades from the top of the wall into the open trucks. Shooting commenced at once but the fighting didn't spread. For Westerners, life went on as usual. The evening moonlight dance was held on the roof of the Hotel de Pekin, the noise of the firefight clearly audible over the orchestra. Although as the conflict widened, Westerners found it increasingly difficult to preserve their normal lifestyle, most were determined not to let the violence around them interfere with their own work and leisure.

Meanwhile, in Nanking and Tokyo the fighting forced the realization that Japan was approaching something far more dangerous than a localized conflict. Once more the Japanese tried to gain control. In Tokyo, Konoe publicly declared the need for a "fundamental solution to Sino-Japanese relations" and Foreign Minister Hirota added, "Japan wants Chinese cooperation, not Chinese territory." Hirota assured the British and American Ambassadors, who were fearful of an all-out attack on Peking, "There are about 10,000 Japanese there. Even if they were to escape into certain areas about the diplomatic establishment, isn't it a certainty that we would not attack that vicinity?"[30] In Nanking the Chinese Foreign Minister advised the Japanese Consul that Chiang Kai-shek was "prepared to accept a 'local settlement of the Marco Polo Bridge incident ... along the lines of the three points covered by the settlement of July.'"[31]

The initiative, however, had passed from the capitals to the field commanders. General Katsuki declared that he had "freedom of action" to deal with the Chinese 29th Army, and he followed up with an all-out assault, falling on the Chinese barracks at Nanyuan and Siyuan, south and west of Peking. In both instances, Japanese aircraft inflicted heavy casualties. At Tungchow, some fifteen miles east of Peking, a battalion of 500 men was annihilated. The Japanese claimed that the Chinese had not only ignored an ultimatum to withdraw but had treacherously killed five Japanese sentries at Tungchow's eastern gate. It was on the basis of this allegation that Japan made a combined aerial and ground assault on the Chinese garrison. Whatever the circumstances, the battalion at Tungchow was hardly a threat to the Japanese army. Anthony Billingham, reporting for the *New York Times* on July 28, had visited the Chinese commander a few days earlier and inspected the barracks. He reported that the men were poorly armed with broadswords and ancient brass-bladed spears. Their only automatic weapons were obsolete air-cooled rifles. Cut off from the outside world, the men had been subsisting on meager rations of ground corn. Two American missionaries nearby witnessed the slaughter. They told Billingham that they had heard no shooting near the mission gate, only the thunder of Japanese artillery at dawn. "If the Tungchow battle today was intended as a warning of what may happen in Peiping, it is a terrible one."

This attack prompted even greater bloodshed at Tientsin, where the Chinese launched a surprise attack early on the morning of July 29. Regular Chinese Army troops slipped into the city dressed in civilian clothes and joined members of the Peace Preservation Corps, the Japanese-armed Chinese militia, in the assault. As more Chinese forces swarmed into the city, the Japanese fought back tenaciously. As fighting raged through the streets, the local inhabitants watched from rooftops or behind shuttered windows. The Chinese captured three railroad stations and part of the Japanese concession, but these were only temporary victories. The Japanese counterattacked with massive air raids, employing some of their largest bombers, to drive out the Chinese. Much of Tientsin was reduced to rubble, including Nankai University, an act of vengeful terrorism in the eyes of foreigners because the students at Nankai had organized resistance against Japan. Pouring in reinforcements, the Japanese managed within forty-eight hours to gain the upper hand and rout Chinese troops from the city. In the aftermath, Tientsin seemed stunned by Japan's ferocity. Billingham found Japanese sentries so tense that they snarled and crumpled passes rather than read them. He found Chinese shops piled high with merchandise left behind when the owners fled in haste.

But at Tungchow, the scene of the massacre just a few days before, the tables were turned on the Japanese in a bloody reprisal. The bulk of the forces that had destroyed the Chinese garrison left for Peking, leaving behind a small contingent to hold the city. Tungchow was the seat of the East Hopei Autonomous Government, and order was normally maintained by the Peace Preservation Corps, which the Japanese had considered loyal. They were mistaken. On the same morning that the Peace Preservation Corps revolted in Tientsin, their brothers in Tungchow rose up against the "dwarf people," as the Chinese derisively called their foe. Over 2,000 militia went on a rampage of murder and pillage. Two-thirds of the 380 Japanese civilians living in Tungchow were slain and their homes looted and smeared with blood. The *Japan Times and Mail* of August 5 reported that many of the bodies were mutilated beyond recognition. Tungchow was a minor episode compared to the Rape of Nanking, but it was symptomatic of the fury that both sides periodically unleashed against each other. Little quarter would be given as the conflict grew.

Although the Chinese had aggressively taken the war to their enemy,

Sung asked that no Central Government troops be sent to Peking and Nanking obliged him. Then, to the surprise of the Nationalist Government, he quit Peking and withdrew his forces west of the Yungting River. Chiang Kai-shek, however, was determined to fight in the north. Some 50,000 troops, supported by aircraft, moved toward Paoting, a key junction south of Peking. In a statement issued on July 29, Chiang vowed that there would be "no compromise and no surrender" by his government.[32]

The Japanese press, which had taken a hard line from the outset, blamed Chiang for prolonging the conflict by persuading the Chinese people that they would prevail. The editors of major newspapers said that they hoped for peace, but that China was responsible for a resolution. The public expressed its support by creating a relief fund for Japanese soldiers at the North China front. Outside a Buddhist temple in the Asakusa section of Tokyo, hundreds of women and girls sewed "thousand stitch girdles" for their husbands and brothers. American G.I.s fighting in the Pacific in World War II often found these "girdles" (belts) on the corpses of Japanese soldiers. They consisted of a narrow strip of cotton on which 1,000 circles, each the size of a dime, were printed, and within each circle a tiny cross-stick was inserted. Every woman who passed the Buddhist temple in Tokyo during the day would add a stitch, thereby giving an unknown soldier her blessing. The girdle was supposed to bear good fortune and bring the soldier home safely. Few men on a battlefield might rely on such a superstition, but each girdle was a bond linking the soldier with hundreds of unknown well-wishers.

There were more signs that the nation knew it was in for something more than an "incident." Flags were flown from many houses and business establishments. There were cheers for groups of soldiers when they marched by, and voluntary collectors for war funds were to be found at every street corner. Forty aggressive members of the Diet called a meeting to condemn the government for being too moderate in trying to localize the dispute in North China and demanded a fundamental solution to the China question. At the same time, there were fears about the financial consequences of the dispute. Asahi announced that an anti-profiteering ordinance was being drafted and tighter trade controls and tax increases could be expected. At risk were the substantial investments that Japan had in China. The Chinese terminated commercial contracts with the Japanese, forcing many Japanese entrepreneurs to abandon their quarters, particularly in districts along the Yangtze River and remote regions in the interior. In some cases, the Japanese left because of business conditions, but in others because they felt their lives were threatened. Many withdrew to Shanghai, where they felt safer, while Chinese who worked in the Japanese Quarter or Concession in Shanghai took refuge in their own section of the city. In Tokyo, more than 500 Chinese students at the city's universities left for home. This widening personal chasm pointedly demonstrated the pessimism that both nations felt about the future.

By August 7 the Japanese had mopped up the area around Peking and begun occupation of the city. A brigade of 3,000 soldiers in full combat gear entered the Southwest Gate and paraded along the Avenue of Everlasting Peace. Overhead, Japanese army planes dropped leaflets proclaiming, "The Japanese army has driven out your wicked rulers and their wicked armies and will keep them out. Although Nanking is preparing a destructive war, do not be afraid. The Japanese army will protect you."[33]

Crowds of Chinese watched impassively as this message fluttered to the ground and the khaki-uniformed men marched by. There was no overt hostility, but rumors were afoot about the possible return of the former boy-Emperor of China, Henry Pu Yi, now the Emperor Kangte of Manchukuo. Meanwhile, Japan lost no time in imposing control over Peking. Japanese plainclothesmen removed the telegraph equipment from the branch offices of the Chinese Government Radio Administration, cutting off wireless communications. Political administration was seized from the Hopei-Chahar Political Council and placed in the hands of Japanese "Maintenance Committees." The police banned all schoolbooks containing Kuomintang principles and bookstores in the western sector of the city were purged of works that the Japanese considered unfriendly.[34]

The Japanese occupiers' behavior was unpredictable. A Red Cross worker thought the troops "made a good impression. The worst offenses were petty theft and occasional meanness." They were described as being "very young, obviously fresh from training school ... helping themselves to the benefits of the countryside and only incidentally making life miserable for the Chinese they encountered." Yet one could never be sure of their intentions. A Japanese patrol stopped at a luxury hotel in the Western hills outside Peking and forced all of the women to line up. They deliberated among themselves and then chose the wife of a Chinese doctor and marched her upstairs at bayonet point. "The others feared the worst, but an hour or two later she came down trembling with fury—but intact. The soldiers had only wanted her to scrub their backs in the bath, a duty which any Japanese woman would expect to perform."[35]

Their behavior was not always so whimsical. Several weeks before the occupation of Peking, there was an ugly incident involving two American women. The Japanese said that the women had crossed the street and tried to look inside sandbag barricades, at which point Japanese sentries asked them to leave. The Japanese claimed that they were merely "pushed on their way" and that one of the women slipped on wet pavement and fell. One of the women, Mrs. Helen Jones of Detroit, sharply disputed this account, saying that she and her friend, Miss Carol Lathrop, a resident of Peking, had had dinner at a nearby hotel and afterward taken an evening stroll. She acknowledged that they were close to the barricades but insisted that they had not looked inside. "The minute we saw the sentries rise up and heard their war whoop, we were terrified and thought only of getting away quickly. A wave of the hand would have sent us on our way only too gladly. ... If being kicked and shoved as we were isn't violence, then I'd hate to meet the real article." It was also her impression that the pavement was dry.[36] The Japanese conveyed their regrets to Ambassador Johnson and the matter was dropped, but this was just the first of a number of apologies that the Japanese would extend as incidents involving Westerners multiplied.

The Western powers were concerned about much more than isolated insults. A Sino-Japanese war would not only disrupt commerce and China's economic life but would also threaten the status quo of the Western presence there. The Nanking Government was quick to recognize this and sought to enlist the Western governments in its cause. In particular, they looked for support to the United States, which had been the architect of the Open Door policy and the prime mover at the Washington Conference in securing a commitment from the nine powers to respect Chinese political and territorial integrity. Three days after the Marco Polo Bridge Incident, Dr. C.T. Wang, the Chinese Ambassador to America, invited Stanley Hornbeck, the State Department's Chief of the Division of Far Eastern Affairs, and the Assistant Chief, Maxwell Hamilton, to lunch. Also present was Dr. H.H. Kung, the Chinese Minister of Finance. The conversation among these men centered on the fighting that had broken out near Peking. Kung raised the issue previously broached by the Nationalists, that the maintenance of foreign troops at Peking under the Boxer Protocol was no longer justified now that the capital was in Nanking and the foreign governments had their embassies there. Ambassador Wang suggested that the foreign governments should withdraw their forces from North China, as the Protocol conditions had changed. Hornbeck replied that if the Chinese government made such a request, the United States would probably comply, and in turn the British and several other nations might do the same. He then asked Dr. Kung whether he wanted American troops to withdraw. Hornbeck later recalled that "Dr. Kung immediately and emphatically replied that they did not, unless such withdrawal would be concurrent with withdrawal of all the other governments of their armed forces. He said that President Roosevelt had asked him that question and he had made the same reply."[37]

Obviously the Chinese were on a fishing expedition. The departure of all foreign troops might be an effective ploy to get the Japanese out of North China. On the other hand, a unilateral withdrawal of Western forces would leave the field to the Japanese. That was most definitely undesirable.

The Chinese weren't the only power thinking of using the Boxer Protocol as a policy instrument. In Paris, the French Foreign Minister, Yvon Delbos, suggested to the American Ambassador, William Bullitt, that the Great Powers might make a simultaneous proposal to Tokyo and Nanking to keep the Peking-Tientsin Railway open.[38] Nothing came of this idea, but it illustrates the attention that the Western nations were giving to the developing crisis in North China.

All that summer, Chinese diplomats in Washington beat a path to Hornbeck's door and to that of the Secretary of State, Cordell Hull. The Chinese hoped that they could play the American card, but Hornbeck and Hull were determined not to deal it. For example, Hornbeck reported:

> I asked Mr. Ing how he viewed the situation. Mr. Ing replied "I am afraid it means war." I made the rejoinder, "Surely you do not mean that either the Chinese Government or the Japanese Government want war." Mr. Ing then said that the Japanese, especially the Kwantung Army, had long wanted to cut North China off from the rest of China and that operations of the Japanese troops last week now appear to be deliberately provocative.

Ing then asked Hornbeck what he advised China to do, but Hornbeck said that he was not in a position to give advice. He did point out that war would be terribly costly for both sides and inimical to the interests of not only their own people but the whole world. That afternoon, Ing telephoned Maxwell Hamilton to read him a cablegram from the Chinese Foreign Office describing the situation in North China as "extremely grave" and asking if the United States could "do something in a mediatory capacity." This was the first direct appeal from China for American mediation. Hornbeck rejected it at once, declaring that it would be "premature and ill-advised" and more "more likely to aggravate than ameliorate the situation." He also suggested to the British Government that it tell the Japanese it could not negotiate Far Eastern issues as long as hostilities between China and Japan continued. Although none of the Western powers really wanted to take the initiative in trying to make peace, lest they find themselves drawn into a quarrel, they were still concerned about the consequences of inaction.[39]

As the situation in North China worsened, Washington, London and Paris exchanged a flurry of diplomatic cables. Wellington Koo, the Chinese Ambassador to France, called on the French Government to invoke Article 18 of the Covenant of the League of Nations against Japan. The French were reticent, believing that this would only demonstrate the League's impotence. Furthermore, since the United States was not a member of the League, and American participation in any outside attempt to resolve the crisis was seen as essential, the French thought it would be better to seek relief for China under the provisions of the Washington Treaty, to which

V. The Marco Polo Bridge Incident 143

the U.S. was a signatory. Clearly France was too occupied with events in Europe to make commitments in Asia that might weaken its ability to address the growing threat across the Rhine and in the Mediterranean.

In London the Chinese sought joint mediation by the United States and Great Britain, but the British said that unless both of the belligerents wished it, mediation was impossible, and the Japanese had given no indication that they wanted outside help. Yet the British did not reject cooperation out of hand. Britain's commercial interests in China were greater than those of any other Western power. They therefore asked America for support in urging restraint on both sides. However, the notion of joint action by the British and American governments was incompatible with the policy in Washington of avoiding any commitment to involvement in a Far Eastern imbroglio. The State Department advised the British that "cooperation on parallel but independent lines would be more effective." It was feared that isolationists in the Hearst press and Congress would see any formal statement of joint action as an attempt to "pull British chestnuts out of the fire" in China.

However, if the Americans and British had been willing to undertake joint diplomatic action, the French were willing to join them. Delbos told Bullitt that France would cooperate "to the fullest extent possible." But both Delbos and Sir Eric Phipps, the British Ambassador to France, advised Bullitt that if China appealed for help, it would be "disastrous to the League of Nations." The League could not refuse to address the question but would be powerless to take effective action. Delbos told the Chinese Ambassador, "You might as well call on the moon for help as the League of Nations."[40] And yet what Japan was doing in China was a clear violation of the League Covenant and the Washington Nine Power Treaty. The Chinese tried to secure support for their cause through private diplomatic channels. When this failed, they felt they had no choice but to make a formal complaint to the League, but in the end, Delbos' observation was proved correct. China's failure convinced the Japanese that they had nothing to fear from Western intervention.

In Nanking, Chiang Kai-shek applied what personal pressure he could. On July 25 he met with Ambassador Nelson Johnson and begged the Americans and British to act more vigorously, not only in defense of their own interests in China but because of their "moral obligation" as signatories of the Nine Power Treaty. He said this was the only way war could be averted. Chiang was convinced that Western help would eventually be forthcoming. He knew that China could draw on a great well of sympathy and goodwill in America, much of it generated by Christian missionaries and the long commercial ties that stretched across the Pacific. China had a place in American hearts that no other nation shared. Chiang was sure that the United States would not allow Japanese aggression to go unchecked. Ultimately, he was right, but in 1937 no American administration would have supported China. Isolation was too firmly entrenched. Nevertheless, Chiang hoped for Western intervention, without which he couldn't win. Had he been a guest at the dinner table with his Ambassador in Washington on the night of July 31, he would have had a more realistic appraisal of the outlook. Hornbeck was Wang's guest at an informal dinner. Once more, Wang tried to invoke the Nine Power Treaty to involve the United States and Great Britain in East Asia. On that issue, Hornbeck deferred to his chief, Cordell Hull, but he was not above giving his host some parting advice:

> I [referred] to statements which have been repeatedly made by Chinese leaders during recent years to the effect that China must [not] expect the foreign powers to fight her battles or [take sides] in relation to Chinese-Japanese controversies. ... I [said] that the safest thing for any country to do is to frame its policies and conduct its activities on the best estimate that it can make of its own capacity without reference to the possibility of assistance from any other country.... If assistance comes from outside sources, so much to the good; but if any country bases its plans on expectation of assistance from others and then when the time comes the assistance is not forthcoming, it may frequently happen that there is not only disappointment but disaster.[41]

Stanley Hornbeck never gave a better piece of advice than that.

On August 1, Chiang Kai-shek called a meeting of his leadership to announce that he was delaying an offensive by Central Government troops against the Japanese. He said that within ten days he expected to establish a front from Paoting east to Tsangchow and once that was done, he would meet force with force. Substantial numbers of Kuomintang troops had already been sent north, but Chiang held back the best of his troops for a purpose that he did not disclose.

Meanwhile, the Japanese continued to pour troops into North China. American Consul General Caldwell reported from Tientsin to the Secretary of State that in the first four days of August, 14,000 troops, ten heavy howitzers, twenty-four 75-millimeter field pieces, four tanks, twenty-five armored cars, and "huge quantities of military supplies" had been brought to Tangku by the Japanese. These were now being transferred to Tientsin and Peking, evidence of the growing concentration of Japanese military strength and preparation for an offensive.

As Chiang attempted to shore up defenses in North China, he was confronted by a command structure so complicated that he often bypassed the senior generals and issued orders directly to their subordinates. The legacy of warlordism denied Chiang the modern chain of command that would have permitted effective planning and execution. At his disposal was a conglomeration of divisions and brigades that looked good on paper but was in reality a force of no more than 60,000. "An illusion of strength was created by sonorous tones of impressive titles and lengthy rosters of army groups, armies, corps, divisions and brigades."[42] The truth was that it was an uncoordinated mass, weakened by jealousy and mistrust of the various commanders and sectional friction between units from central China and those from the south. The fact that northern troops wore gray uniforms and southern forces wore khaki, similar to the Japanese, compounded the problem. More than once, northern troops fired on those from the south, believing them to be Japanese, and the southerners returned the volleys, thinking that they were repelling invaders.

Chiang won pledges from the warlord governors of Yunnan and Szechuan, but their forces were of little help. The Chinese Red Army, renamed the 8th Route Army, was one of the most formidable Chinese fighting forces, led by the redoubtable Chu Teh. Chiang was reported to have made $500,000 available to the Communists for their help in repulsing the invaders. Disciplined and well led, the 8th Route Army would win one of the few engagements in North China in which the Chinese prevailed. The Communists avoided pitched battles unless they were certain of victory, and they excelled in guerrilla tactics, harassing the enemy and confining him to cities and towns. The countryside belonged to the guerrillas.

The Nationalist armies in North China were determined to fight a conventional war, but their divisions were no match for their modern adversaries. The Japanese enjoyed an advantage of two and a half times the Chinese firepower in small arms, twice the power in light and heavy machine guns, four times the power in pack howitzers, and in other artillery, one and a half times the firepower. There was simply no comparison in mobility or ammunition. Even the Chinese War Ministry in Nanking admitted that one Japanese division was equal to five Chinese divisions and that it would take six to eight Chinese divisions to launch an offensive against a single Japanese division. One expert said, "Considering the fumbling inability of the average Chinese commanding general and the deplorable condition of his troops, those ratios or rules of thumb were optimistic."[43]

Japanese newspapers played up stories of Chinese troop trains speeding northward with reinforcements, but although there was some movement to the north in late July and early August it was slow. Throughout August the Japanese pushed northwest of Peking into Inner Mongolia and the Chinese offered little resistance. The warlords of Shantung and Shensi provinces did not commit themselves, preferring to watch developments. There were substantial numbers of troops on both sides, but except for fighting around Peking and at Tientsin, the combatants in North China hardly more than brushed up against each other. The conflict was still local, and some of the leadership in Tokyo were fooled into believing that the worst had passed, and that political settlement was possible.

The origin of peace negotiations is uncertain. One source said that the plan grew out of an audience that Prince Konoe had with the Emperor on July 30, when Hirohito suggested that a diplomatic solution might be found. Another said it came from the Foreign Ministry, where a secret draft proposal was supposed to have been initiated. In any event, the army was brought in and Ishiwara, still laboring away in the General Staff, now became one of the plan's strongest proponents. Indeed, Ishiwara had offered a similar plan to Admiral Shimada, the Vice Chief of the Navy General Staff, on the 30th, paralleling the Emperor's initiative with Konoe. The next day, Ishiwara appeared before Hirohito and warned him "the army can reach the Paoting line but nothing more can be accomplished. The most urgent task awaiting us today is to effect a truce by diplomatic means before we reach the limit."[44]

The Emperor immediately approved this proposal and with the imperial sanction, Ishiwara again approached his military colleagues as an emissary of peace. By August 4 the services had agreed to a plan that was endorsed at a Four Ministers Conference. The truce plan was comprehensive and, by Japanese standards, generous. A demilitarized zone was to be created in all of the Peking-Tientsin regions of Hopei Province and all Chinese troops would evacuate Hopei. Japanese forces would be reduced to their levels prior to the Marco Polo Bridge Incident. The Hopei-Chahar and East Hopei regions would be abolished, along with the multiple agreements affecting North China. The Nanking government would have the right to administer the North, but the only officials who would be appointed were those who were "fitted for the attainment of Sino-Japanese reconciliation."[45] There was an attached companion plan designed to resolve all of the outstanding differences between China and Japan. Its main provisions would have required the Nationalist government to give de facto recognition to Manchukuo, agree to a Sino-Japanese anti–Communist pact, and cease all anti–Japanese activities in China. In exchange, Japan would end its subversion of Nanking's authority in Inner Mongolia and Suiyuan and assist in the abolition of smuggling in Hopei. These were major concessions. Japan was relinquishing all it had gained in North China since 1933. Only Manchukuo would remain firmly in its hands.

Negotiations with the Chinese were entrusted to Shigeru Kawagoe, the Japanese Ambassador to China. His Chinese counterpart was Kao Tsung-wu, the head of the Asiatic Department of the Chinese Foreign Ministry. The two men met in secret in Shanghai because the General Staff and the War Ministry knew that if the terms leaked out, radical army elements would immediately object and might take precipitate action. Indeed, on August 14 the Kwantung Army issued its own outline for a settlement that was far different from the one Kawagoe was carrying. Entitled "Outline for Solving Current Problems," it called for the establishment of autonomous regimes in the five northern provinces of China and the dissolution of the

Nanking government. It specifically rejected the notion of ending the war by diplomatic means.

Kawagoe knew there were untrustworthy elements, but Hirota nonetheless advised him not to discuss his mission with the Japanese military and naval attaches in Shanghai, and told him that he should try to reach an agreement with the Chinese before August 20, because by then, Japan would have the three divisions it had sent to China in place and military operations would be imminent. Kawagoe was told to make informal overtures; if the Chinese were amenable, then they should take the initiative and publicly request that negotiations be opened.

When Kao and Kawagoe conferred, Kao seemed open to a settlement. He told Kawagoe, "It is unsatisfactory to leave matters as they are. We would like to have something done ... in the near future." Kawagoe replied in general terms. "First, eliminate the fundamental causes of the controversy; second, plan the stability of North China; and third, cooperate and seek powers anew." Kao then asked, "Is the first issue the Manchurian problem? ... You say the 'stability of North China.'[46] However, Japan has no territorial ambitions. Namely, there is no thought of infringing upon the sovereignty. Take positive steps to plan the stability of East Asia in the future." Kao's words might well have been uttered by his opposite. In any event, he promised to take the Japanese terms to Nanking for a review and final answer. But Kao never returned. Shanghai soon became the scene of intense fighting, taking the conflict into a new and more violent phase. There would be another attempt at peace, but it would not hold the same promise. By then the Japanese terms were so severe that there was no hope of their acceptance.

VI

The China Incident

> China and Japan are two brothers who have inherited a great mansion called eastern Asia. Adversity sent them both to the depths of poverty. The ne'er-do-well elder brother turned a dope fiend and a rogue but the younger, lean but rugged and ambitious, ever dreamed of bringing back past glories to the old house. He sold newspapers at a street corner and worked hard to support the house. The elder flimflammed the younger out of the meager savings and sold him out to the common enemy.
>
> The younger in a towering rage beat up the eldest, trying to beat some sense of shame and awaken some pride in the noble traditions of the great house. After many scraps the younger finally made up his mind to stage a showdown fight and that is the fight now raging along the North China and Shanghai fronts.
>
> —Yosuke Matsuoka, October 1937[1]

When the Japanese campaign was at its height in China in 1937, foreign correspondents would attend press conferences at the War Office, a surprisingly shabby building in Tokyo where visitors came and went as they wished. The Army seemed to take a perverse pride in the rambling wooden structure with its long corridors and overhanging balconies. Once, asked why the Army did not build a modern headquarters, an Army officer replied, "Why should we? This building holds traditions and memories we treasure. We won the Russo-Japanese War here! We'll win future wars here."[2]

Western correspondents enjoyed playing a charade with the Japanese briefing officer. One of them would open the conference by asking if there was any news about the war in China and the briefing officer would always reply, "There is no war with China." "Well then," the reporter would ask, "do you have any information on the 'China Incident'?" "Ah, yes, the China Incident. I would like to report the following..." And the briefing officer would then recite field reports on the progress of Japanese forces in

China. This egregious fiction was perpetuated for years while the Japanese Army battled with Nationalist and Communist forces. Although within a few months of the onset of the conflict, Japan withdrew recognition of Chiang Kai-shek's government in favor of a rival puppet regime, the "Incident" soon became a war in the real sense with pitched battles and widespread destruction. Both sides poured in men and employed all of the weaponry at their disposal. Like the conflict in Southeast Asia some thirty years later, there was no formal declaration of war, but it was war all the same: bitter, bloody and barbarous.

The second phase of the struggle opened in Shanghai. For Chiang, North China had become a losing battle and his generals, with few exceptions, avoided confronting the stronger Japanese field forces. On the evening of August 7, he held a meeting with his senior civil and military personnel in the meeting room of the Endeavor Society, an officers' club in Nanking. Present were Wang Ching-wei, who would eventually defect to the Japanese; the Shansi Army commander, Yan Xishan; General Bai Chonxi, the most senior commander in the Guangxi Clique; and General Feng Yuxiang from the Northwest Army.

The Army Minister reviewed events and then Chiang told the officials that he wanted everyone to speak frankly. By 11:00 p.m. the decision was made. China would fight and Chiang would open his own offensive in Shanghai.

The cream of his army were divisions trained by Germany. Had war not erupted in 1937, and had Chiang had his German advisers around longer, Japan might not have enjoyed its relatively easy victories. Chiang's German-trained divisions, numbering 11,000 men, had 275 light machine guns, 100 artillery pieces, and a mechanized unit comprising 40 light military vehicles and 70 armored cars. But there was a huge disparity in weaponry. Chinese mortars had a range of 1,200 meters, while the Japanese could strike targets five times farther. Perhaps more one-sided was the disproportionate advantage Japan had in aircraft. The Chinese had only 202 warplanes capable of conducting combat operations and just enough bombs for 22 missions.

The German chief military adviser, Alexander von Falkenhausen, believed that war with Japan would unify China as it had Germany in the Franco-Prussian War in 1870. Chiang was no Bismarck, and China was no Prussia, but von Falkenhausen persisted. His war plan called for two offensives, a more aggressive one in North China to prevent Japanese reinforcement in Shandoung, and the other at Shanghai. If these failed, the Chinese could fall back and fight a prolonged conflict. After Nanking, Chiang's resistance would be reduced to that approach. But von Falkenhausen also recommended fortifying Nanking and Wuhan and the coastline to forestall

Japanese landings that might deprive China of her lines of communication with the outside world. Von Falkenhausen's opinion of Chiang's assets were wildly at variance with reality. The Chinese had neither the forces nor the tactical competence to carry out such an ambitious plan.[3]

Chiang opened his campaign with a bombing attack on the Japanese warships anchored in the Yangtze River. His aviators were notoriously inaccurate, with a reputation of hitting everything but their target. In this case, the missed target was the *Izumo*, the Japanese flagship of its river flotilla, anchored opposite the Japanese consulate. The subsequent fate of the *Izumo* was inglorious, one that could not have been anticipated on that July day in 1937 when Chiang's bombs fell elsewhere in Shanghai. She had been the lead ship in a class of armored cruisers laid down in the 1890s, completed by 1900, and had been present at the Battle of Tsushima in 1905, in which Admiral Togo commanded the Japanese fleet aboard his flagship *Mikasa*, and she was slightly damaged in an exchange of gunfire with the Russian armada. Although by 1937 she was hardly a high seas threat, the navy sent her to the Japanese anchorage at Kure in the Inland Sea, the home of the Imperial Japanese Navy, in 1945. By then she was just a training ship, but still a target for American bombers who could hardly have known her history. And so it was that she met her end eight years after Chiang's bombers failed to sink her. On July 24, 1945, a swarm of American dive bombers and torpedo planes struck the remnants of the Japanese navy at Kure.

The author was there when *Izumo* met her end. For American navy flyers, Kure was the most dangerous target in Japan. Forty-two planes were shot down over a three-day period that month. Normally bomber crews and fighter pilots flew either the morning or the afternoon strike, but the cycle was such that one could be called up for both. Such was the lot of the author's pilot and his two crewmen in their Grumman Avenger torpedo plane. As the belly gunner, my vision was restricted to two small windows or either side of the fuselage and the tail gunner position from which I strafed, but the pilot and turret gunner had largely unrestricted views.

At Kure, the Japanese fired what can best be described as Technicolor flak, anti-aircraft fire that looked like a Fourth of July celebration at home but as lethal as any other kind, as the losses testified. Only on the return flight to our carrier, the *Yorktown*, was I aware of the great peril to which I had been exposed. As we flew back in formation, my pilot, who had completed a combat tour in the Solomons in 1943, flown missions from Guadalcanal, and been shot down on one occasion, called the turret gunner and me on the intercom and said, "If you boys want a drink, come to my quarters and I'll give you a shot of whiskey." He had flown thirty-nine missions and tangled with a formidable fighter component of the Japanese air force, as evidenced by his near-death experience at their hands, but as we winged our way back to our carrier late in the afternoon of July 24, he told us that Kure was the worst he had ever seen. The gunner and I weren't drinkers then and we politely refused, but in the ten missions that we flew with him before the war ended in August, it was the only time he ever offered us a drink.

The *Izumo* was hardly a serious target for us at Kure. The principal ones were the battleships *Ise* and *Hyuga*, all heavily damaged and settled in shallow water, along with the *Haruna*, beached by the Japanese. Lesser vessels were also sunk or neutralized. The *Izumo* just happened to be in the wrong place at the wrong time and was sunk in the rain of bombs that fell on Kure on July 24, 1945.

The rivalry between the Japanese army and navy for funds, of which the army received the lion's share, as well as in roles and missions, manifested itself at Shanghai. The navy had always been skeptical of the army's adventure in China. The navy saw it not only as an error in strategy but also as a waste of resources. However, the war was on, so they divided their responsibilities. The army would take over the fighting in North China, the navy the air war over central and South China. One unusual aspect of this arrangement was that a number of the aviators who participated in the attack on Pearl Harbor also flew many missions against the Nationalists in China, because they were superior to the army flyers.

The botched attack on the *Izumo* was more than the navy could take. On August 10, Navy Minister Yonai briefed the Cabinet on the situation and asked that the government prepare for mobilization. Yonai promised that the navy would act prudently, but it was clear that he saw the matter as serious. The Cabinet went on record as reaffirming its policy of protecting Japanese citizens, and the Navy General Staff now requested the Army General Staff to prepare to order troops to China.[4] The army complied, but not without misgivings about committing troops while operations were ongoing in North China.

On August 13, two divisions were ordered to Shanghai. That evening there was a long Cabinet meeting in Tokyo. Prime Minister Konoe and his colleagues agreed with the army's decision and then stayed up until two the next morning, wrangling over the wording of their official statement. Akira Kazami, the chief secretary, later wrote that the prolonged session created the false impression with the public that a grave crisis had occurred and that the ministers had been deep in discussion. Kazami said that in fact, they had just been wasting time.[5] It is clear that the fundamental policy that Japan should pursue in China was not debated. Reinforcements, classified as the Central China Expeditionary Force, would be sent to Shanghai. By the fall, the Japanese would have more troops deployed in that operation than in all of North China.[6]

This certainly suited Admiral Yonai, who spoke out more strongly about developments in Shanghai and South China at a second Cabinet meeting, on August 14. He called for a campaign to occupy Nanking. Konoe objected to extending the conflict and his Finance Minister concurred, warning that it would be difficult to finance such a war. Sugiyama raised concerns about Soviet forces, which the army regarded as its principal threat in spite of the offensive already under way in North China.

The army had no interest in further operations in Central or South China, and it was concerned about fighting in Shanghai, where geographical conditions were unfavorable. To isolate the Japanese, Chiang had erected a line of fortifications west of Shanghai, running from the Yangtze to the sea. Referred to as "China's Hindenburg Line," it was supposed to isolate the Japanese in the city and protect the capital at Nanking should Shanghai fall. Had Chinese troops been at full strength, their fortifications in place, and all of the German-supplied arms in their hands, this ambitious plan might have worked. Its failure did not deter Chiang, however, and he opened his offensive on August 13 with the 87th and 89th Divisions, his best, against the Japanese Naval Landing Force at Shanghai, his aircraft taking off on their doomed attempt to sink the *Izumo*. He aimed to push the Naval Landing Force into the sea while simultaneously relieving the pressure on his front line in North China.

Outnumbered ten to one against Chiang's best troops, the Japanese General Staff was understandably worried.[7] To subdue the Chinese would require a major military effort, and given the other concerns the army had, a Shanghai operation looked like a dangerous detour. Admiral Yonai initially seemed to oppose a united front, although in fact the army and navy had agreed in October 1936 to provide support for one another should circumstances dictate.

The "North versus South" strategy that divided the two services was revealed within a week after the incident at the Marco Polo Bridge. From the outset the navy had wanted to contain the fighting in North China while preparing for operations in the south. They had wrung from the army an agreement to protect Japanese nationals in Tsingtao and Shanghai, binding the army to the navy's plans. Chiang's offensive preempted Yonai's move, but the navy was still able to provide the army with a formidable backup. They massed 32 ships at Shanghai, an armada that could use punishing naval gunfire to break a Chinese attack. Not surprisingly, Chiang's airmen tried to neutralize the threat with an attack on the *Izumo*.

Subjecting Shanghai to the terrors of modern warfare involved more than the collateral damage and loss of life that Chiang's incompetent aviators inflicted. Shanghai was the principal treaty port of the foreign nations that had forced commercial concessions from China ever since the Opium

VI. The China Incident

War in 1840. The International Settlement, administered by the British, and the French Concession had steadily expanded through eight separate treaties, and by 1937 extended along seven miles of waterfront and from one to five miles inland. Both areas were under the provision of extraterritoriality, which put them outside the authority of the government in Nanking. Crowded within them were 1,575,000 Chinese and some 63,000 foreigners, including 20,000 Japanese, 9,000 British, 4,000 Americans, 2,500 French, and 8,500 White Russian refugees. Small groups of other European and Indian nationals comprised the rest. Besides the civilians, five nations maintained military garrisons in the city. There was the 4th Marine Regiment of 150 officers and 2,600 men and a British force of 90 officers and 2,500 men. The French had 50 officers and 2,000 men; the Italians, 20 officers and 750 men; and the Japanese, a mixed force of 5,000 men, including a specially trained unit of 1,800 men in a fortified barracks at Hongkew, which straddled the north boundary of the International Settlement.

The Japanese treated Hongkew as their own preserve, often holding military exercises there and behaving with the same contempt for their neighbors that they had around Peking. Residents within the Settlement had to put up with parades of Japanese soldiers, artillery and tanks through crowded streets and along the Bund, the wide quay adjacent to the waterfront. Outside this imperial sanctuary lived two million Chinese, in the old walled area known as Chinese City and the nearby neighborhoods: Chapei, Paoshan, Hongkew, Kiangwan and Kiangnan west of the river, and Pootung on the east bank.

Before the fighting began in August there were over 6,500 Japanese living in the Hongkew section of Shanghai and about 1,700 in Hankow, where the Japanese had stationed another garrison; another 1,700 were scattered among the cities along the Yangtze: Nanking, Wuhu, Kiukiang, Changsha, Ichang and distant Chungking. Like the other nationals in China, the Japanese maintained a gunboat flotilla on the Yangtze but with rising tensions, these vessels and the Japanese citizens they were charged to protect were moved downriver to Shanghai. Some 12,000 Japanese also resided along the coast in the ports of Foochow, Amoy, Swatow and Canton. Like their brethren, they would be evacuated by early August after the fighting intensified in Shanghai.[8]

General Sugiyama had no choice but to send two divisions to Shanghai. The Third and Eleventh Divisions under the command of General Iwane Matsui arrived to reinforce the beleaguered navy units. Matsui's troops were designated the Shanghai Expeditionary Army and by August 23 had come ashore at the mouth of the Whangpoo River. It was their largest amphibious operation to date. Taking advantage of a high tide, the two divisions landed along a five-meter-high river dike. Their air force dominated the skies. The fighting would be intense.

Both the military and civilian leadership had difficulty accommodating themselves to this fact. The number of divisions committed to China as the war expanded into the north eventually stretched them to the limit. Prince Konoe, who had vacillated over the army's expansion of the conflict, confided his unhappiness to Kango Koyama, a friend, who recorded their conversation in his diary:

> The Prince looked haggard and said that the government had no idea how the situation in China would develop. With a deep sigh of despair [he] complained, "I have accepted a daunting job at an unfortunate time. I should have known better, for the situation was actually better right after the May 15 Incident. Right now the civilian government is too weak to do anything. Worse, the military is so divided that we do not know who to deal with...." He seemed so discouraged that I tried to lift his spirits; he had undertaken the task, I told him, and owed it to the country to carry it out to the finish. I warned him that publicly he must appear to be fully confident; otherwise he would cause harmful rumors that the prime minister was disheartened by the China problem. As for the future of China, would Chiang Kai-shek be able to maintain his position and negotiate peace with Japan? or would he fall, and with his defeat throw China into utter confusion? If Chiang would only concede at an appropriate moment and seek peace, Japan could avoid a protracted war. If he refused to surrender even after ignominious defeat and persisted in drawing out the hostilities, there would be no way of knowing how the situation would develop. *The prince confessed that he had no idea which way the war would take us.* [italics added]⁹

Publicly, Konoe continued to put up a brave front as his friend had urged, but privately he was miserable. The army was in no better spirits. The fighting at Shanghai forced them to abandon any hope of containing the conflict. The field forces, eager for combat, chafed at the restrictions Tokyo sought to impose. There had always been friction between the Army General Staff and the Ministry of War. One faction wanted to offer concessions to encourage the Chinese to negotiate; the other believed that China could be brought to its knees. Depending on the fortunes of war, these groups occasionally swapped positions as hawks and doves. The army paid for its ineptitude and lack of cohesion in other ways. The need to mobilize resources at all levels should have been anticipated but wasn't. Reinforcements assigned to Shanghai had insufficient ammunition. The high casualties suffered by the army in Shanghai were not due only to Chinese resistance. Had the army managed its campaign more effectively, its losses might have been less.

On the ground, the fighting looked like a repeat of World War I. Trenches and battlefields chewed up by artillery fire were a true no-man's land. It would take the Japanese four months to push out Chiang's forces. In October, the Chinese mounted a night attack with four divisions, although a counterattack threw them back with severe losses.

The man chosen to command the Shanghai Expeditionary Army was an unlikely candidate. General Iwane Matsui stood just five feet tall and he was suffering from tuberculosis when the Emperor summoned him to the palace to receive his commission. Matsui had reached the age where he had been relegated to the reserves, so he viewed this assignment as both an honor and an opportunity, particularly since he had been one of the officers who favored friendship with China. Once war broke out, however, he advocated aggressive military action to capture Nanking and install a government favorable to Japan. He believed that the Chinese people could then be won over by a benevolent occupation and an honest and wise administration.[10]

After kneeling before Hirohito and receiving his command baton, Matsui left the palace in the company of Prince Konoe. As their car drove away, Matsui turned to the Prime Minister and said, "There is no solution but to break the power of Chiang Kai-shek by capturing Nanking. That is what I must do." Soon afterward, he was honored with a farewell dinner by his fellow directors of the East Asia League and told them, "I am going to the front not to fight the enemy but in a state of mind of one who sets out to pacify his brother."[11]

General Matsui did indeed fulfill his vow to capture Nanking, but the occupation that followed was marred by unparalleled rape, slaughter and destruction. The "Rape of Nanking" was a dreadful stain on the already blemished reputation of the Japanese Army, an event so repulsive that it branded Japan as a rogue nation. Although Matsui had not ordered Nanking to be defiled, as commanding general he was ultimately responsible for his soldiers' conduct. It would have been better for him to have coughed away his life, but he lived to be tried as a major war criminal and was hanged with General Tojo and the others at Sugamo Prison. At the age of 70, Matsui was the eldest of the condemned and was allowed the honor of leading them in a final "banzai" for the Emperor minutes before their execution.[12]

As the Germans would learn at Stalingrad in 1942–1943, urban warfare is tortuous. General Matsui had not only to try to dislodge the stubborn Chinese defenders but also to respect the International Settlement and the French Concession. The foreign forces stationed there were not a threat in themselves, but Japan could ill afford to complicate an already difficult military operation by risking an incident with one of the Western powers. Yet minor confrontations with nervous Marines and policemen along the edges of the foreign settlements occurred almost daily. The inaccuracy of Chinese air attacks had already killed people within the Western enclaves, so Matsui went to some lengths to avoid shelling or bombing there. The *New York Times* correspondent, Hallett Abend, wrote that over the three-month period during which he observed the conflict, only one Japanese bomb landed within the Settlement, and that was clearly a mistake. The target was a Chinese warehouse on the north bank of Soochow Creek and the bomb landed just inside the sector manned by American Marines, hitting a streetcar, and killing thirteen Chinese passengers. Abend remarked that it was unnerving to listen to the screaming of Japanese shells as they soared over the International Settlement and the French Concession into Nantao, the Chinese section in the north of the city, but he added, ironically, that none of the American or British observers saw the relative accuracy of Japanese gunfire as evidence of an experienced and competent adversary.[13]

Meanwhile, Chiang had to fight with the Japanese while nervously watching his back. The Communists occupied the interior, as did some of the warlords. They were constantly threatening or making demands on him. If he could defeat the Japanese in Shanghai, he would not only demonstrate his strength but bring his homegrown opponents into his camp and achieve the national unity that was his fundamental goal.

Despite the misfortunes at Shanghai, Chiang's resistance and his willingness to take the fight to the enemy proved to be a watershed in the war with Japan. The public responded enthusiastically, as evidenced by a headline in the *Dagongbao*, China's most prestigious newspaper, which hailed "'the first time that the entire nation' had fought together against a common enemy, thus marking the birth of a new age," and added, "Children of China! We ought to congratulate you [on being] born into this great age!"[14]

For the residents of Shanghai, however, the fighting was anything but welcome. Many foreigners were leaving. On August 21, 1937, the *New York Times* told its readers:

> The last few days have been marked by countless tense scenes when women and children sailed, those saying farewells realizing full well they may never see each other again. The partings were all the more wrenching because the haste of the evacuation in many cases allowed only a few hours for breaking up homes, packing and sailing away.
>
> The bars and lounges of the foreign clubs present an odd atmosphere tonight. Little nervousness is evident, but somber moods prevail, violently contrasting with occasional groups becoming noisy and boastful over an excess of cocktails and highballs. All over the city homes are locked, abandoned and dark, the owners trusting to fate that their possessions won't suffer loss by looting or fire. ... [G]reat buildings stand black and tenantless against a moonlit sky.
>
> Besides personal separations, doubts for the future, fear of the renewal of bombings and aerial flights over the foreign refugee center, there is added depression caused by the hourly losses of large fortunes or the modest savings of a lifetime. As fire areas and hostilities spread, more and more millions go up in smoke or crumble into dust under artillery shells.
>
> The collapse of buildings will, in most cases, mean the permanent loss of investments and ... of many positions.

The persistent Western prejudice that Japan had neither good equipment nor capable pilots or marksmen was not shared by Hallett Abend. He noted the surprise of American aviators in the Philippines in 1941 at how well the Japanese Zero fighters performed. He recalled an earlier article he had written for *The Saturday Evening Post* during a brief furlough in the United States in April of that year. He had titled it, "Yes, the Japanese Can Fight." In his original draft, he had described an influx of hundreds of German aviation experts into Japan following the formation of the Axis. Before their arrival, the maximum known speed of any Japanese plane was 350 m.p.h., but under German tutelage, the Japanese had begun to manufacture a "new mystery plane known as the Zero," which had then seen only limited service in China. Abend commented on what U.S. pilots later learned, that the aircraft was remarkably maneuverable, although the speed of 420 m.p.h. with which Abend credited it was an exaggeration. He submitted his draft to both the War and Navy Departments in Washington before it was to be published, but they deleted his description of the Zero's performance features for reasons they never made clear to him. "Perhaps they didn't believe what I wrote." (Abend later acknowledged that he was mistaken in believing that German aeronautical designers had influenced the development of the Zero. A Mitsubishi design team headed by Jiro Horikoshi had created the plane at the request of the Navy Air Staff, and his prototype was first flown in April 1939.)[15]

American worries about the safety of its nationals in the International Settlement prompted an official protest to the Central Government in Nanking following the bungled air attack on the *Izumo*. Wang Chung-hui, the Chinese Foreign Minister, reacted with undisguised annoyance. Although his reply to Ambassador Nelson Johnson was couched in courteous diplomatic language, it was nevertheless blunt and showed the Central Government's exasperation with the Western Powers' narrow concern over a few thousand acres along the Shanghai waterfront while China was locked in a life-and-death struggle for its very existence. Wang reminded the American Ambassador that before the fighting began in Shanghai, the Chinese had warned that if Japanese troops tried to use any part of the Settlement as a base of operations or as a place of retreat, Chinese forces would have to take action against them. "The Japanese are now still using Hongkew and Yangtzepoo as their base of attack, while a large number of Japanese warships operating in the Whangpoo River are continually bombarding Chinese positions." He went on to say that Chinese aircraft had taken pains to avoid hitting neutral ships or property, but that the proximity of Japanese warships made that extremely difficult. He suggested that, if the Western powers wished to resolve the problem, they could either make the Japanese remove their warships from the Whangpoo or withdraw their own vessels from the danger zone. He concluded by saying, "We believe that the position thus taken by the Chinese government is based on fairness and justice, especially in view of the fact that we are fighting for the security of Chinese territory, including the area of Shanghai."[16]

Admiral Harry E. Yarnell, commander of the U.S. Asiatic Fleet, was more concerned about the security of Americans there. He asked that a force of 1,000 Marines be sent to China as soon as possible, and orders were issued to dispatch the 6th Marine Regiment from San Diego. However, even a Marine regiment would have offered little protection for the isolated Shanghai enclave. The belligerents were coming in divisions, not regiments, and had they put their minds to it, they would have made short shrift of the Western outpost along the waterfront. Sending in U.S. Marines was merely symbolic. The problem confronting the International Settlement and the French Concession was not a direct military threat but the tragic byproduct of war. Hundreds of thousands of Chinese were taking refuge inside, putting an enormous strain on food and health services. Crowding and shortages threatened to break down civil order and made the already difficult task of the Chinese municipal authorities nearly impossible.

The *North China Daily News* described the scene:

> It would seem as if the Japanese forces were being commanded to kill an overflowing cup of bitterness with which their exploits will be associated in the eyes of the world. Here in Shanghai as streams of refugees are [seen] in the streets ... among them hosts of mothers desperately protecting their offspring and gallantly endeavoring to conceal their fears, the thought irresistibly arises that the Japanese mother would be horrified if she could see what is being done to Chinese mothers and their children in the name of her people.[17]

Fighting in the city escalated. By August 17, the fifth day of combat, Shanghai was being rocked by explosions. After sundown, star shells arched overhead as both sides grappled in the unrelenting conflict. Searchlights from Japanese warships shone along the waterfront, picking out targets for their guns that pounded Chinese targets throughout the night. In those first two weeks, while Japan was racing to put reinforcements ashore, the Chinese brought their own troops to within a mile of the Whangpoo riverfront. By the 19th, the *New York Times* reported that Chinese lines stretched from the northwestern edge of the International Settlement along the railroad. through the North Station, and around the Japanese Hongkew positions toward the Whangpoo. On the night of August 18, with a bright moon overhead, the Japanese air force unleashed their bombs on Chinese positions. For Settlement residents this was a spectacular light show. Hallett Abend had a room on the 11th floor of the Broadway Mansions in the International Settlement just north of Soochow Creek. He reported that he could "sit looking downriver and watch the Japanese planes bombarding the North Station and Chapei day after day." From another terrace he could watch them bombing Nantao, the upriver Chinese section of Shanghai.

Viewed from a distance, an aerial attack was a vivid pyrotechnic display, but from close up, it was carnage. Abend wrote a graphic account of what he saw when he arrived in Shanghai on August 18, several days after the ill-fated Chinese bombing raid:

> A whole block of Nanking Road between the Palace and Cathay Hotels was still roped off and closed to traffic. After the hundreds of corpses and maimed people had been removed from the pavement, the sidewalks [were] sticky with clotting blood. Sand and disinfectant had been liberally sprinkled around but the street still smelled like a foul charnel house, and little of the wreckage had been touched.
>
> Out near the racecourse, conditions were still worse. Scores of bodies and fragments of bodies still lay about wrapped in cheap matting, and as yet the spatters of human flesh had not been removed from walls and buildings, billboards or fences. The ... stench of unburied bodies [in] the simmering August heat was unbearable.

The Chinese air force could not be compared to the Japanese. A few of China's pilots had been trained in the United States, but most of them had been taught to fly by an Italian mission sent out by Mussolini. Indeed, Madame Chiang Kai-shek had complained to Ambassador Johnson that while Italy had sent instructors to China to train aviators, the U.S. government would not authorize Americans to do the same. However, during his state visit to Germany in 1937, Mussolini joined Hitler in professing friendship with Japan, and shortly after he returned to Italy, he ordered all of the Italian flight instructors home from China. China's German advisers left soon afterward.[18]

When the air war over Shanghai heightened in August, Chiang Kai-shek offered generous contracts to foreign aviators—a monthly salary of $1,200, a princely sum in those days, with a bonus of $1,000 for every Japanese warplane shot down.[19] Colonel Chennault, an American officer who left the U.S. and his career there to take up the Chinese cause, and who would eventually organize the American Volunteer Group, became Chiang's air combat adviser. The "Flying Tigers," as the AVG group came to be known, would indeed trouble the Japanese bombers attacking Chungking, but they weren't around in 1937, and Chennault could not do much with the feeble and incompetent Nationalist air force.

Now the Japanese were bombing Nanking on a daily basis and Chinese troops endured more or less continuous attacks as Japanese airmen coordinated operations with those on the ground.

On August 21 the U.S. Asiatic Fleet flagship *Augusta* was struck by an unknown bomb or shell; an American sailor was killed and eighteen others were wounded. More than likely, the *Augusta* was hit by a shell fired by one of the Chinese shore batteries dueling with Japanese warships anchored in the Whangpoo. Not knowing for sure where the missile had come from, the cruiser did not attempt to return fire. Admiral Yarnell, the senior commander of the foreign fleets at Shanghai, was determined to keep his ship moored between the Settlement and the contending Sino-Japanese forces, even though the Whangpoo was only 900 feet wide. He insisted that the river be kept open to international navigation in spite of the danger of hostile fire. In this, Yarnell was supported by Secretary of State Hull and President Roosevelt. Senator Key Pittman, chairman of the Foreign Relations Committee, endorsed the Administration's policy. "So long as there are American citizens in China in danger, it is the duty of the navy to remove them to safety regardless of the risks involved."[20] But many Americans in China were getting out as fast as they could. The death of the young sailor aboard the *Augusta* was the fourth American fatality within a week. The previous Saturday three people had died when Chinese bombs fell in the International Settlement.

The same day that the *Augusta* was struck, the Chinese 36th Division launched an attack on the Huishan wharves across the Whangpoo opposite the Settlement. This pushed the Japanese almost back to the river, but heavy naval and artillery fire saved the day for them. The following night, units from the Japanese 3rd and 11th Divisions came ashore near Woosung, ten miles down the Yangtze. A firefight erupted as Chinese machine gunners supported by artillery fought tenaciously to keep the invaders from getting a foothold on the river's mudflats, but under the protection of naval gunfire, the Japanese secured a landing. American naval officers stationed two miles away counted twenty-six Japanese cruisers and destroyers covering one landing with a barrage of eight- and six-inch shells while Japanese planes bombed and machine-gunned Chinese positions.

Franklin Delano Roosevelt: U.S. president, 1933–1945 (photograph by Elias Goldensky).

The landing itself was led by merchant ship masters and Yangtze River pilots in the Japanese naval reserve, men who were familiar with the waters. The first launch was filled with a "death detachment" of seventy men wearing white bands. Disembarking at a ruined jetty, they advanced through a hail of bullets, followed by their comrades who threw hand grenades and swept the Chinese lines with machine gun fire. Their approach was similar to that used by the Japanese in 1932, when they had broken up a stalemate by landing a division at Liuho fifteen miles up the Yangtze, outflanking the Chinese and forcing them to retreat. As the fighting intensified, both sides taunted each other. The *New York Times* reported that Japanese officers said they hoped the Chinese would cling to their positions because that made them easier to annihilate, to which the Chinese retorted, "Let them come on. We are prepared to give them a welcome of a kind they never dreamed of." For all of their boasting, however, the Chinese didn't halt the Japanese advance until it had penetrated four miles inland. A stalemate followed, with attacks and counterattacks as each side tried to gain the advantage. In spite of a lack of adequate naval, air and artillery support, the Chinese grimly hung on. Their losses were severe, and Chiang would pay heavily for decimating his best divisions by trying to hold the city. Eventually the issue was decided, the retreat became a rout, and Chiang had only a remnant of his army for the defense of Nanking. The best of it had been squandered in Shanghai.

The Japanese also suffered heavy losses, particularly the 3rd and 11th Divisions, which had entered the battle of Shanghai early on. The Wachi Regiment of the 11th Division started with 3,500 officers and men; 1,100 were ultimately killed and over 2,000 wounded. The Ishii Regiment of the 3rd Division, also originally 3,500, eventually lost 1,200 killed and 3,000 wounded. Replacements were constantly needed, or the units would have ceased to exist. Before the Chinese were driven out of the city, Japanese losses totaled 9,100 dead and 31,300 wounded. The army's ammunition shortage contributed to its casualties. The War Ministry in 1937 had only enough ammunition to last eight months, sufficient for combat operations by fifteen divisions, yet by the end of the year there were sixteen divisions fighting in China. By mid-September, Japanese artillerymen were limited to a handful of shells per cannon per day. Although they were better prepared than their adversaries, they tried to compensate for their lack of weaponry with *Bushido*, which simply increased their losses. More and more boxes of ashes of the fallen were returned home, their spirits prayed for at the Yasukuni shrine in Tokyo.

A Japanese hospital ship anchored in the harbor cared for the wounded, so that the unlucky soldier who caught a bullet or a piece of shrapnel could be quickly evacuated, and his wounds treated. Shanghai hospitals initially tried to care for Chinese casualties, but they were soon swamped, and the more seriously wounded received little help. Beyond Shanghai, the Japanese tried to provide medical care in the field, but the Chinese had practically nothing. They usually shot their own seriously injured as an act of mercy, knowing they were doomed to die.[21]

As conflict convulsed the city, it became increasingly difficult to control. When the Japanese shelled the municipal jail, the Chinese released several hundred Chinese and European inmates, taking them under guard and setting them free in the countryside. Some 5,500 Chinese prisoners in the Ward jail were not so lucky. They were locked up inside while fighting raged all around them.[22] The Chinese had hoped to free about 5,000 minor offenders in Chinese territory west of the French Concession, but the plan fell apart after only about 500 had been let go. The Japanese had argued that the release of so many petty criminals so close to the International Settlement could result in a serious outbreak of crime.

During late August 1937, classified ads in local editions of the *New York Times* gave an insight on living conditions in Shanghai. On August 21, an apartment was offered "cheap, outside the shrapnel area." Another boasted the advantage of having an observation roof "to detect air bombers." A bungalow was listed at a bargain price, plus "American Marines within easy reach." Then there was "one house, cheap, bomb-proof shelter." Also available was "one auto—free, in return for care until the owner can return." Meanwhile, Chinese stores advertised regulation army-style steel helmets for civilians, "either singly or by the dozen." Ads with slogans such as "save your lives [with] our gas masks" were illustrated with pictures of Chinese men and women wearing them. Other merchants offered sandbags but warned shoppers that there were "only a few left." Given the penchant of Chinese generals for selling off military equipment, it is not difficult to see how this merchandise reached the shelves in Shanghai.

Normal commerce was impossible. The banks had closed almost as soon as the fighting started, leaving foreign currency transactions to the Chinese-owned exchange shops that were little more than a legalized black market. Before the war spread to Shanghai, a hundred U.S. dollars had bought the equivalent of $363 in Chinese money. Within two weeks, the figure had risen to $475 Chinese. Profiteering and inflation went hand in hand as basic necessities soared in price. Hundreds of thousands of Chinese refugees surged into the International Settlement and the French Concession. Desperately hungry and unable to buy food because the Chinese banks had suspended business, they rioted and looted food stores.[23] The police in the French Concession struggled vigorously to drive them out and clear the streets. In the American section, the Marines strung barbed wire along a 7,000-yard stretch and studded the banks of Soochow Creek with machine gun emplacements. Admiral Yarnell issued orders to bar armed Chinese and Japanese troops from the American sector, and if unorganized groups of Chinese should make an attempt, they were to be dispersed with tear gas.[24]

One of the weirdest aspects of the Shanghai theater of war was that the belligerents insisted on observing absurdly diplomatic conventions and customs. For example, maritime etiquette in peacetime required passing warships to salute each other. While shelling targets on shore, Japanese naval vessels remained punctilious about observing this courtesy. Whenever a foreign warship passed while they were engaged in hostile action, the Japanese gun crews would cease fire and stand at attention until the other ship passed, and then resume their bombardment.

Within the International Settlement and the French Concession, the same anomalies prevailed. Every day at 10:00 a.m. and 4:00 p.m., the Japanese held press conferences for foreign correspondents. A few blocks away, between 6:00 and 7:00 p.m., the Chinese held a similar briefing. Japanese and Chinese military and diplomatic officers attended these meetings, often coming from and returning to combat zones without threat or hindrance. Chiang Kai-shek's mansion in the French Concession stood vacant, but it was only a five-minute walk from the home of the Japanese Ambassador, Shigeru Kawagoe, whose residence was undisturbed although not unguarded. One of the highest-ranking Kuomintang officials, T.V. Soong, who would represent Chiang's government abroad, lived so close to the Japanese Consul General that they often passed each other in their automobiles on the way to their respective offices. These paradoxes gave the war a strange character, but after Shanghai fell, the Japanese dropped the charade.

On August 23 another stray bomb fell in the heart of the Nanking Road shopping district, killing some 400 people and wounding 1,000. Lunchtime shoppers who had crowded into the two largest department stores, Wing On and Sincere, were the main victims. The large-caliber bomb struck Sincere, taking out the facade and one whole corner of the seven-story structure. Wing On was heavily damaged as well. Among the casualties were Hallett Abend and Anthony Billingham, the *New York Times* correspondents. Billingham had gone into Wing On to buy a pair of binoculars and was in an elevator in the building opposite the store when the explosion occurred. The force of the blast broke the cables, sending the elevator crashing to the ground. Although he was badly injured, he and a ten-year-old Chinese boy in the cage survived. The rest of the elevator's occupants perished. Abend had been waiting for his colleague in a car on the street when the bomb hit. He suffered a serious injury to his foot but fought his way into the building and managed to locate his friend and lead him to safety. Morris Harris, an Associated Press correspondent, witnessed the carnage and reported it to the *Times* in melodramatic terms:

> I escaped again as I did on that terrible Saturday a week ago, August 14, when the Chinese aerial bomb killed at least 1,000 in the International Settlement. I was just leaving the Wing On store when the projectile screamed toward the [Settlement].
> Suddenly everyone was aware of the danger—but it was too late. It struck with the speed of a meteor, smashing into a bewildered mass of humanity. It was as if a great shell had fallen at noon on Fifth Avenue in New York, or in State Street in Chicago.
> I turned back into Wing On's to find it a shambles. The explosion had ripped

through the walls as if they had been tissue paper. Hundreds lay about, either dead, wounded, or so dazed and white with shock that they appeared dead.

Hundreds, crazed with fear, sought to escape from the wrecked building. Stairways and exits were choked. Scores must have perished in the crush to escape. I thought I had become inured to scenes of horror in this war-engulfed Shanghai, but the scenes in Wing On's would have made anyone sick with horror.

Most of the store's staff were lying about, dead, hurt, or shell-shocked. A few managers who had survived the blast tried to control the crowds, but none heard them. It was a tide of humanity fighting in panic for life and tearing through any open space.

Outside I found sections of two towering stores hanging dizzily over the street. Balconies and railings sagged. Here and there bodies were draped over balustrades. The charred bodies of a Sikh and two Chinese policemen hung grotesquely from a twisted, swaying traffic tower.

Scores of mortally wounded staggered blindly, insanely away from the ruins to collapse and die. They lay there until the police had gathered up those whose lives might be saved. Then they were carted away to the mortuaries.

The Japanese denied any responsibility for the tragedy. Admiral Hasegawa said that none of his warships, artillery or airplanes were in action at the time, and Japanese pilots had been specifically instructed not to fly over the International Settlement while carrying bombs. Given the record of the hapless Chinese Air Force, and the caution that both Hasegawa and Matsui observed with respect to foreign enclaves, a Chinese aviator was undoubtedly to blame, but that was no comfort to the dead and wounded.

Then, on August 26, Japanese aviators attacked the car of the British Ambassador, Sir Hughe Knatchbull-Hugessen, severely wounding him. Sir Hughe had left Nanking for Shanghai that morning with the British flag prominently displayed on his automobile. He was about 40 miles from Shanghai when two Japanese planes dropped their bombs. Although they missed their target, one of the aircraft swooped down and strafed the car, riddling it with machine gun bullets that struck the Ambassador has he stepped from it. The British protested strongly, demanding an apology, indemnification and assurances against a repetition of unprovoked attacks, but the government in London knew it was unable to back up its demands with force, even had it wanted to. Eleven days later, Hirota conveyed his country's regrets to Sir Robert Craigie, but also warned the British that the Ambassador of a friendly power should inform Japanese authorities when traveling through a danger zone. This was a clever tactic on Hirota's part, for if a British official gave such notice, it would be a tacit acknowledgment of Japan's belligerent rights in China.

The day before the attack, there had been another occurrence that had a far greater effect on British interests than Sir Hughe's wounds. Admiral Hasegawa announced a blockade of the South China coast, from a point 690 miles north of Shanghai to just south of Swatow. Although the blockade applied only to Chinese vessels, it put Britain's commercial interests at risk by interfering with the Chinese Customs Administration. However, the blockade had little effect on Chiang's campaign around Shanghai, and since the Japanese did not attempt to stop and search the ships of other nations, no one protested. Some thought it might even prove a windfall for the British, who could take over much of the coastal trade.

Chiang Kai-shek tried to micromanage the battle. On September 6 he ordered his troops to go on the defensive, but his instructions were so detailed that they precluded any individual initiative. As with Hitler's meddling on the Eastern Front in World War II, field commanders found themselves constricted. The battle plan amounted to little more than an order for every soldier to give up his life. Many of them did, but Japanese firepower forced the remainder to retreat. The Chinese covered up their defeat by issuing euphemistic communiqués saying "the battle line was interspersed."[25] Although Chinese lines held elsewhere, by mid-September they had been pushed back over two miles from the Whangpoo and Yangtze.

Both sides had now committed enormous numbers of troops to the field, the Chinese half a million by September 21, and the Japanese 200,000, both less losses previously sustained. At this point the combatants were facing each other along a line west of the Whangpoo River running from the vicinity of the Chapei-North Station to the International Settlement, north through Kiangwan to a salient on Woosung Creek, six and a half miles northwest of the Settlement, and then north again to Liuho on the Yangtze, eighteen miles north of Shanghai. The Japanese were particularly challenged by the Chapei district. Since the southern side was bounded by the International Settlement and guarded by foreign troops, the Japanese could not penetrate it from that direction. Within Chapei, Chinese troops took refuge in basements and buildings constructed of brick and concrete. Relatively safe in these hideouts from Japanese bombers, they could emerge to fight enemy infantry. Japanese soldiers found the going arduous. The diary of Private Tokaji Toshihara, stained with mud and blood, revealed the peril and hardship of combat. Along with two of his comrades, Toshihara had been cut off from his unit at Lotien near Shanghai. Severely wounded, he was later pulled from a swamp where the three of them had hidden for nineteen days, trapped behind Chinese lines. He wrote:

Drinking muddy water. We ate half a portion of dry biscuits.

Sixth day—Flasks empty, and we have no more water to drink. We can hear the enemy all around us. We are still hiding in the swamp and nobody dares go for water because of the danger. Oh! I wish somebody would come get us. It is already 7 o'clock—another awful night coming. There comes a shell again. We don't know if the enemy knows where we are, but there are no rifle shots. Midnight—again shells, but no sign of our own troops. Emperor, Banzai!

Seventh day—I want water, water, water! I am so thirsty.

The diary continued with an account of Toshihara's success in filling his canteen from a nearby creek that was choked with bloated bodies:

> Returned half-hour later. All I can feel is heat and pain. Now we have enough water for the night, but we cannot sleep because of the shells. We can hear talking in the Chinese trenches tonight.
>
> A week already. Not so much pain from the wound this morning. We saw one of our airplanes and I whispered Emperor, Banzai! We are now eating an ear of rice. I examined my pistol and I have 300 rounds. Hope someone will come tomorrow to get us out of this hell.[26]

As the days crept by, one of the three made a run for the Japanese lines, but Toshihara and the other soldier stayed put. Subsisting on rice and tinned meat which they had taken from the bodies of nearby dead, they continued to suffer from thirst. Finally, on the nineteenth day, the Chinese retreated beyond the creek and the two men were rescued by their own forces.

With the initiative now in the hands of the Japanese in Shanghai, Chiang Kai-shek openly appealed to the Western powers to intervene and halt the war. On August 31 he issued a lengthy statement from Nanking to the *New York Times*, declaring that the Chinese were fighting not only for themselves but also for those nations that believed in the sanctity of treaties:

> If the nations of the world recognize the menace of Japanese aggression and wish to prevent its consequences from descending ... directly or indirectly, they should take immediate action. Intervention is imperative not only for China's sake but for international safety.

The next evening the Generalissimo asked Ambassador Johnson to his residence to press his case further, with Madame Chiang acting as his interpreter. Chiang said that he was puzzled by American policy, particularly the Americans' unwillingness to cooperate with Great Britain in trying to restrain Japan. In truth, Britain, beyond asking Washington to join in an offer of "good offices" to the belligerents to settle the conflict, was unwilling to take an active part in the dispute. Both Hull and Roosevelt, wary of the virulently anti–British Hearst press, and mindful of strong anti-interventionist sentiment in the nation, had determined that American action must be independent of that of any other government. Johnson repeated this line to Chiang, telling him that the United States "preferred to act in consultation and when in agreement, independently." Chiang replied that China "was not asking anyone to fight [its] battle for it," but he left Johnson feeling that the United States had failed to take a strong stand by not condemning Japan for its aggression.[27]

More than a month would go by before the West bestirred itself to respond to Chiang's plea. The only immediate reaction was a request by the British, French and American Consuls General in Shanghai for the belligerents to withdraw their forces from the areas near the International Settlement and the French Concession because of the dangers to the Chinese and foreigners residing there. Falling shrapnel and stray bullets continued to take their toll on the unlucky, but it was fruitless to expect that either side would forfeit its advantage in the contest for the city. Chiang's aviators continued to embarrass him by hitting neutral targets more often than the enemy. On August 30, five members of the crew and two passengers on the American Dollar liner *President Hoover* were wounded when a Chinese warplane bombed the ship off Woosung at the mouth of the Yangtze River. This could not have occurred at a worse time, just before Chiang's appeal for Western intervention and in particular his personal plea to Ambassador Johnson for American assistance. The Nanking government could only apologize and offer reparations but privately, Chiang chafed at Western recalcitrance. The foreign powers had enriched themselves at China's expense, clung to their commercial holdings, and refused to recognize that Japan was threatening their investments. Nowhere did Western conduct more epitomize this attitude than in Shanghai. Inside their enclaves, Westerners insisted that China and Japan take their war elsewhere, an attitude that Chiang had never anticipated when he ordered his divisions into the city.

As the Japanese offensive in Shanghai intensified, they also stepped up the air war over Chiang's capital. They had bombed Nanking periodically ever since the early stages of fighting in Shanghai, but on September 25 the city was hit by 80 aircraft in five successive waves over seven hours. The aftermath was like that in Britain during World War II, with cleanup crews clearing streets, repairing broken water mains and restoring essential services. In spite of the prolonged bombardment, casualties were surprisingly light, with fewer than a hundred dead. The worst was yet to come.

Chiang would have liked to retaliate against Tokyo but knew that his air force was incompetent. The American Consul General in Shanghai reported:

> American aviators with experience in handling long distance transport planes and heavy bombers have ... been offered $25,000 to fly over Tokyo at a safe height whence bombs could be released by Chinese accompanying them. There are no Chinese aviators capable of flying such planes over Japan, but foreign airmen may be ... recruited for that purpose.[28]

Gauss added that recent air raids over Shanghai were probably conducted not by Chinese aviators but by foreign pilots. He cited as proof of this that the body of a Russian flyer was found in a plane that had been shot down over the Japanese-occupied area of Shanghai.

Chiang's air force was a reflection of his regime. There was no shortage of exceptional candidates for the flying corps, nor was their equipment so inferior that they could not have given a good account of themselves, but, according to the *New York Times*, their leadership, like the army and the government itself, was "almost fatally handicapped by corruption, nepotism and favoritism." Money that should have gone into training and modernization was funneled into private hands. In an effort to stanch the hemorrhaging of funds, Madame Chiang Kai-shek assumed the position of Secretary General of Aviation, but she was no more able to eliminate the ills of the air force than her husband was of the venal regime over which he presided. In late October, her car was attacked on the road from Nanking. After artillery opened up, Japanese planes strafed the vehicle. Her driver accelerated to avoid being hit but struck a pothole, overturning the car and throwing Madame Chiang into a mud puddle. She suffered a broken rib and a displaced ligament and was knocked unconscious, resulting in headaches that plagued her for the next five years.[29]

Although its air force was ineffective, stubborn Chinese resistance on the ground in Shanghai continued into October. After nearly two months of fighting, the Japanese had failed to dislodge Chiang's forces from the city, and the longer the Chinese held out, the more Japan's military reputation fell. The results were brutal. For the first time, the Japanese used poison gas. Meanwhile, foreign military observers in Shanghai concluded that none of the major powers, particularly the United States, had anything to fear from Japan's armed forces. The *New York Times* reported one of them as saying, "The old bugaboo about Japan being a menace to the Western world, especially to the United States, definitely has been exploded." In the same article, an aviation expert sneered, "A hundred good American bombers and fifty pursuit planes could annihilate the Japanese air force in the Shanghai and Nanking area within a week."

However, another observer said that the Japanese had simply underestimated the strength of their opponent and that the Chinese troops now fighting were "totally different from the rabble Japan had met in previous encounters." The Japanese navy also came in for criticism, in particular for "poor naval gunnery," even though it had 700 naval guns ranging in size from three to eight inches. All of those guns, along with artillery and aerial bombardment, had done little more than push the Chinese back from their shore positions to interior lines of defense.

Six weeks of combat in Shanghai, however, did not lead to an accurate understanding of Japan's military prowess. The Western observers who underestimated the Japanese can be compared to the "experts" who gave the Soviet army a poor rating following its initial reverses at the hands of the much smaller Finnish foe in the "Winter War" of 1939–1940. When Hitler planned his invasion of Russian in 1941, he dismissed the Red Army as a hollow host, citing its early defeats by the Finns while ignoring the fact that the Soviet generals had ultimately breached the Mannerheim Line and forced Finland to surrender. The biased contempt of Westerners, particularly Americans, for Japanese military capability was reinforced by the newspaper reports from Shanghai. World War II would shatter these illusions.

For a people accustomed to victory, the slow progress of Matsui's soldiers was puzzling. The Japanese acknowledged the stubbornness of the Chinese, but the home front was told that the Shanghai area presented unusual problems. Chinese disciplinary units with revolvers supposedly stood behind the front lines, threatening to shoot those who wavered. Moreover, Japanese forces were at a disadvantage because the topography favored the Chinese. The *Japan Times and Mail* reported in October 1937 that:

> There are no mountains or even hills in any of the fighting area. Outside of the settlements the country stretches into miles of rice paddies and Kaoliang fields with here and there a cluster of low buildings, denoting a small village. Because the country is only two or three feet above sea level, even in light rains some parts of the land [are] inundated. A vast network of creeks in width and depth from five to ten or twelve meters or more winds [its] way through the rural districts.... It is usually bordering these creeks that the sandbag[s] and barbed wire ... are placed, several feet inland, to protect the dugouts and trenches of the enemy.

The same correspondent credited the Chinese with constructing a clever system of underground machine gun nests using the mounds of Chinese graves:

> Many of these mounds are so high and so naturally formed, covered with the verdant vegetation of their environs, that strangers to the country often ... think that they are nature's peculiar whim in forming the topography of China. However, the Japanese soon discovered that many of these innocent looking resting places of the dead had become desecrated by the Chinese military when strategically located.

However difficult the situation was outside Shanghai, it was much worse within the city. The Chapei district held out despite repeated attacks. Employing tanks to protect waves of infantry, the Japanese sought to penetrate Chinese positions but were blocked by barriers of railroad tracks torn up and formed into pronged traps. Old China hands watched from crowded rooftops in the International Settlement as landmarks in what had been Shanghai's most popular entertainment district were pounded into rubble. The Chinese hunkered down in the Pantheon Theater, clinging to it tenaciously after bitter hand-to-hand fighting. The cabarets, bars and music halls along Jukong Road, once crowded with foreign soldiers and sailors, were gutted.[30] Losses on both sides were heavy, and an outbreak of cholera added to the woes of the civilian population. There seemed to be no end to the horrors that would be inflicted on Shanghai.

In Tokyo, Baron Harada fretted over the growing demands of the war. The reserves, he said, were worried about their families and finances. The Chinese army was stronger than expected, filled with young men who attacked with a "fatalistic spirit." Harada commented on a letter found in the pocket of a fallen Chinese soldier. It was from the young man's mother, exhorting him not to come back alive. In his diary, as reported in the *Japan Times and Mail* in October 1937, Harada vented his disgust with the Japanese army leadership:

> There seems to be a strong inculcation of [Chinese] patriotism towards the mother country and anti-Japanese spirit. In Shanghai and North China, army surveys are highly incompatible, and ... since the outbreak of the Shanghai incident [in 1932], it was discovered that great defensive works had been constructed in these five years. ... The Army was completely ignorant of this ... because the expeditionary army was occupied [so] entirely with politics and diplomacy that they forgot their main duties.

Winthrop Scott, the American Consul in Kobe, was an astute observer, keeping a close eye on troop deployments and Japanese reaction to the escalation of the conflict. During the first week of August there had been little evidence of military movements in Kobe, but with the opening of hostilities in Shanghai and Japan's decision to send reinforcements, this changed rapidly. On August 10, Scott reported to Ambassador Grew that:

> Since last Sunday evening there has been ... an embarkation of troops from Kobe on a relatively important scale, ... chiefly soldiers from the.... Hanshin district, including a ... large number of soldiers from Himeji. ... [The] indication of the locality has been taken from the soldiers' uniforms so that the place of origin cannot be ascertained directly. The best estimates [are] that ... between 20,000 and 30,000 [infantry and cavalry] have left Kobe. The actual movement of the troops is being carried out very quietly, and although the streets are ... well-filled with soldiers, the "banzais" which were so vociferous a week before are conspicuously absent.
>
> Owing to the fact that under the present system now in vogue in the Japanese army by which the old and the young recruits are mixed in the same units, it is difficult to gauge what class of reserves are being called out. ... [T]he troops withdrawn from local garrison duty are being replaced by very young soldiers. There is no indication ... [of] the destination of the various units, nor is there any announcement as to the various classes called out.
>
> The general psychological reaction in [Kobe] to the North China incident must be reported with extreme caution. Now that his country's prestige and honor are engaged, the average businessman, who so frankly and openly gave vent to criticism of previous government policies, literally "won't talk." Perhaps the attitude in commercial circles might best be summarized by saying that it is one of loyalty but definite unenthusiasm for the newest developments.

Scott went on to say that the move to a war footing was causing great apprehension among business groups, and while there was no thought of pressuring the government to make peace, there was deep worry about the country's financial future.

> The attitude of the humbler classes seems also to be one of restrained patriotism. I have been amazed by the admirable self-restraint of these people. They apparently fully concur in the government's position and stoically accept what fate may be in store for them. There is no very vociferous anti-Chinese spirit in evidence. This of course may develop later.[31]

Three days later, however, Scott wrote Grew that Chinese merchants in Kobe were experiencing a Japanese boycott, and the Chinese Consul had met with them to encourage them to return to China. The feeling toward other foreigners was mixed. Even though the Japanese expected the United States to sympathize with China, they did not think the situation would affect relations with America. This was not the case with Great Britain. Scott argued that this was due to the "typically unfriendly and overbearing position taken by British nationals residing here." He also said that the Russians were viewed "with suspicion and dislike." But what continued to impress Scott was the absence of any great war fever in Kobe. "The school children and patriotic societies are marshaled forth to see the troops leave, but all proceeds solemnly and decorously with little show of enthusiasm."

The unexpected developments in China which had forced the nation into war meant that the conflict could no longer be conducted piecemeal. That at least was the view of the Army General Staff and was shared by Prince Konoe. As Prime Minister, Konoe resented his exclusion from decision-making in the prosecution of the war, particularly the separation of the supreme command from affairs of state. Therefore, the Imperial Headquarters was cloned from one that had first been organized during the Russo-Japanese War. The decision to set it up was initially recommended by a small group within the Army General Staff, but the Emperor formally requested it in early September 1937. Hirohito wanted to bring deliberations and staff planning into the palace. He felt that this would add weight to any decisions, although it did not substantially alter the management of the war.

Of course, the Emperor was commander-in-chief of the armed forces, and overall strategy had to be run past him by Prince Kanin, Chief of the Army General Staff. The General Staff operations office was just 300 yards from the palace wall, which meant that there was a constant flow of aides-de-camp between the two, because the Emperor had to sign all orders for divisional movements. However, Hirohito had to be left out of tactical deliberations, because if he rejected a particular order, some subordinate would lose face and be forced to resign.[32] Creating the Imperial Headquarters would bring the Emperor into the planning process. Not until November 20, two months later, did it become a reality. Even then, it accomplished little to enhance operational effectiveness. One critic called it "a mere change of name of the existing command headquarters to accommodate the wartime system." Another said it was "an organization more concerned with name than with actual accomplishment, one that became a means of propaganda to enhance the war consciousness in people's minds."[33]

Meanwhile, General Matsui continued the struggle in his own theater. In October he issued a statement which was later published in the *New York Times*, saying that he was determined to "scourge the Chinese government and Army" and "eradicate at any cost China's anti–Japan policy." That cost was proving enormous. Matsui had boasted that he could capture Shanghai and defeat the Chinese in three weeks. It had now been almost two months, and the two nations were still locked in heavy fighting along Woosung Creek. This is where Chinese troops first resorted to the use of poison gas. The Japanese authorities voiced outrage and said that it was a violation of humane conduct, ignoring the fact that they had done the same thing to the Chinese. The Chinese protested that they had discharged only non-toxic smoke shells, but British investigators found traces of phosgene.[34]

As the two sides slugged it out, Tachang, some six miles north of Shanghai, became the focus of the battle. The town was a key defensive position for the Chinese in Chapei and Kiangwan. On the morning of October 24, the Japanese began their long-threatened "big push." Much of their success was due to a stroke of luck comparable to the capture of Robert E. Lee's orders dividing his army before the Battle of Antietam in 1862. Four days prior to the Chinese drive, general orders for their offensive were found on the bodies of several of their high-ranking officers. With this information in hand, the Japanese withdrew, luring the Chinese into a deadly trap and then slaughtering them with a torrent of artillery and machine-gun fire. The Japanese then launched their own offensive and pushed into Tachang. Three days later the Chinese, who had held out in Chapei for two months, abandoned their stronghold. They had sworn that if they were driven out they would "leave only masses of blackened ruins" to the Japanese invaders. They kept their oath, setting off a hundred incendiary bombs and turning the once densely populated district into a sea of flames. The Rising Sun flag that was raised over the North Station, the terminus of the railroad to Nanking, fluttered over a funeral pyre.

Japanese forces simultaneously seized Kiangwan, trapping the remaining Chinese defenders. A Japanese Army spokesman gloated to the *New York Times*, "We have closed the outlet of our great net and now we must lift it and count the fishes." The catch, however, was disappointing. The most disciplined Chinese troops had escaped. A regiment of the veteran Chinese 88th Division remained in Chapei to cover their retreat. Heroically dubbed the "Lost Battalion," a sobriquet which had been given to an American unit during World War I, the embattled Chinese vowed to fight to the last man. But after they had lost 200 men, Chiang ordered them to surrender to the British in the International Settlement. Internment may have been less noble, but for the survivors it was certainly preferable.

The fall of Chapei was an occasion for celebration by Japanese civilians who had been confined by the fighting. New flags were raised over Japanese-owned buildings in Hongkew and Yangtzepoo, and fancy kites were flown. Within the International Settlement hundreds of Japanese raced their cars back and forth over the Garden Bridge and along the Bund. In Tokyo, the victory was hailed by a march of 10,000 elementary, middle, and high school pupils. The children waved Rising Sun flags on their march from the various parks and shrines in the city to the plaza in front of the Imperial Palace. Two nights later, 20,000 students and members of the Women's National Defense Association, along with a flag procession of 700 geishas led by a specially trained band of their youngest associates, joined an evening parade from the Palace to the War and Navy Offices. With bands playing and shouts of "Banzai!" resounding through the night, they filed past War Minister Sugiyama, who smiled and saluted them from the veranda of his office.[35]

For the Chinese, it was a harsh defeat. Japanese planes bombed their retreating troops continuously, and although Chinese aircraft made nuisance raids on Shanghai, they could not provide protection for the ground forces. Chiang tried to minimize his losses, declaring that the reverses suffered in Shanghai and North China were not a "determining factor for the remainder of this war," and claimed that his troops had not had time to erect adequate defenses. This was hardly true in Shanghai, where the Chinese had been preparing positions for nearly five years. He told the New York Times, "The nation's real defenses are to the west," and added mendaciously:

> [W]e were forbidden by the Shanghai 1932 agreement from military occupation of the preparation of defenses in Shanghai. But since we were forced to resist Japan to protect ourselves, we did the best possible. This was exemplified by the magnificent resistance of our soldiers in Chapei.

The Generalissimo also blamed his defeat on the failure of the United States and Great Britain to uphold the Nine Power Treaty. In fact the signatories, with the exception of Japan, had agreed to meet in Brussels to address China's complaints, but the result of that meeting was predictable. No convocation of the Western signatories would deter them from their non-interventionist positions. Chiang could not have been so naive as to fail to foresee this outcome, but at the end of October, with his fronts cracking in Shanghai and North China, he pled desperately for help from the West:

> Japan must be stopped in her aggression and imperialism before it is too late. It is also the duty of the United States and England to protect the freedom of the seas, not permitting a Japanese blockade of the China coast, which is detrimental to the trade of these countries.
> American business in China is going to the dogs because the United States government permits Japan to maintain an illegal blockade of the China coast, violating international law. The British and American fleets should exercise their customary duty of keeping commerce free on the entire Pacific.[36]

The only concern that the British and American Asiatic Fleets had at the moment was the safety of their own nationals. The Japanese in the meantime tightened their blockade on South China by seizing the island of Quemoy, opposite the port of Amoy, giving the invaders virtually total control over the city.

The only relief that Chiang received during the early phase of the China Incident was from the Soviet Union. A non-aggression pact had been signed on August 29, under which China and Russia pledged not to support an attacker of either country. Although some aid was forthcoming from Moscow, there was more symbolism than substance in this agreement. To the militants in Tokyo, however, the pact confirmed their suspicion that Communism was tightening its hold on China. They became determined to resolve the China Incident on their own terms. The Nationalist Government must either be forced to its knees or be replaced by a subservient regime.

In Shanghai, Chiang's battered troops dug in on the south bank of Soochow Creek, hoping to establish a line that would contain the Japanese. Both sides brought up reinforcements, facing each other along a five mile stretch from Soochow Creek on the north to the Whangpoo River on the south. The impending battlefield included an area comprising some of the finest residences and private clubs, and the western parts of the French Concession and the International Settlement were also threatened. These prospects exacerbated the alarm of Westerners who still resided in the city, where only a short time before it had seemed that no pleasure could not be gratified, nor any fortune denied. Now, skyscrapers under construction along the Bund stood uncompleted. Traffic trickled along once-busy Nanking Road and Bubbling Well Road. A few cinemas reopened, offering comedies to lift their patrons' spirits, but only Walt Disney's fantasies evoked any real laughter. Hollywood's colorful, lighthearted musicals were such a contrast to their own miseries that audiences found them depressing. Symphony concerts resumed but were sparsely attended, as were the once-popular boxing matches between U.S. Marines, British soldiers, and sailors from various naval ships in the harbor. Those who sought solace in alcohol found the gaiety in the cabarets and bars to be forced.[37] There seemed to be an unspoken recognition of the end of an era. Viewed from the river, the Bund with its Western architecture dominating the skyline still seemed impregnable, a monument to imperial success, but in reality it was a Potemkin village which most of the residents had left, a fragile facade that provided little comfort and less security to those who remained behind it.

Matsui's soldiers, their confidence heightened by their recent victory, found Soochow Creek a minor obstacle. Using junks and sampans, they easily crossed it and established footholds on the south bank. The heavy fighting and the loss of Tachang, Kiangwan and Chapei had decimated

Chinese strength. The 18th and 87th Divisions were reduced from 10,000 to 1,000 men each, and Chinese prisoners said that the 66th Army had been virtually annihilated. Weakened by their stubborn but costly defense of Shanghai, Chiang's forces were not prepared for the blow delivered on November 5.

Late in October four and a half division, totaling 80,000 men, were assembled for embarkation at ports in North China and Japan. Sailing in two formations, "red" and "black," they landed first to the south and then to the north of Shanghai, in a well-conceived pincer movement designed to outflank their enemy. This was a portent of Japanese amphibious operations in World War II. Indeed, the planners in Taiwan had been working for three years on procedures for future landings on Luzon and Java. The commander of the strike force was General Heisuke Yanagawa, a "small, bald, and studious-looking" man. Yanagawa had met Hirohito in Paris when the Crown Prince visited there in 1921. By the 1930s, Yanagawa had risen to the position of Vice Minister of War, and in 1935 was posted to Taiwan, where he helped to develop the amphibious tactics that were now being employed. Until the China Incident, he had seemed destined for oblivion, because he had been one of the generals on the periphery of the February 26 uprising. A summons from the Emperor to oversee the largest amphibious operation in the history of the Japanese Army was a heaven-sent opportunity. Yanagawa said, "It is as if I were crossing the Styx of Hades; I can see the light ahead."

Before dawn on November 5 the "red" task force, observing radio silence, slipped into Hangchow Bay about 40 miles south of Shanghai. Fog shrouded the waterfront of the walled town of Chinshanwei on the north shore. As Yanagawa contemplated the canals lacing the lowlands of the Yangtze River delta, he captured his thoughts in poetry:

> The mist of morning/has still not evaporated./I wait out ninety minutes/ that seem interminable./By the Emperor's/inexorable mandate,/the road I take/is like today's scenery/washed entirely by tears.[38]

Yanagawa came ashore with the first wave of his troops, scrambling down the net into an assault boat along with the lowest ranks. The Chinese had not anticipated the assault, so there was negligible opposition, Even so, Yanagawa was not above using a bit of psychological warfare. Three and a half divisions were landed, but the next day, with the wind blowing onshore, he launched hundreds of balloons with streamers attached reading, "A million Japanese soldiers have landed at Hangchow Bay." The propaganda ploy was unnecessary. The Chinese 109th Division, which had been rushed back to meet this new threat, was overwhelmed by Yanagawa's 6th Division, which spearheaded the drive to Shanghai. Within three days the Japanese had reached Sungchiang, less than twenty miles from their goal. At the same time that Yanagawa's forces began their advance, the Japanese who had crossed Soochow Creek hit the Chinese Center Wing Corps, driving it back. Chiang's army was on the brink of destruction. Still hoping that he could hold back Yanagawa's forces, Chiang dispatched three divisions and a brigade to Sungchiang, but there was no fight left in them. The 11th Reserve Division, which moved south along the Soochow-Hangchow Railway, failed to give battle, and after suffering a few casualties the other two divisions retreated.[39] In the absence of any support, the entire right flank and rear of the Chinese army in Shanghai was in jeopardy. Ever since the Japanese had landed at Hangchow Bay, Chiang had been issuing a spate of frantic and often contradictory orders to his field commanders. On November 8, with disaster looming, he gave the one order that he could be sure would be understood and obeyed: retreat.

As they withdrew, the Chinese in the area near the western border of the International Settlement set fire to the large Japanese-owned Toyoda cotton mills, along with other factories and homes belonging to foreigners. From mid-August to November 12, the fighting in Shanghai destroyed 2,900 of the factories there and cut the east-west railway lines. This was scorched earth with a vengeance. The pullout was accelerated by Japanese aircraft, which harried the retreating Chinese with relentless bombing and strafing. Discipline broke down as commanders deserted their units. The sick and wounded were left behind, most of them to die at the hands of the enemy. Abandoned weapons and equipment of every kind, the refuse of a defeated army, strewed the roads and fields. At night, units unable to tell friend from foe panicked and fired on each other.

Except for the foreign enclaves, Shanghai was now an occupied city. Tens of thousands of terrified Chinese tried to push their way into the safety of the foreign-controlled areas. Hallett Abend noted that each bridge leading into the French Concession was guarded by tanks, a few French soldiers, and "many French ... and Chinese policemen employed by the ... Concession." He told the *New York Times*:

> The approaches to the bridges were guarded by movable barbed wire emplacements. Occasionally a handful of panic-stricken refugees was permitted to enter, those holding passes or market gardeners bringing needed fruits and vegetables. Otherwise old and young and mothers carrying infants were ruthlessly clubbed or beaten back with long bamboo poles when they attempted to attain safety.
>
> Some wept, some knelt begging while the pressure on those behind tore away their clothes and upset the pitiful bundles and baskets containing the few possessions with which they had fled. The background of these scenes was a vast cloud of smoke from the fires set by the retreating Chinese soldiers. Occasionally lurid tongues of flame leaped hundreds of feet high. The pitiful mobs of helpless noncombatants had waited until too late, blindly trusting to the strength of the defense forces.

Stragglers from Chiang's abandoned defenders discarded their uniforms and donned civilian clothes, knowing what their fate would be if they were captured. Others, still armed, tried to force their way past the guards, but French tanks and soldiers barred them. Chiang now rested his hopes on a defensive line of pillboxes across the Yangtze delta west of Shanghai that had been planned by his German advisers. They thought that if he could assemble his demoralized troops for a stand along these fortifications, those troops might still resist. What neither Chiang nor his advisers foresaw was that the Japanese could leapfrog his position and land their forces behind it. On November 12, the Japanese 16th Division, the "black" amphibious formation, landed on the upper reaches of the Yangtze River at Paimou Inlet behind the Chinese lines. Commanding the Division was Lieutenant General Kesago Nakajima, who had recently supervised the *Kempeitai*, the secret police, in Tokyo following the February 26 revolt. Nakajima had a dubious reputation among his peers and was known as a "hard man of sadistic personality."[40] This was the man who would preside over the Rape of Nanking and bring shame on himself and his command.

The Japanese offensive had three prongs: Nakajima in the north, Matsui in the center, and Yanagawa in the south, all pushing the Chinese steadily westward. The terrain was broken by a maze of lakes and canals, but these did not hinder the invaders. Not only had the Japanese brought motorized sampans with them, but scores of owners of Chinese junks and sampans, waving homemade Japanese flags, offered their craft for sale or hire. The capture of Soochow, 50 miles west of Shanghai, presented an even sorrier spectacle. The Japanese called it "the most tragicomic exploit in the history of modern warfare." Two Japanese scouting parties, totaling fifteen men, followed a large body of retreating Chinese troops through the gates of Soochow under cover of night. While the Chinese stacked their arms, the Japanese marched to the administration building and at dawn hoisted the Rising Sun flag. When the sleeping Chinese awoke and saw the Japanese flag flying, they fled the city in panic. Not a shot was fired, and the small band of Japanese soldiers remained in control of Soochow until the main body of their comrades joined them a few hours later. There were reports of the Chinese using "supervisory divisions" (disciplinary troops), which were placed behind the lines to shoot soldiers who wavered, and in a number of instances Chinese soldiers were found chained to machine guns and field artillery pieces.[41] These desperate measures did little to stiffen resistance.

Although the Japanese were known to treat prisoners harshly if they took them at all, they did try to induce the Chinese to surrender. In the Shanghai sector they dropped propaganda leaflets over Chinese positions with a photograph of a Chinese prisoner enjoying a meal in a detention camp. They also persuaded a 17-year-old Chinese girl to exhort her countrymen to give up. Using a microphone with loudspeakers, she described the kind treatment that Chinese soldiers could expect from their captors.[42] These techniques, later to be familiar to soldiers in the Second World War, met with mixed results. A Chinese soldier who believed his situation to be hopeless might take the bait, but any who actually surrendered usually suffered a far different fate from the one promised.

Although the Japanese advance on Nanking now seemed unstoppable, the General Staff in Tokyo announced periodically that the invasion would not proceed beyond certain prearranged lines. However, the field forces pushed on toward their goal. In *Japan's Imperial Conspiracy*, David Bergamini has charged the late Emperor himself with the responsibility for the continued advance of the Japanese army west of Shanghai. He argues that Hirohito, far from trying to restrain the campaign in China, actually encouraged it and issued secret orders to the field commanders to press on. The existence of such orders was revealed by a group of retired generals in 1964.

At the time, an impression was carefully created for foreign observers that the men at the front were out of hand and could not be controlled. The truth was that they had never been more scrupulously obedient, for they knew that a Grand Imperial Headquarters was being established in the palace and that their deeds would be watched by the sacred Emperor in person. The first stop line was drawn across the Yangtze delta on November 7. When all divisions had arrived at it on November 24, it was dissolved by the Emperor's order. The General Staff drew a second line on the same day fifty miles farther west. Hirohito dissolved it unofficially three days later and officially seven days later.

Bergamini says that General Tada, the Vice Chief of the General Staff, opposed an attack on Nanking because he knew that a campaign of terror was planned for the city and thought it would be detrimental to the army's morale. However, Tada could do little more than delay the execution of the Emperor's will and the orders went out. Hirohito's culpability notwithstanding, the success of Japan's field armies in North China, coupled with the victory at Shanghai, had whetted the appetite of his commanders and their men to achieve the total defeat of Chiang's army and capture his capital.

On November 24, the Nationalist government announced that it was moving the seat of government to Chungking, over 1,000 miles to the west. From this remote region of central China, Chiang would be able to conserve his power and preserve his legitimacy. He would make distance and time his allies. The Japanese might harass him from afar, but they would not follow him into the hinterlands. Chiang also knew that he had the sympathy if not the active support of the West, and he counted on the latter to be eventually forthcoming. Patience was a Chinese virtue; having been imprudent in Shanghai, Chiang would await the Japanese-American conflict he believed was inevitable. He had not wanted to give up Nanking, but he was already taking the long view for his cause. He would not exhaust his resources in a fight with Japan. Finally, he had to prepare to settle accounts with his Communist rivals in Yenan. The West would eventually defeat the Japanese and expel them from China. When that happened, Chiang was determined to be strong enough to defeat Mao's peasant armies and bring all of China under his dominion.

For Shanghai the long night of military occupation now began. Confident of their power, the Japanese military authorities swept aside the cautious respect for the foreign enclaves that they had been careful to observe during the fight for the city. On the day that the Nationalists announced the removal of the capital to Chungking, the Japanese presented a series of demands designed to control the activities of the Chinese living in the International Settlement and the French Concession to the authorities there. These would extinguish all vestiges of Kuomintang authority and bring the Chinese firmly under Japanese control. Anti-Japanese propaganda would be suppressed; all national and municipal Chinese administrative institutions would be dissolved; Chinese censorship in all forms would be prohibited; and telegraphic privileges would be denied to the Chinese.

The Japanese claimed that they had the right to take these actions since China had never relinquished sovereignty over the area. They said that, if the Settlement was still part of China, having conquered the region, they were justified in taking whatever measures were necessary to secure their interests.[43] The Settlement authorities yielded, intimidated by the overwhelming military power surrounding them. The American and British governments were not disposed to interfere, although in a speech to the House of Commons on November 23, British Foreign Secretary Anthony Eden argued that the status of the International Settlement was governed by regulations that could not be changed without the consent of the Chinese government. Hardly anyone paid any attention to him. General Matsui's presence was a lot more imposing, and Settlement officials began to comply with the Japanese demands. The Chinese Central News Agency was shut down, along with several virulently anti–Japanese newspapers. All Chinese censorship agencies in the Settlement were abolished and on November 27, the Japanese authorities announced that they were taking over all postal, telegraphic and wireless offices in the city.

In the Hongkew area, where the Japanese had maintained a garrison before the outbreak of fighting in Shanghai, an English language bulletin was published, setting forth new regulations for foreign residents, including:

> Foreigners returning to districts north of the Creek are specifically requested to respect the sentry on duty at the Garden Bridge and at street corners by giving a gentle bow and wishing him a good morning. Foreigners must realize that the Japanese soldier is only doing his duty and represents the *Emperor of Japan*. Special passes will be given to those having Japanese friends and it is hoped that everyone wishing to live in Hongkew will make friends with the Japanese.
>
> Japanese ladies, 150 from Tokyo High School, well versed in English, are moving to Shanghai for the sole purpose of being better acquainted with foreigners. Further details regarding interviews, etc., with these ladies will be furnished at the Japanese Club in the Office of the Secretary to the Commander of the Naval Fleet in Shanghai.
>
> Foodstuffs will be sold at 23¼ percent discount. Sake will be free of charge to those who drink to the health of the *Emperor* and a quantity not exceeding two litres can be taken each day.
>
> In the event of foreigners wishing to employ Japanese maid servants they are requested to make application to the Garrison Commander at the Japanese Club as soon as possible as there are a limited number of Nei Sans. Bachelors need not apply. All single men will be supplied with mates as soon as facts are known. Married men applying for Nei Sans will have to obtain the consent of their wives.
>
> Foreigners who employ Nei Sans will be entitled to one bath a week in any of the undermentioned houses in Hongkew free of charge. Foreign ladies can apply for Japanese male masseurs. Bath houses are situated at: 27D Range Road, 293 Boone Road, 120A Woosung Road
>
> BY ORDER OF THE GARRISON COMMANDER OF THE JAPANESE EXPEDITIONARY FORCES IN CHINA.[44]

Westerners must have viewed these rules with mixed feelings. Bowing to a Japanese sentry would be humiliating, but it was probably seen as a small price to pay for two free liters of sake every day and the 150 "Japanese ladies ... well versed in English," to say nothing of the weekly free bath that came with the Japanese maid.

Nor were criminal elements overlooked. Throughout the fighting Shanghai's opium rings had continued to thrive, their leaders as well as the gangsters who controlled prostitution hiding out in the refuges of the International Settlement and the French Concession. However, their days were now numbered. The Japanese already controlled the lucrative opium market in North China; taking over the trade in Shanghai meant that they could get much-needed revenue to finance their war in the south. Moreover, the underworld leaders, members of the notorious Green Society, had been allies of Chiang Kai-shek ever since they had helped him smash the Communists in Shanghai in 1927. If the Japanese could not drive them out, they could at least force them to share their profits.

VI. The China Incident

The China Incident had now lasted for over four months. The Japanese army in the north had made impressive gains, while the forces in the south were poised for what promised to be a successful drive on Nanking. But the cost had been high. The procession of white boxes containing the ashes of fallen soldiers had become a familiar sight on railway platforms in Tokyo and other Japanese cities. Thousands more bore the scars of war wounds. Except for Nazi Germany and fascist Italy, Japan was increasingly alienated from the world community. Nevertheless, the nation held to its path in China. The military hierarchy might have a few doubters, but the leadership was determined to hang on. The people, obedient and loyal to the traditions of sacrifice and stoicism, gave their husbands and sons to the Emperor's service. They hoped for peace, but they would not turn aside from the struggle.

VII

The Home Front

> Every day and night the cries of "banzai" are heard here and there. At busy street corners young wives with their children on their backs, white-haired old women and lovely girls are asking people to help them prepare sennin-bari (one-thousand stitch vests). I too, like all other women, am offering a helping hand with pleasure. As I sew with a needle and red thread, I pray for the safety of His Majesty the Emperor and for the safety of our country.
> —Miota Otaka, Member, Young Women's Association, Suginami-Ward (Tokyo)[1]

Army officials claimed that the military action in China aroused as much popular enthusiasm as that shown during the war with Russia a generation earlier. But as Hugh Byas had previously reported to the *New York Times*, "it was an organized and inspired enthusiasm," peculiarly Japanese. The nation saw itself as one great family and behaved as one, thinking and acting en masse. When a soldier went to war, he was given a stirring send-off, often accompanied by a festive parade. By the end of August, as more and more reservists were brought to active duty, these scenes became commonplace. Byas described one:

> The central figure in the lengthy procession was a bashful young man in a blue suit and wearing a scarlet sash, showing that he had been called. He was escorted by 200 women wearing the insignia of the Great Japan's Women's Patriotic Association in khaki and many members of the Reservists' Association, the local fire brigade, a group of local elders and a brass band. The procession marched with the prospective hero to a local temple, then to the station.

If the citizen-soldier worked in an office, his departure was always accompanied by a demonstration of support from his coworkers. Furnished with trucks by their employer, they would career through the streets, shouting and waving flags. The novelty of these spectacles soon wore off, however, and passersby began to ignore them. Only following a great victory, as at Shanghai and later with the fall of Nanking, were there orchestrated celebrations that inspired genuine public enthusiasm, mainly because they seemed to promise victory and peace. The deep misgivings that Winthrop Scott sensed in Kobe were confirmed by Byas and others, but publicly the people rallied in support, each member of the greater Japanese family a loyal and reliable sibling.

The army took advantage of this nationalism by portraying itself as a paternal figure to families whose sons were called to service. A few weeks before a conscript was summoned for training, a "letter of instruction" was sent to his family by the military authorities. This may seem strange to Westerners, but it illustrates not only the concept of kinship intrinsic to the Japanese national character but the army's shrewdness in playing upon it.

> Greetings to the Father and Elder Brother
>
> We have learned that your son and brother will shortly experience the greatest joy and satisfaction possible to one of our nation by joining soon our second company. We congratulate you.
>
> When your son and brother enters the barracks, the officers of the company will take your place in looking after his welfare. We will be to him as a stern father and a loving mother. We will always be concerned with is two-fold training, body and mind, so that in belonging to the Army he may become a good soldier and a loyal subject of the Emperor. We want to be able to teach him in such a way that he may be able to realize the highest hope of a member of our race [i.e., to die for the Emperor].
>
> With the company and your home forming a complete circle, we wish to cooperate with you to the fullest extent in order to administer his education and guidance along the most rational lines.
>
> In order to do this, we wish to learn as much as possible from you with reference to his personal history and character and the environment of his home. The information will be kept in confidence. If you have any misgivings, fear it will be difficult to learn your son's exact condition after his enlistment, or that he will not be able to advance in rank, or any other misunderstandings, rest assured we will be glad to discuss the matter with you. That our efforts to guide the young man will not be hindered, we beg you to fill out the enclosed form with the greatest care and return it to us as soon as possible.
>
> The regiment, however, is not concerned entirely with the past life of your son, but in guiding his development—wishing unselfishly to emphasize his good points and strengthen his weak points—to develop all his powers to the end that he may become a good and faithful soldier, maintaining a first-class record in the Army, and put his whole heart into fulfilling the mission of the Imperial Army.
>
> On the day your son enters the barracks, we trust that you will accompany him in order that we may meet you and have an intimate talk with you.
>
> Respectfully yours,
(Commanding Officer)
Imperial Japanese Army[2]

American draftees in World War III joked about the terse postcards they received with "Greetings" on them, saying that a "committee of friends and neighbors" had selected them for induction. A letter like the one above would have made them laugh out loud. It read more like a letter from a summer camp counselor than one of preparation for military service, but to the close-knit Japanese it expressed the qualities of kinship that they cherished.

In the years leading up to World War II, army service was the expected postscript to the adolescence of Japanese males. Some three and a half million boys—some as young as twelve—volunteered for five years of military instruction conducted by Youth Training Schools, wearing uniforms and drilling on their school grounds with standard military rifles. In the autumn, those lads who had participated in the program were sent on maneuvers, an experience unknown to American high schoolers. Over three days, as many as 10,000 Japanese boys would divide into armies and engage in mock battles over a seven- to ten-mile front, under the rattle of rifle fire, the drone of aircraft flying overhead, and the rumble of armored cars, including night attacks.

For a peasant who had lived in a thatched hut and whose day had been one of heavy labor, bearing buckets of fetid night soil to fertilize the fields, barracks life must have seemed a relief. Already toughened by the hardships of rural life, he could easily endure the rugged training imposed on Japanese Army recruits. And since he came from humble circumstances, he wasn't about to complain about his pay. Privates earned between ¥5.50 and ¥6.40 per month, or about $1.25–$1.47 in the rate of exchange at the time. Even a Japanese general received only ¥550 a month—about $126.50. The death benefit paid to the family of a private killed in the line of duty was ¥1200, equivalent to $276. The army virtuously proclaimed, "the Japanese soldier must hold a toothpick between his teeth when his stomach is empty." In other words, he should pretend that he had just eaten. One officer wrote, "We look upon service in the Imperial Army as an honor, with no thought of commensurate financial return.... [Small salaries are regarded] as an honorarium in acknowledgment of high service to the nation."[3]

The Japanese having been raised from childhood on a diet that did little to foster growth, it is not surprising that they were referred to in China as the "dwarf people." The average height of the 1936 class of recruits was 5'3" and the average weight, 117 pounds.[4] There were, of course, some tall Japanese, and the Imperial Marines recruited them for their size, but they were exceptional and not easily outfitted. In November 1937, Ikuo Skeda, a big private in the Japanese Army, lost his shoes in the fighting at Shanghai. The quartermaster was at his wits' end to find a replacement pair for him, since he wore a size 12. An American, Gordon Warner of Los Angeles, a former captain of the University of California swimming team, came to the rescue. Warner was coaching water polo at Meiji University in Tokyo at the time, and since he also wore a size 12 shoe, he donated a pair to Skeda, along with six pairs of socks.[5]

The Japanese soldier's motto was, "Whether I float as a corpse under the waters or sink beneath the grasses of the mountainside, I willingly die for the Emperor." This was no idle pledge, as any of Japan's adversaries would confirm. In the wars of the twentieth century, no other soldiers showed a greater willingness to sacrifice their lives. In writing about the experiences of the Second World War, Fleet Admiral Chester Nimitz said that every aspect of the conflict with Japan had been anticipated in the war games at the Naval War College except the use of *kamikazes*, the aviators who willingly gave up their lives by dive-bombing American warships in an effort to kill their enemies. The conduct of the war in China should have warned the United States that *kamikaze* tactics were not an aberration but a confirmation of the Japanese value of self-sacrifice. One of the most popular monuments in Japan was a memorial to three privates from the Kurume Engineering Corps who had carried bombs into a Chinese position in Shanghai to destroy a barbed-wire barricade which had prevented Japanese troops from advancing. In giving up their lives they became national heroes.

The self-mutilation of sympathizers with the Young Officers who were tried for assassination has been noted. The war in China prompted a new spate of bloodshed and even suicide. The mayor of Kobe received a letter written in blood from a young Japanese maidservant seeking aid in her efforts to be allowed to go to the front:

> Every day I hear all sorts of stories of the bravery of the Japanese soldiers and sailors at the front, either through the radio or the newspapers, and I cannot bear to remain idle at home any longer. Propelled by the irresistible "Yamato Damashi" [Japanese spirit], I am determined to go to the front in order that I may act as a nurse for the wounded heroes of the Empire.[6]

The *Japan Weekly Chronicle* also reported that on October 13, 1937, a 16-year-old boy had jumped in front of a train and killed himself, leaving a suicide note saying that he had done so to encourage his elder brother at the front.

Stories of heroic death on the battlefield or in the skies filled the newspapers. Death-bed scenes were recounted in melodramatic detail. According to a story on September 6, 1937, in the *Japan Times and Mail*, a Japanese officer named Horigane, who was fatally wounded in a Chinese bombing attack, "could not move his hands freely because of the wound, but wrote the words 'Tenno-heika-banzai' (Banzai for his Majesty the Emperor) with the tips of his fingers. Having written these words he quietly passed away." The same article reported the death of a Captain Kasahara on the Shanghai front who was mortally wounded while leading a landing party, saying that his heroic sacrifice would "furnish war history for the world":

> He was smeared with blood. He had to repress his anger for he was taken to a hospital in the evening of [August] 24th. But it was too late; the doctor's operation was of no use. He stared at the battlefield from the blood-stained bed, and all of a sudden he began to sing the national song. When he reached the word "chi" of "kimiga-yoowa ... chi" he breathed his last. The doctors and nurses who were present solemnly prayed for the soul of the dead soldier.

Mothers were expected to show equal fortitude. The *Japan Times and Mail* story quoted a letter of gratitude to the Navy Bureau of Personnel from a woman who declared that it was an honor for her son to sacrifice himself "to die a glorious death for the defense of the Fatherland." She concluded by saying:

> I have three more sons whom I love dearly; I am educating and encouraging them so that they might one day offer their humble service to the State. I respectfully ask the authorities concerned to set their minds at ease for Tatsuo's character was such that even at the last moment he would not forget to preserve the honor of the Imperial Navy.

The army also utilized its own presses to turn out propaganda in support of the war. Pamphlets included such titles as "Our National Preparation in the Face of Crisis," "China's Mistaken Policy Towards Japan and the Powers' Activities in China," "The Principles of National Defense and the Strategy of Economic War," "The International Situation of the Changing Period and Our Japan," and "How to Prepare for Long-Term Hostilities." The last included subtitles such as "Support Behind the Guns" and "Think Always of the Soldiers at the Front." Army booklets and pamphlets of this kind were nothing new. Indeed, "The Principles of National Defense" was first published in 1934. Inspired by General Araki, it had proposed that the Japanese economy be reorganized for military purposes. It opened by saying, "War is the father of creation and the mother of culture. The testing of one's ability against hardship is the motive and stimulus for the development of life and the creation of culture both in individuals and competing nations."[7]

Japan's Foreign Office justified the war in terms similar to those propounded in the Nazi doctrine of "Lebensraum." Nothing was more unfair than for an honest and industrious nation to be denied existence. Although Japan's population had doubled in fifty years, her efforts to seek places for development outside the home islands had been impeded. America had prevented Japanese emigration, an act that was "against the natural laws of mankind."

> There is a struggle between the "haves" and the "have-nots" in the world, and there are growing outcries against unfairness in the distribution of resources and materials If this unfairness is not rectified and if the "haves" refuse to concede their vested rights to the "have-nots," the only ... solution must be recourse to arms.[8]

VII. The Home Front

While these arguments were made in the international arena, they were primarily for home consumption. The Japanese military was sensitive to the army's reputation for brutality and tried unsuccessfully to counter it. The most infamous photograph from the conflict in Shanghai had been of a terrified screaming infant, almost the only human being left alive after the bombing and shelling of the South Station. This picture did more to turn Americans and the West against Japan than any other photograph taken during the China Incident. It was shot by H.S. ("Newsreel") Wong, a cameraman for the Hearst press. All of the Hearst newspapers, with a readership of 25 million, printed it; so did 35 non–Hearst papers serving another 1.75 million. It was also seen in theaters by 25 million moviegoers in a "News of the Day" reel, and Movietone News bought it and ran it as well. Together, both organizations showed it to some 30 million viewers overseas. The total estimated audience for this single scene from the Shanghai South Station was 136 million.[9]

The Japanese press did its best to overcome the military's negative image. Japanese atrocities in China were real enough, but Wong's photograph had been staged, and the Japanese could prove it. In its October 18 issue, the *Japan Times and Mail* featured three pictures. At the top was the familiar one of the crying baby alone on a station platform. Immediately below it were two more shots, one showing a relief worker placing the child beside the tracks and another of him with the waif in his arms. The editor accurately observed, "These photographs show how, through clever posing, war pictures can be made to win the sympathy of people abroad by misrepresenting the truth."

Although Japan did its best to give the lie to pictures and stories of atrocities, another photograph, which was widely circulated in the Western press, had incited even more revulsion than the one of the baby at the Shanghai railroad station. It depicted a Japanese soldier using a Chinese prisoner for bayonet practice. Lieutenant Tan Takahashi of the General Staff was in New York when the picture appeared in the newspapers there. Outraged, he told American reporters that it had been faked by the Chinese. He said that, while it was true that the soldier with the bayonet was wearing a Japanese uniform, Japanese soldiers did not use their bayonets in the way shown in the photo, and that Chinese agents were disseminating anti–Japanese propaganda.[10] Meanwhile, Viscount Hidemaro Konoe, younger brother of the Prime Minister, warned that Japan was losing the propaganda war in America. Returning from a visit to the United States, he declared that the problem was "far worse than Japan thinks." He noted the prominent treatment that news stories from the Chinese side were receiving compared to the scant attention paid to Japanese dispatches from the China front. The same was true of newsreels. "It is quite useless to invite a couple of pro-Japanese Americans to a tea party at the Japanese Embassy and there discuss the China affair." The only solution, he said, was to disseminate moving pictures for propaganda purposes as China was doing.[11]

Viscount Konoe's observation prompted an editorial in *The Japan Times and Mail*, saying that it was doubtful that Japan's image in the West was due to propaganda. The editors said that the fact was, neither the people in the United States nor those in England had any desire to give Japan a hearing:

> They have convinced themselves that we are wrong, and they do not want to hear anything to the contrary. Here is an instance, for the absolute truth of which we can vouch. A certain foreigner in Japan who contributes to the English press has been told definitely by one editor that he wants nothing from him except what is "absolutely condemnatory of Japan."

The editors went on to say that the English and American public had already made up their minds and would believe nothing was true about Japan unless it was bad. Anger, bitterness and scorn followed.

> What is the cause of that? Is it bad propaganda? Our past propaganda may have failed to create the same sympathetic atmosphere for us that the Chinese have managed to get. Certainly the idea of China that the people in the West appear to entertain is an utterly fantastic one. They seem to know nothing about the hundreds of thousands of bandits, of the scores of warlords, of the treaty-breaking politicians, who have created a misery for the Chinese people and a problem for the rest of the world, especially for Japan, her nearest neighbor. On the contrary, they seem to believe that China is a weak little suffering country of saints and martyrs, where every prospect and every characteristic pleases, and only the Japanese are vile.
>
> In this respect, we must admit that our wily neighbors have us completely beaten. But it is no use crying over spilt milk. We have to face facts, and the chief fact is this. Not even the cunning Chinese propaganda would have been so sweepingly successful unless the ground had been thoroughly well predisposed to receive it. As we have said, the British and American public have made up their minds already; and the reason is—it is no use blinking facts—that both Britain and America are themselves opposed to Japan in this issue. They are not interested in China, but in their own investments and prestige in the Far East.[12]

The editors were venting their own frustration in ascribing American attitudes to purely commercial interests or influence in the Orient. In fact, a majority—55 percent—of Americans polled in September 1937 said that they would rather not take sides between China and Japan. Of the rest, 43 percent favored China and 2 percent, Japan. A month later, 59 percent expressed sympathy for China, 1 percent favored Japan, and the rest had no preference. This change was undoubtedly the result of the attack on Shanghai, and the American press, which had given the war extensive coverage, had swayed public opinion. However, Americans were not willing to make any personal sacrifices for the Chinese; 63 percent said that their opinions were not strong enough to keep them from buying goods made in Japan.[13]

Those Japanese editors should have taken heart from the last statistic. They were right that America had an economic stake in Asia, but it was based on profitable trade with Japan, not with China. In 1936, Japan ranked just behind Canada and Great Britain in trade with the United States. Half of all American exports to Asia went to Japan, an amount equal to that shipped to the entire South American continent.[14] The United States received 22 percent of Japan's total exports and supplied 32 percent of her imports.[15] By contrast, American trade with China was negligible. In 1936 the total value of U.S. exports to the latter country was $46.8 million, or about 1.05 percent of all exports. Imports from China were also insignificant.[16] Although in October 1937, American investments amounted to $125 million in China and $60 million in Japan, the foreign dollar bonds sold by each in the U.S. were far different—$7 million from China and $360 million from Japan.[17] As one writer stated, the American stake in China was "an investment equal to a few urban blocks of real estate, and annual trade the fiftieth part of a New Deal budget—this is the aggregate result of a hundred years of American enterprise in the Chinese market."[18] The arguments of the Japanese editors were mistaken.

Nevertheless, it is true that most Americans felt a deep affection for the Chinese. Extensive missionary efforts in China had created strong emotional ties. Chinese laborers had built the western stretch of the trans-continental railroad after the Civil War. Chinese-Americans were a popular minority and not perceived as a threat, whereas Japanese migration to California had been a source of friction and led to the ill-conceived exclusion legislation passed by Congress in 1924. American foreign policy in China continued to rest upon the Open Door, proclaimed in 1899–1900 and subsequently reaffirmed in the Nine Power Treaty of 1922. Japan had violated that agreement, and its attack on China in 1937 was seen as evidence of unbridled aggression. The atrocity stories that were spread by the American media, whether accurate or not, stamped Japan as a brutal bully. Finally, while the photograph of the bayoneted Chinese soldier might have been questionable, there were too many eyewitnesses to the events in Nanking to dismiss the horrors inflicted by the Japanese. But those stories never appeared in the Japanese press, and to his own people, the Japanese soldier was brave and noble.

A Japanese refugee sent a letter about the behavior of Japanese troops in Shanghai to the *Japan Times and Mail*. She said that she had seen them on duty at their headquarters as well as at play on festival occasions and in the parks while enjoying leave. She said they were sometimes "a little noisy and merry but never menacing." She contrasted the care exerted by Japanese pilots in bombing only military targets with Chinese who had committed "acts of hate and revenge against non-combatants."

> There is not one case of Chinese being insulted or killed in Japan. ... Japanese in China have been massacred in cold blood, civilians brutally murdered by reviling, hating, cruel mobs, ships bearing refugees to safety, ... hospital boats flying the Red Cross flag have been continuously and flagrantly fired upon.

For direct propagandizing, the army sent officers to give lectures. No group was overlooked: multiple patriotic organizations, factory workers, schoolchildren, university students, priests, and peasants. Japanese women were a particularly strong source of support for mass allegiance. They were divided into two principal groups: the Patriotic Women's Society, comprising some three million members of the aristocracy and upper classes; and the Women's Society for National Defense, with nearly six and a half million members drawn from the poorer segment of the population. Army officials visited villages, towns and cities, seeking out influential women to organize local clubs. One major persuaded six thousand Tokyo waitresses to get together and pledge a portion of their tips.[19] In myriad personal ways, from stitching the charmed belts worn by soldiers in the field to preparing "comfort bags" of candy, cigarettes and toiletries for their fighting men, Japanese women united in support of the war.

The nation's sudden plunge into war affected all aspects of life. The mobilization of so many men obliged some shops and small businesses to close because their owners had been called up. Storefronts that were locked and shuttered with a Rising Sun flag pinned to the door told the story: the proprietor was in uniform. For those left behind, shortages were more painful signs of a nation at war. Raw cotton and cotton cloth disappeared from the domestic market and chemists in the Department of Agriculture turned to tanning rat skins in an effort to find a substitute for leather. Household items like frying pans became impossible to find; iron was a defense commodity. The Home Ministry issued a notice to factory workers that "twelve hours should be the maximum" workday, but two hours of overtime were permissible "if unavoidable."[20] Far from being "unavoidable," a fourteen hour day soon became routine.

War also adversely affected the Tokyo Stock Exchange. By August 24, prices had fallen between 10 and 30 percent. Spinning companies with mills in China were hardest hit, but a slide in heavy industry stocks also occurred, even though those companies stood to profit from arms and munitions production. Business leaders were well aware of their vulnerability. They knew that the government would have to issue numerous bonds to pay for the war, that lending institutions would be forced to purchase most of those bonds, and that there would be government controls on the private sector. These concerns became a reality when a special session of the Diet convened on September 3 to consider an additional budget of $737 million, of which $592 million was earmarked for the campaign in China. Lending emphasis to the gravity of the situation was the presence of the Emperor, who wore the uniform of a field marshal when addressing the Diet. In his remarks, Hirohito departed from the generalities in which his speeches were usually couched and blamed China directly for the conflict. In succession, Konoe, Hirota, Sugiyama and Yonai followed the Emperor to the podium, reviewing the events that had transpired since the clash on July 7 and professing their desire for peace but stating that Japan was prepared for protracted hostilities. Each man developed his case from the perspective of his cabinet responsibilities: Konoe as Prime Minister; Hirota, foreign policy; Sugiyama, the army; and Yonai, the navy. Sugiyama summarized for all of them:

> The incident has thus developed to a state of an all-front clash and it is difficult to tell how it will develop in the future. But the Army, in accordance with the Imperial will, is determined to punish the Chinese to the bitter end and eradicate their anti-Japanism completely, even if it becomes necessary to wage prolonged warfare. Until the Chinese lose their will to fight Japan, the Army will never cease fighting them. I wish that all of you will cooperate with the Army to lead it to victory and to tide the nation over the national crisis.[21]

The Diet maintained its record of never rejecting a budget proposal and approved the requested amount. Bonds were issued and the nation hunkered down for a long-term fight. No sacrifice was too small to make. According to articles in the *Japan Weekly Chronicle*, 3,000 professors and students at Osaka Imperial University donated money they would otherwise have spent on New Year postcards to the national defense fund, while 56,000 convicts in Japan's prisons sent over ¥46,000 to the army and navy to pay for two airplanes, raising the money by working overtime and giving up their monthly holidays. The *Japan Times and Mail* reported that to conserve salt, the owners of restaurants and geisha houses decided to abolish the tradition custom of *mori-shio*, the practice of placing tiny mounds of salt at their entrances each day to bring good luck. Since there were 7,000 such establishments in Tokyo alone, an enormous amount of salt had been wasted. Abolishing the custom, it was said, would result in annual savings of ¥100,000. Even Japanese living abroad participated in these efforts. The Japanese Residents' Association in Argentina had solicited contributions from its members to pay for a warplane for the Japanese Army, and also prepared 700 comfort bags, which were shipped back on an O.S.K. liner leaving Buenos Aires.

The mobilization of so many divisions created another shortage, albeit a largely ceremonial one. In the Samurai tradition, no Japanese officer felt completely equipped without a sword. Not only were swords in short supply, but many of the new ones were defective. They were brittle and often broke in freezing weather. In North China, where temperatures began to drop in early fall, the new swords snapped at the slightest pressure. To produce new, durable swords, Dr. Kusaka of the Central Laboratory of the South Manchurian Railway Company announced that he was making swords of pure steel, although skeptics questioned whether these could match the ones turned out by the ancient master sword makers whose blades had endured for centuries.[22]

Japan's first air raid drill since the start of the China Incident was held in Tokyo on September 15. It was an extraordinary undertaking, mobilizing 350,000 members of the capital air defense corps and 1,300,000 men and women of "home anti-fire groups." Mock raids were conducted in the afternoon and evening, and all citizens were told to abide by the air defense regulations. Army spokesmen warned that while the Chinese Air Force had been dealt a severe blow, it had by no means been eliminated, particularly since the Chinese were trying by every possible means to reinforce it.[23]

Sobering exercises of this kind put a damper on Japanese night life. The early 1930s had been a peak time for entertainment in Tokyo, Osaka and other large cities. Tokyo's famed Ginza district had been ablaze with lights from cabarets, dance halls, restaurants and bars where hundreds of hostesses waited to charm and divert guests, while the back streets harbored a profusion of cafes, bars, and the summit of all pleasures, the geisha houses.[24] Now, in late October 1937, the *Japan Weekly Chronicle* said that Osaka authorities were reporting that the war in China had adversely affected cafes, tea-houses and theaters, although they added that brothels in Osaka had experienced an upturn in business. The nine "licensed quarters" reported an increase of 177,393 "visitors"—an extraordinary number under any circumstances. The timeline of these statistics was not revealed, but it would seem the employees in these "quarters" had caught the national spirit and were working more than fourteen hours a day. The numbers suggested that war, far from dulling libido, was in fact an aphrodisiac.

As the war progressed, chauvinism intensified. Prizes were offered for new martial songs: *Gunka*, as they were called. A columnist for the *Japan Times and Mail* wrote, "There must be necessary sentiments and excitement, and particularly racial sentiments." Music from the Russo-Japanese War was revived, the words ringing out once more, "Our soldiers of all the world the most brave ... now leave the land that bore and bred them; never to return except as victors." The war brought out Japan's latent xenophobia. Patriotic groups urged their countrymen not to read "intellectual magazines" that might contain "dangerous thoughts" but instead to spend their time on Japanese poetry about patriotic subjects. Perhaps the silliest effort was the attempt to erase English phrases from the language. Baseball players were encouraged not to shout "Play ball!" or "Home run!" but to substitute Japanese words.[25] Of course, that was no more ridiculous than the American term "liberty steak" in place of "hamburger" during World War I (or more recently, "freedom fries" instead of "French fries").

One popular example of home front support was the "comfort bag," which included a variety of items thought to be a practical expression of appreciation for the Japanese soldier's service. A typical such bag contained:

> Comedy sketches 10 sen; popular songs 10 sen; dried plum candy 20 sen; cup-and-ball game 10 sen; shogi chess 20 sen; fan 10 sen; doll 10 sen; notebook 20 sen; set of soap, ear cleaner, razor 20 sen; loin cloth 20 sen; tissue paper 25 sen; stationery 25 sen; needle and thread 30 sen; fava beans, mashed and dried sea bream 60 yen. Total: 2 yen, 90 sen.[26]

Whether deservedly or not, Japan had a reputation in the West as a nation of borrowers, having no indigenous culture of its own but having derived it from the Chinese. In the Meiji era, the Japanese had indeed been forced to adopt Western forms and technology, and nowhere were they more imitative than in the evolution of their armed forces. The Japanese knew that America scoffed at their lack of invention and made jokes about their inability to build anything without Western plans or guidance. But scorn and humor of this kind aroused intense resentment and fueled national pride. Japan had compiled a record of achievement in three generations that was unparalleled by any other nation in modern times. It had emerged from feudalism to become a thriving economic entity and international competitor. Along the way, the Japanese had defeated a major European power in war and, alone among Asian nations, avoided the subjugation of Western colonialists. They were particularly galled by Western prejudices while they were trying to defend the military actions they were carrying out in China, all the more because it seemed to them that the West's bias was based on false premises. As Japan's xenophobia deepened, it seemed to need to denigrate China, in whose shadow Japan had so long existed. An angry editorial in the December 8, 1937, *Japan Times and Mail* was even more heated than the earlier one on American and British attitudes:

> Nothing is farther from the mark ... than to persist in regarding China as still the abode of culture, and still the wise and learned schoolmaster of youthful, barbaric, undeveloped Japan.
> The exact opposite is the case. For centuries China has been culturally dead. She has neglected her own monuments and her own culture. If one wishes to see the best of whatever culture China ever had, he must come to Japan. Japan, thanks to her strong indigenous culture, has taken and employed Chinese culture and brought out

all that was best in it. It is Japan who is today the schoolmaster, and China, the pupil. Has no one ever told our critics in the West that those Chinese who wish to acquaint themselves with the best Chinese culture actually flock to the Japanese universities and Japanese scholars to find it? Thanks to the strength of our own national spirit, and the genius of our culture, we have become the best interpreters of what was best worth interpreting from ancient China.

So, it is with regard to Western culture. It is China that has played the sedulous ape to the West and has in consequence picked up from the West only that which was least worth having, its mechanism and materialism and commercialism. That is why China is in such tragic plight today. On the one hand, there is the vast majority of that vast population, a poverty-stricken, ignorant mass of suffering human beings, laboring under the burden of centuries. On the other hand is an arrogant minority, flaunting a few of the most blatant plumes of the modern West, taking a mechanical, superficial and materialistic view of life, and thinking themselves capable of supplying the deep spiritual and bodily needs of the suffering millions with their smart, shabby modernity.

Whereas by contrast, Japan has been saved from that fate by her strong national spirit. She, like China, has received Western culture and Western influences, but she has chosen the best of what the West has to offer, and has assimilated it to her own needs. Frankly and readily does Japan admit her debt both to ancient China and to the modern West. But because she has employed what she has borrowed on developing her own modern culture, she is now in the position of creditor both to China and the Western world.

Casting China in an unfavorable light was not a sudden propaganda move. For years the Japanese people had been indoctrinated by government-prepared textbooks on history and geography that portrayed China as a backward and unenlightened country. Considering that as late as 1935, fewer than 18 percent of all Japanese had gone beyond the first six years of compulsory education, it is easy to see why the vast majority had so little respect for their mainland neighbor.

Like the *Times and Mail* editors, textbook authors acknowledged a debt to China in Japan's early history but saw contemporary China as a nation sunk in its own past, a barrier to progress in the entire region. The 1910 textbooks said that Japan should reach out and help the Chinese people. The "help" was a thinly disguised policy of exploitation; China was to be developed as a market for Japanese goods. The Japanese, like many Americans, saw China as representing immense trading opportunities. When these did not materialize, the Chinese government was accused of being uncooperative.

Japan's expansionism was euphemistically referred to as "preserving the peace of East Asia," and China's unwillingness to go along was denounced as "insincere" and "obstructionist." The textbooks that appeared after World War I could be read as a primer for the Mukden Incident. They stressed the importance of Manchuria to Japan's economy. They cited

VII. The Home Front

Japan's investments and its role in railroad construction and other developments, as well as Manchuria's suitability for the settlement of Japan's excess population. By the time new textbooks came out after 1931, Manchuria was a Japanese protectorate, and Japanese schoolchildren got an even heavier dose of jingoism. Now the creation of a Japanese empire was spoken of as a necessity, not only to assure the nation's self-sufficiency but to preserve peace in the Orient and throughout the world. Young readers were assured that this goal would benefit all of Japan's neighbors, who would prosper as their economies were integrated with that of Japan. Finally, Japan would assume the role of policeman for the region, keeping the peace—which really meant keeping out the West.

This proprietary role was justified based on Japan's equality with the United States and Great Britain. Once, according to the textbooks' authors, these nations had been Japan's tutors, but now Japan was strong and independent. Moreover, Japan was the "oldest country in the world" and had never suffered the humiliation of occupation. The nation was great "because of the purity of spirit of the Japanese people, the brilliance of the Meiji emperor, her uniqueness, and the new claim that it was a 'god country.'"

But it was China that received most of the authors' attention. With 50,000 loyal subjects of the Emperor already living in China, seeking to develop industry and trade, it was clear that young Japanese now had an obligation to go there as well, to exploit China's natural resources, provide it with an adequate food supply and merge its economy with that of the home islands. The salient point of this benevolent mercantilism was that "China was secondary to Japan's needs." All this was couched in the same terms that Western powers had used to justify their own imperial designs on alien peoples. From Africa to Asia, foreign flags had been planted among new subjects who did not know what was best for themselves and needed the benefit of rule by others more progressive. The Chinese, according to Japan's textbook authors, "should not be criticized too severely, since over the centuries [they] were only concerned with themselves and their immediate environment."[27]

The militarists had long hidden their designs behind the figure of the Emperor. In insisting on his divinity, they excluded the tenets of Christianity. Mission schools were required to change Christian education so as not to conflict with the myth of the Emperor's divinity. No depiction of Christ, even in stained-glass windows, could be above the portrait of the Emperor in any chapel.[28] A story in Tokyo's diplomatic circles told of two Christian missionaries walking down the capital's street when one of them asked the other, "If you saw Jesus Christ and the Emperor coming down the street at this moment, which one would you bow to first?" The other replied, "The

Emperor. I'm sure Jesus would understand."[29] The number of Christians in Japan, of course, was a small percentage of the population, and there was never any question of their patriotism, but Christianity was still an alien religion and not fully trusted. There were hardly any Jews, but anti–Semitism was a tool to be used if it served the Army's purpose. A *Japan Weekly Chronicle* correspondent in China reported in October 1937 that Jardine, Matheson and Company were "the biggest arms merchants in China financed by Jewish capital," and "either through their propaganda organs or by bribing the leaders of anti–Japanese organizations, these merchants did their best to stimulate Chinese sentiment against Japan." The correspondent went on to raise the old specter of Jewish control of the banking and financial systems in China and elsewhere, claiming that British capitalists of Jewish extraction were "eager to help the Nanking government in order to safeguard the enormous investments which they have in China." Jewish influence on the Shanghai Municipal Council was said to be "supreme" because both the chairman, Mr. Arnold, and his predecessor, Stirling Fessenden, were "of Jewish descent." The French Concession was also said to be under the control of Jews helping China to resist.

Veneration of the Emperor reinforced the seams of the national fabric. Imperial rescripts inspired respect and obedience; there was one for every occasion. On major holidays, school principals throughout the country read the Education Rescript. Even though there were no classes, pupils attended the ceremony and listened with their heads bowed. Army recruits were expected to memorize the entire text of the Emperor's Imperial Rescript on the duties of soldiers. Children and soldiers were flogged if they failed to transcribe the characters properly or recite the words smoothly. A young officer who stumbled in his recitation to his troops went to his quarters, wrote an apology to his parents for his lapse and then committed suicide. Even a photograph of the Emperor was entitled to respect. Every pupil had a special place to store a copy, and students and teachers were expected to bow to it when passing. For every Japanese, the Emperor was the source of religious, moral and political authority.[30]

Hirohito did not regard himself as divine. By all accounts, he was modest and unassuming, and resented the deification of his person that the militarists encouraged. The "mystery of the monarchy" seemed to find expression in the Imperial Castle itself that, like the Emperor, was not what it appeared to be. An ordinary citizen or tourist saw only the massive stone walls sloping up from the great moat that surrounded the grounds. Inside, there was no majestic palace but rather a series of temple-like one-story buildings clustered together, sharing a terrace or courtyard and connected by broad corridors. Hugh Byas described the Emperor's quarters and his daily regimen:

VII. The Home Front

Within this private village is a dwelling in no way different from the other buildings. A porte-cochere under which cars and carriages draw up shelters its entrance. It looks out on a simple garden; no fountains, no statues, only undulating greensward and a few flowering bushes. In this structure the Emperor and Empress live.

The rooms are Japanese, comfortably but plainly modified to suit modern tastes. The roofs are coffered, the floors carpeted; an occasional dwarf pine or gold screen relieves its austerity. The living room is a comfortable square room, not very large, with a fine ceiling and a floor of hardwood covered by carpet. A few pictures—personal favorites, not show pieces—hang on the walls.

In summer the Emperor rises at six, in winter at seven. Having no taste for luxurious personal service, he shaves himself. He worships his ancestors in the customary manner, closing his eyes, clasping his hands, and bowing to a miniature shrine that has been constructed in the private apartments. At the same time a chamberlain visits the three official shrines in the Palace compound and formally worships the ancestors on behalf of the Emperor. Breakfast is in "foreign style," this mild luxury being advised by physicians who say that the Japanese diet needs vitamin reinforcement by at least one foreign meal daily. It is simple enough—fruit, cereal, coffee, toast, and in peacetime, bacon and eggs. The Empress usually joins him, and the little princesses may come in before setting out for the Peeresses' School. Then the Emperor glances through the Tokyo newspapers which are laid out on his study table. They are not clipped. He questions his secretary about any item that attracts his attention. Before the China war he used to go to his office in the next room at ten o'clock; now he goes in at nine. He sits at his desk, receiving officials, reading documents and commenting on them, transacting the business of an Emperor, till half past twelve, when he takes an hour off for lunch. In peaceful days he used to spend another hour in the private grounds, playing golf one day, riding another, or walking in the garden. Now he goes right back to his office and stays there until half past six.

A tight khaki field-service uniform is the Emperor's daily wear, generals and admirals his most frequent visitors.[31]

Hirohito's avocation was marine biology, an area in which he acquired considerable expertise over the years. A laboratory was built on the Palace grounds, and whenever he could, the Emperor escaped to it for his experiments. After World War II ended, he was able to indulge in his hobby and often went to his summer residence at Hayama on Tokyo Bay to look for specimens.

Byas' account of the Emperor's daily routine suggests a dutiful, conscientious monarch, simple in his habits but subservient to a government controlled by the military. But was he really a passive instrument, a ruler surrounded by advisers he could no longer trust to keep him accurately informed? Or was he a willing collaborator who encouraged the military to settle the China question by force? Of course, he ruled by divine right. The Japanese constitution was clear on this. Byas quoted the opening paragraph of the Emperor Meiji's Imperial Precept to the Soldiers and Sailors:

> The forces of Our Empire are in all ages under the command of the Emperor.... The supreme command of Our forces is in Our hands, and although we may entrust

subordinate authority, We Ourself shall hold and never delegate to any subject. It is Our will that this principle be carefully handed down to posterity and that the Emperor always retain the supreme civil and military power.

It was for good reason that Prime Minister Konoe had said that only the Emperor could "restrain both the Government and the Supreme Command." The problem was that the Emperor's advisers were either too timid or too unwilling to prod him to make a decision, and Hirohito was someone who needed to be pushed.

Hirohito's devotion to marine biology prompted criticism from reactionary extremists who thought he spent too much time in his laboratory and not enough on affairs of state. Even Marquis Kido, who had been secretary to the Lord Keeper of the Privy Seal and therefore a Palace intimate, told Baron Harada, "[T]he Emperor possesses all the excessive characteristics of a scientist, and hence has no sympathy for the thinking of right wingers and the like. It is distressing that His Majesty is so extremely orthodox."

Hirohito was distressed by these criticisms and soon avoided Palace sentries who might see him going to his lab, for fear they would report that he was not giving enough time to national policy matters. But he wouldn't give up his hobby entirely, and arranged for Professor Hattori, his former biology tutor, to sneak into the Palace in the evenings so that the two of them could study specimens under a microscope without being observed. The grumbling of right wingers was undeserved. What else was the Emperor to do? Far from initiating policy or events, he, like the civilian ministers who served him, was faced with military actions after the fact. On occasion, he did speak up. The record shows that he took his advisers to task for deceiving him about the murder of Marshal Chang Tso-lin in 1928 and also for keeping him in the dark about the Manchurian conquest in 1931. The Emperor's rare direct role in the suppression of the 1936 uprising was further proof of his anti-extremist convictions.

Nevertheless, the final responsibility for what happened in China and the subsequent war in the Pacific rests with him. Not until summer 1945, when the war was irretrievably lost, did the Emperor intervene directly and demand an end to it. Perhaps the most damning verdict can be found in the words of a Japanese friend of this author. When Hirohito died in 1989, I wrote to express my sympathy and recall the Emperor's role in bringing the war to a conclusion, thereby sparing the lives of tens of thousands of Americans and Japanese alike. My friend thanked me perfunctorily, but went on to say that, while it was true that the Emperor had actively sought to secure peace when it was clear that Japan's population was about to be decimated, he had failed to use his powers to prevent the conflict in the first place, capitulating to the militarists and making a mockery of the name that he had chosen for his reign: *Showa*, "Enlightened Peace."

VIII

North China and the Failure of Mediation

> Every indication points to the conclusion that Nanking has considered North China as lost since the outbreak of hostilities. The Central Government has sent only a few of its good troops north, and has held most of its artillery, and all but a few of its planes, south of the Yellow River, which would seem to show that Chiang Kai-shek, despite loud talk to the contrary, never had any real intention to fight for North China.[1]
> —Stilwell Situation Report, October 18, 1937

It was understandable why the world's attention focused on Shanghai when the battle for the city commenced. The significant Western presence there and Chiang's commitment to it of his best troops magnified the event. Shanghai seemed a microcosm of the horrors of modern warfare—the bombing of innocent civilians, the pitiful plight of refugees and the wholesale destruction visited upon a great urban center. Yet the Incident had begun in North China and operations there were no less important than those in the south, at least until the start of the drive on Nanking. Although in some respects the Japanese campaign in North China was more significant, Nanking was a political goal, its capture seen as essential to the dissolution of the Nationalist regime, the fulfillment of Japan's expansionist aims, and the extension of Japanese hegemony beyond Manchukuo and its environs. The Western press duly reported the movement of forces and battles in North China, but with one or two exceptions, the theater was relegated to a secondary status, even though the fighting there was more widespread and was just as intense as in Shanghai.

Colonel Joseph Stilwell, the American Military Attaché, might have had little respect for Chiang, but he positively loathed the Japanese. He found it difficult to deal with them directly and he made no effort to conceal his dislike and contempt for them in his official reports. After the skirmish at the Southwest gate of Peking on July 26, when Chinese soldiers lobbed hand grenades onto Japanese Army lorries, the Japanese Embassy ordered all of their nationals in the city into the Embassy compound. Stilwell said:

> [It] offered a rare opportunity of a glimpse at Japan's pioneers—the ronin, drug-peddlers, pimps and other scum from the Hataman hutungs mingling with the business agents, clerks, etc., of the slightly more reputable types of trade that flourish under the emblem of the Rising Sun. With the sewer rats so much in the majority, the Japanese photographers had to use considerable care in selecting their shots of their oppressed countrymen.[2]

His own prejudice notwithstanding, Stilwell was obliged to go to the Japanese when he wished to visit the front or occupied territories. This was not easy for him, and matters did not always go well. He therefore acquired a Japanese-speaking assistant from the American Embassy in Tokyo, Captain Maxwell Taylor, a future U.S. Chief of Staff. Stilwell was known to be crusty but Taylor liked him, and the two got along well. Yet even Taylor's fluency and tact could not soften Stilwell's attitude or his antipathy toward the Japanese, who sensed that Stilwell was no friend and treated him accordingly. They spurned his invitations to lunch, restricted his movements, and often left him out of tours arranged for foreign attachés. He wrote despairingly, "I guess I am washed up for this war. I am spotted as a friend of the Chinese and a moral leper." However, in spite of his isolation, he was a competent observer and submitted a series of excellent analyses of the conflict.

Stilwell was on hand as the first phase of the Japanese campaign in North China got under way. With Peking in their hands, the Japanese mounted a drive to the northwest with the object of capturing the Nankow Pass, the gateway to Chahar Province. The invaders found themselves battering at China's oldest ramparts, the Great Wall. Built two millennia earlier by the Emperor Shi Hwang-ti, who had first unified the Chinese Empire and named it "China" from his dynasty, the Chin, the Wall was constructed over fifteen years by prisoners of war, criminals and the army. Shi's successors extended it over time until it stretched for 1,500 miles across northern China. In some places it was doubled and tripled, and at Nankow there were ten walls, erected one behind the other. The eastern sections of the Wall, which were rebuilt in the sixth century, were intended to keep out the Mongols, the aggressive central Asian nomads. It failed in that respect, although the Mongols were eventually absorbed like all other intruders. Indeed, caravans between Peking and Mongolia had traversed the Nankow Pass, where an offshoot of the original wall had been built. In recent years the Wall had been breached by a rail line that connected Peking with Kalgan, the capital of Chahar, and had then been extended to Paotow in Suiyuan Province.

VIII. North China and the Failure of Mediation   201

Securing this link would make possession of North China easier for whoever held it. The Wall's builders had never imagined it as a barrier to invaders from the south, and it was no more able to stem the tide of a modern aggressor than it had held off the northern invaders, but the Chinese briefly entrenched themselves against the Japanese among its crumbling stones.

The importance of the Nankow Pass was self-evident, but as had so often been the case, the initial Japanese attack was weak, reflecting either disdain for the Chinese or simply poor planning. In this instance, it was a combination of both, aggravated by bad weather. The commander of Japan's forces was Seishiro Itagaki, Ishiwara's co-conspirator in the Mukden Incident. He had advanced in rank to become the Chief of Staff of the Kwantung Army, and was now a Lieutenant General, although he was eventually doomed to be hanged at Sugamo. The battle began on August 15, when a 3,000-man Japanese force drew fire from a Chinese regiment posted just south of the entrance to the pass. Surprised by the determination of Chinese resistance and handicapped by the rugged terrain, which favored the Chinese, the Japanese called up reinforcements. They soon had 15,000 men in place, but numbers made little difference on a narrow front. The Chinese took up positions in the surrounding hills, laying down mortar and machine gun fire on the attackers. Western observers saw huge chunks of the Great Wall blasted into the air by Japanese shells, but in the defile, artillery was of little avail. Japanese infantry scrambled along the rocky creek bed at the bottom of the pass, sheltering from enemy fire where they could. Then heavy rains fell, forcing them higher up the slopes. They suffered all of the miseries of infantry warfare: an enemy who held the high ground; an absence of natural cover; and torrential rains that robbed them of even the most basic battlefield comforts. A week after the campaign for the Nankow Pass had begun, the Japanese had penetrated only a quarter of the way along its twelve-mile length. In the meantime, Itagaki did what he should have done earlier and launched an attack on the west flank. But he failed to conceal his preparations, giving the Chinese time to dig in and contest it. Four more days of fighting ensued before the flanking forces reached the Great Wall and began to threaten the Chinese rear.

Simultaneously with the drive to capture the Nankow Pass, the Kwantung Army pushed down from the north into Chahar to take Kalgan, the provincial capital and important rail junction on the line to the west from Peking. The movement of Kwantung Army units into Chahar followed an all-too-familiar pattern. In early August, Chinese troops entered Chahar from Shansi Province and threatened the rear flank of the Japanese China Garrison Army, which was in the process of advancing on Paoting. To counter this threat, the high command ordered the China Garrison Army to clear the enemy from the region and directed the Kwantung Army

Commander, General Kenkichi Ueda, to support the campaign with reinforcements from Jehol and Inner Mongolia. While the forces to the south were driving on Nankow, the Kwantung Army made its move into Chahar. It hardly needed encouragement since it had long been in favor of striking a blow in North China and extending the frontiers of the empire to the south. Once Chinese troops had crossed into Chahar, the Kwantung Army declared that Manchukuo was in peril and asked permission from Tokyo to advance beyond the Jehol border. Although the request was denied, elements were sent forward. It was the same old story: the Kwantung Army did as it pleased and the General Staff in Tokyo, faced with a fait accompli, gave way. An Imperial ex post facto sanction was granted, and the Kwantung Army continued its campaign. Three brigades were organized into the Chahar Detachment and placed under the command of the Kwantung Army Chief of Staff, Lieutenant General Hideki Tojo. On August 27, striking south from Dolonnor in Manchukuo, they captured Kalgan. According to a report in the *Japan Times and Mail* on August 31, they got there just in time. Chinese troops had recently imprisoned 130 pro–Japanese residents and shot ten of them. The remainder were under sentence of execution, but the timely arrival of Tojo's forces saved their lives.

In danger of being caught between the Nankow hammer and the Kalgan anvil, the Chinese had no choice but to retreat and they marched off to the southwest. By August 30, the Japanese had pushed all the way to the Nankow Pass and controlled the railroad to Kalgan. Nearly two weeks passed, however, before they could run trains on it. The Chinese had derailed eight American-made locomotives inside a long tunnel under the Great Wall, destroyed several bridges, and tore up sections of the track.[3]

In his military postmortem of the campaign, Stilwell criticized both sides. He also pared the numbers that Western correspondents had often inflated in their reports of the fighting. While dispatches to American newspapers spoke of 150,000 Chinese or 100,000 Japanese troops, the actual figures were far lower. Stilwell estimated that Itagaki had no more than 20,000 men in the Nankow offensive and the Chinese probably fewer. The brunt of the defense was borne by the 89th Division, although the Japanese claimed that parts of at least four Chinese divisions had faced them. Stilwell said, "They were very hazy about the identifications, and it is believed that they magnified.... Chinese strength to glorify their own achievement." He added that if such large numbers of Chinese troops had been present, they could not have escaped the surrounding Japanese. Estimating enemy casualties has often been a test of credibility failed by belligerents, and both sides inflicted far more harm on paper than they did on the battlefield. At Nankow, the Japanese claimed that 2,000 Chinese had been killed while they

VIII. North China and the Failure of Mediation

themselves had lost only 200 dead and 400 wounded. Stilwell estimated that Japan's losses were actually several times higher.

Standing on the sidelines like a frustrated coach unable to make a winning play, Stilwell agonized over the tactical opportunities squandered by the Chinese. He noted that before the thrust from Dolonnor, they could have turned the Japanese right flank and threatened the Peking area:

> The nature of the country east and west of Nankow nullified all the Japanese advantages in materiel; the Chinese, in small groups concealed among the rocks, ... had to be dug out one by one; and the weather was bad continuously, with heavy rain nearly every day, which handicapped the [Japanese] air service. Although the hills extended east and west, and the Chinese had enough strength available to extend their lines indefinitely and oppose the Japanese everywhere with the same advantages in their favor, they confined their efforts to the narrow front on the pass, where the Japanese were able to advance only ... four or five kilometers in two weeks. But the Japanese flanking movement around the Chinese right [put] the flank well east of the Yung Ting Ho, where a high hill was held by some 600 Chinese troops, and when this point was reduced, the whole line gave way.
>
> [T]he Japanese [erred] ... in not occupying the pass before the Chinese did, in sending an inadequate force to reduce it, and [in] wasting efforts on frontal attacks before turning the flank. [Nevertheless] they preen themselves on the operation as a whole [as] a considerable military accomplishment.

As a military professional, Stilwell lamented the poor quality of the Chinese officer corps, particularly at the higher echelons where tactics and strategy were poorly understood. Again commenting on the Chinese position at Nankow, he wrote that Napoleon would have worked for weeks to get between two widely divided enemy forces in order to deal them separate blows, but all the Chinese saw was a threat on two fronts. "The sacrifice of the individual soldier is invariably wasted by the incompetence of his leaders."

Stilwell estimated the total Japanese strength in North China at 150,000 men, as of September 1. Given his own sources, as well as the steady stream of transports debarking troops at Tientsin, this number was probably accurate. However, it was difficult to identify specific units. They were known by their commander's name, not by number. In spite of this idiosyncrasy, positive identification was made of seven divisions and two others were tentatively identified. Stilwell later reported that in occupied Peking, the Chinese were feeling the effects of the war. Restaurants and places of amusement were suffering because many Chinese were unwilling to go out at night unless they had to, and they thought it was unseemly to indulge themselves during a time of national crisis. In addition, a Chinese seen spending freely could be subject to extortion by his own people as well as by the Japanese. Efforts by the Peking Chief of Police to get the owners of Chinese theaters and cinemas to open in the evenings failed. Only two of the foreign-style movie houses ran films, and their evening attendance was low. Nevertheless, the occupying army was putting its best foot forward within the city. For the most part the soldiers there were well-behaved, and the Chinese had little reason to complain about them. In the outlying villages, it was a different story. There, the Chinese were preyed upon by their own, suffering depredations by bandits and plain-clothes troops, remnants of the Chinese 29th Army who were still putting up a show of resistance against Japan. Stilwell expected that after the crops were harvested, the Japanese would take measures to stamp out these elements and other irregular forces that still opposed the occupation.

The key to possession of North China was control of the railroads. There were three lines, with roads parallel to them, that ran south from Tientsin, Peking and Kalgan. On the south side of the Yellow River there was an east-west line, the Lunghai Railway, which ran from Lanchow in Kansu Province to the port of Lienyunkiang on the coast. Within the rail grid that encompassed North China there were two shorter east-west lines connecting the north-south railways, one from Tsinan to Tsingtao and another from Taiyuan, an industrial center southwest of Peking, that linked the city with Kalgan and Peking. Heavy rains fell in the summer of 1937, flooding much of the region and making overland troop movements difficult and in some places impossible. The railroads were not only a strategic prize but also vital to tactical deployment. Most of the fighting during that autumn was at junctions along these rail routes.

While Chiang Kai-shek threw his best divisions into Shanghai, he could hardly be charged with writing off North China as Stilwell had alleged. In fact, Chiang personally assumed command of what was designated as the 1st War Area. He had a large force of 20 divisions, plus one cavalry and three infantry brigades at his disposal. These troops were assembled along the corridor of the Peking-Hankow Railway from the Yung Ting River south of Peking through Paoting to Shihkiachuang, a distance of 130 miles. In early September, more Chinese forces were brought in to defend Shansi Province. Unfortunately, although their numbers looked impressive on paper, they were in reality poorly equipped and ill-trained. They outnumbered the Japanese two to one, but those odds were meaningless. They had little confidence that they could defeat the invaders, and the warlord generals who commanded Chiang's armies had hardly any experience in modern warfare. Yet Chiang was obligated for the service of their soldiers to retain them. Only when their incompetence could no longer be tolerated were they removed, and then they were usually kicked upstairs to meaningless positions where they could do no harm. Not all were useless: some generals, like Wei Li-huang of the 14th Army Group and Shang Chen of the 20th Army Group, were able combat leaders. These men were well born and, more importantly, well educated. If they had a failing, it was their excessive caution, "a characteristic usually more suited to philosophers than to forceful military commanders."[4]

Between August 31 and November 12, 1937, while Japanese forces were breaking out of Shanghai and forcing the Chinese retreat to Nanking, a new North China Army was formed, with General Hisaichi Terauchi as its commander. It was divided into two corps. The First, led by Lieutenant General Kiyoshi Kazuki, advanced along the Peking-Hankow Railway, and the Second, commanded by Lieutenant General Toshizo Nishio, moved along the Tientsin-Pukow Line. Divided into eight divisions, the two armies totaled 100,000 men. Their first major objective was Paoting, the capital of Hopei Province, By September 11, Machang, the advance base of the Chinese right wing in North China, had fallen to the Japanese. Located on the Tientsin-Pukow rail line 35 miles south of Tientsin, it controlled the only direct route from North China to Nanking. The loss of Machang followed a vigorous Japanese assault combining infantry, artillery and air units. The capture of two positions on which their defense had been anchored forced the Chinese to withdraw. As they did so, the Japanese sloshed through waist-deep water in a night attack and turned the Chinese retreat into a rout. By morning, the Rising Sun flag was flying over Machang Castle, which had served the defenders as a barracks. Streaming southward, the Chinese columns abandoned part of their equipment when Japanese planes strafed them. The aircraft also dropped leaflets urging the Chinese to surrender. Few did so, and not many were taken prisoner.[5]

Weather presented almost as many challenges for the invaders. Western correspondents who followed in the wake of the Japanese advance said they had to be transported by railway freight cars, motorboats, a junk, and an ammunition barge before they could walk into Machang. Exploring the area between the city and the nearby Grand Canal, Douglas Robertson, reporting for the *New York Times*, said that it was easy to see why the Japanese were having difficulties in maintaining communications and transporting men and supplies over North China's dirt roads. Late rains had turned them into rivers of mud, in some places more than a foot deep. But the Japanese pushed on.

Japanese forces advanced on other fronts in North China, south and west of Peking. Cavalry, tanks and infantry penetrated Shansi Province, threatening Taiyuan, the capital. After capturing Kwan, 30 miles south of Peking, the invaders swept westward to take Chochow on the Peking-Hankow Railway, blocking the rail line north of Paoting to the main Chinese base 85 miles southwest of Peking. In this operation, some 60,000 Japanese faced off against 100,000 Chinese, but the defenders, outgunned and ill-led, were unable to stem the tide. The commander of the Chinese divisions, General Wan Fulin, had been one of the chief Chinese warlords in Manchuria when the Japanese had conquered the province in 1931. He had fought them off and on for six years, but now, as then, he found himself retreating. The summer rains which had stalled the Japanese offensive ended and as autumn neared, the days turned clear and cool, drying out the land and making troop movements easier. The weak defense of North China became hopeless. The air war in particular intensified as Japanese bombers took to the skies in increasing numbers, striking targets far behind the front lines. However, the gains of war did not come without a price. Although casualties were heavier for the Chinese, the Japanese also suffered losses. Correspondents saw three freight trains arriving in Fengtai on September 16, packed with more than 1,000 wounded. Temporary hospitals had been hastily erected, demonstrating the failure of military planners to foresee the problems of a long campaign.[6]

Boastful press announcements of great victories were made to justify the human cost. General Terauchi spoke of another Battle of Tannenberg in Hopei Province, an envelopment comparable to the magnitude of Germany's destruction of a large Russian force in 1914. Nothing of the sort had occurred, but neither had the Chinese succeeded in stopping the relentless Japanese drive to the south and west. North China was slowly but inexorably being wrested away. If Hopei was to be saved, the Chinese had to hold on to Paoting, the provincial capital 50 miles southwest of Chochow on the vital Peking-Hankow Railway. An old walled city of 200,000, Paoting's reputation rested not on its imperial past but on the presence of the Hopei Medical College and the Hopei Agricultural Institute. Both institutions enjoyed special distinction, especially the latter, which had developed modern agricultural methods for China. By September, the Japanese were within two miles of the city. The Chinese had erected a barrier of concrete forts and now dug in to await the attack.

For one man the advance into North China must have been a personal triumph. Kenji Doihara, whose unsuccessful machinations to take North China a few years earlier had gained him notoriety, was now a Lieutenant General, commanding the Japanese 14th Division in front of Paoting. What he had not been able to win by intrigue he would seize by force. By the morning of September 24, Japanese troops under cover of heavy artillery fire, with a frontal attack from the north and a flanking movement from the west, had broken through the concrete fortifications that had so impressed Western observers. As usual, the Japanese celebrated their victory with a triumphal march through the city's gates. The Domei news agency crowed, "In launching the punitive campaign, the Japanese forces shocked the eyes and ears at home and abroad by their sweeping force which has been displayed to the fullest extent over North China."

VIII. North China and the Failure of Mediation

The eyes of the Japanese at home might have been more shocked by the conduct of their sons and husbands in Paoting upon its capture. A week of pillage, burning, rape and murder followed. Thousands of civilians were killed, and the medical college and agricultural school were put to the torch.[7] It was an omen of what lay ahead for Nanking. Cruelly, crowds of Chinese were forced to gather in front of the former Imperial Palace in Peking and applaud the announcement of the fall of Paoting, the scene filmed by Japanese news photographers for their audiences at home.

The Japanese continued their southward advance along the railway to occupy Shihkiachuang, 60 miles beyond Paoting. It is unlikely that Chinese defenses would have held out for long in any event, but Chiang's meddling made their task harder. He was more than 600 miles away from the battlefield but insisted on ignoring the advice of his senior field commanders and moving their forces into positions of his own choosing. However high his opinion of his own military talents, Chiang could not create a solid front. On the Tientsin-Pukow Railway, a hundred miles east of Paoting, the Japanese were conducting a parallel drive to the south, pushing the Chinese before them. By September 30 they had reached Potowchen, just 35 miles from the Hopei-Shantung border.

The initial Japanese operational plan had not envisaged an advance beyond Paoting, but the intoxication of victory spurred Terauchi's soldiers to pursue the Chinese southward. By early October, the North China Area Army was committed to extending the front into Shantung and pushing their forces across the Yellow River. These objectives exceeded the instructions that had been issued by the General Staff in Tokyo. Terauchi was not alone in slipping the leash. In Chahar Province, Itagaki ignored orders to commit his 5th Division to the Paoting campaign. Together with the Kwantung Army, his troops crossed the border into northern Shansi Province. Like Doihara, he had long coveted North China. He now sent a message to Operations Division Chief Ishiwara, urging that his forces be allowed to go forward and establish a line from Taiyuan, the capital of Shansi, eastward through Shihkiachuang in Hopei to Tsinan, the capital of Shantung, and from there to Tsingtao on the coast. Within the vast area to the north, a new regime could then be organized, fulfilling the imperial goal of the Kwantung Army. Terauchi heartily agreed, saying that the troops should "have the waters of the Yellow Sea as a take-home gift."[8]

Both Ishiwara and Vice Chief of Staff Tada cast a doubtful eye on this scheme. Ishiwara's views on the subject of a China campaign were well known: Japan's principal threat was from the Soviet Union. To commit the Kwantung Army and forces from the homeland to an operation deep in North China was to ignore the peril at their rear. But Ishiwara could no more restrain the army in China than the Chinese themselves. By

September 20 the General Staff had overcome its reservations and endorsed the occupation of North China's five provinces. There was no longer any room at the top for an officer who disagreed; on September 27, Ishiwara was relieved of his office. In his essay in James Morley's *The China Quagmire*, Ikuhito Hata described his departure as a turning point:

> Ishiwara had been the mainstay of the policy of non-extension, and his removal gave encouragement to those demanding an active policy in China. The conflict between him and the activists, which began when the initial decision to dispatch reinforcements was taken, intensified as the war progressed until, in the weeks after the Shanghai campaign, demands for his dismissal within the Army Ministry and General Staff became almost impossible to suppress. ... His departure was followed by a radical change in the direction of the war.

Ishiwara's successor at the Operations Division was Major General Sadamu Shimomura, the former chief of the Military History Division. With his appointment, leadership at Operations took a U-turn. He had already secretly planned a drive into the Yellow River valley and Shantung, and he sent reinforcements to land at Hangchow Bay and outflank the Chinese in Shanghai. These initiatives were the beginning of a vigorous offensive by the North China Army. It had little trouble reaching its objectives and believed that each thrust into China's heartland would weaken the country further and force its capitulation. The reality was painfully different.

During the first phase of the long war in China, when Japan seemed to be on an irresistible march, the Emperor's loyal subjects at home flocked to movie theaters showing newsreels of their army's triumphs. Victory parades in distant provincial capitals and tableaux of conquering soldiers standing on the ramparts of fallen fortifications, waving the Rising Sun and shouting "Banzai!" were an opiate for audiences who were oblivious to the truth that was beginning to dawn on their military leaders. Occupied cities and railroads gave the illusion of conquest, but Chinese peasants toiling in the fields and villages across vast stretches of countryside never saw a single Japanese soldier. When the Pacific War ended in 1945, the million-plus Japanese officers and men stationed in China were no closer to winning than they had been in the fall of 1937.

The Japanese high command was not alone in recognizing that China's heartbeat lay in its hinterland. From the caves of Yenan, Mao Tse-tung grasped the truth and achieved what Japan could not and Chiang would not. Whoever gained the loyalty of the peasants would win China. The Communist revolution hinged on that single assumption, and Mao sent his cadres into the countryside to proselytize and persuade. The Kuomintang had been an urban movement, but Mao knew that the nation's real strength lay in the ancient regions beyond its cities. The Japanese were aware of this

VIII. North China and the Failure of Mediation

new movement—they felt the stings of guerrilla attacks from Mao's regulars and the occasional sharp blow from Chu Teh's 8th Route Army—but were powerless against it.

Shansi Province had the richest coal and iron deposits in China. Since 1912 its military governor had been General Yen Hsi-shan, who prided himself on his benevolence. He had undertaken an extensive public works program to enhance his fiefdom's prosperity, knowing that it would pay off in higher taxes. Like other warlords, he had built a private army, although it was untested against any serious opponent, and he himself had no professional military training. Now old and ailing, Yen had little hope of keeping the "dwarf people" from stripping him of his power. Besides his own unreliable legions and those that Chiang Kai-shek made available, there was only one disciplined fighting force in the area: the Communist 8th Route Army. Ironically, Chiang had seen Shansi as an eastern barrier against the Communists in northern Shansi Province, but now the latter were needed to block the Japanese advance into Shansi. Much has been made of the Kuomintang-Communist alliance against the invaders, but in fact the Communists jealously preserved the integrity of their own forces and refused to merge them with those of the Nationalists. Like Chiang, Mao was preparing for a final showdown for the mastery of China. In 1937, the Communists' field forces numbered only about 50,000 men, but they fought on their own terms, ambushing the Japanese when they could and harassing them with partisan tactics.[9]

The natural ally of the Chinese was the terrain, which was hostile to any invader from the north. A jagged mountain chain guarded the northern and eastern borders of Shansi Province, although several passes admitted entry and rail lines had been driven through them to link Shansi with its neighbors. A determined and well-armed defender could hold these choke points, but the Japanese strategy of using rail arteries to bring up troops and batter their way through had enabled them to dislodge their foes at Nankow and Kalgan. They were sure that what had worked there would also succeed in Shansi. The outer reaches of the Great Wall coiled along the crests of the northern barrier. There were three passes through the mountains on this front, while a fourth in the eastern chain allowed passage between Shansi and Hopei, where a rail line connected the provincial capital, Taiyuan, with Shihkiachuang in western Hopei. The latter city, located about 100 miles south of Paoting, was an important rail junction, connecting the east-west route between Shansi and Hopei with the north-south line of the Peking-Hankow Railroad that ran through Hopei. Shansi was thus vulnerable from the north and east if the passes were breached. Once they were, Taiyuan and the fertile valley in which it lay would be in peril. Like so many other old cities in North China, the provincial capital, with a population of a quarter of a million, was protected only by obsolete walls.

The *New York Times* reported extensively on the fighting. General Yen had 225,000 soldiers under his command, a formidable army on paper but of the same dubious quality that characterized Chiang's forces. Opposing them were some 40,000 men under General Terauchi. Although outnumbered nearly six to one, the invaders were more than a match for the defenders. To take Shansi and capture its capital, Terauchi focused on the passes, attacking from the north and east. His forces consisted of General Itaki's 5th Division, the Kwantung Army Chahar Expeditionary Force of four composite brigades, and nine Mongolian cavalry divisions. As the campaign unfolded, additional Japanese units were brought in from other areas to join the fight.[10] In mid–September they began the multi-pronged operation. Favored by dry weather, the Japanese moved swiftly and by September 28 were within 20 miles of the railroad junction at Shihkiachuang. With an armored train in the vanguard, they were now 50 miles south of Paoting, more than 150 miles from their starting point at Peking, and were meeting little resistance. Simultaneously they were pressing against the Chinese defenses to the north in the Yenmen Pass at the Great Wall, which gave entry from Suiyuan Province into Shansi. As they had done at Nankow, they outflanked the defenders by scaling the mountains to attack from the rear. Taichow, Shansi's second largest city, was just 10 miles away and was now threatened with capture. To the north, in Suiyuan Province, Terauchi's long-haired Mongols, riding their stocky ponies, drove westward, seizing towns along the Suiyuan-Shansi border. By October 30 all of Suiyuan was under Japanese control, although the Chinese put up a spirited defense at Hopei.

The quick drive south of Paoting stalled briefly on the Huto River, eight miles north of Shihkiachuang. As the Japanese struggled to ford its swift current, Chinese machine gunners on the south bank raked them with withering fire. Overly confident from their victory at Paoting and the ease of their drive south, the Japanese were stunned by the Chinese resistance. The *Times* quoted a high-ranking Japanese Army spokesman:

> Something has happened to the Chinese defense. Our attacking force is almost the same as that which took Paoting, but the numbers of the Chinese have been increased greatly. They are offering much more stubborn and desperate resistance and using more artillery. We have found indications that the Chinese may fall back soon, but they still hold on.

Shihkiachuang was the last serious barrier to Hopei. The Chinese, recognizing the consequences of its loss, not only to all of southern Hopei but to the critical rail line leading to Shansi's capital in the west, knew that it

VIII. North China and the Failure of Mediation

had to be held at all costs. The Japanese infantry struggling in the rapid waters of the Huto River encountered a string of concrete pillboxes strung above them along the river's south bank, spewing death from concealed automatic weapons. But the Japanese used their artillery and air power to pound the Chinese positions and interdict Chinese supply lines by destroying the bridges of the Peking-Hankow Railway to the rear. Although the going was still difficult, superior Japanese firepower and persistence paid off and Chinese resistance crumbled. Unable to withstand the continuous bombardment, the first Chinese line broke and those behind, seeing their comrades retreating, fled themselves, in many instances giving up relatively strong positions that might have slowed the Japanese attack. This was to be an all-too-familiar scenario: the Chinese would erect fixed fortifications, but at the first sign of stress, the lines weakened, and the defense collapsed. A trained army with professional leadership would have used flexible tactics and resorted to alternative defensive measures when confronted by reversals, but the Chinese lacked these attributes. Against the Japanese, they fought like the amateurs they were, doggedly adhering to their usual predictable tactics. They had tried and failed at Paoting, tried and failed again at Shihkiachuang, and now they retreated 70 miles down the Peking-Hankow tracks to Shunteh, where more defensive positions were in readiness. Seasoned military observers questioned not just the wisdom of this unimaginative strategy but its effect on the soldiers themselves. If they could not make a stand behind such well-prepared defenses as there were at Shihkiachuang for more than a day, what hope was there for doing any better at Shunteh? As Hugh Byas reported to the *Times*, "It is said the Chinese strategy of resisting and retreating to fight another day is becoming exhausted if, when the other day arrives, the soldiers will no longer fight."

Given the initial fury of the battle, the sudden collapse of Chinese resistance at Shihkiachuang surprised the Japanese, but they now suspected what was apparent to Western observers on the scene: that the Chinese in Hopei were completely demoralized and would not offer further resistance north of the Yellow River. This was confirmed by the fall of Shunteh less than a week later. The expected stand there never materialized, leaving practically all of Hopei in Japanese hands. With its eastern neighbor under enemy control, Shansi's fate appeared sealed. As soon as Shihkiachuang fell, the Japanese drove westward along the narrow-gauge railroad from the mountains to Taiyuan. In Shansi, however, the Chinese did not give up so easily. Both sides reported fierce fighting in the north, in some cases hand-to-hand. The Chinese even used part of their dwindling air force to conduct raids on enemy targets, and the *Times* reported rumors that some of the remaining German advisers had gone north to help coordinate the

Chinese defense. The Japanese, however, continued to press the defenders and on October 26 launched offensives down the highway from Tatung in the north and along the Shihkiachuang-Taiyuan Railway from the east. It took two days for the invaders to push their way through heavy fog and Chinese flanking fire in the valleys and gullies. One front-line officer reported, "Even monkeys [would] find an advance difficult." Yet again, the Japanese succeeded in getting one of their columns around the Chinese flank to attack from the rear. Slowly the Chinese were pried loose from their positions and by the 28th the Japanese had debouched from the narrow defiles of the mountains into the eastern edge of the broad Shansi plain. Taiyuan lay vulnerable 65 miles away, with no natural barriers to protect it, but the Chinese were not going to give up the city without a fight.

Even as the Japanese strove to complete the conquest of Shansi, they announced plans for the administration of North China. From the $1,000,000 building in Peking that had formerly housed China's Foreign Office, Major General Seiichi Kita, chief of Japanese military missions in China, who was also responsible for political affairs, said, "Whatever government is established in North China will be founded only upon the real desires of the Chinese people." This mendacious pronouncement was followed by the far more revealing comment that while the new government would be concerned only with China at first, it might eventually encompass the entire nation should that become possible. The notion of expanding into 90,000 square miles, a region roughly equal in size to the combined area of the states of New York and Pennsylvania, thrilled the heads of Japanese investment and development companies. Plans were laid for cotton mills, power plants and new railways, while shipping lines scheduled more voyages to Tientsin to handle the expected increase in trade with North China, and the South Manchuria Railway and the China Development Company competed for the privilege of exploiting North China's economy. The diminutive president of the South Manchurian Railway, Yosuke Matsuoka, submitted a plan to Tokyo that would give his company virtually total control over all of China's five northern provinces. The China Development Company, on the other hand, argued that it was better suited for the task of cooperating with the new regime to be set up in North China.[11] While these two companies were wrangling, the army was split over the disposition of North China. The Kwantung Army had long advocated an autonomous government for the area, while the Central Army headquarters took a more moderate position. The Japanese command in Korea shared the view of the Kwantung Army, but the command in Tientsin did not. Like the Central Army authorities, they wished to foster economic cooperation between Japan and China and create, if possible, an anti–Communist alliance. Separating North China from the rest of the country, they

VIII. North China and the Failure of Mediation 213

reasoned, would harden resistance. But the Kwantung Army believed that Chiang Kai-shek was losing control and that North China's independence should be expedited in order to avoid anarchy. Since it appeared that the conflict might last longer than had been anticipated, a ruling government should be installed immediately, combining the Tokyo central government departments with those from Tientsin, Peking and the Hopei-Chahar regions. If an advantageous peace was not achieved, the families of the men who had been killed in the fighting would feel that they had died in vain. The Vice Chief of the Manchurian Bureau, Aoki, told Baron Harada that both the families and the soldiers "will say that the Five Provinces will have to be made Japanese territory, or ... that they desire the independence of the Five Provinces under the control of Japan."[12] Putting together a new order in East Asia meant more than establishing a government based on the "real desires of the Chinese people," but the Japanese were not unanimous on the form this government should take.

By the end of October, the first snow of the season had fallen in Peking, and Japanese troops in northern Shansi were feeling the effects of the cold. On the road from Tatung to their goal, Taiyuan, they met strong opposition from the Chinese, who were strung out along a sixteen-mile front. As the fighting intensified, the *Japan Times and Mail* reported that the Chinese were using dum-dum bullets and reported the seizure of 10,000 rounds at Tzechow near the Hopei-Honan border. The paper also accused China of poisoning wells and attacking a Japanese field hospital.

The Chinese held out for five days, but when the Japanese tunneled under one of their key fortifications at Tungshan, 25 miles north of Taiyuan, and blew it up, the Chinese fell back to their last defensive line just north of the city. Sensing that Taiyuan was doomed, a majority of them fled, but a substantial number remained behind to fight for the capital. When the Japanese finally arrived at the north gate on November 5, the Chinese spurned their demand for surrender. The Japanese then launched a furious artillery and aerial assault, breaching the 35-foot wall. Their infantry poured through and rooted out the defenders with hand grenades and bayonets. By nightfall on the 8th, the last of the Chinese garrison had given up and attempted to break out to the west. Only one bridge was open, over the Fen River, and that was choked with refugees scrambling out of the now-burning city. The terrified soldiers shoved the helpless civilians into the water. At dawn, a confused mass of troops and refugees was still clogging the southwest gate and bridge, making a defenseless target for Japanese planes bombing and strafing them.

However, many of the Chinese who escaped did not give up the fight. Some of them took to the mountains, from which they sallied forth periodically to strike back. The Japanese admitted that mopping-up operations would take some time, but increasingly they confined themselves to the cities and connecting rail lines. In the east, they pushed toward Tsinan, the capital of Shantung Province, driving the Chinese across the Yellow River. Although they had seemed an irresistible force, they suffered at least one costly defeat. This was administered by the Communist 8th Route Army. This setback was all the more humiliating because it was suffered by the crack Itagaki Division, when it walked into an ambush.

The Communist force was commanded by Lin Piao, one of Mao's closest comrades until a dramatic break between them nearly forty years later. Lin deployed his division into Shensi Province, concealing his movements from the Japanese, who were brimming with confidence as they marched westward. Lin knew that the Itagaki Division would have to cross the Pinghsing Pass at the Shensi-Hopei border. The terrain was in his favor. He positioned his troops so close to their foes that his enemy could not use its artillery against them.[13] Furthermore, the road that the Japanese were using was sunken from generations of travel, restricting their ability to maneuver. Lin's men struck on September 25, blocking the Japanese in both directions. Trapped and unable to escape, the Japanese soldiers, who had so often surrounded the inept Chinese and cut them to pieces, now fell by the thousands to rifle and machine-gun fire and hand grenades. Over 6,000 Japanese died; Chinese dead numbered just 300. As the decimated survivors fled, Lin's troops melted back into the hills. Thereafter, the 8th Route Army confined itself to guerrilla attacks. It did not engage in another large-scale operation until 1940. But the countryside became a fertile ground for recruitment. By 1945, some 90 million people were living under Communist administrators, and Japanese authority ended at the railroad rights-of-way and adjoining cities.[14] Nevertheless, by the end of November 1937, Japan thought its campaign in North China was over.

Hirohito had been worried for some time about international perceptions of Japan's ambitions in North China. In September, War Minister Sugiyama assured him that the army did not have any territorial ambitions, to which he replied, "You say that, but can you control your subordinates?" Sugiyama answered confidently, "I will be completely capable of assuming that responsibility." Hirohito then said that a press conference should be called for all of the foreign correspondents in Tokyo at which the War Minister could issue a statement to that effect. Sugiyama said that he would follow the Emperor's recommendation, but Baron Harada, who was given an account of the meeting by the Lord Keeper of the Privy Seal, doubted that the British and Americans would be appeased. Great Britain was already unhappy because its interests in South China had been trampled on and Japanese pledges in North China would offer little consolation. Nevertheless, Konoe was sufficiently interested in these overtures to consider

VIII. North China and the Failure of Mediation

sending Imperial Household Minister Matsudaira on a mission to England and Admiral Nomura to the United States. Nothing came of either venture, primarily because Ambassador Grew told Matsudaira privately that President Roosevelt opposed the dispatch of a special envoy.[15] However, four years later, when relations between the U.S. and Japan were at the breaking point and the decision to risk war had already been made in Tokyo, Admiral Nomura was chosen to go to Washington with a final offer for a peaceful settlement of the differences between the two powers.

This preoccupation with American and British concerns over Japanese actions in China was more important to the Emperor and his court advisers than to the military establishment. Baron Kurukei Yuasa, the Lord Keeper of the Privy Seal, knew the Emperor's views. Moving in exclusive circles, he maintained contact between the Emperor and his ministers, arranging all audiences with the Emperor except for those with the Ministers of War and the Navy, who had their own right of access to the throne. Yuasa had held his position since 1936 and was known as "a fusspot with no feelings other than for protocol"; nevertheless, Baron Harada found him to be a useful source of information.[16] Yuasa told Harada that while most Japanese approved of the China policy, they had not been informed of Anglo-American feelings toward Japan. He recommended that English and American newspaper articles be released to the public "a little at a time, so that they will not experience extreme indignation at the end of the war."[17] Moreover, he felt that the Japanese people overestimated the capabilities of the army and navy. China was turning out to be stronger than anyone had anticipated.

It was this aspect of the China venture that worried the wise old *Genro*, Prince Saionji. Early in the fall, he began to express his fears to Baron Harada on a daily basis. Rather than trying to destroy Chiang, he said, Japan should have supported and collaborated with him. But the army had "for some unknown reason ... [taken] a disliking to Chiang ... and the plan fell through." Saionji went on to say:

> During the World War the German Army had hoped for its speedy conclusion and they did not allow a single enemy soldier to enter their country. The reason Germany [was] defeated was because they laid the blame on the statesmen, and while things were in confusion conspiracies arose in the Navy. The final outcome was like that. What is Japan going to do to reach a conclusion? I believe that Foreign Minister Hirota has thought about it, but will you tell the Lord Keeper and the Foreign Minister of my anxieties?

What indeed was Japan going to do? As far as the field commanders were concerned, the enemy forces in North and Central China should be defeated and forced to surrender. Anything less would meet opposition from Generals Matsui and Terauchi at the front as well as from Vice

War Minister Umezu; General Homma, the chief of the intelligence division; and General Ueda, commander of the Kwantung Army. By October 1, the Foreign Ministry had drafted the "Essential Points of Policy Toward the China Incident." By then the military situation in China was far more favorable to Japan than it had been during the summer, when the first feeble attempts at peace had died. The Cabinet approved these "Points" and set forth six basic requirements for a diplomatic solution to the war. First, China would have to extend *de facto* recognition of Manchukuo; second, China would have to sign an anti–Comintern pact; third, China would have to suppress anti–Japanese movements; fourth, the demilitarized zone around Shanghai would have to be enlarged; fifth, the Nanking government would have to recognize the Japanese puppet regime of Prince Teh in Inner Mongolia; and sixth, China would have to pay an indemnity. These terms were far harsher than those proposed two months earlier, especially the demand for indemnity, which concerned those officers like Ishiwara who wanted an early armistice agreement.

The Prime Minister had hesitated to take any diplomatic initiatives with Nanking. He mistrusted the Western powers as mediators. The United States and Great Britain had never recognized the legitimacy of Manchukuo, and the Chinese had already indicated that they were counting on the Nine Power Treaty signatories to pressure Japan. Ultimately, the victories won by the field armies in August and September convinced Konoe and his associates that they could dictate peace terms to Chiang Kai-shek. Tokyo refused to send a delegation to the Nine Power Conference which met in Brussels that fall or to accept an offer from the British government to mediate the conflict with China.[18] However, it was desirable to have a third party broker terms, especially after the fighting around Shanghai persisted far beyond the original calculations of the General Staff. There was one power that could be trusted with that mission: Nazi Germany.

The decision to seek German mediation might have seemed obvious at first glance. After all, given the ideological compatibility between the two powers and the historical connection between German military tutelage and the Japanese Army, Germany appeared to be a trustworthy go-between.

However, there was also a German-Chinese connection. A large number of Chinese students had gone to Germany to study in the 1920s. Many had settled in the neighborhood of Kantstrasse in Berlin-Charlottenburg, where the Chinese Legation was located. Military relations between the two countries originated in the same decade. In those years, when the German Army was limited to 100,000 men and severely restricted in weaponry by the Versailles Treaty, the Soviet Union had provided a secret arena for modernization. The Reichswehr, under the leadership of General Hans von Seeckt, became a shadow army, organizing itself for the day when the

VIII. North China and the Failure of Mediation

shackles of Versailles would be thrown off. However, Seeckt saw in the Chinese Nationalist revolution an opportunity for a long-range coordination of Sino-German economic and military development. While this grandiose scheme never took root, what did materialize was sufficiently important to both sides to grow and bear fruit.

For a time, the attitude of the Weimar Republic toward China was ambivalent. After World War I, Chinese warlords had bought confiscated, obsolete German arms from the victorious Allies and imported German instructors for their private armies. But after 1933 Chiang Kai-shek became the sole beneficiary of German military assistance. That same year, Seeckt accept Chiang's invitation to become his chief German military adviser. General Alexander von Falkenhausen accompanied Seeckt as his deputy and Chief of Staff. When Seeckt returned home in 1935, Falkenhausen succeeded him, a fortuitous choice for Chiang, because he proved to be the ablest foreign adviser in China, a prescient individual whose military skills were matched by his keen political instincts. Falkenhausen served China well, but he was never under any illusions about Japan's strength and the need for Germany to respect it.

Originally, the Germans were to reorganize and train twenty Chinese divisions, but by the time war broke out in 1937, only eight of those divisions were ready. By then, of course, Hitler had shifted his support to Japan, whose military oligarchy and anti–Soviet policy suited his purposes more than preserving a tenuous bond with Nationalist China. But between 1933 and 1936 the Sino-German connection held, and the German officers in China applied their talents to making Chiang's army into a self-confident military force. Seeckt and Falkenhausen admired Chiang, and they and their subordinates came to respect the ordinary soldiers in Chiang's legions. Although they felt that the Japanese soldier was better trained and more energetic and aggressive, they thought that Chinese soldiers were "quicker and more intelligent." As the Nationalist government consolidated its control over Kwangtung and Kwangsi Provinces in South China, Falkenhausen's confidence in China led him to take a more aggressive stance. In April 1936, he advised Chiang to plan for war with Japan and to include guerrilla warfare in enemy-controlled areas, along with intelligence and sabotage operations in Manchuria and Japan itself. In October he recommended that plans be laid for surprise attacks on the Japanese garrisons at Hankow and Shanghai. A month later he proposed an offensive in North China to recover Hopei, using infantry with air cover.

When war finally broke out in July 1937, Falkenhausen spoke for the German Military Missions in China when he sent the following message to General von Blomberg, the Minister of War:

> Chiang is determined to fight. This is not a local war but total war. China's chances for victory are not bad because the Japanese—mindful of the threat of Russian intervention—cannot commit all their forces against the Chinese. The Chinese infantry is good. The Chinese Air Force is about equal to the Japanese. A Japanese victory is far from certain. The morale of the Chinese Army is high. They will put up a bitter fight.

This report was overly optimistic and reflects the bias of a man who had so immersed himself in his role that he could not separate hope from reality. Three years of almost daily contact with his charges had transformed Falkenhausen from adviser to advocate.

When the fighting escalated, the German advisers often accompanied their Chinese units in the field. Falkenhausen faced the same dangers as his adopted soldiers in the battle zone around Shanghai and subsisted for days on "boiled eggs and cognac." In September, the Chinese recognized his contributions by bestowing on him the Military Order of the "Cloud Flag," Second Class, with Grand Cordon. Five other advisers were also decorated for their services on the Yangtze Valley front. As a professional soldier with his own credentials from the Western Front in Europe, Falkenhausen's patience was tested time and again by the mistakes the Chinese made as the Japanese steadily drove them back. Yet he was convinced that China must continue to resist the invaders by whatever means were available. It was against this background that peace overtures, with Germany as mediator, were made.

It is not certain who first proposed a Sino-Japanese peace treaty, but in late August 1937 Foreign Minister Hirota broached the idea with the German Ambassador, Herbert von Dirksen. The Germans reacted cautiously, since the suggestion had come from the aggressors and they did not wish to appear to be collaborators.[19] For the moment they did nothing, nor did the Japanese press them. But as weeks passed and casualties mounted, particularly around Shanghai where Chinese resistance was fierce, the Japanese General Staff concluded that mediation was a less costly alternative, especially if Japanese demands were met. With the help of the friendly German government, a diplomatic solution might be found.

On October 11, the War Ministry decided to make the effort. The procedure was somewhat convoluted, since "face" was at stake and the Japanese wanted the official initiative to come from the Chinese. Accordingly, the German Military Attaché in Tokyo, General Eugen Ott, was asked to approach China to find out if Nanking wanted a settlement. At the same time, the Japanese instructed their own military attaché in Berlin, General Hiroshi Oshima, to prevail upon the Germany Army to serve as a conduit to Chiang Kai-shek. Neither of these ploys worked. Negotiations were ultimately handled by diplomats.

Ambassador Dirksen had apprised the German Foreign Office of

VIII. North China and the Failure of Mediation

Japan's overtures and Berlin sent a message to Ambassador Trautmann in Nanking, instructing him to approach the Chinese. The Germany envoy immediately contacted Vice Minister Chen Chieh, offering his government's services, and urging him to seize the opportunity, saying that the "psychological" time for peace was at hand. Chen Chieh seemed amenable and said that Chiang wanted to know Japan's terms.[20] With this green light, Dirksen was told to proceed.

In the meantime, the Japanese Cabinet adopted a seven-point proposal prepared by the Foreign Minister, and on November 3, Hirota turned it over to Ambassador Dirksen. It was softer than the "Essential Points of Policy" of October 1; no mention was made of indemnity or recognition of Manchukuo. Nevertheless, China would have to make concessions. The points were as follows:

1. Recognition of an autonomous government in Inner Mongolia;
2. Creation of a new demilitarized zone in North China;
3. Creation of an enlarged demilitarized zone in Shanghai;
4. Cessation of anti-Japanese activities in China;
5. Creation of a "common front" against Bolshevism;
6. Reduction in customs duties on Japanese goods; and
7. A guarantee of political and economic rights for Japanese nationals in China.[21]

Hirota told Dirksen that these terms were not subject to change. Nanking could take them or leave them, but if they were rejected, Japan would wage total war and bring China to its knees, and then China would face even harsher terms. Both Dirksen and Ott believed that Japan genuinely wanted peace but would not yield on its demands. Moreover, they felt that the demands were reasonable, and that the Chinese could accept them "without loss of face." Indeed, they said, Falkenhausen should make it clear that China's military position was hopeless, and that Japan's demands must therefore be met.

Chiang did not hesitate. On November 5 he told the German Ambassador that he would accept no terms unless Japan was willing to restore the *status quo ante* of July 7, 1937. In talking to Trautmann, Chiang said that for him to accept such terms would mean he would risk a revolution that he could not survive. The Generalissimo added that he also wished to see the outcome of the Brussels Conference before acting. Trautmann warned him that he should not delay too long, especially if he waited until his military forces were spent. But Chiang procrastinated. While he continued to hope that the Western powers at the Brussels Conference might come to his rescue, the Japanese field commanders were pushing for a campaign in Central China and the occupation of Nanking, while simultaneously moving to establish puppet administrations in Shanghai and North China. Only when Nanking was about to fall and disaster was staring him in the face did Chiang, after consulting with his generals, ask Trautmann to help him reach a settlement with Japan. By then, it was too late. If Tokyo had agreed to the October proposals at that point, the Japanese field armies would have revolted.

In retrospect, it might seem that Chiang's belief that a waiting game was preferable to giving up the fight was just wishful thinking. Yet when one looks back on the news from Western capitals in the early fall of 1937, it is clear that Chiang had reason to believe that the West would act on his behalf. His diplomats in Washington, London and Paris might have been rebuffed, but the leaders in those countries were aware of his plight and of the need to let Japan know that her actions were contrary to Western interests as well as China's. Chiang always believed that America was his best hope. That conviction was reinforced when President Roosevelt delivered a surprising address to America's people and the world from its heartland, Chicago. The speech was a watershed for Roosevelt, his first major challenge to isolationism. His words were more dramatic than their substance, but they heartened the embattled Chinese. With FDR's announcement that the Nine Power Treaty signatories would meet to take up China's grievances against Japan, Chiang was surely encouraged to think that he had been thrown a life preserver.

IX

Quarantine the Aggressor

> It seems to be unfortunately true that the epidemic of world lawlessness is spreading. When an epidemic of a physical disease starts to spread, the community approves and joins in a quarantine of the patients in order to protect the health of the community against the spread of the disease.
> —President Franklin D. Roosevelt, October 5, 1937

Throughout his life Franklin Roosevelt showed a partiality toward China that had been shaped from his youth. His maternal grandfather, Warren Delano II, was a member of Russell and Co., a major Boston firm engaged in trade with China. The President recalled that his grandfather had twice made a million dollars in the China trade, only to lose it by poor investments in the United States. Roosevelt's mother, Sara Delano, had lived with her family in China for a number of years when she was a child. From her and from his grandfather, Roosevelt had heard many stories of life in China and the lucrative China trade. His interest in the Far East continued during his preparatory school and college years. In 1899 he wrote to his parents that a lecturer at Groton "ran down the poor Chinaman a little too much and thought too much of the Japs." Roosevelt's bias toward China not unnaturally aroused a corresponding suspicion and antipathy toward Japan. At Harvard he met several Japanese students, one of whom told Roosevelt an amazing story of Japan's expansionist plans, including the conquest of Korea, Manchuria, New Zealand and Hawaii. When he was Assistant Secretary of the Navy under Woodrow Wilson in 1913, Roosevelt urged the concentration of Far Eastern squadrons in the Philippines based on the war scare resulting from an anti–Japanese bill in California. He also proposed plans for a possible Japanese-American conflict. In January 1914, even after these fears had abated, he pointed out that the weakness of the U.S. fleet put it at risk of destruction, in which case it would be relatively easy for the Japanese to land on 1,800 miles of unprotected American coastline.[1]

In retrospect, Roosevelt's bombshell speech on October 5, 1937, might appear to be saber-rattling, but Sumner Welles said that Roosevelt's apprehension about the Japanese was genuine and ascribed it to the President's association with the Navy. Since the Navy saw Japan as its paramount rival, Roosevelt was bound to have been strongly influenced by naval strategists.[2] This is demonstrated by Roosevelt's advice to the House Naval Affairs Committee during the First World War. Although Japan was an ally, Roosevelt regarded her naval strength as a threat to the United States, pointing out that her naval construction made her fleet the equal of America's in Japanese waters.

In the following decade, Roosevelt's fears seemed to abate, not only because of the new climate produced by the Washington Conference but also because his political instincts probably told him to adopt a more conciliatory point of view. In a 1923 magazine article in *Asia*, "Shall We Trust Japan," Roosevelt said it was natural that suspicion arose between the two nations in the years following 1898. The Japanese, he said, must have regarded the American acquisition of the Philippines as a potential threat. Both sides were expanding their navies, Japan because of the presence of a new Western power in their "south yard" and America because of its fears for the security of the islands. But the Washington Conference had eliminated many of the causes of friction, so there was no longer any reason for mistrust. While the Open Door was part of America's foreign policy, the U.S. should "recognize the greater necessity to Japan of the markets and the raw products of the Chinese mainland contiguous to her shores." Japanese immigration and land ownership problems in the U.S. could be disposed of if both nations would apply the Golden Rule: Americans did not move in large numbers to Japan, therefore Japanese should not migrate en masse to America. When one remembers that the Exclusion Act was passed the following year, Roosevelt's article seems remarkably prescient.

By 1928, Roosevelt was planning to run for President. He was aware of public sentiment against a return to internationalism. That year, he published an article in *Foreign Affairs* in which he stated his unequivocal opposition to American membership in the League of Nations. Just eight years earlier he had run for Vice President on a Democratic platform calling for participation in the League. Now he attacked President Coolidge for approving a costly cruiser-building program for the Navy instead of supporting a ban on cruiser construction at the recent disarmament conference in Geneva.[3] His friends and associates in the Navy must have been scratching their heads. As the Democratic convention approached in 1932, he continued to repudiate the League, and after his election he deferred to the isolationists, primarily because he wanted their support for the New Deal. However, he no longer maintained a benign attitude toward Japan.

This was due to the Manchurian Incident in 1931. While he made no public remarks that would alarm the isolationists, he did reveal his feelings to some of his subordinates. At a dinner party at James Farley's home in January 1933, Roosevelt voiced his apprehension about Japan's aggressive ambitions, and at his second Cabinet meeting he went so far as to discuss military strategy against Japan.[4]

However, he had little time to waste on such musings. America was suffering the most dangerous economic crisis in its history and he was keenly aware that he had enough problems to deal with at home. Indeed, his second inaugural address on March 4, 1937, concentrated on domestic issues and made no reference to foreign affairs. His concern was with a nation in which a third of the populace was "ill-housed, ill-clothed, ill-nourished," and he declared that he intended to turn over to his successor on January 21, 1941, "a Nation intact, a Nation at peace, a Nation prosperous."

It was nevertheless impossible to ignore what was happening elsewhere in the world. Americans were watching uneasily in 1936 as Mussolini conquered Ethiopia and civil war broke out in Spain. Both Germany and Italy were sending aid to the Spanish insurgents, while Russia was supporting the Loyalist cause. The struggle appeared to be a dress rehearsal for a future conflict. When and if it came, however, the American people were determined not to be drawn into it. Nothing more emphatically demonstrated their outlook than the passage of special legislation to ensure U.S. neutrality in the event of another war in Europe.

The attempt to legislate neutrality stemmed from the disillusionment that followed participation in World War I. The conviction grew that the war had not been an idealistic crusade after all and that the Allies, particularly the British, had used America to pull the chestnuts of France and England out of the fire. The reluctance on the part of most of the Western powers to pay their war debts fueled growing anti–European sentiment, and when they defaulted on their payments, Congress retaliated, prohibiting future loans to the defaulters. Moreover, after Czarist, German and Austrian archives were opened, and subsequent revelations followed from the foreign offices of the British and French, Europe was revealed to be a continent of grasping states with mutual designs on each other's power and territory. American authors such as Walter Millis in *Road to War* indicted the Wilson administration for its failure to maintain neutrality during the war, while a Senate committee headed by Gerald K. Nye conducted sensational hearings on the munitions manufacturers, who were dubbed "merchants of death."

Popular surveys were just beginning. In September 1935, the American Institute of Public Opinion, after a long period of experimentation with the technique, began regular publication of its polling results. These revealed the public's determination to avoid foreign entanglements. The general deterioration of international relations strengthened Americans' isolationist attitudes. Of those polled that August, 95 percent advocated remaining neutral in the event of another war in Europe.[5]

Congress shared its constituents' feelings but was not united on how neutrality should be maintained. One group, led by Senators Hiram Johnson (R–CA) and William E. Borah (R–ID), believed that the government should concentrate on "making democracy work at home" and provide only for the defense of the American continent.[6] In the event of a war overseas, America could best protect its interests by adhering to its neutral rights and duties under international law. The other faction, led by Senators Champ Clark (D–MO), Gerald Nye (R–ND), and Arthur Vandenberg (R–MI), agreed that America should refrain from international political commitments, but felt that many of the rights of a neutral state would be lost by the risks attending foreign trade during wartime. This problem could best be avoided by neutrality laws. However, if the Clark-Nye-Vandenberg theory were carried out, the nation might have to abandon its foreign trade, after the fashion of Jefferson's embargo in 1808. Few Senators would go that far, especially the Johnson-Borah group, who had too much pride to submit the United States to such a condition. However, both groups were equally disillusioned by the results of America's participation in World War I and were determined to avoid their repetition. Thus the neutrality laws were born.

The first act was temporary, to be effective from August 31, 1935, to February 29, 1936. It stated that whenever the President proclaimed the existence of a war, he could ban the sale or transportation of munitions to the belligerents. The President was also given discretion to warn Americans that they traveled on belligerent ships at their own risk, a clause that had its roots in the sinking of the *Lusitania* in 1915, when 128 Americans lost their lives. When the first law expired, Congress passed the Neutrality Act of 1936. The second law included the basic provisions of the first, but the President's discretion to impose an arms embargo was removed. If he found a state of war to exist anywhere in the world, the embargo would take effect automatically. Moreover, remembering their bitter experience with loans to the Allies in the previous war, Congress included them in the embargo. Only the Latin American countries were exempted from the provisions of the law, and that was in the event of a state at war with a non–American nation. The drafters of this legislation were like those generals who believe that future wars will be like the last one. Both acts were intended to prevent American entry into a war that had been over for eighteen years. This became glaringly obvious after civil war broke out in Spain in July 1936. When Congress convened the following January, the President submitted an urgent request for authority to impose an arms embargo on Spain. Congress passed a joint resolution granting it to him.

The 1936 law was due to expire on May 1, 1937, so Congress then considered a permanent law to replace it. By the end of February, the bills had been reported out of their respective committees in the House and Senate, and floor debate began. There was hardly any debate on an embargo on arms and loans to belligerents, but there was a sharp difference of opinion with regard to the export of other materials and the protection of American ships on the high seas.

Debate centered primarily on the question of "cash-and-carry," which would permit foreign trade with belligerents, except in the case of arms and other war materiel, only if the belligerents transported American goods in their own ships and paid cash for them. In this way the U.S. would not be responsible for the fate of such goods or vessels on the high seas or in war zones. A majority in Congress was willing to try cash-and-carry as an experiment but was unwilling to apply it automatically at the outbreak of any war. Many wars, they felt, were not serious enough to warrant such severe restrictions on the American merchant marine and foreign trade in general. In the end, the President was given discretion on both the matter of when a given foreign conflict constituted a war, in which case the prohibitions on arms sales became automatic, and whether to prohibit or allow the cash-and-carry provision to be invoked on the sale and transfer of other commodities.

Roosevelt was not entirely satisfied, but he signed the laws when they came to his desk. He believed that there were "just," and "unjust" wars and he wanted the right to distinguish between aggressor and victim and the discretion to prohibit all trade with an aggressor power. In fact, when the first law was being drafted in 1935, Roosevelt urged Congress to include this discretionary power, and the State Department prepared a model bill providing for it.[7] However, Congress would not permit the President to take the side of the United States in favor of one belligerent against another. Roosevelt did not make an issue of this, and for good reason. The success of the New Deal was his primary goal. To achieve it he needed the support of progressives like Borah, Nye, LaFollette and Burton K. Wheeler, men who championed neutrality and would fight any attempt to draw the nation away from it. Finally, public opinion did not favor wide discretionary powers for the President. In January 1937, while the Third Neutrality Law was under consideration, a Gallup poll showed that 69 percent of those surveyed felt that Congress should be responsible for America's neutrality policy, while only 31 percent thought that it belonged in the hands of the President.[8]

Although the Neutrality Law of 1937 was not purposely framed to benefit Great Britain, that was its effect. Since England would undoubtedly control the seas in the event of a European war, she would be able to take advantage of the cash-and-carry principle and purchase non-military goods from the United States. A continental enemy could not. The law also did not take into account developments in Asia. Senator Hiram Johnson, who stood for the traditional rights of neutrality and had opposed cash-and-carry, declared that the law made Britain an ally in the Atlantic and Japan in the Pacific.[9] In a sense, he was right. In the event of a Sino-Japanese war and the subsequent invocation of the Neutrality Law, China would suffer from its provisions far more than Japan. Lacking Japan's naval power, China would be in the same position as any foe of Britain in the Atlantic. She would be denied access to American goods. For those who sincerely desired neutrality this would not matter, but when fighting broke out between China and Japan in the summer of 1937, Roosevelt was markedly reluctant to apply any measures that might weaken China. In this regard, he showed his thinking with regard to the type of neutrality that he thought America should observe. The Neutrality Law was thus subjected to its first test in an area that no one had anticipated. When the President failed to invoke it, many of its sponsors came to see as a mistake the discretionary power given to him to determine whether a foreign conflict was a "war."

As noted previously, sentiment in the United States swung in favor of China as hostilities escalated in the late summer and fall of 1937. But that sentiment did not translate into a call for intervention or any other step that would put American neutrality at risk. No one was in a hurry to apply sanctions to Japan. Between July 1937 and January 1938, only five resolutions calling for sanctions were introduced in Congress. None of them were acted upon, and all were assailed by Congressional isolationists.[10] Still, a vocal minority outside Congress, including various civic organizations made up of educators and professional men and women, wanted a ban on the sale of Japanese products. On October 1, 1937, 10,000 people rallied at Madison Square Garden to protest Japan's actions in China and to urge a boycott of her goods.[11] A few days later the American Federation of Labor and the Committee for Industrial Organization passed resolutions against the purchase of Japanese goods. Many people refused to wear silk garments, turning to rayon instead, while three of the largest five-and-dime store chains announced that they would no longer stock items made in Japan.[12] Numerous student and labor groups sent telegrams to the White House urging the President to lead the nation in the boycott.[13]

Would such pressure have been effective? Perhaps. An embargo on all trade with Japan would certainly have been a serious blow to its economy. In 1937, Japan produced 5.3 million tons of steel, over a third of which was made from American scrap and pig iron. Besides the raw materials for Japan's furnaces, the U.S. sold her a million tons of new iron and steel in various unfabricated forms. Seventy-five percent of the fuel used by Japan for her army, navy and air force came from America. The U.S. also sold her immense quantities of high-speed metal-working machinery of all kinds. In 1937 alone, Japan purchased $34 million worth, which was more than she had bought from the entire world in the preceding year.[14] Cutting off these commodities would have severely limited Japan's war-making capabilities.

However, the shortage could have been largely made up from other sources, principally the British Empire and the Dutch East Indies. For economic coercion to have been effective, the United States would have needed the cooperation of the British, French and Dutch. Moreover, a combination of sanctions and boycotts would have been a two-edged weapon. A boycott would have hurt American silk manufacturers, and Japan was America's biggest buyer of raw cotton.[15] In 1937, at the height of the Depression, the U.S. could ill afford additional setbacks to its economy. It would also have been difficult to make sanctions stick. The experience with Italy during the Ethiopian crisis had shown that it was not easy to gain international cooperation in imposing sanctions on an aggressor nation. Finally, it is well to remember that, after the 1940 embargo on all oil and scrap iron shipments to Japan, the latter's militarists were driven to conquer Southeast Asia and to make war on the United States and Great Britain. Any decision to use sanctions or boycotts against Japan would have had to be joined with a willingness to back them up with force.

Nevertheless, the British considered sanctions against the Japanese. A wave of pro-sanction feeling swept the kingdom. Labor and Liberal newspapers took up the theme, and at the Labor Party Congress in early October, Clement Attlee called for an economic boycott of Japan. A similar argument was made at a mass meeting at the Albert Hall on October 5, followed by an intense campaign in the press to convince the public that effective economic measures could be taken without dragging Great Britain into war. The Labor Party hailed President Roosevelt's quarantine speech in Chicago on October 5 as evidence that the United States would support such a program.[16] The Chamberlain government, however, did nothing to encourage the hopes of those who wanted sanctions. Instead, the British Foreign Office, using the private channels of diplomacy, decided to get in touch with the State Department and sound out the Americans on the subject. On October 1, the British Chargé handed a note to the Secretary of State in which the British declared their willingness to explore the possibility of an economic boycott against Japan, if America wished it.[17] The State Department was even less interested in a boycott than was the British Foreign Office, and sidestepped the issue by replying that, since the signatories of the Nine Power Treaty would be meeting soon, the two governments could then consult with each other on what policy to adopt in the Far East. This response seemed to satisfy the British, who regarded American policy as one that "left the door wide open."[18] That description was more accurate than the British realized. As far as the Roosevelt administration was concerned, what to do in the Far East was indeed a wide-open door, although there was considerable uncertainty about how to proceed through it.

Although there have been numerous biographies written about Franklin Roosevelt, he remains something of an enigma. This is especially true of his role as the architect of American foreign policy. Cabinet officers like Frances Perkins and Henry Morgenthau described him as a man "of bewildering variety of moods and motives," while his wife declared that she never knew anyone who was less influenced by other people.[19] Not since Woodrow Wilson had there been a President who was so conscious of the prerogatives of his office, but Roosevelt often exasperated his Cabinet members by refusing to adhere to conventional organizational procedure. In arriving at an executive decision, he would bypass department heads, to their chagrin, and instead call their subordinates to the White House for consultation. This unorthodox approach seems to have stemmed from an innate desire to deal personally with individuals and issues. Thus, many people were able to telephone him directly, without bothering to state their business first to a secretary. Government officials with anything serious on their minds had little difficulty in scheduling appointments.

While Roosevelt scanned half a dozen leading newspapers daily and read an enormous number of official memoranda from State Department cables to government reports, he preferred to get ideas and information through conversation. He also amassed a wealth of miscellaneous intelligence from his periodic trips around the nation. He was stimulated by the crowds and by chance conversations with ordinary citizens. Because he was physically disabled, he often relied on others to observe for him. Mrs. Roosevelt frequently served him in this way, and he placed great store by her observations. Mail to the White House was another source of knowledge; at least 5,000 to 8,000 letters arrived daily and in critical times many more. He closely watched the trend of his mail and would select letters at random "to renew his sense of raw contact."[20]

Within his administration, Roosevelt believed that all key decisions were his responsibility, and for this reason he preferred a competitive organization in which none of his subordinates had complete authority and all of their jurisdictions overlapped. Of course, this led to some confusion and annoyance at the departmental level, but in a bureaucracy of ambitious men eager for power, he kept the final say.[21] On important matters, he often procrastinated. Much of his success was due to his ability to gauge

Congressional feelings and public opinion. He would wait for a situation to develop and would delay action on a matter until conditions were favorable to him. On some occasions he might be forced to back off, but he would regard these as temporary setbacks and would soon resort to other tactics to reach his goals. Frances Perkins remarked that Roosevelt "rarely got himself sewed tight to a program from which there [was] no turning back."

Nowhere were all of the President's characteristics more obviously displayed than in his handling of foreign affairs and his relationship with the State Department. Although Roosevelt sometimes spoke of himself as his own Secretary of State, that title was officially held by Cordell Hull, a former Tennessee Congressman of long standing. Hull, a conservative, was unduly cautious, a trait that greatly annoyed the State Department's other leading figure, Sumner Welles.[22] Hull was obsessed with his trade agreements program and saw the lowering of economic barriers in the world as a cure-all for international ills. When confronted with what he saw as a breach of international conduct, Hull indulged in "preachments" to the world at large, while privately he would lecture or even berate foreign diplomats in his office. This seldom had any practical results. Nevertheless, Roosevelt and his Secretary of State agreed on fundamental issues. At heart, the President shared Hull's internationalist sentiments, although he was more pragmatic about lowering tariffs.

Besides serving as Roosevelt's "internationalist conscience" in economic matters, Hull, according to Welles, had some qualities that could not be overlooked. These were "a physical facade that appealed to the American people" and an influence in Congress that enabled the State Department to maintain a fairly good relationship with the legislative branch of the government.[23] Within his department, Hull relied on informal deliberations with his staff. These conversations, which probably stemmed from the Secretary's Congressional experience, often took place on Sunday mornings when Hull and some of his advisers would gather in his office.

The Under Secretary of State, Sumner Welles, was the second most important individual in that department. In some respects, he was actually its paramount figure, because the President liked him personally and because his ideas harmonized with Roosevelt's own philosophy of foreign affairs. Like Roosevelt, Welles had attended Groton and Harvard and was independently wealthy. In the Foreign Service he had become an expert in Latin American issues. He had served as Ambassador to Cuba, and much of the direction of the Good Neighbor policy had been in his hands. After his appointment to the State Department in May 1937, Welles advised the President not only on the conduct of Latin American policy but also in other areas of American foreign relations. He was temperamentally the exact opposite of Hull. Dr. Stanley Hornbeck described him as a man of "great native intelligence who made up his mind quickly."[24] He often lost patience with the deliberate Hull, and friction between the two men sharpened over the years. Other factors contributed to the breach. Hull had wanted R. Walton Moore for the post of Under Secretary after William Phillips vacated it, but Roosevelt chose Welles.[25] The Under Secretary had access to the White House and often conferred with the President without Hull's clearance, a procedure that was normal to Roosevelt but displeased Hull.[26] Finally, the two men had fundamentally different views on the conduct of foreign affairs. Welles saw Hull's belief in free trade as a panacea for the world's troubles and his lofty statements of moral principles as inadequate to halt the "triumphal march of the dictators."[27] Welles thought that the President should circumvent the normal channels of diplomacy and play a direct role on the world stage to achieve peace. His memory of Hull's schemes was still bitter when the author interviewed him in 1960.

Dr. J. Stanley Hornbeck, J. Pierrepont Moffat and Norman Davis were less influential than Hull but still important men within the State Department. Hornbeck, Chief of the Division of Foreign Affairs and later political adviser to Hull, was regarded by his contemporaries as extremely able. He had spent many years as a teacher in China and, as a member of the Foreign Service, still felt a deep affection for that country. He demonstrated this in 1931 during the Manchurian crisis, when he tried to prod Secretary Stimson into taking a stiffer attitude toward Japan.[28] Moffat headed the Division of Western European Affairs, a post to which he succeeded in 1937 after having served as Consul in Australia. The son-in-law of Ambassador Grew, he was an able administrator. Unfortunately, as Hornbeck later said, he was easily alarmed and overly cautious. Davis was not a career diplomat, but he served the Roosevelt administration occasionally as a foreign policy adviser and roving ambassador. He was popular with everyone at State and enjoyed the highest confidence of both the President and the Secretary. When the President decided to speak out against the aggressor powers, Davis supplied him with much of his verbal ammunition.

Roosevelt was not particularly friendly toward the State Department as an institution. He felt that many of the men who had been appointed to it and to the Foreign Service had been chosen solely on the basis of their social connections. Furthermore, Roosevelt saw the notorious leakage of information from the Department as purposeful attempts by his opponents within that agency to embarrass him, even though both Hull and Welles tried to persuade him that his suspicions were groundless.[29]

Roosevelt's Cabinet did not play a significant part in the formulation of foreign policy, although some of its members were quick to suggest how the State Department should conduct its business. Henry Morgenthau, the Secretary of the Treasury, was the department's most vocal critic and confided in his diary that its approach to foreign affairs was "timorous and conventional" and was dominated by a "foreign office mentality." Although Morgenthau admired Welles and Herbert Feis, Hull's economic adviser, he felt that Hull the Secretary was "obsessed by his trade agreements program and misled by the Anglophilism and the hesitancies of career diplomats."[30] Morgenthau tried as far as he could to use the Treasury Department as an agency of American foreign policy. Meanwhile, Harold Ickes, the Secretary of the Interior, also offered advice to the State Department, but Hull was not the only Cabinet member to be subjected to the benefits of Ickes' wisdom. The "Old Curmudgeon," as Ickes was nicknamed, was convinced that no one else's department was administered as efficiently as his own.

The Administration's foreign relations representative in Congress was Key Pittman (D–NV), the Chairman of the Senate Foreign Relations Committee. He was not the strongest link in the Roosevelt chain and his position was not enviable. The Committee included such spokesmen for internationalism as Tom Connally (D–TX), Robert F. Wagner (D–NY), and later Claude Pepper (D–FL). But Roosevelt's opponents on the Committee were more powerful. These were William Borah (R–ID), Hiram Johnson (D–CA), Arthur H. Vandenberg (R–MI), Arthur Capper (R–KS), Robert M. LaFollette, Jr. (Pro–WI) and Henrik Shipstead (Farm-Labor–MN). Senator Pittman was buffeted between both groups, and while he provided leadership for the internationalists and supported the Administration's foreign policies, particularly with regard to action against Japan, he nevertheless shared some of the opposition's views and was reluctant to risk a fight with them. Pittman was extremely cautious about the strength of the Congressional opposition and frequently warned the Administration against moving too quickly in foreign policy, which could only have fortified Secretary Hull's characteristic wariness.[31]

These, then, were the players and agencies that contributed to the formulation of America's course of action in dealing with the Sino-Japanese conflict. The President, however, would ultimately decide whether the neutrality law should be invoked. He saw himself as the helmsman who would steer American foreign policy, and his appointment of Sumner Welles to the post of Under Secretary showed that he wanted someone of his own stamp assisting him. While in the earliest phase of the war in China, Roosevelt had made no move of his own, deferring to the Secretary of State, when the Far Eastern crisis became more acute, he became decisive.

The clash between Chinese and Japanese forces was barely a week old before Hull set in motion his plan to restore order. On July 16 he sent to all the world's governments a note asking them to sign a pledge based on the Eight Pillars of Peace. This was a statement of principles that Hull had proclaimed at the Buenos Aires Conference in the previous December. They called for observance of international law, cooperation among nations for the respect of treaties and the sovereignty of one's neighbors, and the adoption of "commercial policies to bring each the prosperity upon which enduring peace is founded."[32]

The Japanese were unimpressed. Ambassador Grew reported that the Japanese press carried an extensive summary of Hull's remarks, but there was no official and little editorial comment on them.[33] By mid–August the three so-called aggressor nations, Germany, Italy and Japan, had sent replies to Hull indicating their agreement with his proposal. However, the Japanese qualified their consent by saying "the objectives of these principles will only be attained in their application to the Far Eastern situation by a full recognition and practical consideration of the actual particular circumstances of that region."[34]

By the time America received this reply the situation in Shanghai had worsened and the fighting in North China had assumed large proportions. Obviously, Japan was paying only lip service to Hull's circular. What was to be done? Neither the Chinese nor the Japanese wanted mediation except under circumstances that were unsatisfactory to both. The Cabinet met on August 7 and discussed the Sino-Japanese war for nearly an hour. Vice President Garner questioned the wisdom of keeping Marines and soldiers in China, but Hull argued that to withdraw them would convince Japan that the United States was weak and subject America to insult. Harold Ickes wrote:

> As I listened to him, it occurred to me that on other occasions he has seemed to be obsessed with the idea that if we did or refrained from doing certain things in the Far East, the Japanese would "insult" us. His attitude with respect to Japan seems to be entirely different from that with respect to other countries with which we have diplomatic relations.[35]

A week later the matter came before the Cabinet again and Garner returned to the attack, but Hull put up the same defense. Ickes wrote that, while Roosevelt deplored conditions in China, he felt that he could not withdraw the Marines at that time. Admiral Leahy, present in his capacity as Acting Secretary of the Navy, summarized the disposition of American forces in China. The President expressed apprehension about the safety of Americans in Shanghai.

Throughout August and early September, Welles, Moore, Hornbeck, Moffat and some lesser officials met in Hull's office to discuss what course to follow in the Far East. Moffat noted in his diary that there was "a slight rasping of nerves and considerable wear and tear on the part of the group." At one office meeting on August 27, Hull proposed to issue another statement about his "Pillars of Peace." Everyone present tried to discourage

IX. Quarantine the Aggressor

him. The Secretary, wrote Moffat, could not understand why the other powers would not take their cue from him and "try to arouse public opinion through statements of principle in favor of peace." Hornbeck bluntly responded that no European power believed in words, and that unless and until we were prepared to talk deeds, they would not take anything from Washington seriously.[36]

The main issue around which these conversations revolved was whether the Neutrality Act should be invoked. Should the United States wash its hands of Far Eastern perils, or should it hold to its commitments as one of the great powers in the Orient? To apply the law would give notice that America regarded the struggle impartially and was removing itself from any possibility of involvement. The practical consequences of the Act were apparent to the Roosevelt administration. It would deny China access to American loans and munitions that were not as vital to Japan in her prosecution of the war. On the other hand, America's failure to invoke the law would show partiality to China and allow her to make use of U.S. resources for her defense. The Administration did not want to become a belligerent, but how neutral could it be?

By mid-August 1937, the White House had received hundreds of telegrams and letters from peace groups and private citizens in favor of the Neutrality Act. Editorials in the *Washington Post*, the *Philadelphia Record* and Midwestern journals called for its invocation. Only a few newspapers, such as the *New York Times*, questioned its wisdom. Far more formidable was the pressure from Congress, much of it from members of the President's own party. Roosevelt expected this from outspoken isolationists, but they were joined by rank and file Democrats.

The State Department decided to consult its representatives in Nanking and Tokyo on the possible reaction in those capitals if the Act were invoked. The replies were predictable. Ambassador Johnson in China cabled Hull that the Chinese press would express "keen regret" if the United States, a friend of long standing, should be the first country to deny them effective aid, and would use this both at home and abroad to explain their reverses. "The Chinese government cannot rid itself of the feeling that the powers party to the Kellogg Pact and Nine Power Treaty should have done something in the past and still should do something now or in the future to restrain Japan."[37]

Ambassador Grew reported from Japan that its press and some government agencies might regard invocation as a sign of American disapproval of Japanese policy but that the

> ... predominant reaction would most probably be favorable. It would probably be regarded as evidence of the intention of the United States to make no exception in policy in a case arising in the Far East as contrasted with similar cases which might

occur in other parts of the world. It would probably be regarded also as further manifestation of intention by the United States to refrain from intervention.[38]

Grew did not believe that invocation would materially affect Japan, except for the loss of the aircraft it imported from America as models for adaptation. The same day that this cable arrived at the State Department, Hull and his advisers gathered in his office for two and a half hours to discuss whether they should advise the President to invoke the law. After a visit to Hull's house with Hornbeck (to play croquet!) Pierrepont Moffat wrote in his diary on September 7:

> In one sense these conferences where we go round and round may seem a terrible waste of time; on the other hand, not an argument, not even a shading, can be missed.... Later in the day ... [Hull] confessed that he was putting all his strength into determining the right course of action and that it was the biggest thing he had faced in five years. He is looking pretty haggard and [Hornbeck] too is looking pale and drawn.

While the leaders at State were wringing their hands in indecision, Roosevelt appeared to have decided not to apply the neutrality measure. In a day when reporters still agreed to take comments off the record, he addressed the issue. Sitting at his desk in the Oval Office, with the press corps gathered around him, he indulged in memories of his maternal grandfather's ties with China, the conditions that existed there in those days, and the imperial system that had grown up there. Eventually, he came to the point. The present situation in China, he said, was considerably different from the one that had existed between Italy and Ethiopia at the time of the conflict between those two countries. Then, each side had withdrawn its diplomatic representatives from the other's capital and the Italian army "commenced a perfectly definite war in Ethiopia with the full recognition on the part of both governments that a state of war existed." In the current Sino-Japanese quarrel there had been no break in diplomatic relations and consequently it was not in the same category.[39]

For the record, Roosevelt said that technically, no war had been declared between China and Japan and the two nations were at peace. Privately, he and Hull agreed that the Neutrality Act should not be applied unless circumstances required it. However, technicalities did not enter into their decision. Hull later wrote that to have shut off supplies would place aggressor and victim on the same footing, and while Japan did not need them, China did.[40] Roosevelt had backing from his principal lieutenant, Key Pittman, Chairman of the Senate Foreign Relations Committee. In a radio broadcast on August 23, Pittman reiterated the President's assurance that no formal declaration of war had been made by either China or Japan. At the same time, he defended the presence of U.S. military forces in China, saying that their withdrawal would be cowardly and unpatriotic.

However, advocates of the Neutrality Act would not be silenced, and on September 14 Roosevelt threw them a sop. He announced that henceforth no merchant ships owned by the U.S. government would be allowed to transport to China or Japan any of the arms or munitions listed in the neutrality bill of May 1, 1937. Any other merchant vessels that tried to transport any of the listed articles to either country while flying the American flag would do so at their own risk. The President's critics were not satisfied. Congressman Hamilton Fish (R–NY) called Roosevelt's policy "half-baked, milk-and-water," while a writer in *Amerasia* dubbed it "make-believe ... nourished on the flimsy hope that the conflict will soon be over."[41] Ultimately, the only ship that was affected by the President's order was the *Wichita*, operated by the Maritime Commission. It had been en route to China with a cargo of nineteen Bellanca airplanes and a limited quantity of small arms, but when it arrived from Baltimore at San Pedro, California, this cargo was removed, much to the delight of the Japanese and the chagrin of the Chinese.[42] This was the closest Roosevelt came to an actual prohibition of the transportation of weapons to the belligerents.

Whatever the President might have said or written in the past, he had now concluded that the United States could not remain aloof in a world that was witnessing a steady succession of aggressor triumphs. Hitler, in defiance of the Treaty of Versailles, had remilitarized the Rhineland. Ethiopia had fallen to Italian conquest. Events in Spain made it clear that Hitler and Mussolini were actively assisting Franco in establishing another fascist state. In conversations with Sumner Welles in 1937, Roosevelt said he was aware of the future threat to the U.S. if Europe came to be dominated by Nazi Germany, but his main concern was with Japan. He was clearly troubled by the invasion of China. As he was wont to do, he speculated out loud about possible courses of action. He told Welles that he might consider a naval blockade if Japan persisted in trying to conquer the rest of Asia.[43] Such a scheme would have been fraught with peril at home and abroad if he had suggested it publicly, but it gave a clue to his thinking. To Admiral McIntyre, the White House physician, Roosevelt said that he regarded the Japanese as "the Prussians of the East and just as drunk with their dreams of domination."[44] His resolution became clearer as he reviewed his options.

Early in the summer of 1937, Roosevelt decided to supplement the moral support of the Stimson Doctrine for China with more tangible aid. Dr. H.H. Kung, the Chinese Minister of Finance, came to Washington to negotiate the sale of 50 million ounces of silver to the United States. Secretary of the Treasury Henry Morgenthau was reluctant to buy that much but prodded by the President he softened his attitude and eventually bought 62 million ounces at 45 cents apiece. When Morgenthau gave Kung the good news on July 8, he explained that Roosevelt had instructed the Treasury

Department to do everything it could to keep China strong. Pleased by the turn of events, Kung praised the American action, declaring that a strong China would mean peace and security in the Far East. The Marco Polo Bridge skirmish had occurred only the day before.

By summer's end, the President was becoming increasingly anxious about how long China could be kept "strong." Withholding application of the Neutrality Act might enable the Chinese to buy the arms they needed to resist Japan, but in his view, this was not enough. He had so far refrained from making a public statement about his true feelings regarding the conflict in Asia. Hull's pronouncements had proved useless. Roosevelt now decided to take the initiative and seek to rally the American people in a clarion call for action.

Few Presidents in American history have matched Franklin Roosevelt's ability to put forth ideas in catch phrases and clever metaphors—what we would now call "sound bites." He came by this ability naturally. His Republican uncle who had occupied the White House a generation earlier had this talent, and so did Woodrow Wilson, whom he had served so faithfully. Clichés are a useful way to promote national policy. They enable a President to sell an idea or program that might seem arcane or dangerous. Depending on the objective, a President might seek to lull or even dupe his audience with vague words, leaving them to interpret his message. If his phrasing is sufficiently general, the President has an escape hatch if public reaction is hostile. Roosevelt's "quarantine" speech falls into this category. What he said privately before the speech makes clear what he had in mind before he delivered it. What he said afterward were the words of a man retreating from his own convictions.

In the summer of 1937, with hostilities escalating in China, the President revealed his thoughts to at least two of his contemporaries: Harold Ickes, the Secretary of the Interior; and Sumner Welles. He told Welles that he had in mind imposing a trade embargo on Japan, to be enforced by units of the American and British navies stationed at strategic points in the Pacific. The plan was similar to an earlier one that he had mentioned to the Under Secretary but was more specific. In retrospect, the proposal was not only unthinkable in the existing political climate but was terribly naive and amateurish. Yet Roosevelt seriously argued its merits. He told Welles that Japan needed American and British markets and could not continue her China policy if these were denied to her. When Welles asked if this might not lead to war, the President replied that he did not think so because Japan was already heavily committed in China, and with her trade shut off "she would bog down long before she could get access to oil and other raw materials in Southeast Asia."[45] Welles wondered what assurance there was that Great Britain would support the U.S. in such a radical program. Roosevelt said that the Chamberlain government was stronger-minded than its predecessor and must realize that it could not allow Japan to jeopardize the vast British financial interests in the Far East. If Roosevelt really believed that Chamberlain would endorse such a dangerous plan, he was engaging in wishful thinking bordering on fantasy. With the looming German threat in Europe, the very last thing the British government would do would be to risk a conflict in Asia. Moreover, Chamberlain had little confidence in America's reliability in a crisis beyond its own shores. Even after Roosevelt delivered his quarantine speech, Chamberlain privately declared that it was best not to count on more than words from the United States.[46] Of course, nothing came of Roosevelt's musings with Welles, but the idea of a trade embargo persisted in his mind. In September 1937 he told Harold Ickes that he was thinking of writing a letter to all of the nations of the world, with the possible exception of Germany, Italy and Japan, suggesting that if any nation should "invade the rights or threaten the liberties of any ... other nation, the peace-loving nations would isolate it." By this, Ickes concluded, the President meant to cut off trade with any offending country and deprive it of raw materials.[47] The proposed letter was never sent, but part of the plan formed the basis of Roosevelt's speech in Chicago in October.

Even more revealing than these disclosures is a memorandum of a conversation in early July 1937 between the President and Clark Eichelberger, a State Department assistant. Roosevelt discussed the international situation and suggested a program of economic measures, disarmament, and an overhaul of the existing peace machinery. He noted the principle of consultation among non-belligerents which had been included in the agreements reached at the Inter-American Conference in Buenos Aires in 1936. These, he said, might be projected throughout the world. If other nations subscribed to the doctrine, the American people would follow suit and adopt economic measures against an aggressor nation. Significantly, he hinted to Eichelberger that he might one day make a dramatic speech which would "lead the world on the upward path."[48]

In late summer 1937, the President decided to travel to the West Coast, visiting some of the areas where extensive publics works projects had been undertaken and speaking to the people at several pre-selected places. Most of these addresses were to be concerned with various phases of the New Deal, but Cordell Hull and Norman Davis suggested that Roosevelt also talk about foreign affairs, "particularly in a large city where isolation was entrenched."[49] They settled on Chicago, where Roosevelt had been asked to dedicate the Outer Drive Bridge over the mouth of the Chicago River. It was time for the "dramatic speech."

The President's train left Hyde Park on September 22 and began the long trip that was to take him across the northern United States to the

Pacific Northwest. Before leaving, he asked the Secretary of State and Norman Davis to provide him with speech material for his Chicago address. This was compiled and given to him before his departure. Hull and Davis also prepared a first draft in Washington in the form of two memoranda. Davis wrote two more memos in New York and read them over the telephone to James Dunn of the State Department, then forwarded them to the President.[50] As Roosevelt's train sped across the West, he took all these drafts and put them together to create what has become popularly known as the "quarantine speech."

Characteristically, the President did not tie himself to what others had written. All of his public addresses reflect his unique style. Roosevelt accomplished this by amalgamating the drafts prepared by Hull and Davis, changing a word here and a phrase there and adding a few key sentences or expressions to convey his own point of view. Furthermore, there were two or possibly three other unwitting contributors to the quarantine speech. The first was author James Hilton, whose *Lost Horizon* had become a best seller. Some months after the famous address, Roosevelt wrote to Hilton that he had enjoyed his book and that it had given him just the "questions" he needed when he was preparing to speak in Chicago.[51] The second was Frank W. Sterrett, Episcopal Bishop of Bethlehem, Pennsylvania, who had written to the President three days before he left Hyde Park for the West. Roosevelt was so moved by the letter that he incorporated part of it into his talk.

The final contributor to the quarantine speech was Harold Ickes. A man of some controversy in his own right, he claimed to have suggested to Roosevelt the word "quarantine." On October 9, Ickes wrote in his diary that he had talked with the President just before the latter's trip. Ickes said that in discussing the international situation, he told Roosevelt that Italy, Germany and Japan were like a "contagious disease in a community" and that "neighbors had a right to quarantine themselves against a contagious disease." At this, he wrote, "the President said, 'That is a good line; I will write it down,' which he proceeded to do."[52] But Samuel Rosenman, another Presidential speechwriter, got a letter from Sumner Welles which said that Roosevelt had used the word "quarantine" several times that summer in discussing with him the trade embargo against Japan that he had in mind, long before the address was drafted.[53]

It is no longer important who originated the word. The President's use of it, however, was enormously significant because many people saw it as a fundamental change in foreign policy, with serious consequences for the United States.

The speech was weighing on Roosevelt's mind as he traveled westward. In September he wrote to Lord Tweedsmuir, the Governor General of Canada, "I do not dare to be away from Washington long because of the international clouds. I am, as you know, an impatient soul and it is especially difficult not 'to speak out loud in meeting.'"[54]

With the drafts from Hull and Davis in his hands, the President began to put in final form the ideas that he had been developing for the past months. On the afternoon of the day that he spoke at the Bonneville Dam in Oregon, he dictated some letters to his secretary, Grace Tully. When he was done, he asked her casually, "Child, what are you doing tonight?" Miss Tully said later that she knew from long experience what that meant: an evening of dictation. With the intimate charm he reserved for his inner circle, he told her, "You'd better come back and have some dinner and if you're good, I may even give you a little cocktail. Later we'll do some thinking out loud on the first draft of my speech at Chicago."[55] And thus the quarantine speech was born.

In three brief paragraphs the President described the peaceful and prosperous conditions he had found on his cross-country trip and contrasted them with what was happening elsewhere in the world. He then inserted the drafts prepared by Hull and Davis. The points made in these were that: (1) the world's hopes for peace engendered by the Kellogg-Briand Pact had been threatened by the "present reign of terror and international lawlessness"; (2) ruthless unjustified warfare was being perpetrated on helpless civilians, including women and children. On the latter point, he called attention to the fact that these atrocities had taken place without a declaration of war, an indictment clearly leveled at Japan.[56] At this point, Roosevelt quoted from *Lost Horizon*, to fit the mood he was trying to create:

> Perhaps we foresee a time when men, exultant in the technique of homicide, will rage so hotly over the world that every precious thing will be in danger, every book and picture and harmony, every treasure garnered through two millennia, the small, the delicate, the defenseless—all will be lost or wrecked or utterly destroyed.[57]

The President returned to the Hull-Davis drafts for a few paragraphs before inserting parts of Bishop Sterrett's letter: "It seems to me that something greatly needs to be said in behalf of ordinary humanity against the present practice of carrying the horrors of war to helpless civilians, especially women and children."[58] He then went back to the memoranda of Hull and Davis to declare that it was impossible in the modern world for any nation to isolate itself from economic and political upheavals and that it was vitally important for the United States to see that "the sanctity of international treaties and the maintenance of international morality be restored." The peace, freedom and security of 90 percent of the world were threatened by the remaining 10 percent. "Surely," he said, "the 90 percent who want to live in peace ... can and must find a way to make their will prevail."⁵⁹

After these words, Roosevelt generally adhered to the text sent to him by Davis. Part of it seemed to fit the "quarantine" concept that he had included. "War is a contagion, whether it be declared or undeclared. It can engulf states and peoples remote from the original scene of hostilities." The President concluded by condensing the paragraphs of Davis's draft that had advocated a course of positive efforts to preserve peace. "America hates war. America hopes for peace. Therefore, America actively engages in the search for peace."

The address, combining as it did the ideas of several authors, was something of a cut-and-paste effort, but Roosevelt arranged it to express his own viewpoint. Without the quarantine phrase, it probably would not have aroused any controversy. He certainly knew that it was no ordinary expression to use in a major discussion of foreign policy. His choice changed the temper of the speech from a simple protest against international lawlessness to a speculative suggestion of collective action in terms such as no President had uttered since the days of Woodrow Wilson.

When Roosevelt arrived in Chicago on the morning of October 5, some 750,000 people gathered to see him as he drove from the railway station to the dedication ceremony at the Outer Drive Bridge. According to a *New York Times* reporter, they "remain[ed] silent most of the time but applaud[ed] his demands for world peace. It was evident from comments made in the crowd afterward that the tenor of the address was a surprise, but general approval was heard." Grace Tully later recalled that when Roosevelt returned to the train, he had the "air of having made a profound decision and commitment and of being glad that the step was taken."

If all of the "quarantine" arrows before the speech had pointed toward economic sanctions, they lost their direction afterward. Before the President boarded his train for the return trip to Hyde Park, he lunched at the residence of Cardinal Mundelein, Archbishop of Chicago, and the two men apparently discussed his remarks. The next day, Mundelein wrote to Amleto Cicognani, the Apostolic Delegate in Washington, "[Roosevelt's] plan does not contemplate either military or naval action against the unjust aggressor nation, but rather a policy of isolation, severance of ordinary communications by all the governments in the pact."⁶⁰

The President also talked the next day with William Phillips, a former Ambassador to Italy, who visited him at Hyde Park. Phillips told Roosevelt that he had read the address in the newspapers that morning and had misgivings about it. He asked, what did the President mean by a "quarantine"? Roosevelt replied that while he was dictating the speech, he had searched for a word that was not "sanctions" and had finally settled on "quarantine," which he thought indicated a "drawing away from someone." In developing this idea, he said that he was willing to go very far in drawing away.⁶¹ Roosevelt continued to backpedal at a press conference in which he answered several questions about his definition of "quarantine." He first warned the reporters that his replies were off the record, after which they asked him what measures he had in mind with reference to quarantining and whether these could be reconciled with the neutrality laws passed by Congress. He sidestepped these questions by referring to the last line of his speech, "Therefore America actively engages in the search for peace." The reporters wanted to know if this meant any positive steps had been taken, which the President admitted was not the case. One of them asked if "quarantine" meant economic sanctions. "No," he said, "not necessarily. Look, 'sanctions' is a terrible word to use. They are out the window." When asked if there would be a conference of peace-loving nations, the President replied, "No; conferences are out of the window. You never get anywhere with a conference." This was a strange answer, since the United States was then preparing to meet with the Nine Power Treaty nations to seek a settlement in the Sino-Japanese dispute. When told that foreign papers were saying that this was an attitude without a program, Roosevelt acknowledged that it was an attitude but indicated that his administration was looking for a program.⁶²

The reporters continued to press the President for clarification but succeeded only in working up a case of frustration. Ernest Lindley had the following exchange with him:

> Q: You say there isn't any conflict between what you outline and the Neutrality Act. They seem to be at opposite poles to me and your assertion does not enlighten me.
> THE PRESIDENT: Put your thinking cap on, Ernest.
> Q: I have been for some years. They seem to be an opposite poles. How can you be neutral if you are going to align yourself with one group of nations?
> THE PRESIDENT: What do you mean, "aligning"? You mean a treaty?
> Q: Not necessarily. I mean action on the part of the peace-loving nations.
> THE PRESIDENT: There are a lot of methods in the world that have not been tried yet.
> Q: But at any rate, that is not an indication of a neutral attitude–"quarantine the aggressors" and "other nations of the world."
> THE PRESIDENT: I can't give you any other clue to it. You will have to invent one. I haven't got one.
> Q: Do you agree or disagree with what apparently amounts to the conclusion of the British, that sanctions mean war?
> THE PRESIDENT: No. Don't talk about sanctions. Never suggested it ... don't get off on the sanctions route.
> Q: I meant that in general terms; going further than moral denunciation.
> THE PRESIDENT: That is not a definition of "sanctions."
> Q: Is a "quarantine" a sanction?
> THE PRESIDENT: No.

Q: Are you excluding any coercive action? Sanctions is coercive.
THE PRESIDENT: That is exactly the difference.
Q: Better then to keep it in a moral sphere?
THE PRESIDENT: No, it can be a very practical sphere.

Thus the press conference ended with the newsmen knowing nothing of what Roosevelt had in mind with his "search for peace," except that he did not regard a quarantine as the application of economic sanctions. Lindley might have felt that he had experienced an "Alice in Wonderland" moment with the President, but although the latter's definition of "quarantine" remained enigmatic, Roosevelt chose that word for a definite purpose. He had always liked to put ideas and programs into easily understood terms. The twelve years of his Presidency are filled with them. His domestic reforms were the "New Deal." He popularized, if he did not originate, the term "Good Neighbor" to describe America's relations with the other states in the Western hemisphere. He used "Lend-Lease" and the analogy of offering a neighbor one's garden hose to put out a fire to provide a clever explanation for the non-neutral act of sending direct military aid to Great Britain in 1941. Depending how well the phrase "quarantine the aggressor" caught on, he could then have undertaken one or more of the courses he had been contemplating over the previous year. As it turned out, his boldness inspired neither his foreign policy advisers nor Congress to follow him, and the media were so divided that he could not find a consensus there. The Hearst press was downright vitriolic in its denunciation of him.

Pierrepont Moffat was in Hull's office when the ticker service relayed the text of the President's speech in Chicago. Moffat wrote in his diary that the Secretary was delighted, and said that almost everyone else in the room agreed that the public would strongly approve, but he also observed that "the sentence regarding the quarantine was a surprise" and might "ultimately drive us much further than we wish to go."[63] If Hull was in fact initially enthusiastic about Roosevelt's words, he soon had serious misgivings. He later said that what he had had in mind was a speech conforming to his own recent pronouncements, voicing concern about the threat to peace abroad and perhaps appealing to all nations to abide by recognized principles of international morality. Hull felt that the quarantine speech had the effect of "setting back for at least six months our constant educational campaign intended to create and strengthen public opinion toward international cooperation." If the Administration proceeded gradually, without undue opposition, its words and actions, "though not dynamic or far-reaching," would have more influence in the world at large than "startling pronouncements" or "precipitate action." Others in the State Department were also alarmed. Stanley Hornbeck told the author that while he was glad the President had suggested action, as a member of the Department he regretted the way Roosevelt had gone about it. "I felt that the idea should have been discussed in camera in advance of its being sprung in public."

The words of these officials demonstrate the wariness and discipline that guided them in their conduct of foreign affairs. Boldness was equivalent to rashness, and rashness was anathema to men whose careers were guided by circumspection and orderliness. The maverick among them was the Under Secretary of State. Sumner Welles was enthusiastic about the speech, and the failure of Hull and his followers to support the President not only disappointed Roosevelt, he said, but slowed the latter's momentum in leading the nation toward collective security.

In the Cabinet, only Harold Ickes, Henry Morgenthau and Henry Wallace supported the President's stand, while in Congress, a storm of opposition was raised by those Senators and Representatives who feared abandonment of the neutrality program. Hardly anyone in Congress favored changing America's foreign policy. Even those who praised Roosevelt's remarks emphasized the portions that did not imply forceful measures. Senator Borah spoke for them when he said that the vital part of the speech was the President's statement, "It is my determination to pursue a policy of peace and to adopt every practical measure to avoid involvement in war."[64]

Curiously, those people who expressed their feelings directly to Roosevelt, by writing letters or sending telegrams, were overwhelmingly in favor of the Chicago speech. Five thick folders at the Franklin D. Roosevelt Library in Hyde Park are stuffed with hundreds of messages praising his remarks. These came from well-known figures and from ordinary citizens. Raymond L. Buell, President of the Foreign Policy Association, wrote to James Roosevelt that he had just returned from a meeting of the National Policy Committee in Memphis, Tennessee, where some fifty people from the South and Midwest had come together to discuss the nation's agricultural problems. Buell had asked them for their reactions to the President's remarks:

> The people I talked with are not professional peace advocates, but are dirt farmers, labor leaders, and editors. I was pleasantly surprised to hear them all say that their part of the country was enthusiastic about the new note struck by the President.[65]

Fewer than 100 individuals around the country expressed disapproval, but they were vitriolic in their denunciations. One furious New York resident wrote, "Your outrageous speech for war, a war to help the Jews, and incited by Barney Baruch and Jew bankers, is meeting with universal condemnation in America."[66]

Press reaction was mixed. Roosevelt got high marks from the *Des Moines Register, Cleveland Plain Dealer, Los Angeles Times, San Francisco*

Chronicle, and the *Atlanta Constitution*. The *St. Louis Globe Democrat* came closest to the truth when it said, "this address was a declaration of principles, not a program of action." Some were more cautious in their descriptions. The *New York Times* asked what the President meant by "concerted action" and if he had a specific plan or was simply giving a "well deserved rebuke" to the law-breaking nations. Other newspapers were less restrained. In an editorial entitled "Go Slow, Mr. President," the *Boston Herald* wondered what "positive endeavors" the President had in mind. The *Chicago Tribune* was far harsher:

> Those Chicagoans who went yesterday to see a bridge dedicated, those who gathered at the curbstones to see a President pass in a shower of ticker tape, and those who sat at their radios to hear some words of peace, these and many more found themselves the center of a world-hurricane of war fright. President Roosevelt came to Chicago to bless the bridge that spans two delightful and peaceful park systems.
> He talked war.

The Hearst press was openly hostile. A questionnaire went out to members of Congress, using the quarantine speech as its point of departure and asking if the United States should take sides in the Sino-Japanese conflict or avoid war entirely. As the replies came in, Hearst newspapers ran them over the next two weeks. The Hearst verdict was that Congressmen from the "Atlantic to the Pacific, from Canada to the Gulf" had "roared back their determination for today, tomorrow and forever to keep the United States out of foreign wars."[67]

The fear expressed by the opposition press was that "quarantine" meant war, while the publications that supported Roosevelt's speech did so without endorsing measures that would involve America in conflict with an aggressor power. This is not as paradoxical as it might sound. One segment of the press interpreted the address as a major threat to U.S. neutrality; the other chose to regard the President's words simply as an expression of concern over the threat to world peace. The latter interpretation was no more seen as a call for America to take direct action in the Far East than was the former. Roosevelt must have recognized this as he scanned the newspapers in the days following his address, but he was far less likely to be influenced by what the press was saying than by his lack of support in Washington. The failure of his allies in Congress to rally behind him, and the opposition within that body and in the State Department, made a deeper impression on him and led him to soft-pedal his approach toward dealing with aggressors.

If the Chicago speech had gotten him into hot water, another one might get him out. A week later, on October 12, he gave one of his familiar "fireside chats" over the radio. Those who expected him to propose a new formula for American foreign policy were either disappointed or relieved,

IX. Quarantine the Aggressor

depending on their point of view. Most of his talk was devoted to domestic matters. He referred only briefly to world tensions: "I want our great democracy to be wise enough to realize that aloofness from war is not prompted by unawareness of war. In a world of mutual suspicions, peace must be affirmatively reached for." He went on to mention that the United States was going to participate in the conference of the Nine Power Treaty adherents that was scheduled to convene shortly. He said that this was an example of one possible path to follow in the search for peace. He concluded by saying:

> Meanwhile, remember that from 1913 to 1921 I personally was fairly close to world events, and in that period, while I learned much of what to do, I also learned much of what not to do. The common sense, the intelligence of America agree with my statement that "America hates war. America hopes for peace. Therefore America actively engages in the search for peace."[68]

Apparently Hull and others were placated by the moderate tone of these remarks. In his diary entry of October 12, Pierrepont Moffat observed that they were reassuring but "did not mark any apparent retreat from earlier announcements." The *New York Times* reported a similar view in diplomatic circles in Washington. Moffat was mistaken. The retreat was to become all too obvious when the American delegation turned up at the conference in Brussels.

While the President was attempting to dispel fears with his fireside chat, the echoes of his quarantine speech were reverberating around the world. Among both the prospective quarantiners and the prospective quarantinees, it had aroused intense interest. The Japanese saw it as an attack on their New Order. Ambassador Grew reported that a Foreign Office spokesman had said that, "if the 'haves' refuse to concede to the rightful demands of the 'have-nots' peace will be very difficult to maintain." Grew went on to relate that the two principal Japanese newspapers, *Asahi* and *Nichi Nichi*, were also critical. The editor of *Asahi* had agreed that the ideals of world peace voiced by the President were desirable but said that the facts upon which Roosevelt's arguments were based were in need of revision. *Nichi Nichi* had declared that so far, American behavior with regard to the Far Eastern conflict had been fair, but that Roosevelt's address was imprudent and lacked his usually keen political insight.[69]

Grew was almost as upset by the speech as were the Japanese. He felt that all of his efforts to build good will over the previous five years had been for naught. In his diary, he lamented the turn American foreign policy had taken:

> If this sudden turnabout in policy could possibly help the situation either now or in the future, if our branding Japan as an aggressor and our appeal to the Nine Power

Treaty and the Kellogg Pact and our support of the League of Nations could serve to stop the fighting in China or limit is sphere or prevent similar aggression in the world in the future, my accord with this step would be complete and wholehearted. But alas, history and experience have show that Real Politik and not ethereal idealism should govern our policy and our acts today. With Manchuria, Abyssinia and Spain written in big letters across the pages of history, how can we ignore the practical experience of those events and the hopelessness of deterring them *unless we are willing to fight*? Moral suasion is ineffective; economic or financial sanctions have been shown to be ineffective and dangerous to boot.... Why, oh why, do we disregard the experience and facts of history which stare us in the face?[70]

All of the American Embassy staff shared Grew's view, and he felt it necessary to call them together to warn them against uttering statements which might indicate that they did not fully back Washington's policy. "The members of the staff, I think unanimously, felt so bitter about this new development that I feared they would sputter about it outside."[71]

In Germany, another unnamed aggressor, press criticism of the President's speech was restrained. The semi-official *Diplomatische Korrespondenz* suggested "Mr. Roosevelt would do well to consider the fate of well-meaning President Wilson and not start something he cannot finish." That paper took him to task for not citing the "Bolshevist menace" in his denunciation of those nations who would disturb the peace. Significantly, although a report of Roosevelt's speech appeared in early editions of German newspapers, it was lifted from later ones.[72] Officially, however, there was a great deal of interest in Roosevelt's remarks. From Washington, Ambassador Dieckhoff wired the German Foreign Ministry that the speech was directed against Japan, but as far as his Military Attaché could determine the United States was not planning any military measures. The perceptive Dieckhoff said there was no evidence that the Administration intended to go beyond "moralizing admonitions." He added that even if the forthcoming conference were held the United States was unlikely to assume a leading role. This accurate prediction concluded with an equally amazing prophecy:

> [T]he passive role of American foreign policy in the Far East as well as in Europe would probably be abandoned only if a world conflict should break out in which Great Britain is involved. Then, of course, we will have to expect that the weight of the United States will soon be thrown into the scales on the side of the British.[73]

It would be interesting to know who Dieckhoff's contacts were within the State Department or elsewhere in the Administration in 1937, because he was getting a steady stream of information about the quarantine speech that enabled him to draw realistic conclusions. On October 15 he advised Berlin that the original drafts of the speech provided by the State Department had not contained the quarantine phrase; it was incorporated by the President himself. The German Ambassador was not sure what had prompted Roosevelt to insert the quarantine reference, but he opined:

> The intensification of the Japanese campaign in China probably alarmed him.... [H]e was undoubtedly influenced against Japan during his trip through the Northwest, particularly on the West Coast, which always keeps a sharp lookout in the direction of the Far East. Possibly there many have been a domestic factor, too, i.e., the attempt to drown out and perhaps silence the public discussion of the Black case, which was embarrassing to [him], by a spectacular fanfare in the field of foreign policy.... One thing at any rate is certain: the sharp tone of the Chicago speech can only be attributed to the intensification of the Far Eastern conflict.[74]

Ambassador Dieckhoff concluded his report by saying that the general negative reaction to the speech in the U.S. had caused the President to "blur the impression made by his sharp words" by announcing in his October 12 radio address that the Nine Power conference would attempt to resolve the Far Eastern situation through agreement and with the cooperation of China and Japan. The German detected some skepticism about the conference within the State Department. He predicted that America "would avoid anything which might have the appearance of coerciveness of an economic or military nature against Japan." If Dieckhoff had been representing the British Foreign Office, the London government might have been spared the disappointment that came at Brussels a month later.

The Western powers were guardedly enthusiastic about the quarantine speech. The British press publicized it widely, the *Times* declaring that Roosevelt's appeal to his own as well as other freedom-loving peoples would "nowhere meet with deeper satisfaction than in Britain and the dominions." But other papers were more reserved, warning their readers not to expect too much. The *Manchester Guardian* said, "It should certainly encourage the British Government to ask how far the United States is prepared to go in joint action even if the answer is (as it may well be) that the United States Government cannot tell because it does not know."[75]

It was precisely this question that prompted Foreign Secretary Anthony Eden to have the British Chargé d'Affaires in Washington call on Sumner Welles to seek an interpretation of the President's remarks. Welles' reply could not have provided much comfort. He said that the President did not have in mind "immediate or imminent application of quarantine measures" and suggested that the Chargé listen to Roosevelt's "fireside chat" that night, since it would help the British government understand what the President had in mind in his Chicago speech.[76] Surely the Chargé did so but was not the wiser for the experience.

The French were also skeptical. They applauded the speech, but their newspapers advised readers not to expect too much from the United States. Premier Camille Chautemps told Hugh Wilson, the American Chargé, that he would like to be able to sit down with the President and ask him exactly what he thought the peace-loving nations could do to oppose treaty violations.[77] It is unlikely that Chautemps would have learned any more than Ernest Lindley did at the off-the-record press conference at Hyde Park.

In China the embattled Chiang Kai-shek greeted the speech with an optimism born of desperation. He declared that President Roosevelt had "deeply touched the overridden Chinese" and "aroused those powers who advocate the construction of perpetual peace on the foundation of international ethics."[78] Chiang added that he felt a ray of hope had dawned now that the League and the Department of State were taking steps to censure the Japanese.

The Chinese were heartened further when the State Department announced the day after the quarantine speech that the United States was going to participate in a parley of the signatories to the Nine Power Treaty. Many in America and abroad saw a connection between the two events and assumed that a new era of diplomacy was about to be ushered in. Moreover, the United States had endorsed the League of Nations' position that Japan had violated the Treaty. The juxtaposition of the two events seemed to offer proof of a carefully coordinated plan. In fact, it was nothing more than a terribly misleading coincidence. For Chiang especially, it was a cruel twist. The President's bold words and the near-simultaneous announcement that the Western powers were about to meet to consider his plight fed his conviction that they would rescue him. He believed that his ill-fated Shanghai campaign might be vindicated after all. This was certainly a factor in his rejection of the German mediation effort.

None of these events had any influence on the Japanese. They had invested too much to turn aside from their China venture, no matter what the outside powers might do. They did not interpret Roosevelt's speech as a prelude to action. If sanctions were imposed, they were prepared to defy them just as Mussolini had successfully done during his war with Ethiopia, but they did not think sanctions were likely or that any outside power, including the United States, was prepared to use anything stronger than words against them.

However, two aspects of these developments did bother them. First, the Nine Power action gave China encouragement that would only prolong its resistance and thereby delay Japan's ability to end the conflict on favorable terms. Second, the Japanese were disturbed that the United States had formally aligned itself with the League and branded Japan as an aggressor. They had heretofore viewed America as a friend, and the Japanese press had praised it for its "fair and just neutrality." Now they saw themselves as increasingly isolated. From Tokyo, Hugh Byas wrote for the *New York Times*:

IX. Quarantine the Aggressor

Whatever the press may say in inspired moments, the mass of the Japanese people are much more sensitive to British and American opinion than to any other foreign opinion. Mussolini's approval is no compensation for the loss of Anglo-American goodwill, and his greeting Japan as a fascist power is offensive to the great majority of Japanese.

For the moment, though, attention shifted from the battlefields in China to the Palais des Academies in Brussels, where the Nine Power Treaty was to be given its severest and final test.

X

Charade at Brussels

> We all know quite well that whatever action is taken in this Far Eastern dispute does depend essentially upon the cooperation of the United States. I say without hesitation that in order to get the full cooperation, on an equal basis, of the United States Government, in an international conflict, I would travel not only from Geneva to Brussels, but from Melbourne to Alaska, particularly in the present state of international affairs.[1]
> —Foreign Secretary Anthony Eden, November 1, 1937

> What I cannot understand is that you Americans from time to time talk as if you really intended to act in the international sphere when you have no intention of acting in any way that can be effective. I understand how much the President may desire to do something today to preserve peace; but I should like infinitely rather to have him say nothing than make speeches, like his speech in Chicago, which raised immense hopes when there is no possibility that in the state of American opinion and in the state of mind of the Senate he can follow up such speeches by action.[2]
> —Premier Camille Chautemps, November 10, 1937

Although the French Foreign Minister had said that the Chinese might as well call on the moon for help as the League of Nations, Geneva was a lot closer. On September 12, after fruitless consultations in Washington, London and Paris, the Chinese formally appealed to the League Council, asking that the Nine Power Treaty be invoked on their behalf. The appeal was not a surprise. As early as August the Chinese had indicated that they were contemplating such a move by presenting to the League's Secretary General a statement reviewing the sequence of events in their conflict with Japan and charging the Japanese with aggression in violation of the League Covenant, the Kellogg Pact and the Nine Power Treaty. Technically, this statement was not an appeal to the League but simply a résumé of the specific acts of which they alleged Japan was guilty. The Chinese government asked that it be sent to the members of the League and of the Far Eastern Advisory Committee that had been established in 1933 with the adoption of the Lytton Report. The American Consul in Geneva took note of China's move, cabling Hull that the Chinese would probably make a formal appeal to the League during the Assembly session and that, if the appeal were simultaneously made to the Advisory Committee, the United States, as a non-voting member of that body, would be drawn into the deliberations. Furthermore, such an appeal would indicate that China considered the present conflict to be a continuation of the Manchurian affair. The Chinese strategy now became clear. Their appeal would set the stage for a future petition to the League that would prompt discussion of the Sino-Japanese struggle in a world forum and marshal international opinion against Japan. This was an aim not only of China but of Britain and France as well.[3]

On September 3 Ambassador Wang called on Hull to tell him that China had definitely decided to take her quarrel with Japan to the League. He said that he hoped the United States would led "moral support" by serving on the Advisory Committee, a somewhat superfluous request. Hull was unenthusiastic. He warned against the introduction of sanctions, which had been so ineffective against Italy, and questioned the League's ability to accomplish anything.

Hull was on the horns of a dilemma. He had little faith in the League, but America would draw adverse attention if it were conspicuously absent from the Advisory Committee on which it had previously been represented, albeit in a non-voting capacity. So, he instructed Leland Harrison, the American Minister to Switzerland, to sit with the Committee, while at the same time telling Harrison not to answer any theoretical questions. Hull suspected that Chinese and Western delegates might seek assurances of American action. He cautioned, "We have sometimes found that the hypothetical conditions did not develop and that, due to our replying to such hypothetical questions, the United States found itself far in advance of other powers in commitment."[4]

In their appeal to the League Council the Chinese requested that Article X of the League Covenant be invoked. This article required member nations to respect and preserve each other's territorial integrity. They also asked that Articles XI and XVII be implemented. The former called for arbitration or inquiry by the Council in the event of a dispute between League members, and the latter invited non–League members to submit their disputes to the Council. If the invited power refused the invitation and resorted to war, this would be regarded as war against all of the League members. Woodrow Wilson and other framers of the Covenant might have had this course of action in mind, but not those who now sat in Geneva. As expected, China's appeal was referred to the Far Eastern Advisory Committee, with Leland Harrison in attendance. When the Committee met on September 21, China, Japan, Germany and Australia were invited to join in the deliberations of the 22 nations already represented. The Japanese and Germans refused the invitation, the former declaring that the dispute with China could best be settled by the two belligerents themselves. Germany had quit the League in 1933, and Hitler's pro-Japanese policy would not be served by attending a meeting that gave every indication of being sympathetic to the Chinese.

The United States found itself drawn into a tighter circle when the French representative, Yvon Delbos, proposed that a subcommittee be created from the powers directly interested in the Far East. When Hull learned of this, he fretted anew, cabling Harrison that this approach would negate the universal character of the attention which should be given to developments in Asia. What was happening in China should concern the whole world.[5] Hull huddled with his usual advisers to consider the situation. Pierrepont Moffat wrote in his diary on September 23 that everyone but Stanley Hornbeck had favored accepting membership on the grounds that it would be impossible to explain how America could sit on the Advisory Committee but not on a working subcommittee. Hornbeck complained that it was "a move to get further and further away from action and that we should not be a party thereto." Reluctantly, Hull authorized Harrison to join the subcommittee, which began its deliberations on October 2. It included Australia, Belgium, the United Kingdom, China, Ecuador, France, the Netherlands, Poland, Sweden, Russia, the United States, Latvia and New Zealand. Not all of the countries represented could be said to have Far Eastern interests, but it was felt that their inclusion would bring balance to the debate. In any event, the subcommittee agreed to address the matter of Japanese forces in Chinese territory, Japan's relevant treaty obligations, and the question of justification for Japanese actions.

While the subcommittee was absorbed in these discussions, a British proposal was circulated in the League Assembly, calling for a meeting of the Nine Power Treaty members. Dr. Wellington Koo, China's spokesman, reminded his colleagues that all League members had an obligation under Article X and the Nine Power Treaty could not relieve them of it. The least that the member nations could do, he said, was not extend aid to Japan in its aggression against China, nor take steps that would weaken China in her fight to defend herself. Bringing together the Nine Power signatories and other interested parties might involve too much delay in the face of a grave situation.

In the meantime, the subcommittee adopted two reports which were accepted by the Advisory Committee. The first noted that there was nothing in the relations between China and Japan which could not be settled amicably. It also declared that the Japanese military operations then under way were out of all proportion to the incident, and that Japan's actions were in contravention of its obligations under the Nine Power Treaty of 1922 and the Pact of Paris (Kellogg-Briand Pact) of 1928. The second report urged that further efforts be made to secure the restoration of peace by agreement and recommended that the Assembly call upon those nations that were parties to the Nine Power Treaty to initiate consultation provided for by the Treaty. Other states with special interests in the Far East might join this conference. Finally, the Assembly should express its moral support for China and recommend that members of the League should "refrain from taking any action which might have the effect of weakening China's power of resistance" and should also "consider how far they can individually extend aid to China."[6]

On the afternoon of October 6, the League of Nations Assembly adopted the reports of the Advisory Committee. Leland Harrison reported that he had heard on good authority that several delegations had been influenced by the President's Chicago speech to vote for the adoption. Otherwise, he said, they might have abstained. Among these were the Canadians, who had delayed their vote in the Advisory Council until they received instructions from home.[7]

Although as a member of the Advisory Committee and the subcommittee, the United States had been a party to the preparation of the two reports, Hull tried to preserve the fiction of "parallel action" in order to create the illusion of independence. In his office, he and his advisers hammered out a statement to the effect that the American government had come to the same conclusions as the League. This was no easy task. Pierrepont Moffat wrote in his diary that they went through three or four revisions to "avoid the pitfalls of its proving an anticlimax in tone to the President's speech on the one hand and being provocative in its language on the other." Their final draft took note of the action taken by the Advisory Committee and the League Assembly. It then summarized the position of the United States as contained in two of Hull's previous "pronouncements" and mentioned the Chicago speech, particularly that portion of it that called attention to respect for treaties and international morality. But its last paragraph made America's position clear:

> In the light of unfolding developments in the Far East, the Government of the United States has been forced to the conclusion that the action of Japan in China is inconsistent with the principles which should govern the relationships between nations and is contrary to the provisions of the Nine Power Treaty ... regarding principles and

policies to be followed in matters concerning China, and to those of the Kellogg-Briand Pact.... Thus the conclusions of this Government with respect to the foregoing are in general accord with those of the Assembly of the League of Nations.[8]

Coming on the heels of the President's explosive remarks in Chicago, many thought that a new era of American diplomacy was about to be ushered in. Pierrepont Moffat was none too happy. He worried that the United States had put itself in the same position that England had been in during the Ethiopian crisis two years earlier. Then, he wrote in his diary, all the nations were willing to apply sanctions against Italy because they were sure that if trouble occurred, the British would suffer the brunt of it. Should the same conditions prevail in the Orient, America would bear the responsibility. "Once again, Great Britain would have someone to fight her battles for her." Moffat's fears were premature. America was not going to fight anyone in 1937.

The Japanese press reacted to the State Department's announcement with newspaper extras and special editions, but the Government showed no signs of alarm. The Far East presented new conditions, it said, so the Nine Power Treaty and the Kellogg Pact, which had been signed years before, were no longer applicable.[9] Clearly Japan was not going to be influenced by resolutions drawn up in Geneva or Washington. The chances of the Government's meeting with the Nine Power signatories were so remote as to virtually cancel its participation in the forthcoming conference.

Pierrepont Moffat's suspicions about British intentions, however, were not entirely groundless. On October 6 the British Embassy presented an *aide-memoire* to the Department of State in which London raised some questions about the pending meeting. What opinion did the United States have regarding consultations; issuing invitations; the form they should take; invitations to Germany and the Soviet Union; and the location of the conference? The Foreign Office said that it would "warmly concur" if America would call the conference or offer to hold it in Washington.[10]

Britain's proposition got a cold reception from Hull and his advisers. The last place they wanted to hold a meeting was Washington. Norman Davis cast his vote for London but withdrew it when his colleagues observed that Japanese hostility toward England would render a conference in London pointless and that the delegates would be at the mercy of the British-controlled press. Better, they said, to hold it in a small European capital. Although the meeting was eventually held in Brussels, Davis objected because of its climate, usually cold and rainy in the fall. Ultimately, the British were simply told that the conference should not be held in Washington or any other large capital city.[11] As for the other issues raised in the *aide-memoire*, the State Department made the following recommendations:

X. Charade at Brussels

1. The issuing of invitations should be decided by the signatories of the Nine Power Treaty who were also members of the League of Nations, or the six original parties, leaving out China, Japan and the United States, might jointly suggest a meeting.
2. The invitations should be "couched in as broad language as possible" with the suggestion of time and place of meeting coupled with that part of the Assembly resolution to the effect that the purpose of the meeting was to find a method of ending the conflict.
3. The meeting should be held as soon as practicable.
4. The United States did not object to sending invitations to the USSR and Germany, but asked whether, since the meeting would be called under the Nine Power Treaty, it might be advisable that the signatories, when assembled, should consider the question of inviting other powers. Did the British consider the issue of such invitations advisable? What would be the probable attitude of the USSR and Germany if they attended?[12]

The day after this message was given to the British Chargé, the President returned to Washington to make preparations for the conference. He summoned Hull, Davis and Welles to the White House for a two-hour meeting to propound some of his own ideas on the forthcoming parley. First, he wished to have Prime Minister Van Zeeland of Belgium issue invitations to those non–League members who were parties to the Nine Power Treaty. Second, he wanted the conference held in Brussels so that it would not be under British control. Third, the first item on the agenda should be the question of an invitation to the non-signatory states. He indicated that he wanted Norman Davis to represent the United States, despite the latter's reluctance to go. Pierrepont Moffat suspected that Davis was hesitant because he would be lost in a French-speaking country. Moffat's opinion of the meeting was cogent: "As to substance, the President is thinking far more in constructive terms than in terms of sanctions. He has some definite ideas and will not cross other bridges unless and until necessary."

Roosevelt's suggestions were immediately cabled to London. Now that Washington had been rejected, the British proposed the Hague as a possible meeting place, but in the event the Dutch demurred they were prepared to try Brussels. They also felt that the delegates to the conference should be of high diplomatic rank and hinted that Eden would attend, particularly if the American Secretary of State did. Finally, they invited the U.S. delegation to London for a preliminary meeting.[13]

Because of the extent and vulnerability of their possessions in Asia, the Dutch refused to make their capital available for the Nine Power Conference. The Belgians were equally unenthusiastic. Although it seemed that nobody wanted to give the impression of taking the lead in calling the meeting, Belgium eventually gave in. Its Foreign Office dispatched Baron Guillaume, its Ambassador to China, to London to work with the British on the wording of invitations to the other powers. The Belgians said that they would invite the other parties as long as it was made clear that they were doing so "at the request of the American and British governments."[14] America's reaction must have exasperated those on the other side of the Atlantic. The State Department insisted that the wording of the invitation be changed to read that the conference was being held "at the request of the British Government and with the approval of the American Government."[15] To Washington, it still seemed that Britain was trying to place responsibility for calling the conference on the U.S. In Whitehall, it appeared that America was engaging in semantic somersaults. However, London accepted the change and the Belgians sent out the invitations the next day.

The next issues were whether to invite the Germans and the Russians to the meeting and what courses of action the Brussels Conference should consider. The British defended the inclusion of Germany because it was third among all nations in trade with China, while the Soviet Union was an Asiatic power of considerable strength and should therefore be invited on its own merits. The United States wanted to suspend invitations to Berlin and Moscow until the conference opened but capitulated to British pressure. Far more important was the strategy to be followed at the conference. In retrospect, Great Britain took a far more realistic approach than did America. On October 19, the British delivered a long message to the State Department in which they laid out the circumstances as they saw them. This was "not a statement of policy" but an "appreciation of the difficulties which must be faced." They expressed doubt that Japan would attend the conference, and without its presence a peaceful agreement between the two belligerents was unlikely. In that case, there would then be only three alternatives. First, the conference could defer any action in the hope that a change would occur in the Far Eastern situation, particularly in Japan's economic or military position. Second, the conference could confine itself to moral condemnation of Japan. Or third, it could adopt a program of positive action in the form of either active aid to China or economic pressure on Japan. The British dismissed the first two courses as "tantamount to acquiescence in aggression." Moreover, the second of them would only produce additional ill feeling in Japan. That left the third alternative, in which both the United States and Great Britain would go to Brussels "in the full realization of [its] implications."[16]

Most of the memo was devoted to the last point. The British pointed out that it would be very difficult to supply China by sea, because the Japanese might extend their blockade to neutral ships, and sea routes could not then be kept open except by force. It was also doubtful whether economic measures against Japan would work. They could only be undertaken via cooperation among the United States, all of the nations of the British Empire, and some six or eight other countries. Furthermore, there was no guarantee that sanctions would be effective in time to change the course of the war, and there was always the danger that the Japanese would resort to violence if they found economic reprisals intolerable. In that event, every country participating in the sanctions would have to pledge mutual military support to the others. Finally, it would be necessary to guarantee the territorial integrity of those nations. However, these assurances might deter Japan from retaliating, and the possibility that sanctions might be successful would cause her to sue for peace.

If the British had hoped for a comprehensive reply to their *aide-memoire* they were disappointed. The Americans dodged the third and most important point of the note by saying that they did not feel it would be considered by the conference. Instead, the U.S. government advanced two proposals of its own. The first was to induce the two belligerents to enter into an armistice, and the second was to find a way to stabilize conditions in the Far East. The State Department would not go beyond these suggestions in its pre-conference position.[17]

Meanwhile, the Japanese adopted an increasingly hostile attitude toward the Brussels Conference. On October 15 Ambassador Grew called on Foreign Minister Hirota and urged Japan to accept an invitation to meet with the other powers. Hirota told Grew that the invitation had not yet been received, but in any event, it was unlikely that Japan would attend, the League of Nations having already sided with China. Similar overtures from the British Ambassador also came to naught.[18] Yet Grew continued hopeful that the Japanese government might still be persuaded to go to Brussels. As late as October 20, *Asahi*, one of Japan's leading newspapers, questioned whether Japan should attend the Nine Power Treaty Conference. The editor wrote that, if the purpose of the conference was to sit in judgment of the Japanese or attempt to implement the policy of the League of Nations, then Japan should not go. But if the conference was going to examine the causes of unrest in Asia, Japan would be able to demonstrate that the Nine Power Treaty was obsolete, and that China had long followed a policy of hostility toward Japan. Grew said that many influential Japanese had told him that they favored going to Brussels for the same reason, but the military was opposed.[19]

As anticipated, when the Japanese finally received the invitation from the Belgian government, they rejected it. In refusing to attend, they declared that their action in China was "outside the purview of the Nine Power Treaty." They also complained about the League's moral support of

China and charged that there was a direct connection between the League's resolution calling for a meeting of the Treaty's members and the invitation to Brussels, which they said had been sent at the behest of the British with the support of the United States. As a result, they felt that they would not be treated fairly at the conference. Furthermore, a meeting of so many powers with Asiatic interests of varying degrees would only complicate matters and would not lead to a solution. They concluded by saying that China was responsible for the conflict. It was the Chinese, they said, who were guilty of "disseminating anti–Japanese sentiment and encouraging anti–Japanese movements in China and who, in collusion with the Communist elements, have menaced the peace of East Asia by their virulent agitation against Japan."[20]

Although the conferees would not consider this refusal final and would later attempt to draw Japan into their deliberations, the Tokyo government had for all practical purposes abandoned any idea of going to Brussels. Ambassador Grew, who had seen his own independent and impartial course in dealing with the Far Eastern crisis go by the boards, complained in his diary about the Administration's movement toward an anti–Japanese policy, which he considered hopeless unless America was willing to fight. He felt that moral suasion would be ineffective, while economic or financial sanctions would be not only ineffective but also dangerous.

While Grew was lamenting the course of events, the American delegates were preparing to leave for Brussels. They were not a very large group. In accordance with the President's wishes, Norman Davis was to be the spokesman for the United States. Stanley Hornbeck and Pierrepont Moffat would be his advisers. Robert Pell was the press officer, and Charles Bohlen, who would become famous a generation later as a Soviet policy expert, served as secretary. A few clerks and typists filled out the delegation.

When the London Foreign Office learned that Davis would be going to Brussels instead of Hull, Anthony Eden telephoned him and tried to persuade him to come to London first so that they might "talk things over beforehand." Davis declined, saying that it might appear improper, and suggested they meet in Paris or Brussels a day or two ahead of the conference instead.[21] Davis knew that if he went to London, the press would magnify and perhaps distort the meaning of the visit. In that event, any chance of getting Japan to attend the conference would, in view of Tokyo's suspicions, probably be lost entirely. The Anglophobic Hearst press in particular would seize the opportunity to argue that the United States was about to be duped again by smooth-talking British diplomats.

The State Department also objected to a tête-à-tête in London. Hull gave comprehensive instructions to Davis before the latter's departure, saying that the purpose of the conference was to examine the situation in the

X. Charade at Brussels 259

Far East and to seek a peaceable end to the conflict there. Davis should be guided by Hull's previous public statements and keep in mind that America's first objective was to protect its national security, that peace must be kept by "practicable means," and that as a signatory to the Pact of Paris, the United States was pledged to settle its disputes by "none but pacific means." He also told Davis to bear in mind "public opinion in the United States has expressed its emphatic determination that [the nation] keep out of war."[22]

Hull's directives were clear: Davis was not to undertake any measures that would compromise America's neutrality. The day after Davis received the Secretary's letter, he drove from New York City to Hyde Park to confer with the President about his mission. Hull's instructions had been general; Roosevelt spelled out specifically the role that Davis should play at the conference. In a sense, the talk at Hyde Park was a continuation of a discussion between Davis, Roosevelt and Hull the previous week in Washington. At that time Davis had told the President about the two schools of thought in the State Department that Moffat had previously noted in his diary. Roosevelt agreed with the faction that saw Japan as an eventual enemy if she continued on her present course unchallenged. He declared that the sanctity of treaties must be upheld; otherwise, international anarchy would endanger American security and stability. Under the circumstances, the President told Davis, he hoped there would be a determined effort to bring about a truce between Japan and China. If the war in Asia was allowed to continue, America would "run the risk of awaiting the outcome of a situation which is already becoming a most disturbing and dangerous factor in world peace and progress."[23]

The question then arose as to what alternatives would be followed if the Conference at Brussels failed. Roosevelt felt that the United States could not quit if mediation efforts did not succeed, because if Japan persisted in her determination to conquer China, public opinion in America and the rest of the world would probably demand that something be done. What, exactly, was unclear. However, the President did tell Davis that the word "sanctions" should not be used at the Conference if mediation was unsuccessful. In that event, the assembled powers should ask Japan what her objectives were in order to embarrass her, and as a result, public opinion and moral force might be mobilized to put pressure on her. If this approach was unsuccessful, the countries might offer China every facility to acquire arms. However, the President hastened to add, because of the Neutrality Law the United States could not participate in that effort. In line with his quarantine address, he also suggested that the neutral powers could ostracize Japan by breaking off diplomatic relations, though he admitted this would not be practical in the absence of overwhelming world support. As for America's role at Brussels, Roosevelt agreed with Davis that the United

States should not go out on a limb by itself. Cooperation with Britain was fine, but it should not be "one-sided." To make this clear to the British, Roosevelt dictated a memorandum to Davis, suggesting that Davis show it to them when he met with Eden. In summary, the memo reminded the British that public opinion mattered a great deal in America. It stated that the U.S. would not be a party to joint action with the League, but neither would it permit itself to be pushed out in front to lead any action against Japan. It stressed that all of the powers should act as one, and that while American wanted to cooperate with the British government, this must be "independent cooperation, [with] neither one trying to force the other into something. ... This means that final resulting action can perfectly well be identical, though not necessarily joint."

To mollify his critics, Roosevelt had released a statement that Davis was going to the Brussels Conference "without any commitments on the part of this Government to other governments."[24] Not only did the Hearst press charge the Administration with playing England's game, but one of the principal isolationists, Senator Hiram Johnson, was quoted in the *Philadelphia Record* as saying, "Mr. Davis would not be going to Brussels unless in advance a program had been agreed on between England and this country." If the President's words had allayed those suspicions, they simultaneously raised doubts in other quarters about the utility of the Conference. The *Los Angeles Times*, which had backed Roosevelt's Chicago speech and the State Department's endorsement of the League's resolution, observed, "If this statement is literally correct, it means that the conference at Brussels will be purely exploratory and almost certainly futile." Nothing could have been more prophetic.

Sailing on the S.S. *Washington*, the American delegation arrived in Brussels on the night of October 28, having first stopped off in Paris, where Davis conferred with the American Ambassador, William Bullitt, and the Chinese Ambassador to France, Dr. Wellington Koo. At a luncheon with Bullitt at the American Embassy, Davis got some discouraging news, a harbinger of what awaited him in Brussels. The French had stopped shipments of arms and munitions through Indo-China to the Nationalist Government because the Japanese had threatened to bomb the portion of the railroad inside Chinese territory unless the shipments were immediately ended. Moreover, in a thinly veiled warning, the Japanese Ambassador in Paris told Premier Chautemps to his face that if France became involved in a European war, she would lack the means to protect her colonies in the Far East, and the Japanese were "a people who remembered those who had been friendly and those who had been unfriendly, and that it would be a very good thing for France to have a friendly Japan in case she should be at war in Europe." Relaying this story to Bullitt, Chautemps said that France

X. Charade at Brussels

was too exposed in Indo-China to persist in activities that would anger Japan unless Great Britain and the United States would promise to protect French interests in Asia.[25]

Bullitt had more bad news for Hull. The Russians seemed to be playing a double game. Maxim Litvinov, the Soviet Foreign Minister, had told the British that Russia would attack and defeat Japan if the British would promise to restrain Germany from attacking Russia during the process. To the French, Litvinov had said that the longer the Sino-Japanese war lasted, the more Japan would exhaust herself, and this would leave Russia free to play a larger role in European affairs. Bullitt and Davis suspected that the Soviets would try to embarrass all of the great powers in turn at Brussels and if possible prevent an agreement until Japan had exhausted all of her resources. The conference had not even opened and Davis was already getting a glimpse of a world of international blackmail and intrigue to which he had come armed only with resolutions of moral force and public opinion.

Following his talk with Ambassador Bullitt, Davis, accompanied by Stanley Hornbeck, went to the Bristol Hotel in Paris and had a short meeting with Dr. Koo, who was to represent China at the conference in Brussels. Davis and Hornbeck suggested that the Chinese might make a statement of their position at the meeting and then withdraw from the deliberations. When Koo protested this strategy, the two Americans tried to reassure him that they simply wished to make it impossible for the Japanese to argue that only one side was being heard. With the Chinese out of the room, the delegates of the other powers could have the "full and frank" discussion that Article VII of the Nine Power Treaty provided for. Koo had some suggestions for them. He said that while China was in favor of mediation by the powers in Brussels, she wished it only if the proposed terms were harmonious with the terms of the Treaty. He also proposed that arms and munitions be withheld from Japan and supplied to China. Now it was Davis's and Hornbeck's turn to balk; they pointed out that this would involve them in a non-neutral way. On this inconclusive note the discussion ended, and early that evening the American party left for Brussels.[26]

If Davis had been unpleasantly surprised in Paris, he found no relief in Brussels. Ambassador Gibson told him that the Belgian government was still uneasy about being the host country but had been relieved to hear that the Americans were not going to spring any startling proposals that would embarrass them further. The general public, however, expected that Davis would make a speech in the same dramatic vein as the one given by Charles Evans Hughes at the opening of the Washington Conference. Meanwhile, Paul Henri Spaak, the Belgian Foreign Minister, who was to preside at the Conference, was upset because he had never before supervised an international conference and was deeply involved in a cabinet crisis within his own government. At least the conference would be spared one potential problem. The Germans, who could hardly have been expected to play a constructive role, had announced that they would not attend, declaring that the conference was too closely linked with the League of Nations.

Having already confined Davis in a straitjacket of instructions, the State Department was unwilling to allow him any freedom in Brussels. Although he and his advisers spent two days working on his opening address, going over it sentence by sentence before submitting it to Washington for approval, what they got back was a lengthy telegram telling them that the State Department was drafting one for him that would incorporate its words with his own. Pierrepont Moffat wrote in his diary that even after editing the new draft they felt betrayed, having been promised a free hand before they left. To add to the delegation's frustrations, they were beset by press troubles. Hearst had sent over one of his star reporters, Carl von Wiegand, and another man "fresh from California" who had orders to disrupt the work of the Americans at the conference. Moffat said:

> He tried twice to make Pell [the press aide] lose his temper and say things he shouldn't. Whether he will accuse us of concocting a Hoare-Laval plan, or whether he will accuse us of allowing the conference to drift aimlessly, or both alternatively, it is too early to say. The main difficulty is that he is out to make trouble.

By November 1 the delegations of the other nations had begun to arrive in Brussels, and nine of them took up residence in the Hotel Metropole along with the Americans. The room of the British and American delegations, said Moffat, "were interlarded" in a manner that Stanley Hornbeck thought indiscreet.

Meanwhile, before the American and British delegations got together, Anthony Eden, the British Foreign Secretary, had stirred up a hornet's nest with some misleading remarks in the House of Commons. On the eve of the opening of the Brussels Conference he said that whatever action was taken in the Far Eastern dispute depended essentially on the U.S. He declared that while it was a small matter in itself, "I feel I ought to make it quite plain that the initiative for holding the conference ... never came from us at all, but from the United States government itself."[27] The reaction to this statement was instantaneous. There was a flurry of telephone calls between Washington and London before the latter made it clear that Eden was speaking only of Brussels as the meeting place. The American delegation could not decide whether Eden was being very clever or merely disingenuous. What bothered them most was the implication that the success or failure of the conference lay with the United States.

When Eden arrived in Brussels on November 2, a meeting between the two delegations was arranged, and the Foreign Secretary made a bid

X. Charade at Brussels 263

for Anglo-American solidarity, citing the rising perils in Europe and the Far East. He said that while he felt that the democracies would eventually wake up, he questioned whether they could do so in time to cope with the threat of the dictatorships. Therefore, under the present circumstances, he assured Davis that Great Britain would go as far as the U.S. in the present crisis, but no farther. In reply Davis outlined the suggested Roosevelt-Hull approach of proceeding along parallel lines rather than one power or the other taking the lead at the conference. Continuing to follow his instructions from Hull and the President, Davis spoke of moral pressure being brought to bear on Japan before any other action was considered. Finally, he reminded Eden of public opinion and Americans' suspicion that England was trying to maneuver them into "pulling her chestnuts out of the fire for her." Eden acknowledged this feeling but emphatically denied that the United States would have to bear the brunt of Japanese retaliation if Anglo-American policies provoked it. He admitted that Britain would have to keep most of her fleet in Europe to watch the Germans and Italians, but she would be able to send a few ships to the Orient for a joint naval operation. The British Admiralty, he said, regarded the Japanese Navy as grossly overrated by the general public both in England and in the U.S. Dismissal of the Japanese Navy as an effective military force betrayed the same ignorance born of prejudice shared by so many others in the West. This did not stop Eden from saying that if constructive efforts to end the fighting in China failed, the British would be willing to join America in direct pressure on Japan, but if this was objectionable, they would not embarrass the U.S. by advocating it. Finally, he declared that he would second any American proposal and Britain would base her policy on that of the United States.[28] On hearing this, the American delegation had a right to feel that no matter what they did they would be out in front, either in peace or in war.

Eden's statement essentially recapped the points that had been made in the original British overture in its *aide-memoire* presented in Washington. That Great Britain was now willing to embark on a sterner course than the one she had pursued toward Japan in 1931–1932 may be ascribed to several factors. First, the earlier Japanese military operations in Manchuria had not approached in scale the undeclared war in China in 1937. Britain's economic interests in China then had not been in jeopardy. More than half of British business investments in China had been located in the area of Shanghai, an area which saw heavy fighting only briefly in 1932. It had since become a principal Japanese objective following Chiang Kai-shek's abortive offensive in 1937.[29] The transfer of Japanese military activity from an area of little consequence to Great Britain to one of immense importance would surely cause concern to His Majesty's government. If America could be enlisted in a common front against Japan and perhaps assume a major role in that effort, Britain's stake in China could be made secure. Furthermore, with the Italian fleet a potential menace in the Mediterranean and Hitler a growing threat in mainland Europe, Britain could not singlehandedly challenge Japan and could well make use of the United States as an ally in the Pacific. Finally, if America could be weaned from isolation long enough to cooperate in collective security in the Far East, she might be drawn into an Anglo-French partnership to check Axis advances on the Continent. This was a long shot but worth a try.

Late on the afternoon of November 2, Davis, accompanied by Moffat, went to the Belgian Foreign Office, where Spaak held a meeting with the three leading delegates, Davis, Eden, and Yvon Delbos, the French Foreign Minister. Since Davis did not understand French very well, Moffat translated for him. Both Delbos and Spaak believed that the conference should be adjourned as soon as possible. By this time it was clear to them that the Americans had come only to talk, and the notion of improving public opinion that Davis had advanced held little appeal for them. Moffat noted in his diary that even Eden seemed to be trying to hurry matters along so that he could get back to London. Davis was hard pressed to obtain even one public session, since Spaak and Delbos felt that a series of keynote speeches would merely emphasize the differences among the delegates rather than the similarity of their views.

By the end of the day Davis felt that his mission had been fruitless. That evening he prepared a memo outlining conditions as he saw them and suggesting some possible courses of action. He was perceptive enough to see that America had two contradictory ideas. It didn't want to assume a leadership role in the conference, but it wanted the conference to "accomplish something constructive."

> Whether we like it or not, the other powers will try to throw the leadership to us, and unless we take it—in some form and in some degree—the chance that the Conference will accomplish something constructive seems slight. ... [I]t will be up to the American delegation to supply the ideas both as to courses of action and as to strategy.[30]

But what to suggest? The other powers believed that the choice was between words and the use of more forceful means.

In the Far East the Japanese, although they had refused to attend the Brussels Conference, nevertheless kept a close eye on its proceedings. The ever cautious Grew cabled Hull that the conference should confine itself to promoting peace by agreement and not assign blame for the conflict. Mediation would have a chance only if there were impartiality. Perhaps the conference might appoint a smaller number of interested powers to keep in touch with the situation and if the circumstances seemed favorable, collective mediation or mediation by one of them might be offered.

Grew warned that measures adopted by the conference could affect internal developments in Japan. There were rumors that Hirota's position as Foreign Minister was shaky and that the military wanted to replace him with Yosuke Matsuoka. If this happened, Japan would probably take an even more ruthless position toward a settlement with China.[31] The State Department ignored Grew's fears, but the first part of his message had an interesting parallel. Shigeru Yoshida, the Japanese Ambassador to Great Britain, told the American Ambassador, Robert Bingham, that the Brussels Conference should refrain from condemning Japan and instead organize a subcommittee to confer privately with the Japanese government.[32] When Eden revealed that Yoshida had told him the same thing it was thought that Yoshida was acting on instructions from Tokyo, but several cables from Grew dismissed these reports. Grew said that Yoshida was imaginative and probably interested in restoring good relations between Japan and Great Britain; furthermore, he was not on good terms with the military, so it was safe to assume that he had acted on his own and therefore nothing could come of his suggestions.[33]

On this unfortunate note the conference opened in Brussels. Forty-four delegates representing nineteen nations assembled at the Palais des Academies in a room that Pierrepont Moffat described in his diary on November 3 as a "long, dignified but rather dreary hall, with the press at one end and the long green-baize horseshoe table at the other, with three or four boxes occupied by the diplomatic corps, the Belgian Ministers of State, etc." Among the countries represented were the original signatories of the Nine Power Treaty who were members of the League of Nations: Belgium, China, France, Great Britain, Italy, the Netherlands, and Portugal. Australia, New Zealand, Canada, India and the Union of South Africa became signatories after the Statute of Westminster, and Bolivia, Denmark, Mexico, Norway and Sweden later adhered to the treaty. The Soviet Union, although a member of the League, was not a signatory, and the United States was a signatory but not a member of the League.

After the formality of electing Spaak as president of the conference was over, Norman Davis was called upon to speak. His remarks were predictable. He reviewed the conditions of the Nine Power Treaty which was now challenged by the armed conflict in China and expressed his hope that it could be resolved peacefully. Moffat noted that the address was received politely but not enthusiastically. This could hardly have been surprising; Davis had not offered any positive plan for peace, nor had he placed the U.S. on record for any dramatic course of action.

Anthony Eden spoke next. He limited himself to a three-minute talk which amounted to little more than a seconding of what Davis had said. He declared that his government agreed fully with Davis's every word and that

Davis had "so well defined the task and the conditions in which our work will be carried out that I have little to add."[34] Eden also borrowed part of Roosevelt's quarantine speech, noting "war is a contagion" which though confined to the belligerents inevitably had adverse effects upon all nations. His words provoked a sarcastic reaction from Moffat. After Davis spoke, Eden had smilingly told him that he had made one of the great speeches of their time. He went on to tell Davis that the latter had expressed so eloquently the points he, Eden, had wanted to make that he had decided to throw away his own address. Moffat recalled that at ten o'clock the night before, Eden had told the Americans that he actually had not prepared a speech. The deceit rankled Moffat, who noted in his diary that he was particularly annoyed by Eden's habit of "laying flattery on with a trowel."

The French and Italian delegates followed in succession, Delbos with a brief endorsement and the Italian caustically saying that the two belligerents should be left to settle their differences between themselves and that the conference should avoid direct or indirect coercive measures called for "in certain quarters, nor even a more or less moral 'quarantining' of one or the other of the parties in the conflict."[35] That afternoon, Maxim Litvinov, the Soviet delegate, took the floor and indulged in some very plain talk. Far from seeking to cause mischief as some had anticipated, he said that after attending many conferences he had come to the conclusion that a conference would all too often regard its own success as more important than finding a successful solution to the difficulty it had been called upon to meet. The Russian expressed his antipathy toward Japan by warning the delegates against a settlement that would compromise the rights of the victim of an aggressor.

Dr. Wellington Koo was the last speaker of the day. He presented China's case to the conference. His was a long address but he was determined that his country be heard. Although he made no specific recommendation for action, he asked for justice. Moffat found his speech to be eloquent and distinguished, but its length caused the delegates' minds to wander. According to Moffat, the general reaction was, "Well, he made some very telling points but after all we are not sure just what he is after."

That evening Delbos and several of his advisers huddled with Davis and the rest of the American delegation in Davis's room at the Hotel Metropole. Eden did not attend but sent two of his aides. Delbos told Davis that he doubted whether a peaceful solution could be found to the Sino-Japanese conflict, and therefore France, England and America should devise some means of providing aid to China. He spoke about the supply line through Indo-China and the difficulties they were having with the Japanese, adding that while he did not expect Britain and the United States to guarantee protection to Indo-China, he thought they should do something to keep supply lines open. Davis was not encouraging, repeating his instructions that the American delegation had come to Brussels only to seek an amicable end to the quarrel between China and Japan. Beyond that he could make no commitments on behalf of the U.S. government.

Delbos then spoke of the democracies aligning themselves against the dictators of the world and suggested that President Roosevelt call a world conference to settle the international problems facing them. Davis observed that the President would have little appetite for calling such a conference, although he must have known it was Hull who would be more reluctant than Roosevelt. When the meeting ended late that night, Delbos summarized the French position. There was no hope for a peaceful solution to the war in China. The Western powers could help China only by extending aid to her. However, without military guarantees from the Americans and British, France could not risk the safety of her Far Eastern possessions in order to supply China.

Over the following days the conference struggled to put together a message to Japan, inviting Tokyo to meet with a small group selected by the delegates to exchange views on means of ending the conflict. By the morning of Saturday, November 6, the message was adopted, although with little hope that the Japanese would accept the invitation. The conference then recessed briefly to wait for a reply. Nearly a week passed while the conference waited for Japan's answer. This gave the Americans time to take stock of what had happened since they had come to Brussels and to send their views home. Moffat and Davis collaborated on several cables to the President and Secretary of State, giving their estimate of the situation. They were understandably pessimistic. They reviewed the defeatist attitudes of the continental powers; the desire of the Belgians to close the conference quickly; the interest of the French in securing Anglo-American protection for Asiatic possessions and their hope that Western democracies would present a united political front; the Soviet Union's wish for close cooperation with the British and Americans to block Japan; and the failure of most of the nations in attendance to play an active role in the deliberations.[36] Moffat, who had come to regard Eden with suspicion, and was convinced that the British had come to the conference for the purpose of tying the United States to direct action with them against Japan, wanted to include a critical paragraph on Britain's attitude, but Davis vetoed the idea.

The press in Europe mirrored the feelings of the continental delegations. They were fed a steady stream of information concerning unofficial as well as official conversations. In a letter to George Gordon, American Minister to the Hague, Moffat wrote:

> I have never known a Conference where everything that transpired leaked to the press; Geneva is hermetically sealed in comparison with Brussels. The morning papers even

carry accounts of what went on in small drafting committees, while texts that were prepared for discussion in secret meetings were somehow or other broadcast.³⁷

Hardly any of the French or British newspapers were optimistic about the success of the conference. *Echo De Paris* mocked the moral condemnation that Norman Davis was proposing, declaring that words had no value; only acts were important. The London *Daily Telegraph & Morning Post* observed, "It requires a very robust optimism to believe that the so-called Brussels Conference ... can snatch much success from the unfavorable conditions which obstruct the path to peace." More cogently, the *Manchester Guardian* contrasted what had been said at the opening speeches in Brussels with Roosevelt's Chicago address and concluded that it was "more an indication of a changing outlook than the expression of immediate policy."

American newspapers were equally unenthusiastic. Frederick T. Birchall covered the Conference for the *New York Times* and cabled home that it was moving toward "the futility which has ended so many League-born assemblies." The Anglophobic *Detroit Free Press* charged that England was shaping its diplomacy and propaganda "with a single eye to convincing the American people that civilization is doomed if they do not stand shoulder to shoulder with it in defense of democracy. This is pure bellywash." These and other acerbic comments must have irritated the President, because on November 12 he sent a memorandum to Sumner Welles, saying:

> Frankly, I do not believe that these newspapers carry any particular weight as expressions of public opinion, nor do I believe that any editorial writer—I repeat "any"—has the knowledge of facts and circumstances open to the Administration; therefore, instead of quoting a newspaper you are merely quoting one member of the staff or the opinion of an individual owner.³⁸

Roosevelt had apparently forgotten that he had specifically told Norman Davis before he left for Brussels to have the State Department cable him a daily summary of press reaction in the United States so that he could keep abreast of public opinion.

The Brussels Conference got little encouragement from Congress either. Rep. William Barry (D–NY) said that it was obvious to him that Great Britain was trying to push the United States to the fore. "I feel that we should continue our policy of isolation and should beware of being sucked into any kind of united front."³⁹ Rep. Hamilton Fish (R–NY), a perennial adversary of Administration foreign policy, called on his colleagues to remember what he termed the "ancient slogan emanating from London, that the 'British Empire expects every American to do his duty.'" The American slogan, he said, should be, "Millions for defense but not one single dollar to join European or Asiatic wars." Far from urging support for a policy of coercion against Japan, many Congressmen were demanding invocation

X. Charade at Brussels 269

of the Neutrality Law. On November 17 a lively debate took place in the House between Reps. Fish, White and Knutson on the one hand and Rep. Samuel McReynolds (D–TN) on the other, and McReynolds was hard pressed to defend the President's policy. Amidst this outcry on the home front against foreign intervention, Norman Davis was caught in a dilemma in Brussels—how to proceed in a conference that the Japanese had not the slightest idea of attending and where the delegates were totally uninterested in moral suasion as a course of action.

Davis spent his time while the conference was in recess trying to bolster his position and keep the conference from falling apart. He met with Malcolm MacDonald, the British Secretary of State for Colonies, who was standing in while Eden was away, and with Maxim Litvinov, the Soviet Foreign Minister. Davis asked MacDonald what Britain might do if the conference failed and was told that unless the Americans were willing to take more positive action, there wasn't much that Britain could do.[40] Litvinov's main complaint was that the Western powers were trying to keep Russia out of any negotiating committee that might be set up.[41] Some of the small powers voiced skepticism about the success of the conference and declared in no uncertain terms that they would not be a party to pressure against Japan. According to Moffat and Hornbeck, the Scandinavian delegates were particularly vocal on this subject.[42]

In the meantime, the French kept up their strategy of trying to extract assurances of American protection of their Far Eastern possessions, especially Indo-China. Since Delbos had failed to get a commitment from Davis in Brussels, Jules Henry, the French Chargé d'Affaires in Washington, tried to secure a pledge from the President. After Henry expressed concern about the consequences of stopping arms shipments through Indo-China, Roosevelt commented that some of the great powers were behaving "like scared rabbits."[43] Henry then asked what the attitude of the United States might be if Japan did make aggressive moves in Southeast Asia. The President replied that this was a hypothetical question but if such aggression did occur the repercussions would be so widespread that the United States could not be unaffected. Henry interpreted this to mean that the American fleet would protect not only the Philippines but also Indo-China, and so informed his government.[44] He was mistaken, and Ambassador Bullitt had the unenviable duty of telling the French government that its chargé in Washington had misunderstood the President. Premier Chautemps, far from being angry with his diplomatic representative in America, vented his ire on Roosevelt for raising false hopes.

As the conference prepared to reconvene, Davis sent a long telegram to the President and Secretary of State apprising them of his predicament and suggesting some possible lines that the United States might pursue. In the face of Japan's almost certain rejection of the invitation to attend, the delegations might return home and consult with their governments about what future steps should be taken. A standing committee could be created to receive their recommendations and would be available should Japan later decide to take a more conciliatory approach. Davis admitted that little was likely to come from such a move and that it would be an admission of the conference's failure to settle the Sino-Japanese dispute. A second alternative would be for the conference to adopt "some form of united pressure upon Japan in the fields of trade and shipping." However, he simultaneously dismissed this because he did not feel that the "setting" was right and the action would not only be attributed to the United States but would draw Washington into a coalition with the European democracies. Davis's final proposal was that the conference might adopt a resolution in which the powers agreed to one or all of the following: take no action that would hinder China in her military effort; take no action that would force China to agree to "unwilling concessions"; refrain from acknowledging changes in China that were not compatible with the Nine Power Treaty; make no loans or credits available to Japan which might encourage her aggression; and/or give no military aid to Japan in the event she became "embroiled" with any of the conference powers before a settlement was reached with China.[45]

Davis urged "serious and immediate consideration" be given to these steps. In the same message he criticized the Neutrality Law, which he felt nullified the stand which the United States had taken on righteous principles and its need to put moral pressure on Japan. He went on to suggest a recommendation to Congress that the law be suspended insofar as the Far Eastern conflict was concerned. This, he said, would "startle and worry Japan" and would encourage the Chinese and make a "dynamic" impression on the rest of the world.

This was not the Norman Davis who had set sail for Europe just a few weeks earlier. Clearly, Davis's pride had been stung by the barbs of "do-nothingness" thrown by his European colleagues and the European press. As an internationalist he felt that America had a responsibility to do more than just "talk" at Brussels. Given the political atmosphere at home, he knew that it was hopeless to speak of coercive measures against Japan, let alone suspension of the Neutrality Law. But in Brussels he had been cut off from domestic influences, and rather than see the conference break up in failure he felt compelled to seek an alteration to his original instructions so that he could seek the adoption of a program that would enable him to offer his associates something more than moral pledges.

Of course, there was no chance that the President or the State Department would reverse their policy. Hull cabled Davis that it was impossible for the United States to carry out any of the proposals in his third alternative. While Hull was prepared to admit that the conference could not long remain in session, he felt that it should not admit its failure when it adjourned. Instead, a pronouncement should be made that Japan had refused to cooperate; the principles of the Nine Power Treaty should be reaffirmed; and there should be "an expression of determination on the part of the governments participating in the Conference to watch the situation closely" and continue to exchange views which would keep the principles of the treaty alive.[46] Several days later Hull sent another cable to Davis, this one rebuffing his recommendation that the Neutrality Law be suspended.

By the time these messages reached Brussels, the conference had reconvened. Eden and Delbos continued to press Davis for concrete American commitments but he was unable to make any. At lunch with his British and French colleagues on November 10, Davis was told that they could not remain in Brussels indefinitely and that the sooner they "got down to brass tacks" the less ultimate delay there would be. Delbos, who seemed unable to talk about anything except getting guarantees for the security of French Indo-China, repeated this, promising that France would reopen munitions traffic to Chiang Kai-shek if he could get adequate assurances. Like Eden, he said that he was prepared to go as far as the United States as long as there was complete solidarity. He noted that Japan was deeply involved in China, and while China was not holding up as well as the West had hoped, the Japanese were now tied up and would scarcely risk hostilities with the West if they knew the Western powers were united.

Eden reiterated much of what Delbos said but added that consideration might be given to "stopping all sales to and purchases from Japan." He admitted that this would not be a popular move in Great Britain because of the Ethiopian precedent, but His Majesty's government was prepared to carry it through and, if both Britain and the United States should take such a stand, the smaller powers might follow suit.[47]

Davis was unable to offer any hope of a change in America's position. He agreed that the conference could not go on much longer, but he said that the Administration's hands were tied by the Neutrality Law. Moreover, public opinion would ultimately guide the decisions of the U.S. government.

On Friday, November 12, the expected refusal of the Japanese government to meet with the subcommittee of the conference was received. No one was surprised, but it served to further increase the gloom that already prevailed in Brussels. According to Pierrepont Moffat, although everyone now sought some means to close the conference, "even those who are most anxious ultimately to do something to Japan have pretty well come around to the feeling that the Conference is not the place to do it." The Americans, British and French were unpleasantly surprised to learn that whatever strategy they agreed upon would not automatically be accepted by the other powers. The day before, the Canadians had said that under no circumstances would they approve of sanctions. The Scandinavians were reluctant to identify themselves with resolutions that even criticized Japan. Aubert, the Norwegian delegate, told Moffat that Norway was interested only in "self-preservation," which meant staying out of the quarrels of other nations. He said that if anything was going to be done, it had better be done by the powers that could do it; there was little hope of educating public opinion as the Americans proposed.

The following day, the conference reached a turning point, in that the delegates abandoned hypothetical questions and for the first time discussed what they could actually do. Wellington Koo opened the morning session with a direct appeal for aid:

> Now that the door to conciliation and mediation has been slammed in your face by the latest reply of the Japanese government, will you not decide to withhold supplies of war materials and credit to Japan and extend aid to China? It would be, in our opinion, a modest way in which you can fulfill your obligation of helping to check Japanese aggression and uphold the treaty in question.[48]

Koo's plea was ignored. Davis, Eden and Delbos made statements that were so similar, Birchall suspected they had been written in collaboration, as indeed they had. They amounted to nothing more than an appeal for respect for law and international agreements. After the Western "big three" had spoken, Litvinov declared that his government would support whatever action the conference might take. There was little risk in this pledge. Obviously, the conference was not going to do anything of substance. Yet it could not adjourn without a face-saving statement.

Doing even that much proved tortuous. It was so difficult that the delegates recessed for the weekend so that they could consult their governments. Davis sent another lengthy telegram to the State Department, bringing Hull up to date on developments. He said that Eden was still trying to form an Anglo-American bloc to force some kind of action. The Foreign Secretary had reiterated that Great Britain was willing to do anything that the United States was willing to do, and while he had doubts about the efficacy of an embargo, he would be willing to proceed with it if the Americans were agreeable. Delbos raised new fears. The Japanese, he said, were threatening to occupy the island of Hainan and take other retaliatory measures if the shipment of arms went forward. All of this pressure got to Davis. Once more he pushed for strong measures. "The minimum step that will in my opinion hold [Japan] in line would be the adoption of a resolution calling for non-recognition of changes brought about by armed force, prohibition of government loans and credits and discouragement of private loans and credits."[49]

His appeal was in vain. Hull replied that moves of this kind were outside the scope of the terms of the invitation to the conference, and he reminded Davis that the nations of the League had avoided adopting such measures.[50] There seemed to be no way out for Davis, try as he might to secure a modification of his instructions from home. He had to be satisfied with the twelve point declaration that the conference produced. In substance, it expressed regret that Japan would not enter into an exchange of views in order to end the conflict with China; it declared that, although Japan regarded the hostilities as outside the sphere of the Nine Power Treaty, the representatives of the states at Brussels did not; it condemned the use of large military forces by Japan against China to make her "renounce her present policy" as unlawful; and said that because there was no promise of a solution which would give permanent peace and security for the rights and interests of other countries, the situation was a matter of concern to the whole world. It noted that the Chinese had agreed to cease hostilities in order to exchange views through the conference or a small group of powers chosen for that purpose, and added that it was difficult to understand Japan's persistent refusal in light of this agreement. Although they hoped that Japan would not continue to reject peaceful overtures, the powers at Brussels would have to

> ... consider what is to be their common attitude in a situation where one party to an international treaty maintains against the view of all the other parties that the action which it has taken does not come within the scope of that treaty, and sets aside provisions of that treaty which the other parties hold to be operative in the circumstances.[51]

On this resolution the Italian delegate voted no, to no one's surprise. Italy's attitude had been negative since the first day of the conference. But what did stun Eden, Davis and Delbos was the abstention of the Scandinavians. Aubert told Moffat that they feared the phrase "consider what is to be their common attitude" implied possible consideration of sanctions. Somewhat later, Moffat learned that the Swedish delegate would have preferred to vote for the declaration but did not do so because he did not want to break the Scandinavian front.

Following the resolution's adoption the conference, which by now seemed to be spending more time in recess than in session, prorogued its meetings until the following Monday, when it would meet to consider a final declaration and formula for adjournment.

The end was now approaching, and the outcome of the conference was taking shape. The Scandinavians were not the only ones who were disturbed by the implications of the declaration's final point. The day after the conference approved it, Koki Hirota called Grew to the Japanese Foreign Ministry and gave notice of his government's displeasure. Hirota's view was that it would have an "unfortunate effect" on Japanese public opinion. The Minister told Grew that he had received information that the United States had not only taken the initiative in calling the conference but was also taking the lead in Brussels. Up to this point, he said, the Japanese people believed that Great Britain was the country which was trying to establish a united front against Japan, but if the Japanese press learned that it was the United States, then the onus of unfavorable public opinion would rest on America.[52] Hirota was playing a role that was part of an overall Japanese scheme to divide the Brussels Conference. Indeed, in order to discredit America, the Japanese Ambassador to Brussels, Saburo Kurusu, was telling the newsmen covering the conference that the American delegation's instructions were to do nothing but use the conference as a blind to cover a retreat from the President's Chicago speech.[53]

Hirota knew that Grew attached great importance to America's good reputation in Japan. He played upon this in the hope of shaking the United States loose from participation in any possible coercive measures that might be attempted by the conference. The French had been frightened by threats against Indo-China, and one can only speculate about the techniques if any that might have been used against the British, but this was clever and effective diplomacy.

Having indulged in this mild intimidation, Hirota then told Grew that the military situation in China looked favorable and that therefore it was in China's interest to sue for peace. The best thing that the United States could do would be to encourage the Chinese government to open negotiations with Japan. If peace was made, Japanese demands would be "reasonable" and not a foot of Chinese territory would be seized. This mailed fist–velvet glove approach was further amplified by Seijuro Yoshizawa, Director of the American Affairs Bureau in the Japanese Foreign Office. He told Grew "confidentially" that the Japanese government was prepared to consult either individually or collectively with the United States and Great Britain and other powers with substantial interests in the Far East, but would not respond to any invitation within any framework of collective security, be it the League of Nations or the Brussels Conference.[54]

Hull's reaction to Hirota's charges of American leadership at Brussels was instantaneous. The Secretary of State instructed Grew to tell the Japanese Foreign Minister that his statements were groundless and to say that he had misunderstood the last point of the declaration adopted at Brussels.[55] This was a reaction that could not have failed to please Hirota.

The Japanese followed up their Tokyo strategy by encouraging the Americans to believe that they could act as mediators in the Far East. Mr. Suma, the Japanese Counselor in Washington, called on Assistant Secretary of State Hugh Wilson and said that his government was willing to entertain any suggestions that the U.S. government might have to offer to end the struggle in China. He went on to ask Wilson whether it might play the same role in the Sino-Japanese conflict that Theodore Roosevelt had performed in the Russo-Japanese War in 1905. Wilson replied that he could not speak for the Secretary of State, but he felt that America was obligated to act under the provisions of the Nine Power Treaty and would therefore be reluctant to assume any other negotiating role. As for the United States following in the footsteps of Theodore Roosevelt, Wilson said that to answer Mr. Suma's question would "enter ... upon the realm of wildest speculation," since no one could tell what the future might bring, although it was conceivable that at some stage it might offer assistance.[56] At first glance one might think that the Japanese were sincere in offering America the opportunity to end the war in China. However, as Japan had never given serious consideration to America's previous offers of mediation, and no references were made to Suma's suggestion in subsequent discussions between American and Japanese officials, one can only conclude that the offer was merely part of the Japanese plan to separate the United States from any united front that might be formed in Brussels.

The last full week that the American delegation spent in Brussels was in many ways the most miserable one. Everyone came down with a cold, and Davis was so ill that he took to his bed. To add to his misery, he was still at odds with the State Department over the conduct of affairs in Brussels. A steady stream of telegrams, some of them critical, flowed in from Washington, with the net result that he became more discouraged than ever about his mission.

The differences between Davis and the State Department continued to revolve around the issue of whether or not the conference could do more than reaffirm moral principles. Hull positively would not permit, and in fact with prevailing public sentiment could not permit, Davis's suggested prohibition of government loans as well as the declaration against private loans and credits to the Japanese. Davis gave in, but he did so with undisguised disappointment. On November 17, he cabled Hull,

> I bow to your judgment and hope that it will be possible to make such a strong reaffirmation of the principles which underlie international relationships that it will not fall flat. However, all of the large and most of the small powers believe that a mere reaffirmation of principles, after a week's adjournment, will not contribute to a solution of the concrete pressing problem which the Conference assembled to consider.[57]

Davis then asked the Department to consider including as part of the final declaration a statement to the effect that if in the near future it was not possible to secure negotiations toward a settlement of the Sino-Japanese conflict, the powers would not recognize "situations created in contravention of obligations" and would not be "justified in extending or encouraging loans and credits to the Japanese government" as long as it continued its present course of action. Hull, however, would not even make this concession, and advised Davis "at this moment the temper of the country is not disposed to favor a course of pressure or threats."[58]

The Secretary of State was also bothered by press reports coming out of Brussels. He told Davis that these were spreading the impression that other states were willing and eager to adopt coercive measures against Japan as long as the United States would do so. "The tenor of these reports is that the United States is solely responsible for determining what attitude the Conference will take in this respect."[59] What most upset Hull was that the British and French Embassies were consciously fostering this idea in various capitals throughout the world. Hull was not the only one who was disturbed by the way blame was being placed on America for what had transpired in Brussels. Pierrepont Moffat accused Charles Peake, the British press officer, of passing out propaganda poison along with a "limitless supply of good Scotch whiskey" to reporters at the conference. Norman Davis was so perturbed that he personally told Malcolm MacDonald that it was absolutely necessary for the United States and Great Britain to assume joint responsibility for whatever was or was not done at the conference.[60]

As the time approached for the conference to reconvene, the Chinese again tried to secure something more tangible than moral platitudes. Dr. Koo called on Hornbeck to inform him of the grave military situation that confronted his country. The government, Koo said, was being removed to Chungking, although Nanking and the areas to the east of the capital would be defended. Now that the French had shut down their transit facilities for weapons and munitions, and other transportation routes had been blocked, the best way to help China was to make a forceful demonstration of a united front. While China had not held much hope for assistance before the conference opened, the calling of it had aroused substantial expectations. If it closed now without accomplishing anything, the Chinese would be profoundly disappointed. Hornbeck, of course, could promise nothing, and by this time Koo himself must have realized that China's chances of getting aid from the Brussels Conference were almost nonexistent.[61]

In the last two days before the conference reconvened, Davis and his staff worked, primarily with the British, on the final draft to be adopted by it. The absence of Eden and Dalbos, who had failed to return to Brussels and had left affairs in the hands of their subordinates, made it clear that London and Paris saw the draft as a lost cause. Litvinov was also convinced that the conference would not amount to anything and had left following the previous adjournment. Soviet affairs, too, were now left in the hands of an underling, Vladimir Potemkin.

Fearing that the Chinese might take their concerns back to Geneva, the British delegation, now led by MacDonald, tried to persuade Davis to have the conference adjourn in such a way that the Chinese would be deprived of their justification for doing so. This could be done by having the United States and Britain make a joint offer of mediation to Japan, or at least announce their willingness to mediate. The conference could then end without the appearance of failure. Davis said he did not feel the time was ripe for such a move, but the truth was that he did not want to make a public pronouncement tying American to Great Britain. Instead, he offered a compromise. The conference could adopt a resolution calling upon Japan and China to suspend hostilities and couple with it a standing offer to help negotiate an armistice. A second resolution could direct the powers to stay in touch with each other and continue to exchange opinions on the Far Eastern conflict. These proposals bear the stamp of Cordell Hull, who had sent Davis a long cable embodying them just two days before Davis conferred with MacDonald.[62]

The British still clung tenaciously to their own formula. On the day before the conference reopened, the Americans learned that MacDonald's draft resolution completely ignored the proposals from Davis to which the British had agreed the previous day. Moffat wrote in his diary that they had drawn up "a restatement of the unvarnished case in favor of an immediate joint Anglo-American mediation." This made it necessary for the two delegations to renegotiate all over again, and they remained in session until a compromise was worked out at 2:30 a.m. on the following day. The Americans were not only exhausted but exasperated to learn that the British had been circulating the story that they had proposed mediation, which the latter said they thought would be effective, but that the Americans had turned them down and wanted to adjourn instead.

The next morning, the French delegation, without Delbos, arrived back in Brussels for the afternoon session that would reopen the conference. They informed Davis that they wished to be associated with the United States and Britain in sponsoring the declaration that had been worked out the night before. When it was shown to them, they disagreed with its contents but accepted it rather than be left out. Over the rest of the morning the British and Americans showed advance copies to the other delegations. The British approached the Dominions, Italy and Portugal, while the Americans went to Russia, the Netherlands, the Scandinavian countries, Mexico and Bolivia. Davis took it upon himself to talk to Potemkin. Moffat was given the task of calling on all the others. Only the Norwegians and Mexicans proved difficult. The Norwegian delegate tried to monopolize the conversation and justify Norway's policy of independence. Moffat said that the Mexican delegate was the most trying of all. He "just didn't know what it was all about and kept reverting to the League of Nations when no one else wanted to speak about it."

When the session began in the afternoon, Dr. Koo took the floor for his final address. In acid tones he attacked the body for its impotence. This accomplished little more than to annoy the other delegates. The rest of the session was devoted to tentative drafts of the final report and declaration to be adopted by the conference. The last hours were somewhat frantic. The Dutch delegate, who had previously been silent, suddenly told the Americans that the conference should either take action and aid China or else adjourn with no more than a factual report. He said that the draft resolution was weak and that education by moral force was nothing but an alibi for inaction. Not until the morning of the last day did Davis bring him into line. Koo, who seemed to blame the U.S. for the conference's failure to take a more determined stand, got in a parting shot by telling the press that the British had praised his final speech and were China's friends, while America was letting China down.[63]

It was on this sour note that the conference assembled for the last time on the afternoon of November 24. The session lasted for only two and a half hours and the declaration, which was entitled simply "Report of the Conference," was adopted with virtually no amendments. It was an innocuous document addressed to no one in particular, to be forwarded through diplomatic channels to the world's governments. It consisted of twelve typewritten pages, comprising a historical survey of the circumstances under which the conference had been called, the documents it had produced, and the pointless conclusion it had reached. It ended with a declaration of principles which deplored the use of force in settling disputes, affirmed the provisions of the Nine Power Treaty, urged a prompt suspension of the hostilities between China and Japan, declared that the conflict in the Far East was one that was of vital concern to all the powers assembled at Brussels, and announced that the conference was suspending its sitting temporarily but would reconvene if the president or any two of its members "shall have reported that they consider that its deliberations can be advantageously resumed."[64]

As each delegate was called upon to vote on the adoption of the Report, short speeches were made. Only the Italian representative voted against it. Count Aldrovandi-Marescotti declared that his government regarded not only the report but the conference itself as superfluous and useless. His verdict was correct. Dr. Koo reluctantly voted for adoption, saying:

> The new draft, like the old one, reaffirms certain general principles which China has always accepted. But in view of the continued raging of the hostilities in the Far East, the Chinese delegation believes that a mere reaffirmation of these principles cannot be considered as a satisfactory result of the Conference, because it is not adequate to deal effectively with the grave situation.[65]

X. Charade at Brussels

Koo concluded by saying that he regretted that the conference had not followed Chinese suggestions for "positive and concrete measures" against Japan, measures "indispensable in any effort to restrain Japanese aggression and hasten the restoration of peace in the Far East."

Norman Davis gave the conference's valediction. While his words were optimistic, everyone in the room knew they were meaningless. The *New York Times* reported them:

> It should be particularly emphasized that this recess does not in any sense signify that the problem we have been considering is to be dropped or that our interest in its solution is to be in any way lessened.
>
> The fact that we have been unable thus far to bring about negotiations looking to a peaceable settlement by agreement of the Sino-Japanese conflict in no way diminishes our effort, our interest, or our concern....
>
> Those who may be discouraged or impatient over the delay in achieving the objectives sought should realize that we are not ending the Nine Power Conference. We are merely going into recess. Nothing has been lost and much has been gained through the fact of our having engaged in an exchange of views and having exerted the efforts thus far made.

Davis's words were obviously intended to put a good face on what everyone realized was a failure. He was not very persuasive. The European press had long since dismissed the conference as a fiasco. Not a single American newspaper of any consequence could fail to arrive at the same conclusion. The *New York Times* said, "one is now justified in wondering why the Conference was held anyhow." Most editors harked back to the President's Chicago speech, which was regarded as having triggered the convocation at Brussels. The *Los Angeles Times*, which had greeted the quarantine speech with enthusiasm, observed:

> It seemed to be a sound and statesmanlike utterance, but if there was no intention of following it up, which seems to be the case, it is removed to a different classification. "Speak softly and carry a big stick" was another Roosevelt's idea of foreign policy. This Roosevelt seems to have reversed it.

Although the American delegates resented the attacks made by the press, they knew that the criticisms were mostly justified. For Norman Davis, the Brussels Conference was probably the three most frustrating weeks of his life. Although he said nothing in public, when he arrived home, he told Sumner Welles that he felt his government had let him down and had not supported him properly. Welles asked him, what more could the President or the State Department have done? The answer, of course, was nothing. Pressed by the other conference participants to take a more vigorous stand against Japanese aggression in China, Davis finally suggested a weak formula of financial coercion, although in his heart he might have liked to do more. Even this went beyond his original instructions, and Hull would not have permitted him to exceed those. So Davis was buffeted by the British, the French, the Chinese, and to a lesser extent by the Russians, as he vainly sought for a proposition that would not be rejected by the Department but would enable him to refute the charge that Americans were all talk. His dilemma reveals the real reason for the failure of the conference.

One sympathizes with Davis's predicament. It would be interesting to know what the attitude of Britain and France might have been had Davis been authorized to propose coercive measures to Eden and Delbos. Stanley Hornbeck told the author that he clearly recalled how impressed he was by Eden's sincerity (in contrast to Moffat!) in arguing that something should be done to stop Japan in China.[66] However, any moves on Britain's part would have been governed by developments in Europe and the degree of cooperation that England could have offered the United States would have been limited by them. Eden strongly disapproved of appeasing the Axis, and it was over Chamberlain's insistence on following that line that Eden resigned in February 1938. This tends to support Hornbeck's impression that Eden had argued earnestly in favor of collective security in the fall of 1937.

It is impossible to say what effect sanctions might have had if they had been applied. By November, the Japanese had won Shanghai and all of North China. The drive on Nanking was under way, and Tokyo was confident that the capture of China's capital would shatter Chinese resistance. If Chiang Kai-shek did not come to terms in the meantime, a puppet government could be created in his place. Japan's military extremists might well have driven their leaders to a more radical course if sanctions had been imposed and put their imperial gains in jeopardy. Indeed, it was the American embargo on oil and petroleum products in 1940 that drove the military to launch its campaign to seize all of Southeast Asia in December 1941, even though this meant war with Britain and the United States. By then, of course, the Japanese had been at war with China for four years and they had far more at stake than in the fall of 1937. In any event, the unpredictability of the military radicals would have made sanctions risky because, as Grew pointed out, to be effective sanctions would have to have been total and backed up by a willingness to use force. The lesser powers at Brussels had made it clear that they would have nothing to do with such sanctions.

Direct aid to China, in the form of either armaments or loans, was a more realistic policy, but here again the Western powers would have had to demonstrate a measure of solidarity and with it, a willingness to resort to force in the face of a common enemy. Consideration of this course was abandoned when Britain and France realized that Davis could not commit his country to any policy that would impair its neutrality. Small wonder

X. Charade at Brussels 281

that they hastened to close the conference and go home. Once they did so, the Nine Power Treaty was finally buried and hopes for collective action in the Far East dissipated. American policy was thoroughly discredited and the hopes that had been raised among the Europeans and the Chinese following the President's Chicago address and the State Department's statement of early October were dashed completely.

In Tokyo and Nanking, the collapse of the Brussels Conference ensured that the war was now completely theirs. The Japanese saw that they no longer needed to be concerned about outside interference. They were undoubtedly emboldened to tighten their controls on Shanghai in violation of Western privileges in the city. They could get on with their campaign and Chiang Kai-shek would either submit or they would deal without him. They self-confidently drew up harsher terms for peace, which they felt they were now able to impose on a government that had been deserted by the West.

Chiang's disappointment was deep and bitter. Although he would never have blamed himself for the reverses that he had suffered on the battlefield, he believed that the encouraging statements made in Chicago and Western capitals as well as Geneva offered hope of at least indirect help so that China could continue to resist. In the aftermath of the Brussels Conference, he was faced with the cold truth: China stood alone. This fact drove him to wage a different kind of war. He would defend Nanking with the remains of his shattered divisions even if their loss was foreordained. He would keep fighting, making the vastness of the land his ally. But he did not give up on the West. He knew that ultimately they would not tolerate Japanese hegemony in Asia and that a larger conflict was therefore inevitable. In this respect, Chiang showed far more wisdom than his adversaries, whose military adventurism continued to feed on itself.

XI

The Rape of Nanking

> Mercy to enemies has been a characteristic of Japanese warriors in the past and is still the thought of the modern military men of the country....
> Although the entire nation is now eagerly awaiting news of the fall of Nanking, they are also hoping that Nanking will peacefully surrender as they are against unnecessary destruction and fighting. From the very beginning of the incident, Japan has had no intention of killing Chinese soldiers and people, and of destroying buildings, residences and other structures. Damages already done in Shanghai and North China were caused by the resistance of the Chinese.
> —Editorial, *Japan Times and Mail*, December 11, 1937

It was not often that a Japanese publication spoke with caution about the war in China, especially in the fall of 1937 when the Imperial Army seemed invincible. In late November, however, the *Japan Weekly Chronicle* made a sobering assessment of the conflict to date, taking note of the progress the army had made to end Chinese resistance. In spite of the heavy losses inflicted on Chiang Kai-shek's forces and the shattering of his best divisions in the fighting at Shanghai, there was no sign of his surrender. True, the editor of the *Chronicle* wrote, Chiang's armies could expect little in the way of arms and munitions from abroad and had few resources at home. For these reasons, effective resistance against a Japanese offensive aimed at Nanking was unlikely, although the Chinese could be expected to fight with whatever means were available. The editor then made a remarkable prediction:

> They will make the Japanese advance as costly as possible and when forced to do so, will retreat still further up the Yangtze, falling back to Hankow. This retreat is along the route taken by the victorious Kuomintang army in 1926–1927, and can be continued into the mountainous wilds of Szechwan and in the South-West until Canton. Where it will finally end depends solely on the impetus of the Japanese drive, and the decision of the Imperial General Staff. All that can be said now with any confidence is that the occupation of the Chinese capital quite evidently will not mean the end of

XI. The Rape of Nanking

the war. The phase will be changed, battles will become skirmishes, and the Chinese troops will adopt guerrilla tactics, but all indications are that they will fight on.[1]

In the euphoria that followed the fall of Shanghai, however, and the anticipation of the fall of Nanking, the Japanese field commanders were not thinking beyond their immediate goal. They were sure that raising the Rising Sun flag over the Chinese capital would crown their military exploits. Nanking was the finish line, a finite object within their grasp. Victory would be the culmination of their success in China; the capture of the enemy's capital must oblige her to accept defeat and come to terms. This after all was how wars had been fought and won since men had taken up arms. But China was not a Western nation with limited boundaries. Nanking was a political entity, its loss irrelevant in the larger struggle for a country whose cities were not the source of her strength and powers of resistance. The editor of the *Chronicle* was right. The Chinese would fight to defend Nanking, inflicting as heavy losses as they could on the invaders, but they would lose the capital. Then would come the new phase when battles would become skirmishes and the real struggle for China would begin. The *Chronicle* did not speculate on the outcome, but its editor must surely have had his doubts. For the moment, though, the fate of Nanking was the center of attention.

In the meantime, the Japanese military forces in the Shanghai region were reorganized. On November 7 Yanagawa's 10th Army was merged with Matsui's Shanghai Expeditionary Army to form the Central China Expeditionary Forces. General Matsui was named overall commander. What followed was the familiar pattern of military developments in North China, in which field commanders initiated offensive operations on their own, expanding the war against the wishes of the General Staff back in Tokyo. Even before Matsui arrived in China to take command of the Shanghai Expeditionary Army, his comments revealed that he intended to drive onto Nanking, and although the official policy of the General Staff was to confine operations to the Shanghai area, the Operations Division Chief, Shimomura, and the other army expansionists shared Matsui's aims. On the day he assumed command, Matsui was authorized to advance to a line between Soochow and Chiahsing.[2]

By November 19 Matsui's troops had reached their immediate objectives, but neither he nor Yanagawa meant to stop their offensive and they now pressed the General Staff to extend the demarcation line further to the west. Indeed, Yanagawa did not even await permission but ordered the 10th Army forward. As noted earlier, the Vice Chief of Staff, General Tada, strongly objected to expanding the war and countermanded Yanagawa's order. Tada opposed what he saw as a "war of annihilation," believing that it would hinder the army's armaments and production expansion plans. But Tada not only had to contend with Matsui and his allies in the General Staff Operations branch, he found himself at odds with the Foreign Minister. Hirota had come around to the view that capturing Nanking would destroy Chiang's political viability and end the legitimacy of his government. Others outside the military establishment shared his belief. The Japan-China Business and Industrial Association, which represented the principal business leaders, favored setting up a military government for all of China. Even Konoe abandoned his customary handwringing and said that the nation had no choice "but to deal a blow in a determined manner."[3]

Although permission was granted on November 24 to extend operations to a line between Wusih and Huchow, Tada held out against an advance on Nanking until November 28. By then, Matsui had sent word that Chinese forces were so disorganized that Nanking should be taken in a short time. Shimomura was able to talk Tada around, and on December 1 an official order to attack Nanking was sent to Matsui.[4] The Japanese field army now surged forward to seize its prize.

The announcement on November 20 by the Nationalist government that it was removing itself to Chungking prompted a mass exodus from Nanking. On November 18, Tillman Durdin, the city's *New York Times* correspondent, had already reported that

> Crowds and traffic were still dense on the main streets and the river front, but in many areas homes, offices and shops for blocks were already shuttered, and only a few vehicles and pedestrians were moving through the roadways, littered in many spots with bomb wreckage, papers, bedding and household goods left behind in the hurry of departure.
> In most of the government offices virtually all the staff members have departed, only a few executives remaining. [O]n Wednesday, a low mist accompanied by an intermittent drizzle added to the gloom of the depression and at the same time saved the city and the long trains, fleets of ships, and endless trails of automobiles forging their way into the interior from the further panic of Japanese air raids.

The commander of the Nanking defense forces, General Tang Shing Chih, recommended that all foreigners leave who did not have urgent business in the city. There had been disorders, he said, primarily because of the poor quality of the Chinese garrison troops, and while all efforts would be made to protect foreign lives and property, foreigners should be forewarned. Most embassy personnel heeded his advice and departed, leaving behind only skeleton staffs.[5]

The Chinese, depending on their station in life, fled Nanking on foot or by oxcarts drawn by plodding water buffalo, in the case of peasant refugees from the villages east and south of the city, or by car along the muddy roads to Hankow and Changsha for those lucky enough to own private automobiles. All but the most precious possessions they could carry had

XI. The Rape of Nanking

to be abandoned. The government itself was able to remove only its most essential equipment and important papers. Everything else was consigned to huge bonfires stoked by records and books from the various ministries. Cabinet members lingered only briefly. When the enemy drew near only the most foolhardy remained, trusting in divine providence or Japanese assurances to protect them.

By November 26 the Japanese had captured Wusih, an industrial city near the northern shores of Lake Tai, fracturing the Chinese line that ran from Wusih northward to the Kiangyin Forts on the south bank of the Yangtze River. According to Major David D. Barrett, the forts proved "a fairly tough nut for the Japanese to crack," but by the 29th they were in Japanese hands. Once again the Chinese failed to hold an important position that they could easily have defended. What made their loss particularly significant was that they had commanded a boom that had been thrown across the Yangtze as a river barrier. The boom was comprised mostly of junks and other boats loaded with concrete and sunk in the river. A narrow channel had been left through the boom, but it was difficult to navigate even for ships that were not threatened by fire from shore batteries. A series of forts on the north side of the Yangtze opposite Kiangyin commanded that end of the boom, which made it an even more formidable barrier to Japanese warships. These positions were not taken until December 8, and the boom was not breached until the next day. The Chinese erected another boom above Kiangyin at Chinkiang and the Japanese were unable to force their way beyond it until December 13, but by then the fate of Nanking had already been sealed.[6]

Japan's infantry advanced so rapidly in their race to capture Nanking that their munitions and supply trains had a hard time keeping up with them. Lake Tai proved no obstacle as their forces encircled it and then used hundreds of Chinese junks, ferries and small steamers to transport soldiers and supplies to the west. Major Barrett found himself following newspaper reports of the routes of the Japanese offensive. He learned from Hallett Abend's *New York Times* column on November 30 that a three-pronged assault was in progress, one along the Shanghai-Nanking Railway, a second on the highway from Ihing just west of Lake Tai, and the third on the highway through Kwangteh south of Nanking. However, the successive booms across the Yangtze barred Japan's navy from playing more than a minor role in the conquest of Nanking. With the exception of navy aircraft, it was an all-army show.

At home the Japanese people followed with pride the deeds of their soldiers. A dispatch from the Shanghai front on December 6 gave details of a bet between two officers as to which of them would be the first to slay a hundred Chinese with his sword.

Sub-Lieutenants Toshiaki Mukai, 26 years old, and Tsuyoshi Noda, 25 years old, laid a wager on the accomplishment and have since been trying hard to win.... At last accounts they were approaching the end of the contest, for [in] the fighting for the capture of Kuyung in the advance on Changchow, Mukai claimed 89 victims and Noda 78. Mukai's best day was set down as 55 slain in a raid on Wusih and Changchow. A condition of the match is that no victims shall be counted unless they were resisting when killed.[7]

Grisly as this story was, it captured the imaginations of Japanese readers, who learned a week later that the two young officers had extended their goal to 150 because those monitoring the contest were unable to tell which of them had reached 100 first. The *Japan Advertiser* reported that Mukai's blade had been slightly damaged in the competition as a result of his having cut a Chinese in half. He characterized the game as "fun."[8]

Editorials now filled Japanese newspapers, speculating on the fighting and urging the Nationalist government to sue for peace before it was too late. On November 23 the editor of *Kokumin* wrote:

> Already Soochow and Wusih have fallen into Japanese hands, and the fall of Nanking is expected not so far distant. Who then will be able to save China from her apparently inevitable collapse? Only the Chinese nation itself and no other, we do not doubt. Besides it is a fact already made clearly known ... that the saving of the Chinese nation ... from its possible collapse may materialize not in a fight with Japan but by an armistice with our nation.

Mukai and Noda, two Japanese officers who had a contest to see which of them could kill the most Chinese during the Nanking massacre, one of many atrocities committed by the Japanese.

XI. The Rape of Nanking

The editor of the *Japan Times and Mail* surmised that in spite of Chiang Kai-shek's defiant posture, he had to be considering capitulation. With this in mind, the editor said he hoped that the peace imposed would be neither too strong nor too weak. The definition of a peace that was neither did not necessarily conform to Chiang's perceptions.

General Matsui behaved as if the war was already won. On November 30 he gave a long interview to Hallett Abend in Shanghai. Foreign holders of bonds secured by Chinese maritime customs had expressed concern that their claims were in jeopardy now that Japan controlled Shanghai customs. He said they had nothing to fear, nor did any of the residents and investors in the International Settlement. The Japanese government did not intend to interfere with their properties. He assured Abend that bond holders and other investors would be protected. Then, with a stern expression, he said:

> I have been made very, very angry by cabled reports from England and American revealing foreign expectations that the Japanese Army under my direction would grab everything in Shanghai and would imperil all foreign rights and interests here. Nothing is further from my thoughts.

This was an act. Matsui finally could not contain himself and began to laugh so hard that he had to wipe tears from his eyes before he could go on.

> New York, Washington and London seem to think that I am something akin to the ordinary looting Chinese warlord. Please disabuse the public abroad. My original broad statement still stands. We as the military conquerors of this area hold ourselves entitled to assume all the rights and prerogatives previously exercised in the Shanghai area by the Chinese government, nothing less, nothing more, but this does not mean we intend exercising those rights irritatingly or encroachingly as did the Chinese.[9]

The general went on to say that, although he needed every available man for his offensive against Nanking, he was ordering an entire division to return to Shanghai to take over police functions and make the city safe so that foreigners could return to their homes and places of business.

The day after Matsui spoke so paternally of his concern for the welfare of Shanghai's Western inhabitants, the Japanese sent a very different message. They announced that their soldiers would be parading through the British and American sectors of the city, while a victory flight of warplanes would fill the skies above. This martial display would make an unmistakable statement: only Japan's unchallenged military could protect Western economic and financial interests. The American and British commands protested that they would not be responsible for any incidents that might occur, although they promised to keep the routes free of refugees.

On Friday, December 3, the parade came off as scheduled, but so did the feared incident. As elements of the Fukui and Yamada regiments marched down Nanking Road, a Chinese in the curbside crowd threw a hand grenade, wounding a Japanese soldier and civilian as well as two municipal policemen. The police shot him dead, but a provocation had taken place.¹⁰ It might have been worse. The Japanese immediately occupied an area of more than thirty blocks, stringing barbed wire barricades and closing streets to traffic deep within the American defense sector. Despite the risks involved, Colonel Charles Price, commander of the Fourth Marine Regiment, under orders from Brigadier General John Beaumont, commander of the U.S. Marines in Shanghai, took several members of his staff and drove through the lines to Japanese headquarters, which was guarded by machine-gun emplacements. Colonel Price demanded that all Japanese soldiers, sentries and barriers be removed from the American defense sector at once and threatened that if they weren't, his Marines would clear them. He must have displayed an intimidating presence, because the Japanese commander apologized profusely and gave hurried orders to his troops to pull out.

By the next day all of the Japanese had withdrawn from the occupied area but they had made their point: the Western enclaves were vulnerable. In the twenty-four hours that they had been in control, they gave the Americans and British a look at what life would be like under Japan's rule. The Park Hotel, the Shanghai Race Club, the Grand Theater, the YMCA and the China Park Apartments were isolated and inaccessible. Surly Japanese sentries were posted at the doors of all of these establishments and refused to allow foreigners to enter or leave.¹¹

By December 6 Matsui's soldiers were within 25 miles of Nanking. With the city's fall imminent, rumors began to fly in Tokyo that mediation was a possibility. Word of the Trautmann mission had leaked out, but the press assumed that the German Ambassador's actions would be confined to encouraging Chiang Kai-shek to open direct negotiations with Japan. Given the developing relationship between the Third Reich and the Japanese, no one thought that Germany would offer to mediate, particularly in light of a recent statement by Premier Konoe that the Imperial Government would never allow intervention or mediation by a third party.¹² As is often the case, the press reports were partly true and partly creative writing. Ambassador Trautmann had indeed urged Chiang to accept Japan's terms but had been turned down. Now, following the failure of the Brussels Conference and the impending capture of Nanking, Chiang reversed course. On December 3 he notified the German Ambassador that he was prepared to settle the conflict on the basis of Hirota's conditions of November 3, so long as China's territorial integrity was preserved. Chiang's message was immediate transmitted through the German Foreign Office in Berlin to Ambassador Dirksen in Tokyo. Once again, however, events had outrun diplomacy. Hirota told Dirksen that the November peace proposals were no longer applicable because the field armies would never accept them.

This may have been true, but the General Staff, with the exceptions previously noted, saw an opportunity to get a settlement and extricate the nation from the China quagmire. The far-sighted General Tada recommended an armistice at once, to be followed by a peace similar to that negotiated by Bismarck after the Prussian victory over Austria in 1866, when generous terms had made a friend of a former enemy. Once Japan had achieved this goal it could then focus its attention on its real adversary, the Soviet Union.

The mercurial Konoe, who after the war with America had blamed the military for denying him freedom of action, lost his last chance to act as a statesman. He was no longer interested in dealing with the Nationalists, believing that once Nanking was taken, Chiang's government would collapse and Japan could then withdraw recognition of it. General Tada rebutted him, saying that Japan would have to pursue the Nationalist forces into South China, which would widen the war even further. Simultaneously, Japan would be stuck with the task of organizing a new Chinese government. He pointed out that resolving the China Incident would be a political problem, and to settle it meant dealing with Chiang. To this end, with the support of the service ministries and the naval general staff, Tada demanded that Konoe call a Liaison Conference between the Inner Cabinet and the Supreme Command. Only in this forum "could the government systematically consider the strategic and political issues involved in Chiang's latest overtures for a negotiated peace."[13]

Two days before the meeting, Baron Harada visited Konoe and found him in a fretful mood. "I can no longer bear it," Konoe suddenly blurted out. "When Nanking falls, Chiang's government will fall. Japan will issue a statement of non-recognition of Chiang's government. I think that is the time for me to withdraw and I shall resign at that time." Harada rejected the notion out of hand, telling Konoe that it was not an appropriate time for him to quit, and that not only would he be behaving irresponsibly but that the "public confidence of the Japanese people will practically fall to the ground. It will mean that you are betraying the trust of the people." Konoe groaned that if he did not resign now he would be kept on forever. At this point, Marquis Kodo entered the room and saw Konoe's anguish. Told that the Prime Minister wanted to resign, Kido said that it was out of the question, but to soften his words he offered hope. "When expectations for the future are set up and everything quiets down, you can resign." Like their mentor, Prince Saionji, the two peers treated Konoe like a spoiled child, enduring his selfish pique while trying to instill in him a sense of duty. Harada was disgusted. He concluded his diary entry describing the encounter by noting, "Kido and Konoe left for golf, but I went home."[14]

Konoe's behavior was not only self-indulgent, it was deceitful. Baron Harada was his friend and confidant, yet he failed to tell Harada of an important Cabinet appointment that he had made. On the evening of the 12th, the very day that Harada and Kido had dissuaded him from quitting his post, the newspapers announced that Admiral Suetsugu was going to assume the position of Home Minister. The decision to appoint him had been made on the 11th but Konoe said nothing to Harada when they met on the 12th. "He probably thought I would oppose if it he told me. Or else he probably thought I wouldn't agree to it," Harada observed afterward. Konoe's deception of the Navy was worse. Courtesy demanded that the Navy Minister be consulted or at least informed about Admiral Suetsugu's appointment before it was announced. Instead, when the Navy Minister visited the Imperial Palace on the 11th to have lunch with the Emperor, he ran into Konoe in the hall and asked him, "What's up today?" According to Harada, Konoe replied, "It's nothing important."

It was, of course, enormously important on the eve of the Liaison Conference. Admiral Suetsugu's chauvinism was well known and his agitation of the young officers in the Navy had led to his forced retirement. For all of Konoe's private talk about wanting to resign, he showed a Machiavellian skill in bringing Suetsugu into his Cabinet. Now he had an ally against the General Staff. That the Admiral shared Konoe's view on the China war became apparent in a press interview following the announcement of his appointment. It was December 14, a date that coincided with the fall of Nanking and the meeting of the Liaison Conference to consider whether to undertake negotiations with the Nationalists to end the war or pursue other military/political options. Suetsugu declared his preference for the latter, dismissing Chiang Kai-shek as just another "old warlord" and saying "special regimes" would have to be set up not only in North China but in South and Central China as well. He concluded with his favorite thesis, that Japan's mission was now to end white domination and bring about the liberation of the "colored races." Obviously, retirement had not mellowed Admiral Suetsugu.

Bringing this firebrand to the Liaison Conference set a precedent. The Home Minister was not a member of the Inner Cabinet and had not sat in it since its creation in 1933. It was at Konoe's express request that Suetsugu was now invited to participate. The result was predictable; the meeting was a stormy one. Konoe began the session by observing that Chiang Kai-shek had said he was willing to negotiate for peace, and then asked General Tada for a military summary. Instead, Tada brought up the terms that Chiang had agreed to accept. Under the circumstances, Tada said, the General Staff advocated an armistice and the pursuit of diplomatic negotiations. Then it was the Foreign Minister's turn to speak. Hirota commented on the changed military conditions, which he said should be taken into account if new terms were adopted, but he offered no specific recommendations.

XI. The Rape of Nanking

At this point, Konoe called on Admiral Suetsugu. If what followed had not been previously orchestrated, it might as well have been. Suetsugu offended Tada not only by criticizing the conduct of operations in China but by giving him some unwarranted advice on coordinating the campaigns in the North and South. An irate Tada replied that military matters were not Suetsugu's business. At this point Konoe declared a recess to let passions cool, but when the conference reconvened Suetsugu continued his provocative behavior. When General Sugiyama and Admiral Yonai said they were willing to use the Cabinet's peace terms of October 1 as the basis for negotiations with the Nationalists, Suetsugu immediately demanded to know whether the Japanese people would be willing to accept them after the heavy losses incurred in the capture of Nanking. He was joined by Akira Kazami, Konoe's secretary and a senior member of the Seiyukai Party, prompting Tada to ask "sarcastically whether the government intended to determine national policy on the basis of public opinion or the long-term security interests of the empire." The Prime Minister decided not to prolong the debate and declared that, since the Liaison Conference could not agree on a policy, the meeting was adjourned.

Whatever hope there might have been for a settlement was now dashed. By bringing Admiral Suetsugu into his Cabinet and giving him a seat at the Conference, Konoe had ensured that it could not succeed, but he was far from done. On December 17 he called a meeting of the Cabinet to discuss new peace terms to be offered to the Nationalist government. He turned again to Suetsugu. The Home Minister recommended four basic demands: (1) the Nationalist government would have to sign an anti–Communist pact with Japan; (2) special regions and demilitarized zones "in areas desired by the two governments" would be created; (3) there would be a guarantee of close cooperation between China and Japan; and (4) China would have to pay an indemnity. Konoe and Hirota undoubtedly knew and approved of Suetsugu's proposals before they were presented to the Cabinet. In light of Konoe's expressed views on refusing recognition of the Nationalist government, he and the others knew that Chiang Kai-shek would never accept conditions that practically amounted to capitulation and the loss of political and economic independence. Konoe would have his cake and eat it too. He would go through the motions of offering peace terms in order to placate the General Staff, but the terms themselves guaranteed that they would be refused. Japan could then get on with dispensing with Chiang and the Nationalists and seek out Chinese who would be willing to cooperate and adopt "a good attitude" toward Japan. The game, however, had to be played to its conclusion. Hirota advised Ambassador Dirksen on December 23 of the new conditions for peace. The German Ambassador was understandably perplexed by their vagueness and asked for further details, telling

Hirota that Chiang was unlikely to accept them without some clarification. A week passed before Hirota authorized Dirksen to tell the Chinese that based on "conversations with leading Japanese personalities," the points included "(1) a recognition of Manchukuo; (2) a recognition of Prince Teh's government in Inner Mongolia; [and] (3) the continuation of the existing 'demilitarized zone' in North China, plus an enlarged demilitarized zone in the Yangtze region."[15] Dirksen was sure that these conditions would be rejected, and he was right. The harshness of the Japanese terms confirmed in Chiang's mind the wisdom of retreating to Chungking and conducting a different kind of war against the invaders. Moreover, the unrestrained rape and slaughter by Matsui's soldiers in Nanking had shown that Japan would accept only unconditional surrender. Chiang had labored too long to unify and liberate his country to settle for that.

Late in the afternoon of December 6, Japanese troops occupied the tomb of Sun Yat-sen on Purple Mountain in the suburbs of Nanking. The Chinese people had been resigned to the loss of their former capital, but the seizure of the tomb of their revered patriot, the father of modern China, confirmed the disaster that had befallen them. However, they would not give up the city itself without a fight. The Japanese would still have to breach the massive walls built by a Ming emperor centuries earlier. Thirty miles long, these walls were the last barrier that Japan's troops would have to overcome to capture Nanking. They had left a trail of death and destruction in their wake after breaking out of Shanghai. An American missionary described conditions:

> My companion and I had to drive carefully to avoid running over the bodies of the dead lining the roads and scattered over the fields. When we arrived, looting by Japanese soldiers was proceeding in lively fashion. Mission property, as yet, had not been molested. From that time until December 11, we went into Soochow every day. We saw that every bank and shop and every residence had been forced open. Japanese soldiers were passing in and out of them, like ants loaded down with bales of silk, eiderdown quilts, shop goods and household effects of every description.
>
> The dead bodies we saw in the streets of Soochow on our first visit there after the Japanese occupation lay there for ten days or more. On our later trips to the city, we observed that the street dogs were noticeably fatter. Equally ghastly were the buildings, damages amounting to more than a million dollars.
>
> None can possibly estimate the number of women ravaged by the lust-mad Japanese army.... And should anyone believe that the Japanese army is in this country to make life better and happier for the Chinese, then let him travel over the area between Shanghai and Nanking, a distance of some 200 miles, and witness the unbelievable desolation and destruction. This area, six months ago, was the most densely populated portion of the earth's surface, and the most prosperous section of China.
>
> Today the traveler will see only cities bombed and pillaged; towns and villages reduced to shambles; farms desolated; and only an old man or woman here and there digging in the once "good earth." The livestock has been either killed or stolen, and

USS *Panay*: American gunboat sunk while on the Yangtze River by Japanese aircraft fire (National Archives).

every sort of destruction that a brutal army, equipped with all the modern implements of war, can inflict ... has been done.

It is shameful, indeed, in the face of all this, that the Japanese, who control communication lines, are proclaiming to the world that they are inviting Chinese back to their ancestral homes to live in peace and plenty.[16]

With the invaders closing in, most of the remaining Westerners in Nanking were urged to leave before the huge gates of the city were shut against all chance of escape. The few Americans were told to board the gunboat *Panay*, which was standing by in the Yangtze River. A handful of American Embassy personnel, led by Second Secretary George Atcheson, now evacuated the mission, Ambassador Johnson having left for Hankow nearly two weeks earlier. Japanese air attacks had forced the suspension of all civilian shipping on the Yangtze, and the bombing of Pukow, just across the river from Nanking, cut off escape by rail to the north. Since the Japanese were approaching from the east and south, these routes were closed as well. Nevertheless, some foreigners were determined to stay behind and tried to organize a neutral zone within Nanking as a safety area for refugees. The Chinese authorities tolerated this, and the Japanese promised that they would not attack the area so long as it was demilitarized and did not interfere with military operations. Other foreigners, led by the Rev. John Magee, an American, sought to form a Nanking branch of the International Red Cross and put the military hospitals in the city under their supervision to protect thousands of wounded Chinese soldiers.[17]

The city now prepared for a siege. Its massive gates were backed up by sandbag and cement breastworks twenty feet thick. Public utilities sputtered out as power died in many neighborhoods. Telephones became inoperable, water supplies were uncertain and public transport disappeared. As the neutral zone was marked out with flags and signs, public buildings, including the Ministry of Justice and the War College, were opened to the homeless. Although Chiang Kai-shek had moved his capital and his ministries had departed, he remained in Nanking until December 7. Early that morning, he and his wife took a private airplane, piloted by Americans, to Hankow. The next day, the last of the foreign embassy personnel left to take up quarters aboard ships in the Yangtze, having come to the common realization that it was too dangerous for them to remain in the city.

While Japanese troops paused before their final assault, a significant change in command was ordered. General Matsui was still the overall commander of the Central China Army, but the Emperor appointed his uncle, Prince Asaka, to lead the forces investing Nanking. Asaka was a lieutenant general with thirty years of experience. Fifty years old, he walked with a limp, the result of an automobile accident outside Paris in 1923. At that time, he had been serving as an intelligence officer, ironically in the company of two men who were now playing key roles in the Shanghai-Nanking campaigns, Generals Yanagawa and Nakajima. Asaka had fallen out of favor at the court in 1936 due to his sympathy with the army mutineers, and his command at Nanking was offered as an opportunity to redeem himself. That "redemption" took the form of overseeing the brutalization of thousands of captured Chinese soldiers and helpless civilians.

It was the hapless Matsui who paid with his life after the war for the atrocities committed by Japanese soldiers in Nanking, rather than Prince Asaka. As the senior Japanese officer, Matsui was held ultimately responsible, although there is no evidence that he condoned what happened after the fall of Nanking. Indeed, prior to the assault on the city, he issued specific instructions that troops entering it should be especially chosen for their discipline and under all circumstances should avoid plunder and other unlawful conduct. To ensure proper behavior, he recommended that military police be stationed in the city. In contrast to this injunction, Prince Asaka's headquarters issued secret orders for the killing of all captives. A staff intelligence officer, a lieutenant colonel, later told his friends that he had forged the orders himself. If this was so, he went unpunished, remaining in the army until his death during the Okinawa campaign in June 1945. Asaka was never tried, and Matsui bore the blame for the crimes committed under his command.[18]

On December 9, a Japanese plane flew over General Tang Sheng Chih's headquarters inside Nanking and dropped a "note of advice" from General Matsui. It called on the Chinese commander to surrender within twenty-four hours or face an all-out assault by the Japanese Army. As usual, Japan prevaricated; Matsui claimed that he had a million men ready to attack but said that he wanted to spare the city the horrors of war and destruction. Believing that the Chinese were about to capitulate, the Japanese Army dispatched two dozen bombers from Shanghai, loaded not with bombs but with hundreds of cases of champagne for its officers to toast their triumphal entry into Nanking.[19] Not only the Army was preparing to rejoice. Flags, banners and large paper lanterns were in place on the main streets of Tokyo, and arrangements were made for huge celebrations as soon as word was received that Nanking had fallen. These included nearly 800,000 girls' school students and primary school children from all sections of Tokyo. Fifty thousand of them were scheduled to march to the plaza in front of the Imperial Palace to shout banzais. Another 20,000 middle school boys, members of young men's associations, air defense corps and reservists' associations were to gather at various parks and at the Yasukuni Shrine for a lantern parade to the Palace. Ceremonies to honor the war dead at Yasukuni were also planned, including an appearance by War Minister Sugiyama.[20] "PEKING, SHANGHAI, NANKING!" crowed the editor of the *Japan Times & Mail* in a lead column on December 12, praising Japanese military success in capturing China's three major cities.

> [W]hen we see the glorious result, after four short months, our minds are divided between amazement and pride. We have always had great confidence in our splendid army and navy, but their achievements in the past four months have surpassed our fondest expectations. We never for a moment doubted their ability and determination to do their duty and bring us victory in the end. But we never expected such a victory in so short a time.

Rumors flew that Chiang Kai-shek was about to retire from office and turn over the reins of government to Wang Ching-wei, Chairman of the Central Political Council. Wang would in time become Japan's puppet, but Chiang quickly dispelled any notion of his giving up his office or resistance.

Nor would Chiang hand over Nanking without a fight. The city's ancient walls had not been built to withstand twentieth century artillery fire and aerial bombs, but they were a formidable obstacle, nonetheless. Forty-five feet high and thirty feet thick, dotted with pillboxes, shelters and gun emplacements, they enabled the defenders to put up stubborn resistance. The first breach came late in the afternoon of December 11, after the expiration of General Matsui's ultimatum. The Kwangha Gate was forced when Chinese reinforcements mutinied and refused to go to their posts. There was heavy fighting elsewhere as well. Japanese tanks led the assault on the landward sides of the city, while two observation balloons gave Japan's artillery a better range on targets within the walls. Inside Nanking tens of thousands of terrified refugees streamed into the so-called neutral zone.

Fourteen American missionaries and three German businessmen labored day and night to provide food and shelter for them.[21] By December 13, Japanese troops had penetrated the Chungshan Gate and were pouring into the city. Japanese flags were flying along the entire south wall, but the Chinese fought on in spite of heavy losses and the crumbling of their defenses. However, the day before the Japanese broke through, there was another incident some distance up the Yangtze. Compared to the slaughter in Nanking it was a minuscule moment of violence, but it abruptly diverted the attention of the Konoe government from crushing Nationalist resistance to appeasing two angry Western powers.

Early on the morning of December 12, Lieutenant Masatake Okumiya had taken off in a navy dive bomber on a routine mission from his base near Shanghai in support of Japanese troops battling Chinese defenders at the Chungshan Gate. When he returned, he was told that an advance army unit had reported that seven large merchant ships and three smaller ones filled with Chinese troops were fleeing Nanking. Estimates were that these were about twenty miles above the city and beyond the reach of ground forces. Okumiya's 13th Air Group, comprising bombers, dive bombers and fighters, was asked to intercept them. The young aviator and his flying mates were thrilled at the prospect of attacking naval targets. Until then, they had been under strict instructions to avoid bombing vessels on the Yangtze because of the danger of hitting neutral ships. Finally they could make use of their training. Okumiya even began to imagine a unit citation, which would be a feather in the caps of men who had only recently arrived at the front.

Nine fighters and six dive bombers from the 12th Air Group and three bombers and six dive bombers from the 13th were soon airborne and heading up the Yangtze in search of their prey. Halfway between Nanking and Wuhu, near Hoshien, Okumiya spotted four ships and some smaller vessels. Years later, he described his feelings:

> Having complete faith in Army intelligence, and seeing small boats plying between the ships and a dock, I was convinced that these vessels were loaded with enemy troops and pointed them out to the other pilots of my squadron, who seemed to go wild with joy. I looked about for possible enemy aircraft and seeing none, banked my plane as the signal to prepare for attack. As my squadron lined up in a single column behind me, I surveyed the ships below, observed the second one from the north to be the largest, and selected her as our target.

The dive bombers approached at an altitude of 13,000 feet, with the horizontal bombers 1,600 feet below them. The latter attacked first, each of the three planes dropping six 132-pound bombs, two of which struck one of the smaller ships at the southern end of the group. Okumiya put his plane into a 60-degree dive and watched his target grow in his bombsight as he plummeted toward earth. At 1,600 feet he released his bomb and pulled out of his dive. As he did so, he was surprised to see that not only had he missed, but none of the other dive bombers in his group had scored hits either. The fighters peeled off for a strafing run and the other bombers dropped their loads, again without effect. Only the horizontal bombers had been successful. Okiyuma scanned the scene below him:

> All of the ships were now milling confusedly. The one that had been hit was moving up river and seemed to be sinking slowly by the bow. She was followed by the large ship, unsuccessfully attacked by my squadron, which seemed to be trying to come alongside her. Other ships were being run aground but when I took a last look before returning to base, there were not more than two ships in any danger of sinking; the others were only lightly damaged, if at all.

Returning to base, Okumiya reported the results of the attack and recommended another one. The planes were rearmed and the squadron took off for a second rendezvous with its Yangtze targets. None were to be found at the site of the earlier strike, so the raiders turned back toward Nanking. Ten miles from the city, Okumiya caught sight of a fairly large ship headed downstream, with three more anchored nearby. Selecting the large vessel as his target, Okumiya again put his bomber into a dive and released his bomb. As he pulled out, he suddenly saw a British flag on one of the ships.

> I was struck with terror at the thought of the blunder I had committed. I shook the control stick right and left vigorously, waggling the plane as a signal for the following planes to hold off their attack, but it was too late. In they came, and the only thing I could do was hope that the bombs might miss.
>
> The 40 seconds following my sighting of the Union Jack were like a lifetime—dark moments indeed. The ships had opened with antiaircraft fire just before we dived to attack but had stopped by the time my planes had regrouped. With a total of nine unused bombs in our racks [not all of Okumiya's flight had dropped theirs], I decided to unload them on targets in Nanking. After hitting enemy positions just inside one of the city gates about sunset, we returned to Changchow, where it was dark by the time we landed.[22]

Okumiya's squadron had attacked more than a group of British warships. They had sunk the American gunboat *Panay* on their first mission and inflicted damage on three Standard Oil tankers, the *Meian*, *Meiping* and *Meisian*, forcing them to be beached. Three men aboard the *Panay* were killed, while twelve were seriously injured and thirty-eight suffered minor wounds. Captain Carlson of the *Meian* also lost his life. The incident provoked the worst diplomatic crisis since the war in China had begun.

The *Panay*, after taking aboard American nationals and diplomatic personnel at Nanking, had left the area because of bombing raids on Pukow nearby. British gunboats, which had been targeted by shellfire from shore, also moved to escape. On the morning of the 12th, HMS *Ladybird* was struck by artillery fire that killed one sailor and wounded several others, including her captain. The man behind the attack was Colonel Kingoro Hashimoto, who told the British that he had orders to fire on all vessels in the Yangtze River. Upon learning of the incident, Sir Robert Craigie filed a protest with the Japanese Foreign Office in Tokyo. Meanwhile, continued shelling forced the *Panay* and the three Standard Oil ships to move still further up the Yangtze. George Atcheson, the American Embassy's Second Secretary, who was aboard the *Panay*, sent messages to Japanese authorities in Tokyo and Shanghai advising them that the convoy was proceeding to Hoshien, 27 miles southeast of Nanking. The Japanese Consul General in Shanghai acknowledged receipt of the messages and the *Panay* steamed on her way. By 11:00 a.m. the gunboat and her charges arrived at their destination and dropped anchor. Because it was a clear day and there were no hostilities near Hoshien, it seemed there was no cause for further concern. Commander J.J. Hughes, the captain of the *Panay*, kept the ship's guns covered. The vessel was well marked, with American flags painted horizontally across her top deck awnings. Besides her five officers and fifty crew members, the *Panay* carried twenty passengers, including Embassy staff who had evacuated and a number of American and foreign civilians, including several newspaper correspondents and cameramen. The ever-alert Atcheson dispatched a communiqué to his colleague Gauss in Shanghai, advising him of the *Panay*'s newest location and asking him to notify the Japanese Embassy, which Gauss promptly did. On the military side, Admiral Yarnell had informed Vice Admiral Hasegawa of the *Panay*'s movements, and Hasegawa in turn had conveyed this information to the Japanese air operations officer, Lieutenant Commander Kurio Toibana. However, since the army's intelligence had been so specific, Toibana authorized the strike against what it had said were Chinese vessels. Hours later, he realized that the *Panay*'s location was "ominously similar to the position given by army intelligence."[23]

The attack came at 1:37 p.m. The *Meisian* was lying at anchor about 500 feet ahead of *Panay*; *Meiping* 300 feet from *Meisian*'s starboard quarter; and *Meian* some 700 feet directly behind *Panay*. All three tankers were flying American flags fore and aft. *Panay* was struck on her port bow, destroying her forward 3-inch gun and wrecking the pilot house, sick bay and radio room. Commander Hughes was wounded. The *Meian* came under a hail of bombs from the first wave of planes that set her afire and adrift. As the second wave of aircraft swooped down, the crew of the *Panay* manned .30 caliber machine guns, but this token resistance proved futile. By 2:00 p.m. the gunboat was *in extremis* from repeated bombing and strafing. With her boiler smashed and portable pumps inoperable, *Panay* was sinking. Hughes gave the order to abandon ship, and the lifeboat and two motor sampans were pressed into service. Meanwhile, the Japanese planes continued their attack with bombs and machine guns, wounding the survivors as they made for shore, where they hid among the reeds until the raiders had

XI. The Rape of Nanking

departed. Dead were two seamen, Charles Ensminger and Edgar Hulsebus, and an Italian correspondent, Sandro Sandi. Among the seriously wounded was J. Hall Paxton, a Second Secretary to the American Legation in Nanking. George Atcheson, however, was among those unscathed in the attack. He later described what he had seen from his hiding place ashore:

> After the *Panay* had been abandoned and was settling by the starboard bow, two Japanese Army patrol boats came down the river, machine-gunned the vessel with several bursts, boarded it for about 5 minutes and then departed. *Panay*'s flags were flying in plain view at this as at all times until the vessel sank about 3:50 p.m. The patrol boats then started upriver again and then turned back heading toward our landing point but we were hidden and they departed upriver. Japanese planes soon appeared over us, however—a flight of three bombers. The circling of one plane above the marsh reeds where we had concealed our wounded and ourselves and the previous action of the patrol boats, in connection with the incredible fact of the bombing of the *Panay*, gave us every reason to believe that they were searching for us in order to destroy the witnesses to the bombing.
>
> At dusk we moved [the] wounded to farmhouses about 2 miles away where we improvised stretchers from bamboo beds, doors and a pig pen, and then proceeded to Hoshien, 5 miles distant and 3 miles inland. This town had already been attacked 3 times by Japanese patrols. Next afternoon about 1,000 Japanese troops were reliably reported to have landed near where we went ashore and we decided to move further inland, but before night came Japanese planes circled time and again over the town flying at only 400 feet above the little thatched roof hospital where we had our wounded. Fortunately the planes did not see us; one bullet in the thatch would probably have set the roof on fire and burned to death the 13 helpless wounded we had on stretchers there. That night we proceeded along the creek by small junks to Hanshan 20 miles inland with the object of proceeding to Luchowfu, where there is an American hospital, and the unwounded to continue on toward Hankow.[24]

When he retired for the night at his air base, Lieutenant Okumiya was still unaware that he had led an attack on an American warship. His only concern was about the abortive bombing of the British vessels in the Yangtze. He was soon to learn the enormity of his error. He had hardly gone to bed when he was awakened with an urgent message from Admiral Hasegawa: "Squadron commanders of the flying units which attacked vessels on Yangtze River are ordered to report to flagship *Izumo* tomorrow morning." Okumiya misunderstood the reason for the message. He thought that he and his fellow officers were going to be commended for their attack on Chinese ships, but when he and the other three squadron commanders reached the flagship the next day, they immediately noticed the tense atmosphere on board. Toibana was waiting, and told them that they had struck the *Panay* and a ship belonging to the Standard Oil Company. He then explained that although the Shanghai consulate had received word that the *Panay* had moved upstream, he had delayed the announcement of the gunboat's move until her new location had been determined in order to avoid any confusion that might result from a multiplicity of messages. He said it had never occurred to him that the airmen might mistake neutral vessels on the river for enemy ships. He felt "naval pilots could be counted on not to commit any blunders."

Not until 5:00 p.m. on the 12th had Toibana learned the new position of the *Panay* from the Japanese consulate, and then only following a flurry of telephone calls. During that time, American diplomatic and military officials had besieged the Japanese with inquiries because they had lost contact with the *Panay*. Toibana said he felt terrible. He told the assembled pilots that "his faith in our air force had led to the worst mistake of his whole life. The real magnitude," Okumiya recalled, "was first brought home to us as Toibana concluded his narration with a profound bow." Then it was time to face Admiral Hasegawa.

> We were ushered in to present our explanation of the error to the assembled Third Fleet staff. We had not been aware of the presence of neutral ships in the vicinity of Nanking. Our violation of the restrictions on ship bombing was a product of our temporary excitement inspired by a reliance, in fact an over-reliance, upon the information conveyed to us by the army. We had approached our targets at high altitude certain that they were Chinese. The number of ships and their location made them reasonably fit the description supplied by army intelligence. We cited the similarity of appearance of gunboats of all nations, making them hard to distinguish from the air; and that the Murata group, which had apparently hit *Panay*, had done so from an altitude of 2,500 meters, which meant that they were some 4,000 meters distant from the ship at the time of bomb release. It was absolutely *anything* but a premeditated attack that was carried out on *Panay*. This tragedy was solely the result of a terrible mistake.

Admiral Hasegawa and his staff had no reason to believe otherwise of their young aviators. Okumiya, however, was not out of the woods yet. He and the other pilots who had led the attack on the *Panay* and the tankers received letters of reprimand from Admiral Yonai, the Navy Minister. This was an unusual step. Normally a division commander would be disciplined by his group commander, whose punishment in turn would be set by his superior, and so on up the chain. The fact that the letters came from the Navy Minister himself was proof of the importance the Navy attached to the matter and their desire to settle it and avoid any repetition.

(Fortunately for Okumiya, his career was far from finished. He must have been born under a lucky star. Following his service in China in 1937, he returned home to become a dive bomber test pilot. Injured in a crash, he was temporarily retired but was recalled to active duty in 1941 as an Air Staff officer. He served aboard the carrier *Ryujo* in the Aleutians campaign in April 1942 and also saw action aboard the *Junyo*, the flagship of carrier division 4, during the Battles of Santa Cruz and Guadalcanal. He survived

Allied air attacks on Rabaul, more combat action on the *Junyo*, and duty on Okinawa in July and August 1944. He ended the war on the Naval General Staff as Air Staff Officer with the rank of commander.[25])

Three days elapsed before the *Panay* survivors were found and taken to Shanghai. This enabled the powers to let tensions subside and gave the Japanese time to defuse the crisis. Admiral Hasegawa, on hearing of the attack, immediately sent two flying boats with medical officers and supplies to the scene. The next day, he made a personal call on Admiral Yarnell to apologize. In Tokyo, Foreign Minister Hirota went to the American Embassy, an unprecedented action, to inform Ambassador Grew about the sinking of the ship and express the Japanese government's "profound regrets." Grew remembered the sinking of the *Lusitania* in 1915 and feared that a diplomatic break might be imminent. But Roosevelt, like Wilson, remained calm. The loss of an American gunboat in China was not important enough to warrant drastic action, as long as Japan took full responsibility and agreed to pay reparations. When the Japanese Ambassador called on Hull the next day,[26] Hull gave him a strongly worded message from the President advising the Japanese to tender a formal apology, provide full compensation for losses suffered, and guarantee that there would be no future attacks.

The diplomatic crisis with the Americans was compounded by a simultaneous one with the British. Royal Navy gunboats were performing the same service on the Yangtze as their Yankee counterparts, seeing to the evacuation of British subjects and looking after British interests. Early on the morning of the same day that the *Panay* was attacked, HMS *Ladybird* was shelled by Japanese artillery between Wuhu and Nanking. Over a hundred 6-inch shells were fired, several of which struck *Ladybird*, killing a sick bay attendant and wounding several others in the crew, including the captain. Colonel Kingoro Hashimoto, the local Japanese commander, took responsibility for the attack, informing the British that he had orders to fire on all river shipping on the grounds that the Chinese were using the Yangtze to escape from Nanking. The *Ladybird* had been flying the Union Jack, but Hashimoto dismissed this, saying that his soldiers had difficulty distinguishing various flags and that the Chinese had frequently fired at Japanese troops using the British flag as cover. Moreover, he declared that British soldiers looked like Chinese soldiers—a ridiculous claim since the Chinese Army wore khaki. Reminded that British tars wore navy blue, Hashimoto said that the provincial soldiers wore different colored uniforms.[27] His arguments were of course specious. Hashimoto was a firebrand and a troublemaker, the kind of officer who was the bane of authorities at home and an embarrassment to commanders like Matsui who tried to conduct the war within bounds.

During Christmas week in 1937, Hallett Abend showed up at General Matsui's headquarters to address the aftermath of the *Panay* sinking. At their meeting, Matsui blamed Hashimoto for the incident. "Things have reached such a pass," he said, "that either Colonel Hashimoto must be recalled or I must relinquish my command and go home." When Abend asked if this was the same Kingoro Hashimoto of Wuhu, Matsui said yes. "That's the man. He's arrogant and insubordinate, even mutinous. And he's ignorant and dangerous. He wants Japan to fight the whole world—right now!"

As Matsui related the affair to Abend, Hashimoto was short of army bombers and asked that naval aircraft be made available to "act under orders of various regional army commanders." He said that a squadron of navy bombers had flown to Wuhu and landed near Hashimoto's Yangtze command, and that Hashimoto then ordered the navy planes to "bomb everything that moved on the Yangtze River above Nanking." When the squadron commander pointed out that there were gunboats on the river from several neutral countries, as well as neutral passenger and cargo vessels, Hashimoto "flew into a terrible rage and threatened the navy commander with execution on the spot on the charge of insubordination in a combat zone if he did not carry out the orders." Matsui said that Hashimoto had been able to get away with this unauthorized behavior due to his political connections. He alleged that Admiral Hasegawa knew the truth, but was unwilling to expose Hashimoto and allowed the navy to take the blame. More insultingly, when Matsui went to Nanking to make his formal triumphal entry into the city, Hashimoto showed up uninvited and rode in behind him on a "magnificent white saddle horse, a mount which entirely outclassed that of the commander-in-chief."[28]

Whatever General Matsui thought of Colonel Hashimoto, there is strong reason to doubt that the latter's culpability extended beyond the shelling of the *Ladybird*. Before Okumiya wrote his postwar account of the episode, he consulted the military records and talked with former officers from the Navy Ministry and the Third Fleet with firsthand knowledge of it. The renowned naval historian, Samuel E. Morison, had apparently picked up the Hashimoto story from Abend and other sources and repeated it in his book, *The Rising Sun in the Pacific*, but Okumiya declared that Morison was in error:

> Admiral Morison has written that Japanese naval air units attacked the American vessels in accordance with orders from Colonel Hashimoto. But army and navy commands were absolutely separate, as was made abundantly clear in the findings of the Tokyo war crime trials. Authority for either service to have issued orders to the other would have necessitated a direct command from the Emperor. It is true that Captain Miki [Okumiya's immediate superior] ordered the attack on the basis of an army

report, but his reliance in this was based upon the complete confidence he reposed in Commander Aoki, who had relayed the message which resulted in the final blind command for action. At the time of the *Panay* incident we naval pilots did not even know of Colonel Hashimoto's existence.[29]

While Washington and Tokyo were trying to resolve the situation, the British were not above taking advantage of it to try to get the United States to act jointly with them. In London, Sir Alexander Cadogan, the British Undersecretary of State, met with the American Chargé to suggest a united Anglo-American front. His manner conveyed the feeling that the British "were not displeased that America's interests should have been so decidedly involved by these unfortunate incidents."[30] It was easy to see Eden's hand in this initiative. When it was clear that the United States was going to make its own arrangements to settle the dispute with Japan, Eden dispatched his Ambassador to see the Secretary of State. The British Government, he said, was disappointed that Washington had not coordinated its action with that of London. It was Eden's view that the uncontrolled behavior of Japanese military officers in the combat zones warranted a large scale show of force "to arrest their attention, their movements, and their policy of firing upon the nationals and warships of other countries in a most reckless, criminal and deliberate manner."[31] Whatever Eden was trying to sell, Hull wasn't buying it. All signs indicated to him that Japan was anxious to settle the affair as quickly as possible.

Ambassador Grew reported from Tokyo that he had received expressions of regret from Japanese from "many walks of life" that convinced him that the people were profoundly distressed by the incident and were worried that it would injure the friendship between the two nations. A Tokyo Stock Exchange broker visited the Foreign Office and gave ¥500 to be forwarded to the families of the *Panay* victims. A middle school boy brought one yen to the American Embassy, and five primary school girls took three yen to the Foreign Office along with letters of sympathy addressed to President Roosevelt and Ambassador Grew.[32] These examples and the prompt response of the Japanese government with an offer of an immediate apology persuaded Grew that the country's remorse was genuine. He quoted Hirota as saying, "I cannot possibly express how badly we feel about the incident and I wish to do everything in my power to maintain good relations with your country."[33]

There was an exchange of diplomatic correspondence in which the Japanese took full responsibility for the bombings, which they attributed to pilot error, and promised full indemnification. They also pledged to take action against those who had ordered the attack and to issue strict measures to prevent a recurrence. Roosevelt sent a note insisting "American nationals, interests and property in China" must be respected. This was more than he had originally demanded, but for all practical purposes, the *Panay* incident was closed. All that remained to be done was the settling of details and the ensuring of Japan's compliance with American conditions. The Japanese went out of their way to convince the United States that the attack had been a mistake. On the night of December 23, a joint army-navy delegation led by the Vice Minister of the Navy, Admiral Isokoru Yamamoto. spent three hours in Ambassador Grew's study, with maps strewn across the floor, explaining what had happened on the Yangtze. Grew and his staff, including the military and naval attachés, were impressed by the sincerity of the Japanese in making their case. The next day the Japanese government delivered a note confirming their original pledge and formally accepting America's terms. Washington moved quickly to accept and Grew was instructed to so inform the Japanese. On Christmas Day, a euphoric Grew called on Hirota to relay the news. The Foreign Minister, he said afterward, greeted it with "tears of relief."[34]

In the meantime, private donations that eventually amounted to $5,000 poured in as ordinary Japanese citizens sought to atone for the unintentional loss of American life and property. At Grew's suggestion, Hull agreed that the money should be placed in a trust fund to finance a number of humanitarian projects in Japan, thereby serving as a symbol of friendly relations between the two nations. Official indemnification came later in the spring of 1938 for the deaths and personal injuries suffered aboard the *Panay* and *Meiping* and for the loss of the *Panay* and the three Standard Oil ships together with their equipment, supplies and personal effects. For the deaths and injuries, the amount was $268,337.35. For the vessel and property losses, the bill was $1,945,670.01. A check for these sums was presented to Eugene Dooman, the Counselor for the American Embassy in Tokyo, on April 30. The Japanese had not quibbled about any part of the costs, paying them down to the last cent. A similar settlement was made with the British.[35]

On the day that the *Panay* was sunk, Nanking's ordeal began. By Sunday night, December 12, the city was in Japanese hands. Nanking was now shut off from the rest of the world and a terrible silence settled over it. Western correspondents in Shanghai who sought information were told that transmission was slow because General Matsui had moved his headquarters. Westerners who remained in Nanking, however, were eyewitnesses to butchery unknown in modern times. Hours before the city fell, thousands of terrified Chinese crowded the Ichiang Gate on the Yangtze, their only escape hatch. These were the death throes of Taiyuan to be revisited many times over. George Fitch, the regional secretary of the YMCA, saw cars and trucks jammed, overturned and burning at the gate; piles of dead bodies; and "terror-mad" soldiers scaling the walls to get to the river,

XI. The Rape of Nanking

where an inadequate fleet of junks waited. These were soon swamped by a frantic horde, causing them to capsize and drowning thousands. The few who managed to escape fell victim to Japanese naval launches which raked the helpless junks with machine gun fire, slaughtering those who had won a brief respite from death.

Those Chinese soldiers who could not get out began to discard their uniforms and begged for admission to the neutral zone. The Germans and Americans disarmed them and assured them that the Japanese would treat them as prisoners of war. They were quartered in a separate building until they could be handed over as a group to the occupying forces, but many escaped to mingle with civilian refugees, fearful of their fate if they should fall into Japanese hands. According to General von Falkenhausen, the first combat troops entering the city were well-behaved.[36] For that reason, many of the local Chinese greeted their arrival with relief, believing that the horrors of war were behind them. Within two days, however, all discipline had broken down and the Japanese army began an orgy of murder, pillage and rape. We have the account of one example of their conduct from Xia Shujin, who was seven years old at the time, one of five daughters in a family of nine. Her father was forty years old, a laborer. Her mother was the same age. She had two older sisters, ages 15 and 13, and two younger sisters, one 4 years old and the other an infant of a few months. Her maternal grandparents, both 60 years old, also lived with them. The family lived in a compound with rooms rented on either side to various families. This was her story:

> At about nine o'clock on the morning of December 12, 1937, the Xia family had just finished breakfast and were starting their household chores. Xia Shujin had nothing in particular to do, so she went out into the central courtyard.
> Suddenly she heard someone pounding vigorously at the main gate. The old man who lived next door ran toward it, and he tried to undo the bolt. Xia's father also came running and headed toward the gate. The next instant the bolt came undone, the door swung open, and some Japanese soldiers burst in, saying something in Japanese. Not understanding what they wanted, the old man simply stood there, flustered, and the soldiers shot him down. Seeing this, Xia's father panicked, but as he turned to flee, the soldiers killed him with a shot in the neck.
> Horrified, Xia ran into the innermost family rooms and she and her sisters, except the baby, crawled into a bed and covered themselves with a quilt and the mosquito net that the family typically kept hanging from the ceiling, even during the winter.
> Soon they were aware of a large mob of soldiers rushing into the house—in her excitement, Xia had forgotten to shut the door. They heard the sound of boots tramping on the floor and a murmur of voices and then, almost at the same time, gunshots. Being under the quilt, they could not see what was happening, but their grandfather, who was near the door, was being killed.
> Just after that, the quilt was torn away from them with the tip of a soldier's bayonet. The large room was packed with Japanese soldiers. Xia's grandmother was in front of

the bed, trying to protect the four girls huddled there, but someone shot her with a pistol and whitish bits of her brain flew through the air.

Then the soldiers grabbed the two older sisters to take them away. Terrified, Xia Shujin began screaming and at that instant, she was stabbed with a bayonet and lost consciousness, so she did not see what happened after that. She did not realize it at the time, but she had been stabbed in three places: the left shoulder, the left side, and the back.

She does not know how long she was unconscious, but she became aware of her four-year-old sister, who lay uninjured but crying under the quilt, which was wadded up against the wall. When the Japanese had ripped the quilt and mosquito net off the bed, they had evidently thrown them on top of her. At this point there was no sign of the Japanese, and all was strangely quiet, but the room was filled with an eerie light. Their 13-year-old sister lay dead at the other end of the bed, naked below the waist, her legs trailing on the floor. In front of the bed was their grandmother's body. Against the opposite wall was a desk, and their 15-year-old sister lay dead on top of it, also naked from the waist down and her legs trailing on the floor. Xia could not tell whether her sisters had been stabbed or shot to death. There was no sign of their mother or the baby.[37]

Many civilians were shot or bayoneted, and anyone who ran in fear or excitement, or was caught on the streets after dusk, was likely to be killed on the spot. The soldiers who had been sheltered in the refugee zone were tied up in batches of fifty and marched away. No one doubted their fate. Looting was systematic as Japanese soldiers impressed Chinese to bear their loads of booty. Thousands of private homes were plundered. Hundreds of refugees in camps and shelters were stripped of their money and valuables. Not even the University Hospital staff was spared, in spite of the fact that the building was flying American flags. Foreigners viewed the rape of Nanking with a mixture of rage and helplessness. Writing to friends in Shanghai after watching the city's agonies for two weeks, one Westerner said:

> It is now Christmas Eve. I shall start with ... December 10. In these two short weeks we here in Nanking have been through a siege; the Chinese army has left, defeated, and the Japanese have come in. On that day, Nanking was still the beautiful city we were so proud of, with law and order still prevailing; today it is a city laid waste, ravaged, completely looted, much of it burned. Complete anarchy has reigned for ten days—it has become hell on earth. Not that my life has been in danger at any time; though turning lust-mad, sometimes drunken soldiers out of a home where they were raping the women ... is not altogether a safe occupation; nor does one feel perhaps too sure of himself when he finds ... a revolver at his head and knows it is handled by someone who heartily wishe[s] him out of the way. For the Japanese Army is anything but pleased at our being here after having advised all foreigners to get out. They wanted no observers. But to have to stand by while even the very poor are having their last possessions taken from them—their last coin, their last bit of bedding (and it is freezing weather), the poor ricksha man his ricksha; while thousands of disarmed soldiers who sought sanctuary with you together with many hundreds of innocent civilians are taken out before your eyes to be shot or used for bayonet practice and you

XI. The Rape of Nanking

have to listen to the sound of the guns that are killing them; while a thousand women kneel before you crying hysterically, begging you to save them from the beasts who are preying on them; to do nothing while your flag is being taken down and insulted, not once but a dozen times, and your own home is being looted; and then watch the city you have come to love and the institution to which you had planned to devote your best deliberately and systematically burned by fire—this is the hell I had never before envisaged.[38]

The neutral zone remained the only haven for thousands of Chinese. On December 1, knowing that the city was doomed, Mayor Ma turned over 2,000 tons of rice and 10,000 bags of flour to the International Committee for the Nanking Safety Zone. To provide security, 450 Nanking police were placed under its authority. George Fitch was one of eighteen Americans who stayed behind to serve on the Committee. When the first Japanese soldiers appeared at the entrance to the Zone on the 13th, they showed no hostility. The reign of terror began on the next day when Japanese troops poured into the city. Fitch's diary was a catalog of savagery:

Friday, December 17: Robbery, murder, rape continue unabated. A rough estimate would be at least a thousand women raped last night and during the day. One poor woman was raped thirty-seven times. Another had her five-months infant deliberately smothered by the brute to stop its crying while he raped her. Resistance means the bayonet. The hospital is rapidly filling up with the victims of Japanese cruelty and barbarity.

Sunday, December 19: A day of complete anarchy. Several big fires raging today, started by the soldiers, and more are promised. The American flag was torn down in a number of places. At the American School it was trampled on and the caretaker told that he would be killed if he put it up again. The proclamations placed on all American and other foreign properties by the Japanese are flouted by their soldiers, sometimes deliberately torn off. Some houses are entered five to ten times and the poor people looted and robbed and the women raped. Several were killed in cold blood for no apparent reason whatever.

Monday, December 20: Vandalism and violence continue absolutely unchecked. Whole sections of the city are being systematically burned. At 5:00 p.m. Smythe [Dr. Lewis S.C. Smythe, American University of Nanking] and I went for a drive. All Taiping Road, the most important shopping street in the city, was in flames. We drove through showers of sparks and over burning embers. Further south we could see the soldiers inside the shops setting fire to them and still further they were loading the loot into army trucks.

Wednesday, December 22: Firing squad at work very near us at 5:00 a.m. today. Counted over a hundred shots. The University was entered twice during the night.... The Japanese military police recently appointed to duty there were asleep. Mr. Wu, engineer in the power plant, which is located in Hsiakwan, brought us the amusing news that forty-three of the fifty-four employees who had so heroically kept the plant going to the very last day and had finally been obliged to seek refuge in the International Export Company, a British factory on the river front, had been taken out and shot on the ground that the power plant was a government concern—which it is not. Japanese officials have been at my office daily trying to get hold of those very men so that they could start the turbines and have electricity. It is a small comfort to be able to tell them that their own military had murdered most of them.

Thursday, December 23: At noon a man was led to headquarters with head burned cinder black—eyes and ears gone, nose partly, a ghastly sight. I took him to the hospital ... where he died a few hours later. His story was that he was one of a gang of some hundred who had been tied together, then gasoline thrown over them and set fire....

Friday, December 24: A Chinese at the U.S. Embassy reports that the Chinese staff and their relatives living in the Embassy were all robbed last night by an officer and his men ... three cars stolen from the compound and two more this morning. Later I had the pleasure of telling Tanaka [Sueo Tanaka, Attaché, Japanese Embassy] that Mencken's car, which I had promised him the use of yesterday, was among those stolen. Registration of Chinese started today. The military say there are still twenty thousand soldiers in the Zone and that they must get rid of these "monsters." I question whether there are a hundred left. Anyway, many more innocent must suffer and all are fearful and nervous. Constant interference from the Japanese today: more of our sanitary squad taken, also the policeman at the University gate, and they are constantly trying to get our trucks.

Christmas Day: [T]he American flag was taken from the Rural Leaders' Training School; seven soldiers spent that night and the night before in the Bible Teachers' Training School and raped the women, a girl of twelve was raped by three soldiers almost next door to us and another of thirteen before we could send relief. There were also more bayonet cases; Wilson reports that of the 240 cases in the hospital, three-quarters are due to Japanese violence since the occupation. At the University, registration commenced. The people were told that if any ex-soldiers were there and would step out, they would be used in the labor corps and their lives would be saved. About 240 stepped out. They were herded together and taken away. Two or three lived to tell the tale and, by feigning death after they were wounded, escaped and came to the hospital. One group was machine gunned, another was surrounded by soldiers and used for bayonet practice. We have had quite a number of cases where the men have faced the execution squad, escaped with only a wound or two, perhaps lying all day and into the night covered by the corpses of their comrades to escape detection, and then getting to the hospital or friends.

Thursday, December 30: When I called at the Japanese Embassy they were busy giving instructions to about sixty Chinese, most of them our camp managers, on how New Year was to be celebrated. The old five-barred flag is to replace the Nationalist flag, and they were told to make a thousand Japanese flags for that event. Camps of over a thousand must have twenty representatives present, smaller camps ten. At one o'clock New Year's Day the five-barred flag is to be raised over the Drum Tower, there will be "suitable" speeches and "music" and of course, moving pictures will be taken of the happy people waving flags and welcoming the new regime. In the meantime the burning of the city continues, three cases of girls of twelve and thirteen being raped or abducted are reported.[39]

From antiquity to the present, the record of rampaging armies is full of examples of cruelty and horror. No nation's history is unstained by wholesale or individual instances of inhuman conduct. Yet when large-scale atrocities occur, they prompt not only revulsion but bafflement, as though such actions must stem from some abnormal national traits. Westerners who lived

XI. The Rape of Nanking

in Asia tried to explain the behavior of Japanese soldiers in this way. Stoicism and self-sacrifice were bred into them. A rigid social structure bound them, expressed outwardly by elaborate courtesy and good manners. The young men were sent off to China on a crusade to redeem the entire Orient. They had been instilled with the belief that their noblest fate would be to die for the Emperor. Their foes were inferior beings, unworthy of humane treatment, so the more their enemy resisted, the stronger their hatred grew, particularly as they suffered the stresses of battle and their own losses mounted. What had begun as a mere incident became a bloody unforgiving slaughter and in this charged environment, the emotional dam of the soldiers broke. Away from home, free of cultural restraints, they went berserk.[40]

Yet when reports of Japanese atrocities filtered back to Japan, there was consternation. Lewis Bush was an Englishman who was married to a Japanese woman and taught in a Japanese school. After the rape of Nanking, Western newspapers began to publish eyewitness accounts of what had happened there. Bush said that everyone he knew was shocked, and the Japanese press tried to counter with charges of "malicious Chinese propaganda." Nevertheless, the reports disturbed his students. "What do you think?" one of them asked. "Do you believe that we are capable of such terrible behavior?" Bush said that living among them, working with them, and having seen firsthand the "fundamental kindness of the ordinary people," in particular the farmers from whom most of the army was recruited, he found the charges hard to believe. His views were shared by many British and Americans living in Japan, but one American said to him:

> But what can you expect? In the code of the Army, the end justifies the means; a soldier must think of nothing else but death in the service of the Emperor, is denied the right to be taken prisoner and must forget family ties, is forbidden to carry even photographs of his wife, and [is] molded as far as possible into a veritable human bullet.

Now, Bush's friend said, the younger generation of soldiers had no respect for world opinion and would like nothing better than to drag Great Britain into a war in the Far East. Moreover, the Japanese soldier, who regarded being taken prisoner as dishonorable, saw no reason to offer mercy to his enemy. The brutality of the soldiers was due to their indoctrination. They had been told that they were destined by divine right to rule East Asia, that they were superior to other races. They had been purged of all the finer feelings through harsh and even inhuman methods of training.[41]

If there had been any doubt about brutality as a policy instigated by the Japanese Army's senior officers, the diary of Lieutenant General Kesago Nakajima would dispel it. He was merciless:

> [I]t is our policy not to take prisoners, so we have decided to tidy up. If we capture a group of one thousand, five thousand or ten thousand, we can't even divest them of

their weapons. It's just they completely lose the will to fight and come after us in big groups, and even though they are safe, once they do make a disturbance, finishing them off is a problem, so I get reinforcements with trucks and make them responsible for guarding and guidance.

According to what I learned later, the Sasaki Unit alone dealt with fifteen thousand; the one company commander assigned to guard the Taiping Gate dealt with thirteen hundred; seven or eight thousand gathered in the vicinity of the Xianhao Gate; and they still keep coming to surrender.

In order to dispose of seven or eight thousand people, quite a large trench is needed. So as not to be seen in the act, one plan is to divide them into groups of two hundred, lead them to a suitable place, and deal with them there.

Killing was accompanied by pillaging. Nakajima wrote that he was surprised that enlisted men were acting as thieves for their commanding officers. Many of them took stolen Chinese paper money, exchanged it for yen in Shanghai, and sent it home. However, at least some of the senseless killing backfired on the Japanese. Nakajima observed that until the morning of December 13, electricity and running water had been available in Nanking, but the engineers who had kept the utilities functioning were among those who had been rounded up and executed, the soldiers taking the occasion to "test" their swords in beheading a few.[42]

The loss of human life in Nanking was appalling. In the first six weeks of the Japanese occupation, no fewer than 200,000 Chinese soldiers and civilians were murdered. The city's burial societies, which kept meticulous records, counted more than 150,000 bodies, the majority of whom were found with their hands tied behind their backs. These records did not include the additional thousands whose bodies were burned or thrown into the Yangtze. At least 20,000 women had been raped, and almost a third of Nanking was destroyed by fire.[43] The total number of Chinese deaths will never be known. China claims that 300,000 were killed; Japan says the toll was only a few thousand to perhaps as many as 100,000.[44] China has neither forgotten nor forgiven this terrible episode. A monument to the victims is in place in Nan[j]ing. It is not in the Japanese character to apologize for wartime atrocities, nor for what they did in China nor their brutality during the Second World War. But the records have laid bare the truth.

Not a word of what happened in Nanking appeared in the Japanese press. On the contrary, *Asahi* expressed horror at the destruction and blamed it on Chinese soldiers. The editor of *Japan Weekly Chronicle* wrote piously, "This demonstration of the destructive nature of the Chinese people is in keeping with the ruthlessness with which they have hitherto pursued their absolutely unwarranted anti–Japanese policy."

Japan's attention was now focused on the ceremonies celebrating the fall of Nanking. At 1:30 on the afternoon of December 17, General Matsui, riding his chestnut charger, made a triumphal entry through the

Chungshan Gate. His moment was spoiled when he turned around and saw Colonel Hashimoto riding on a finer horse behind him, but what followed was even worse. When he led the assembled troops in a triple "Banzai!" for the Emperor, he was shocked by a drunken chorus of laughter punctuating the cheers. Now he realized that the city had been invested by an undisciplined horde. He confessed to his aides the next day that he found no joy in the victory. He visited the tomb of Sun Yat-sen, with whom he had once shared a deep friendship and a vision of a united Asia. Only Matsui would be punished for the rape of Nanking. He was the least culpable, but he willingly accepted his fate.

XII

Aftermath

Ignorant of their army's true conduct, the Japanese people saluted its conquest of the Chinese capital with parades and victory processions. Over two days of celebration, three million lanterns and four million flags were waved. In Tokyo, 120,000 primary school children and 15,000 girls' high school students demonstrated, while 9,000 workers from Mitsubishi marched through the city's main streets. Japanese newspaper editors saw the fall of Nanking as a chance for peace. *Asahi* said the loss of Nanking "would afford General Chiang a chance to reconsider his attitude, but it is doubtful whether he will take this opportunity to do so, for it appears that his anti-Japanese feelings and his regard for 'face' are too strong to allow him to take this course."[1]

Asahi predicted that Chiang could not keep the support of the Chinese people and that the Nanking government was "fast heading for ruin." It called for a new administration in China, one friendly to Japan. *Tokyo Nichi Nichi* also anticipated a new beginning. The editor saw in the capture of Nanking a prelude to a new China that would encourage recognition by the other powers in China. He predicted that a new regime in North China would replace Chiang's government and thereby bring "good administration for the welfare of the Chinese people."[2]

This turned out to be wishful thinking, but there was no denying the gravity of Chiang's predicament. Colonel Stilwell summed it up at the end of December, two weeks after Nanking fell:

> The Chinese have had serious losses in planes, guns, tanks [and] trucks, and facilities for their air service and artillery are reduced to a small fraction of their needs. The tank corps was never more than a beginning. The losses in personnel have been large, but the reserve of manpower is enormous; this presents no problem except number of replacements. The force defending Nanking [is] now split and scattered; part is north of the Yangtze, part is in southern Anhui, part is in Chekiang. Cooperation between commanders at best was very poor; it is now worse than ever. What little cohesion existed during the first few months has been shattered. The disintegration of the army has been considerable, and is apparent from the ease of Japanese movements, the inability of the Chinese to establish a front or take any combined action, and the

XII. Aftermath

increasing talk of guerrilla warfare. Many units are out of hand and simply living in the country.

A semblance of control exists which may give orders that issue from the High Command, as for example the designation of commanders for the various fronts, but the mixture of units from neighboring provinces in these several localities makes effective control impossible. The unit commanders do not want replacements supplied by the central authorities; they prefer to recruit their own people. To get order out of this mixture of defeated and depleted units scattered in Kiangsu, Anhui, Chekiang and Kiangsi is probably beyond the power of the Central Government. Instead of attempting to fill up and reorganize the units that have been in action, a new command seems now to be forming new units and concentrating its efforts on the Hankow-Nanchang-Changsha area where they are trying to build up a force while awaiting the developments that events will force on them.

I believe the High Command has no other plan beyond further retreat to the west ... most likely in case of attack, and that they are pinning their faith on the size of the country, overextension by the Japanese, possible intervention by Russia, possible internal trouble in Japan, and an effective development of the Red campaign against ... Japanese communications. ... [A]ny offensive by the Chinese is out of the question, and it is very doubtful if a force capable of offering any further serious resistance can be created.[3]

As hopeless as Chiang's position seemed, he was nevertheless determined to resist. On Christmas Eve he sent a message to President Roosevelt reviewing the events of the previous five months. As usual, he described the conflict in universal terms. China was fighting not only for its own liberty but "against the common menace of all mankind." He expressed his appreciation for the moral support that had been rendered by the United States and praised Roosevelt's leadership, but he renewed his plea for help so that China could continue its struggle.[4]

The day that Chiang Kai-shek sent this communication to the President, the Konoe Cabinet moved to establish a new political mandate in China, one that excluded Chiang altogether. In a resolution entitled "Outline of Measures for the China Incident," the government announced its decision to organize a new regime in North China that would ultimately represent the central and southern regions of the country as well. The area occupied by the Shanghai forces would also be overseen by a new administration tied to the one in North China. Put bluntly, China would be governed by a puppet directorate in Peking with satellite operations elsewhere. This resolution was inconsistent with the continuing peace negotiations, but the Cabinet got around this by stating that if a settlement was reached with the Nationalist government, the new regime would be accommodated within its terms. What followed was a farce. Hirota did little to advance this proposal, and with the green light from Tokyo, the field commanders began to organize satrapies. Hirota, like the boy who murdered his parents and then asked the court for lenience on the grounds that he was an orphan, blamed the field armies for the new China policy.

General Tada was furious and demanded that an Imperial Conference be held. Since the Liaison Conference of December 20 had declared the government's intention to seek a negotiated peace with Chiang, reconfirming it in the Emperor's presence would make the field commanders fall in line. This would undercut Hirota's plans and oblige the Konoe administration to bargain seriously with the Nationalists. At a third Liaison Conference on January 10, 1938, Konoe tried to dodge Tada's move and restrict the discussion to the issues of ending recognition of the Nationalists and legitimizing the regimes being established by the field armies. But Tada stood his ground, reminding the Conference that the Supreme Command was unanimous in its support for negotiations and could abolish the field commanders' puppet authorities if a vow to work with the Nationalists was made in the Imperial Presence. The Chief of the Naval General Staff, Admiral (Prince) Fushimi, supported Tada and declared that the Emperor ought to be able to ask questions at the Imperial Conference since members of the Supreme Command were not allowed to express their views "on the grave political issues involved in the China Incident." The unanimity of the military forced Konoe's hand; an Imperial Conference would be called.

General Tada's strategy was born of desperation. Involving the Emperor in a major policy dispute was not only rare but was regarded in court circles with grave misgivings. Not even Prince Saionji, who favored peace with Chiang, wanted the Emperor drawn into a political quarrel. But in hindsight, this meeting would rank with two future ones that determined Japan's fate: the decision to go to war with the United States in 1941 and the decision to end the war in 1945. Only in the latter did Hirohito exercise his personal powers and intervene directly. Had he been served by wiser and less timid advisers in 1938, or had he seen the pitfalls ahead for his country, he might have held his ministers more accountable. This was not to be. The advisers agreed to the Imperial Conference but said that the Emperor's role would be restricted to clarifying the issues, and his comments should not be considered instructions for either the Cabinet or the Supreme Command.

Konoe was determined to limit Hirohito's input even further. When he presented his petition, he asked that he be allowed to "manage the procedure of the conference because [its] purpose ... was one of deciding our national policy." Furthermore, he said that since he was presenting a policy that had already been approved by the government, the Emperor should not ask *any* questions. Konoe's action was reprehensible. It reveals him to be a conniver, his character still that of the young man who had embarrassed the *Genro* in Paris nearly twenty years earlier. In his efforts to thwart General Tada and Admiral Fushimi, Konoe totally circumvented the will of the Liaison Conference. Nor was this the end of his machinations. He asked

XII. Aftermath 315

that Baron Hiranuma attend the Imperial Conference on the grounds of Hiranuma's friendship with Admiral Suetsugu and their shared view that negotiations with Chiang should be terminated. As president of the Privy Council, Hiranuma's presence would give credence to Konoe's position. The General Staff would see that the political leadership of the nation was united behind the Cabinet.[5] Having stacked the deck, Konoe was ready to play.

Early on the afternoon of January 11, the parties assembled in the East Room of the Imperial Palace. Everyone was conscious of the meeting's significance. There had not been an Imperial Conference since 1914 when Japan declared war on Germany. The setting was oppressively formal, the room adorned with gold screens and a famous wall painting entitled "The Thousand Sparrows." The chiefs and vice chiefs of both general staffs, the Inner Cabinet, Admiral Suetsugu and Baron Hiranuma filed in and sat stiffly at tables covered with rich brocades. The military officers wore their uniforms, the civilians, frock coats. At length the Emperor entered and took his seat on a raised platform. He was dressed in a khaki uniform.[6] Konoe opened the conference with the announcement that the Cabinet had that morning adopted a "Fundamental Policy for the Disposition of the China Incident," which he then asked the Foreign Minister to read. The "Fundamental Policy" was nothing more than a rehash of previous Cabinet statements on Japan's relationship with China and a series of peace proposals that embraced a few of the prior terms and added some new ones. He declared that Sino-Japanese relations must be reorganized, which meant an arrangement between China, Japan and Manchukuo based on three goals: "(1) to promote the joint economic welfare of the three countries; (2) to unite in an anti-Communist military alliance; [and] (3) to eradicate all issues which might 'soil their mutual relationship.'" To achieve these ends, the Nationalist government would have to accept the following conditions:

    1. A formal recognition of Manchukuo;
    2. A formal renunciation of its anti-Japanese and anti-Manchukuo policies;
    3. The creation of neutral zones in North China and Inner Mongolia;
    4. The establishment of new political organs in North China that would confirm the sovereignty of the Nationalist government and would "be suitable to the realization of the co-prosperity of Japan, Manchukuo and China";
    5. The formation of an "anti-Communist and autonomous government in Inner Mongolia" that would possess the same status under international law as Outer Mongolia;

6. A promise to cooperate with Japan in an anti–Soviet policy in East Asia;

7. An agreement by which Japan and China would, in the zones occupied by the Japanese army in Central China, "cooperate in order to maintain public order and to develop the economies of those zones";

8. A pledge that Japan, Manchukuo and China would conclude "necessary" agreements in the matter of customs, trade, aviation and transportation; and

9. The payment of reparations to the Japanese Empire.

Tada must have winced as he listened to Hirota enumerate these demands. They were closer to a call for unconditional surrender than a basis for negotiations. Hirota foreclosed that possibility further when he announced that unless the Nationalists requested a settlement within seventy-two hours, Japan would "annihilate the Chinese central government" and "rejuvenate a new China" by establishing new governing authorities. When the Foreign Minister finished, the Imperial Conference was silent. Then Prince Kanin, the Chief of the Army General Staff, gave his benediction to the proceedings. He said that he doubted whether the Nationalist government was finished but declared that the Supreme Command would accept the "Fundamental Policy" adopted by the Cabinet.[7] On this note the meeting ended. Less than an hour after the Emperor had taken his seat, he left the East Room of the palace. Konoe must have congratulated himself; Hirohito had never uttered a word.

For Tada, it was a bitter defeat. The tables had been turned on him in his own forum, although he had at least put the Premier and his Cabinet on record. *They* would be responsible for what followed in China, not the field armies. Whether or not Tada's plan would have worked, given the undisciplined zeal of the field forces, is beside the point. Konoe, who had complained that he possessed no freedom of action and was forced to bow to the military, showed himself to be remarkably astute in outmaneuvering his military adversaries when he put his mind to it, stooping to lies and deceit to achieve his goals. The plea he made to history shortly before he took his own life rings hollow. Never again would Japan have such an opportunity for peace with China. Instead of making allies of General Tada and other like-minded members of the General Staff, Konoe spurned them and took the path of the radicals whom he professed to oppose.

Hirota was also culpable. After the Imperial Conference he merely went through the motions of seeking a settlement. Following the meeting, he sent a note to the German Ambassador saying that Chiang had seventy-two hours to accept the four terms that had been put forward on December 23, or Japan would take a harsher approach. Continuing to use the German conduit, the Chinese Foreign Minister replied that the peace terms were too vague and should be clarified. Ambassador Dirksen sought further details from Hirota but was told that the Foreign Minister should consult with the Premier. Hirota had no intention of going on with mediation, for the simple reason that he was committed to a military resolution to the China Incident. When the Liaison Conference met on January 14, Hirota reported that the Nationalists had shown no interest in accepting the conditions adopted at the Imperial Conference, so there was no alternative but to pursue "a long-term war." A heated discussion followed, with the army split on whether or not to continue negotiations. Sugiyama agreed with Hirota that these should be cut off, but the indefatigable Tada reminded them that a prolonged war with China would weaken Japan in the face of its principal foe, the Soviet Union. He said he would be willing to fly to China and confer directly with Chiang to seek an end to the conflict. At that, Admiral Yonai reminded him that they had agreed in the presence of the Emperor to break off relations with the Nationalist regime. If Tada persisted in his demands, "either the Army General Staff or the Cabinet must resign *en masse*." With the military divided, Konoe called for a two-hour break to give the General Staff time to reconsider its position.[8]

During the recess Prince Kanin went to the palace and asked to see the Emperor, but the cautious Hirohito would not grant him an audience, fearful, as he told Baron Harada, that it "might definitely be a scheme to overturn what had already been determined." This sealed the matter once and for all. When the Liaison Conference resumed its session, Tada capitulated, agreeing that it would be unwise to change the government. He would support the Cabinet's policy. The Liaison Conference then rubber-stamped the proposal and the meeting ended. Later that afternoon Hirota met with Ambassador Dirksen to inform him that Japan no longer required the services of the German Foreign Ministry, since the government was severing its ties with the Nationalist regime. The Ambassador was surprised and visibly disappointed. Before leaving he cautioned Hirota that a long war with China could reap "three unhappy consequences." The war, he said, would "alienate the Anglo-American countries, lead to the Bolshevization of China, and weaken Japan vis-a-vis the Soviet Union." The warning was remarkably prescient. It was the same alarm that General Tada had sounded from the beginning of the conflict, but Hirota dismissed Dirksen's concerns just as he had those of his own countryman.[9]

On January 16 a public statement was issued confirming the rumors that were already circulating. It was as much propaganda as it was a policy announcement. The Japanese government had offered China a final opportunity for peace. "However, the Chinese government, without appreciating the true intentions of Japan, blindly persist[s] in [its] opposition against Japan with no consideration either internally for the people in their miserable plight or externally for the peace and tranquility of all East Asia." The decision to end relations with the Nationalist government was now official, and Japan would deal instead with a new Chinese administration with which it would seek "harmonious cooperation" to build "a rejuvenated China."[10] Shortly afterward, Konoe spoke even more sharply, announcing that Japan would set a new precedent in international law "by both refusing to recognize the Nationalist government and simultaneously trying to destroy it." This statement was egregious in the extreme. Japan had already displayed contempt for international law in her violation of the Nine Power Treaty and the Pact of Paris. To suggest that an addendum of this kind was akin to any provision of international law was a sham. No matter what the Japanese government might call the "provisional government" set up by army authorities in Peking, it was a puppet regime.

The nation sensed that a turning point had been reached. When the euphoria that had swept the Japanese with the capture of Nanking abated, they realized that nothing had really changed. The conflict was still referred to as an "incident," but Japan was at war in every sense of the word. When the Diet had convened in December 1937, the Konoe Cabinet confounded the legislators by presenting them with bills that would put electric utilities under state control and mobilize the nation. The implications of this were immediately apparent to the business community and political parties. If Japan went to war, the Imperial Diet would lose what little was left of its already diminished powers, and industry would be dragooned into a wartime economy. The Seiyukai and Minseito members were vehement in their opposition, but the military had the support of right-wing parties and began a campaign of intimidation to bring the Seiyukai and Minseito into line. There was a rumor of another Young Officer coup, and a group of radicals seized the Seiyukai and Minseito party headquarters. Another rumor said that the Diet would be dissolved. By March, the two major parties had been cowed into submission. The national mobilization bill passed without amendment and the electric power state control bill was ratified with only minor revisions.

Fumimaro Konoe now began to realize that he had opened a Pandora's box of troubles. Gone was the craftiness he had coolly displayed in January when he outmaneuvered General Tada and forced the policy decision that had led the government to its present pass. He began to have misgivings. He had not just allowed the opportunity for peace to slip through his fingers; he had washed his hands of it. Thoughtful Japanese recognized that the bombastic declaration of January 16 had not been an assurance of victory but the harbinger of an endless conflict. In truth, Konoe had no idea how to extricate himself from the situation. When his friend Kiya told him about the criticisms that were being levied against him, Konoe fell back on his customary excuse that he had "very little control over things."[11] Yet years later, when the Pacific War was drawing to a close, he admitted that he had made a terrible mistake. "The announcement of January 16, 1938, brought no favorable results, a fact of which I am well aware without having anyone point it out to me. I myself confess it was an utter blunder."[12]

When the Diet exploded over his proposed bills, Konoe crawled back into his shell and told Baron Harada that all he wanted to do was quit. After the Diet adjourned, he went to the palace and told the Emperor how helpless he felt, "like a mannequin—dragged along without being informed of anything."[13] His whining exasperated his mentor, Prince Saionji, who told Baron Harada that Konoe would just have to stick it out; if necessary, the Emperor should oblige him to do so. Nearly a year would pass before Konoe was able to shed the position that now tormented him. During that time the war continued to spread through China as Japan's army swept up the remaining cities, including Tsingtao, Canton and Hankow. He made some changes to the Cabinet, but none of these led to harmony or relief from the stress of office. A Chinese collaborator had even surfaced, a vice president of the Kuomintang, Wang Ching-wei, who had always felt that China should preserve close relations with Japan, but peace was not forthcoming. Konoe issued another declaration on December 22, 1938. This one bore his name. In lofty language, it spoke of carrying on the war against anti–Japanese Kuomintang forces and called for "far-sighted Chinese who shared Japan's ideals and aspirations" to join in establishing a New Order in East Asia.[14] It echoed the January manifesto. Beneath the grandiose words, however, could be seen the grasping hand of the military. Far from being willing to yield anything, the army wanted to preserve its gains. Eventually, on January 5, 1939, the Konoe Cabinet resigned and the Prime Minister's ordeal seemed to be over. Not surprisingly, the army was not happy about his departure. They had used him well, and he was not always an unwilling tool. But his career was not yet at an end. In July 1940 he would be called again to take what by then was a rudderless helm, and for a year he would struggle against even stronger forces. His final meaningful efforts to ward off the Pacific War never had a chance, and he had to turn over control to General Hideko Tojo, whose appointment foreordained the coming conflict. By then the old *Genro*, Prince Saionji, had died, spared the worst trial of the nation and the humiliation that followed.

For the field armies, whose successes continued to feed on themselves, the conquest of the remaining urban centers brought them no closer to victory than had the capture of Nanking. It was maddeningly frustrating to pile triumph on triumph and yet be denied the ultimate prize. Since the birth of the Empire there had never been a war like this one. The army continued to form provincial governments and send home pictures of happy Chinese villagers welcoming Japanese soldiers come to liberate them from their local rulers, but as a *New York Times* reporter noted, "the 'peace preservation commissions' seem to get nowhere, and not much peace seems to be preserved. The Japanese troops seem to have to go on fighting." It soon became apparent that creating and propping up puppet governments was costly, especially in North China, where Communist harassment proved to be a perpetual thorn in the side of Japan's military. Tokyo hailed the new provisional regime in Peking but failed to say that its dominion extended no further than 100 miles beyond the city.

From his vantage point as Ambassador in China, Nelson Johnson cabled his assessment to the Secretary of State in early February. The report was both perceptive and prescient. Johnson reviewed the events of the previous seven months and noted Japan's ephemeral triumph. Within its grasp were the entire Yangtze and Yellow River valleys, where most of the Chinese people lived and from which they drew most of their food supply. Yet even with this prize in their hands the Japanese military were a long way from conquering or occupying the whole of China. Johnson then wrote of what would ensue.

> The intellectual life which has dominated the areas thus occupied and which has given character to modern Nationalist China will then have to be drive into the western, more mountainous and less fertile areas. There is no apparent evidence that this intellectual leadership and what is left of its armed forces are prepared to capitulate and make peace. It is true that what is left of China's armed forces will be without equipment necessary to enable it to wage effective offensive war on the plains, but it will have access to sufficient quantities of small arms and ammunition to enable it to equip mobile units which will roam the country attacking trains, destroying crops and supplies, attacking Japanese and those working with them. The Japanese military will therefore have to garrison its holdings and police every mile of the lines of communications along which supplies for its forces must be carried. The future prospect for the plains occupied by the Japanese for the next 3 or 4 years promises little in the way of peaceful development. I believe that conditions throughout those areas will be chaotic in the extreme, with robberies, assassinations and kidnappings.
>
> The prospect for the immediate future is hopeless unless Japan is prepared to send far greater forces into China to enable her to garrison and police the occupied areas. Trade is and will continue to be completely disrupted. Chinese industry no longer exists. Travel in the interior is already well-nigh impossible.
>
> The situation as between China and Japan at the present time is therefore at a stalemate, with Japan's armies carrying destruction into the very areas from whose population she apparently expected to receive cooperation and where she expected to market her goods.
>
> A declaration of war will not in my opinion materially affect this situation. It will have its effect upon trade through Hong Kong and possibly Hanoi, but it will

not lessen the necessity for Japan to continue the present heavy expense and future military operations. It will not close China's back doors through India, Burma and Turkestan. Japanese hostilities have entered the stage of long-time operations to pacify immense areas where the populations have been impoverished and terrorized. Japan must soon come to a realization that up to the present time all that her efforts have netted her has been hostility abroad and expense in China.[15]

Even had Johnson sent his message to Tokyo instead of Washington, it would probably have fallen on deaf ears. The Ishiwaras and Tadas in the military had been silenced. Unchallenged, the new policy had imprisoned its creators. Japan was in for a protracted struggle. The national mobilization that had been ordered made that evident, but the battlefield exploits that had so thrilled the Japanese in the first six months of the war began to lose their luster. Although tightened censorship meant only positive news, or none at all, there was no concealing the mounting casualties. More and more farmers' sons were drafted. These were green troops. In China they found themselves required to make continuous, futile sweeps in an effort to destroy enemy formations. In 1939 the North China Army alone fought 17,500 separate engagements: in 1940, over 20,000. By the time the war ended in 1945, there had been 23 campaigns, 1,117 major battles and 38,931 engagements in China.[16] One can only speculate how long this war of attrition might have lasted had not the European war begun in 1939. The Japanese thought they saw the opening of a door of opportunity if the Western colonial powers were defeated, and a chance to break the stalemate in China by aggressively expanding their empire.

Meanwhile, the attitude of the United States was hardening. Not only was America openly helping Chiang Kai-shek, it was beginning to take hostile measures against Japan, including the cutting off of oil exports.

Thus, what had begun as a minor skirmish near a bridge in North China led to the final defeat and ruin of the empire. Although possible detours presented themselves along the way, they were ignored. In some respects, the destination was inevitable. The modernization of the military had not eliminated the samurai tradition and its *bushido* code; it had only made them more dangerous. The frail constitutional institutions borrowed from the West had no national roots, and once challenged proved utterly incapable of either asserting civilian control over the government or deflecting the army extremists from their course. Japan was already on the way to becoming a garrison state before July 1937. Once the China Incident began, totalitarianism was on its way. The impending catastrophe could have been foreseen, had the leadership at home not been blind and had the brutal forces in the field not been shortsighted. Japan said that it wished to have a friendly and fruitful relationship with China, but it could not have done more to deny these goals by its treatment of its neighbor. Japanese expansionists fed their nation's arrogance by proclaiming their racial superiority and laying claim to their paramount position in the Orient. This unrestrained chauvinism did indeed lead to a new order in Asia, but from the ashes of Japan's defeat, it created an Asia beyond the imagination of those who had wrought their own destruction.

Chapter Notes

Introduction

1. Mayo, Marlene J., ed., *The Emergence of Imperial Japan*, Lexington, MA: D.C. Heath & Co., 1970, ix.
2. Morley, James William, ed., *The China Quagmire: Japan's Expansion on the Asian Mainland, 1933–1941*; Hata, Ikuhito, "The Marco Polo Bridge Incident, 1937," trans. David Lu, New York: Columbia University Press, 1983, 243–286.
3. Coox, Alvin D. and Hillary Conroy, eds., *China and Japan: A Search for Balance Since World War I*, John Hunter Boyle, "Peace Advocacy During the Sino-Japanese Incident," Santa Barbara: ABC-Clio, Inc., 245.
4. Montgomery, Michael, *Imperialist Japan: The Yen to Dominate*, New York: St. Martin's Press, 1987, 387.

Chapter I

1. Lu, David J., *From the Marco Polo Bridge to Pearl Harbor*, Washington, D.C.: Public Affairs Press, 1961, 12.
2. Hoyt, Edwin P., *Japan's War: The Great Pacific Conflict*, New York: McGraw-Hill, 1986, 3.
3. Ward, Robert E., and Danwart E. Rustow, eds., *Political Modernization in Japan And Turkey*, Roger E. Hackett, "The Military," Princeton, NJ: Princeton University Press, 1964, 329–330.
4. Hoyt, *op. cit.*, 3.
5. Hackett, Roger E., *Yamamoto Arigomo in the Rise of Modern Japan, 1832–1922*, Cambridge: Harvard University Press, 1971, 330.
6. Hoyt, *op. cit.*, 5–10.
7. Hackett, *op. cit.*, 332.
8. Hoyt, *op. cit.*, 12.
9. Hackett, *op. cit.*, 332.
10. Lory, Hillis, *Japan's Military Masters: The Army in Japanese Life*, New York: Viking Press, 1943, 153–154.
11. James, David H., *The Rise and Fall of the Japanese Empire*, London: Allen & Unwin, Ltd., 1951, 113.
12. Gowen, Herbert H., *An Outline History of Japan*, New York: D. Appleton & Co., 1927, 308–309.
13. James, *op. cit.*, 113.
14. Gowen, *op. cit.*, 309–310.
15. Huish, Marcus B. Ed., *Fifty Years of New Japan*, Vol. 1, Okuma, Shigenobu, London: Smith, Elder & Co., 1970, 84.
16. *Ibid.*
17. *Ibid.*, 312, quoted from McLaren, W. W. "Japanese Government Documents," "Translations of the Asiatic Society of Japan," May 1984.
18. Mayo, Marlene J., ed., *The Emergence of Imperial Japan*, Yoshitake Oka, "The Meiji Restoration and National Independence," Lexington MA: DC Heath and Com., 1970, 2.
19. Gowen, *op. cit.*, 319.
20. James, *op. cit.*, 119.
21. Gowen, *op. cit.*, 320.
22. James, *op. cit.*, 119.
23. Kublin, Hyman, "The Modern Army of Early Meiji Japan," *The Far Eastern Quarterly*, IX (1949), 20–21.
24. Presseisen, Ernst L., *Before Aggression: Europeans Prepare the Japanese Army*, Tucson: University of Arizona Press, 1955, 25–26.
25. Kublin, *op. cit.*, 28–29.
26. Drea, Edward J., *Japan's Imperial Army: Its Rise and Fall*, Lawrence: University of Kansas Press, 2009, 29.
27. Drea, Edward J., *In the Service of the*

Emperor: Essays on the Imperial Japanese Army, Lawrence: University of Kansas Press, 2009, 79.
28. Drea, *Japan's Imperial Army*, 30.
29. Drea, *In the Service of the Emperor*, 77–78, 81.
30. *Ibid.*
31. *Ibid.*, 89.
32. Hackett, *op. cit.*, 336–339.
33. Hoyt, *op. cit.*, 336–339.
34. Drea, *Japan's Imperial Army*, 45.
35. Presseisen, *op. cit.*, 57.
36. Presseisen, *Ibid.*, 79–142. The author is indebted to Dr. Presseisen for his generosity in permitting him to draw liberally from his work in developing Chapter 1 of this book.
37. Lone, Stewart, *Provincial Life and the Military in Imperial Japan*, New York: Routledge, 2010, 27.
38. Presseisen, *op. cit.*, 143–144.
39. Lane, *op. cit.*, 31. *op. cit.* p. 349.
40. Hackett.
41. Lane, *op. cit.*, 44.
42. Tanin, O., and E. Yohan, *Militarism and Fascism in Japan*, with introduction by Karl Radek, Westport CT: Greenwood Press, 1973, 61.
43. Presseisen, *op. cit.*, 144.
44. Harcave, Sidney, *Russia: A History*, Chicago: J. B. Lippincott, 1956, 347–348.
45. Presseisen, *op. cit.*, 145–149.
46. Harcave, *op. cit.*, 348.
47. Lone, *op. cit.*, 44.
48. Presseisen, *op. cit.*, 145–149.
49. Asada, Sadao, *From Mahan to Pearl Harbor: The Imperial Japanese Navy and the United States*, Annapolis: Naval Institute Press, 2006, 10.

Chapter II

1. Silberman, Bernard S., and H.D. Hartoonian, eds., *Japan in Crisis: Essays on Taisho Democracy*, H.D. Hartoonian, "Introduction: A Sense of an Ending and the Problem of Taisho," Princeton, NJ: Princeton University Press, 1974, 7–8.
2. *Ibid.*, 9–10.
3. Mosley, Leonard, *Hirohito: Emperor of Japan*, Englewood Cliffs, NJ: Prentice-Hall, Inc., 1966, 35.
4. Storry, Richard, *A History of Modern Japan*, London: Cassell & Co., Ltd., 1960, 149–150.
5. Gowen, *op. cit.*, 367–368.
6. Storry, Richard, *Japan and the Decline of the West in Asia, 1894–1943*, London: The MacMillan Press, Ltd., 1979, 104.
7. Gowen, *op. cit.*, 368.
8. Storry, *Japan and the Decline of the West in Asia*, 105–106.
9. Mayo, *op. cit.*, 4–5.
10. Borg, Dorothy, and Shumpei Okamoto, eds., *Pearl Harbor as History: Japanese-American Relations, 1931–1941*, Seiichi Imai, "Cabinet, Emperor and Senior Statesmen," New York: Columbia University Press, 1973, 54.
11. Storry, *Japan and the Decline of the West in Asia*, 107.
12. Tuchman, Barbara W. *Stilwell and the American Experience in China, 1911–1945*, New York: The MacMillan Company, 1970, 48.
13. Shigemitsu, Mamoru, *Japan and Her Destiny*, London: Hutchinson of London, Ltd. 1958, 41.
14. *Ibid.*, pp. 48–49.
15. Cameron, M. E., T.H.D. Mahoney, and G.E. McReynolds, *China, Japan, and the Powers: A History of the Modern Far East*, New York: The Ronald Press Company, 1960, 526.
16. Silberman and Harootunian, *op. cit.*, 218.
17. Gowen, *op. cit.*, 372.
18. Bailey, *op. cit.*, 637.
19. Murakami, Hyoe, *Japan the Years of Trial, 1919–1952*, Tokyo: Kodansha International Ltd., 1982, 20.
20. Storry, *Japan and the Decline of the West in Asia*, 111.
21. Bailey, Thomas A., *A Diplomatic History of the American People*, New York: Appleton-Century-Crofts, Inc., 1958, 636.
22. Storry, *Japan and the Decline of the West in Asia*, 112.
23. Bailey, *op. cit.*, 611.
24. Storry, *Japan and the Decline of the West in Asia*, 113–114.
25. Bailey, *op. cit.*, 611.
26. Storry, *A History of Modern Japan*, 158.
27. Storry, *Japan and the Decline of the West in Asia*, 116.
28. Bailey, *op. cit.*, 637.
29. Storry, *Japan and the Decline of the West in Asia*, 119–120.
30. Gowen, *op. cit.*, 383.
31. Storry, *A History of Modern Japan*, 160–161.

32. Storry, *Japan and the Decline of the West in Asia*, 120.
33. Mosley, *op. cit.*, 56–57.
34. Storry, *Japan and the Decline of the West in Asia*, 121.
35. Bailey, *op. cit.*, 644.
36. Storry, *Japan and the Decline of the West in Asia*, 121.
37. Quigley, Harold S., and John E. Turner, *The New Japan: Government and Politics*, Minneapolis: University of Minnesota Press, 1956, 20.
38. *Ibid.*, p. 21.
39. Ward and Rustow, *op. cit.*, Ike, Nobutaka, "Political Leadership and Political Parties," p. 403.
40. Lu, *op. cit.*, 8–9.
41. Storry, *A History of Modern Japan*, 170.
42. Lu, *op. cit.*, 8–9.
43. Quigley and Turner, *op. cit.*, 18.
44. Lu, *op. cit.*, 10.
45. Storry, *A History of Modern Japan*, 171.
46. Craigie, Sir Robert, *Behind the Japanese Mask*, London: Hutchinson & Co., 1945, 20.
47. Maki, John M., *Japanese Militarism: Its Cause and Cure*, New York: Alfred A. Knopf, 1945, 162.
48. Lory, *op. cit.*, 157.
49. Byas, Hugh, *Government by Assassination*, New York: Alfred A. Knopf, 1942, 133.
50. Lory, *op. cit.*, 158.
51. Jansen, Marius B., *Japan and China: From War to Peace, 1894–1972*, Chicago: Rand McNally, 1975, 323.
52. Hane, Mikiso, *Japan: A Historical Survey*, New York: Charles Scribner's Sons, 1972, 442.
53. Lory, *op. cit.*, 167.
54. Montgomery, *op. cit.*, 277.
55. Lory, *op. cit.*, 169.
56. Storry, *Japan and the Decline of the West in Asia*, 131.
57. Tuchman, *op. cit.*, 116.
58. Storry, *Japan and the Decline of the West in Asia*, 132.
59. International Military Tribunal, Far East, Exhibit, 1946–1953, Testimony of Ryukichi Tanaka.
60. Borton, Hugh, *Japan's Modern Century*, New York: The Ronald Press Company, 1970, 357.
61. Li, Lincoln, *The Japanese Army in North China, 1931–1941: Problems in Political and Economic Control*, Tokyo: Oxford University Press, 1975, 23–24.
62. Hane, *op. cit.*, 445.
63. Storry, *A History of Modern Japan*, 177–178.
64. Hane, *op. cit.*, 446.
65. Borg and Okamoto, *op. cit.*; Asada, Sadao, "The Japanese Navy and the United States," p. 227.
66. Storry, *Japan and the Decline of the West in Asia*, 135.
67. Gow, Ian, *Military Intervention in Pre-War Japanese Politics*, New York: Routledge Curzon, 2004, 156.
68. Hane, *op. cit.*, 450.
69. Asada, *op. cit.*, 228.

Chapter III

1. Borg and Okamoto, *op. cit.*, Shigeo Misawa, and Saburo Ninomiya, "The Role of the Diet and Political Parties," 375.
2. Storry, Richard, *The Double Patriots: A Study of Japanese Nationalism*, Boston: Houghton Mifflin Company, 1957, 54.
3. Borg and Okamoto, *op. cit.*, Ito, Takashi, "The Role of Right-wing Organizations in Japan," 492–493.
4. Hane, *op. cit.*, 456.
5. IMTFE Exhibits 49536-8.
6. Jones, F., *Japan's New Order in East Asia: Its Rise and Fall*, London: Oxford University Press, 1954, 14–15.
7. Harries, Meiron, and Susie Harries, *Soldiers of the Sun: The Rise and Fall of the Imperial Japanese Army*, New York: Random House, 1991, 17.
8. Jones, *op. cit.*, 6.
9. Yanaga, Chitose, *Japan Since Perry*, New York: McGraw-Hill, 492.
10. Harries and Harries, *op. cit.*, 180.
11. Yanaga, *op. cit.*
12. Hane, *op. cit.*, 458.
13. Storry, *op. cit.*, 60–61.
14. Yanaga, *op. cit.*
15. Montgomery, Michael, *Imperialist Japan: The Yen to Dominate*, New York: St. Martin's Press, 1987, 307.
16. Tohmatsu, Haruo, and H. P. Willmott, *A Gathering Darkness: The Coming of the War to the Far East and the Pacific*, Lanham, MD: SR Books, 2002, 26.
17. Shunsake, Tsurumi, *An Intellectual History of Wartime Japan, 1931–1945*, London: KPI, 1986, 77.

18. Hane, op. cit., 464.
19. Tohmatsu and Willmott, op. cit.
20. Hane, op. cit., 465.
21. Shigemitsu, Mamoru, *Japan and Her Destiny*, London: Hutchinson & Co., Ltd., 74–79.
22. Hane, op. cit., 46.
23. Shigemitsu, op. cit., 74–79.
24. Hane, op. cit., 467.
25. Shigemitsu, op. cit., 74–79.
26. Craigie, Sir Robert, *Behind the Japanese Mask*, London: Hutchinson & Co., Ltd., 1946, 29–30.
27. Shigemitsu, op. cit., 74–79.
28. Craigie, op. cit., 29–30.
29. Shigemitsu, op. cit., 74–79.
30. Montgomery, op. cit., 344.
31. Allen, Louis, *Japan: The Years of Triumph*, New York: American Heritage Press, 197, 92.
32. Close, Upton, *Behind the Face of Japan*, New York: D. Appleton Century Press, 1942, 323.
33. Ito, Masanori, and Roger Pineau, *The End of the Imperial Japanese Navy*, New York: W. W. Norton, 1962, 327.
34. Ibid., 333.
35. Piggot, F.S.G., *Broken Thread*, Aldeshot: Gale & Polden, 1950, 265.
36. Ito, op. cit., 333.
37. Craigie, op. cit., 31.
38. Ito, op. cit.
39. Craigie, op. cit.
40. Ito, op. cit.
41. Hane, op. cit., 468.
42. Hane, Mikiso, trans., *Emperor Hirohito and his Chief Aide-De-Camp: The Honjo Diary, 1933–1936*, Tokyo: University of Tokyo Press, 1982, 75.
43. Morley, James W. ed., *Dilemmas of Growth in Prewar Japan*, Akira Iaiye, "The Failure of Military Expansion," Princeton, NJ: Princeton University Press, 1982, 75.
44. Hane, *Japan: A Historical Survey*, 469.
45. Morley, op. cit.
46. Hane, op. cit., 460.
47. Asada, op. cit.
48. Hane, *The Honjo Diary*, 120–125.
49. Asada, op. cit., 242.
50. Hoyt, Edwin P., *Yamamoto: The Man Who Planned Pearl Harbor*, New York: McGraw-Hill, 1990, 84.
51. Drea, Edward J., *Japan's Imperial Army: Its Rise and Fall*, Lawrence: University of Kansas Press, 2009, 177.
52. Harries and Harries, op. cit., 184.
53. Shillony, Ben-Ami, *Revolt in Japan: The Young Officers and the February 26, 1936, Incident*, Princeton, NJ: Princeton University Press, 1973, 64.
54. *Japan Weekly Chronicle*, op. cit.
55. Heinrichs, Waldo H., *American Ambassador Joseph Grew and the Development of the United States Diplomatic Tradition*, Boston: Little Brown & Co., 1966, 225.
56. Shillony, op. cit., 123.
57. Craigie, op. cit., 334.
58. Hane, *Japan: A Historical Survey*, 476.
59. Shillony, op. cit.
60. Hane, trans., *The Honjo Diary*, 213.

Chapter IV

1. Shigemitsu, op. cit., 111.
2. Oral interview with Joseph C. Grew, August 23, 1960.
3. *Japan Weekly Chronicle*, June 21, 1934.
4. Ogata, Taketori, "The Real Hirota," *Contemporary Japan*, March 1934, Vol. II, No. 4, 622–633.
5. Hirota, Koki, "Japan as Bulwark of Peace in the Far East," *The Japan Magazine*, March 1934, Vol. IV, No. 2. Speech to the 65th Session of the Imperial Diet, January 23, 1934, 12–14.
6. Shigemitsu, op. cit., 111.
7. Crowley, James B., *Japan's Quest for Autonomy: National Security and Foreign Policy, 1930–1938*, Princeton, NJ: Princeton University Press, 1966, 248.
8. Connors, op. cit., 187.
9. Asada, op. cit., 243.
10. Shigemitsu, op. cit., 115.
11. Asada, op. cit., 244.
12. Peattie, Mark, *Ishiwara Kanji and Japan's Confrontation with the West*, Princeton, NJ: Princeton University Press, 1975, 277.
13. Hane, *Japan: A Historical Survey*, 479.
14. *Japan Weekly Chronicle*, February 21, 1935.
15. Shigemitsu, op. cit., 111.
16. Craigie, op. cit., 60.
17. Okamoto, Shumei, and Patricia Murray, eds., Yoshitake Oka, *Konoe Fumimaro: A Political Biography*, Tokyo: Tokyo University Press, 1983, 11–13.
18. Oka, op. cit., 41.
19. Ibid., p. 46.
20. Shigemitsu, op. cit., 135.
21. Oka, op. cit., 190.

Notes—Chapters V and VI

22. Ibid., 49-50.
23. Records of the U.S. Department of State Relating to the International Affairs of Japan, 1930-1939, Reel No. 2, Message from Ambassador Grew to the Secretary of State, February 19, 1937.
24. Peattie, op. cit., 268.
25. Cox and Conroy, eds., op. cit., Kahn, Winston B., "Doihara Kanji and the North China Autonomy Movement, 1935-1936," 178-179.
26. Kahn, op. cit., 190-191.
27. Montgomery, op. cit., 299.
28. Kahn, op. cit., 192-193.
29. Tuchman, op. cit., 159-160.
30. Peattie, op. cit., 275.
31. Boyle, op. cit., 251.
32. Peattie, op. cit.
33. Ibid., 289.

Chapter V

1. Japan Weekly Chronicle, December 13, 1934.
2. Abend, Hallett E., My Life in China, 1926-1941, New York: Harcourt, Brace & Co., 1943, 242-245.
3. Butow, Robert J. C., Tojo and the Coming of the War, Princeton, NJ: Princeton University Press, 1961, 91.
4. Saionji-Harada Memoirs, Chapter 244 (14 July 1937), 1818.
5. Bisson, T.A., Japan In China, New York: MacMillan, 1938, 4.
6. Ibid., 6.
7. O'Connor, Richard, Pacific Destiny: An Informal History of the U.S. in the Far East, 1776-1969, Boston: Little, Brown & Co., 1969, 420-421.
8. Tuchman, op. cit., 164.
9. Shigemitsu, op. cit., 139.
10. Dorn, Frank, The Sino-Japanese War, 1937-1941, New York: The MacMillan Company, 1974, 4.
11. Morley, op. cit., 248.
12. Ibid.
13. Ibid.
14. Peattie, op. cit., 297.
15. Morley, op. cit., 249.
16. Ibid., 250.
17. Ibid., 251.
18. Crowley, op. cit., 330.
19. Ibid., 330-331.
20. Ibid., 331.
21. Japan Weekly Chronicle, July 13, 1937.
22. Stilwell Situation Report, July 3-16, 1937, Report no. 9580, July 16, 1937.
23. Oka, op. cit., 55.
24. Peattie, op. cit., 301-302.
25. Saionji-Harada Memoirs, Chapter 245 (27 July 1937), 1842.
26. Oka, op. cit., 56.
27. Dorn, Frank, The Sino-Japanese War, 1937-1941, New York: The MacMillan Company, 1974, 6-7.
28. Coox, Alvin D., "Effects of Attrition in National War Effort: The Japanese Army Experience in China, 1937-1938," Military Affairs, XXXII: 2 October 1968, 57-61.
29. Peattie, op. cit., 307.
30. Wilson, Dick, When Tigers Meet: The Story of the Sino-Japanese War: 1937-1945, New York: The Viking Press, 1982, 18-20.
31. New York Times, July 27, 1937.
32. New York Times, July 30, 1937.
33. New York Times, August 9, 1937.
34. Counselor of Embassy in China (Lockhart) to Secretary of State, August 9, 1937, Foreign Relations, 1937, III, "The Far East," 361-362.
35. Wilson, op. cit., 27-28.
36. New York Times, July 22, 1937.
37. Memorandum by the Assistant Chief of the Division of Far Eastern Affairs (Hamilton), July 10, 1937, Foreign Relations, 1937, III, "The Far East," 132-135.
38. The Ambassador in France (Bullitt) to the Secretary of State, Paris, July 19, 1937, 213.
39. Memorandum by the Chief of the Division of Far Eastern Affairs (Hornbeck) of a Conversation with the Counselor of the Chinese Embassy, Washington, July 12, 1937, 142-143.
40. The Ambassador in France (Bullitt) to the Secretary of State, Paris, July 15, 1937, 173-175.
41. Memorandum by the Chief of the Division of Far Eastern Affairs (Hornbeck), Washington, August 2, 1937, 312-313.
42. Abend, op. cit., 248.
43. Dorn, op. cit., 10.
44. Morley, op. cit., 262-263.
45. Jones, op. cit., 43.
46. Saionji-Harada Memoirs, Chapter 249 (20 August 1937), 1859.

Chapter VI

1. New York Times, October 10, 1938.
2. Lory, Hillis, Japan's Military Masters:

The Army in Japanese Life, New York: The Viking Press, 1943, 125.

3. Van den Ven, Hans, *China at War: Triumph and Tragedy in the Emergence of the New China*, Cambridge, MA: Harvard University Press, 2018, 77.

4. Morley, James W., ed., *The China Quagmire: Japan's Expansion on the Asian Mainland, 1933-1941*, New York: Columbia University Press, 1983, 265.

5. *Saionji-Haada Memoirs* (20 August 1937), 1859.

6. Paine, S.C.M., *The Wars for Asia, 1911-1949*, U.S. Naval War College: Cambridge University Press, New York, 2012, 132.

7. Elleman, Bruce, *Modern Chinese Warfare, 1795-1989*, Routledge, Taylor & Francis Group, 11 New Fetter Lane, London, 2001, 203.

8. Dorn, Frank, *The Sino-Japanese War, 1937-1941*, New York: MacMillan, 1974, 68.

9. Okamoto, Shumei, and Patricia Murray, eds., Yoshitake Oka, *Konoe Fumimaro: A Political Biography*, Tokyo: Tokyo University Press, 1983, pp. 60-61.

10. Coox, Alvin D., and Hilary Conroy, eds., *China and Japan: A Search for Balance Since World War I*, Santa Barbara CA: ABC-Clio, Inc., 1978, 336.

11. Bergamini, David, *Japan's Imperial Conspiracy*, New York: William Morrow & Co., Inc., 1971, 79.

12. Sebald, William J., *With Macarthur in Japan: A Personal History of the Occupation*, New York, W.W. Norton, 1965, 173.

13. Abend, Hallett, *My Life in China, 1926-1941*, New York: Harcourt Brace & Co., 1943, 266.

14. Van den Ven, *op. cit.*, 88.

15. Abend, *op. cit.*, 265-266.

16. The Ambassador in China (Johnson) to the Secretary of State, Nanking, August 17, 1937, *Foreign Relations*, 1937, III, "The Far East," 428-429.

17. Mitter, Rana A., *A Bitter Revolution: China's Struggle with the Modern World*, New York: Oxford University Press, 2004, 170.

18. The Ambassador to China (Johnson) to the Secretary of State, Nanking, September 7, 1937, *Foreign Relations, op. cit.*, 516-517.

19. *Japan Times and Mail*, August 18, 1937.

20. *New York Times*, August 21, 1937.

21. Coox, "Recourse to Arms," *op. cit.*, 304-309.

22. Brice, Martin, *The Royal Navy and the Sino-Japanese Conflict, 1937-1941*, London: Ian Allen, 1973, 52.

23. *Japan Times and Mail*, August 21, 1937.

24. The Commander-in-Chief, U.S. Asiatic Fleet (Yarnell) to Chief of Naval Operations (Leahy), Shanghai, September 1, 1937, *Foreign Relations, op. cit.*, 501-502.

25. Dorn, Frank, *The Sino-Japanese War, 1937-1941*, New York: MacMillan, 1974, 73.

26. *New York Times*, October 3, 1937.

27. The Ambassador in China (Johnson) to the Secretary of State, Nanking, September 1, 1937, *op. cit.*, 503-504.

28. Consul General in Shanghai (Gauss) to the Secretary of State, October 4, 1937, *Foreign Relations, op. cit.*, 578-579.

29. Payne, Robert, *Chiang Kai-Shek*, New York: Weybright & Talley, 1969, 229-230.

30. *New York Times*, October 3, 1937.

31. Records of the U.S. Department of State to the Internal Affairs of Japan, 1930-1939, Reel 11. Winthrop R. Scott, American Consul (Kobe) to Ambassador Joseph C. Grew, August 13, 1937.

32. Bergamini, *op. cit.*, 14.

33. Morley, *op. cit.*, 272.

34. Dorn, *op. cit.*, 76.

35. *Japan Times and Mail*, October 27-30, 1937.

36. *New York Times*, October 25, 1937.

37. *New York Times*, November 1, 1937.

38. Bergamini, *op. cit.*, 14-16.

39. Dorn, *op. cit.*, 76-77.

40. Bergamini, *op. cit.*, 17.

41. *New York Times*, November 15-23, 1937.

42. *Japan Times and Mail*, November 6, 1937.

43. U.S. Military Intelligence Reports: China, 1911-1941, Reel 2, Report No. 9614, November 7-27, 1937. Military Situation Report of Major David D. Barrett, U.S. Assistant Military Attaché.

44. "Regulations Pertaining to Residents Desiring to Return to their Homes in Hongkew," Bonnewell File.

Chapter VII

1. *Japan Times and Mail*, September 27, 1937.

2. Lory, *op. cit.*, 25-26.

3. *Ibid.*, 48-49.

4. Randau, Carl, Leane Zugsmith, *The Setting Sun of Japan*, New York: Random House, 1943, 39.
5. *New York Times*, November 21, 1937.
6. *Japan Weekly Chronicle*, October 7, 1937.
7. Lory, *op. cit.*, 200-201.
8. *Japan Weekly Chronicle*, October 14, 1937.
9. LIFE, October 4, 1937, 102.
10. *Japan Times and Mail*, October 3, 1937.
11. *Japan Weekly Chronicle*, October 21, 1937.
12. *Japan Weekly Chronicle*, November 4, 1937.
13. Wickware, F.S., "What We Think About Foreign Affairs," *Harper's Magazine*, 179, September 1939, 405.
14. Lockwood, William W., "American-Japanese Trade: Its Structure and Significance," *The Annals of the American Academy of Political and Social Science*, May 1941, 87.
15. Utley, Freda, "Japan Fears a Boycott," *The Nation*, 145, October 2, 1937, 341.
16. Johnstone, William C., *The United States and Japan's Order*, New York: Oxford University Press, 1941, 168.
17. *St. Louis Globe Democrat*, October 11, 1937.
18. Homan, Paul T., "Must It Be War With Japan?" *Political Science Quarterly*, LIII, June 1938, 176.
19. Lory, *op. cit.*, 205.
20. Boyle, *op. cit.*, 243.
21. *Japan Times and Mail*, September 5, 1937.
22. *Japan Times and Mail*, October 22, 1937.
23. *Japan Times and Mail*, September 16, 1937.
24. Bush, Lewis, *Land of the Dragonfly*, London: Robert Hale, Ltd., 1959, 177.
25. Lory, *op. cit.*, 207.
26. Gibney, Frank, ed., Cary Beth, trans., *Senso: The Japanese Remember the Pacific War*, New York: M. E. Sharpe, 1995, 198.
27. Coox and Conroy, *op. cit.*, Harry Wray, "China in Japanese Textbooks," 118-127.
28. Lory, *op. cit.*, 212.
29. Mosley, *op. cit.*, 132-133.
30. Shunsuke, *op. cit.*, 27.
31. Byas, *op. cit.*, 300-303.

Chapter VIII

1. Stilwell Situation Report, October 18, 1937, Report No. 9601, October 1-18, 1937, U.S. Military Intelligence Reports: China, 1911-1941, Reel 2, Library of Congress.
2. Stilwell Situation Report, August 8, 1937, Report No. 9583, July 17-August 8, 1937, Reel 10.
3. *New York Times*, September 2, 1937; Stilwell Situation Report, September 17, 1937, Report No. 9590, Reel 10.
4. Dorn, *op. cit.*, 103-107.
5. *New York Times*, September 12, 1937.
6. *New York Times*, September 17, 1937.
7. Dorn, *op. cit.*, 107.
8. Morley, *op. cit.*, 274-275.
9. Levi, Werner, *Modern China's Foreign Policy*, Minneapolis: University of Minnesota Press, 1953, 216.
10. Dorn, *op. cit.*, 120-121.
11. Stilwell Situation Report, November 6, 1937, Report No. 9606, October 20-November 6, 1937, Reel 2.
12. *Saionji-Harada Memoirs*, Chapter 250B (9 October 1937), 1887-1888.
13. Ebon, Martin, *Lin Paio*, New York: Stein & Day, 1970, 24.
14. Rice, Edward E., *Mao's Way*, Berkeley: University of California Press, 1972, 94.
15. *Saionji-Harada Memoirs*, Chapter 250B (3 October 1937), 1878-1879.
16. Mosley, *op. cit.*, 112, 156.
17. Saionji-Harada Memoirs, *op. cit.*, 1880.
18. Crowley, *op. cit.*, 352-354.
19. Presseisen, Ernst, *Germany and Japan: A Study in Totalitarian Diplomacy*, New York: Howard Fertig, 1969, 134.
20. Liang, Hsi-Huey, *The Sino-German Connection: Alexander Von Falkenhausen Between China and Germany, 1900-1941*, Amsterdam: Van Gorcum, 1978, 23-127.
21. Crowley, *op. cit.*, 355.

Chapter IX

1. Neumann, William L, "Franklin D. Roosevelt and Japan, 1913-1933," *Pacific Historical Review*, XXII, May 1953, 143-145.
2. Sumner Welles, personal interview with the author, Bar Harbor, Maine, August 24, 1960.
3. Davis, Kenneth S., *Fdr: The Beginning*

of *Destiny*, New York: G.P. Putnam's Sons, 1971, 817.

4. Range, Willard, *Franklin D. Roosevelt's World Order*, Athens: University of Georgia Press, 1959, 80-81.

5. Wickware, *op. cit.*, 403.

6. Donovan, John C., "Congressional Isolationists and the Roosevelt Foreign Policy," *World Politics*, III, January 1951, 300.

7. Adler, Selig, *The Isolationist Impuse: Its Twentieth Century Reaction*, New York: Abelard-Schuman, Ltd., 1957, 261-262.

8. Cantril, Hadley, ed., *Public Opinion, 1935-1946*, Princeton, NJ: Princeton University Press, 1951, 966.

9. Toynbee, Arnold J., *Survey of International Affairs, 1937*, I, London: Royal Institute of International Affairs, 1938, 265.

10. "Report on American Public Opinion (Far East)," January 23, 1943, Department of State MSS.

11. *New York Times*, October 2, 1937.

12. Shepardson, W.H., and W.O. Scroggs, *The United States in World Affairs, 1937*, New York: Harper & Brothers, 1938, 224.

13. Official files, 197-A, Japan Miscellaneous, Franklin D. Roosevelt MSS, Franklin D. Roosevelt Library (FDRL), Hyde Park, New York.

14. Janeway, Eliot, "Japan's Partner: Japanese Dependence on the United States": *Harper's Magazine*, 177, June 1938, 6-8.

15. *New York Times* editorial, October 12, 1937.

16. British Public Opinion Following the Outbreak of Undeclared War in China, 1937, September 22, 1942, Department of State MSS.

17. British Embassy to the Department of State, Washington, October 1, 1937, United States Department of State, Foreign Relations Of The United States, Diplomatic Papers, 1937, III, "The Far East," Washington, D.C.: Government Printing Office, 1954, 560.

18. Memorandum by Assistant Secretary of State Wilson of a Conversation with the British Chargé (Mallet), Washington, October 5, 1937, United States Department of State, *Foreign Relations of the United States: Diplomatic Papers*, 1937, III, "The Far East," Washington, D.C.: Government Printing Office, 1954, 582.

19. Langer, W. L., and S.E. Gleason, *The Challenge to Isolation, 1937-1940*, New York: Harper & Brothers, 1952, 2.

20. Schlesinger, Arthur M., Jr., *The Age of Roosevelt: The Coming of the New Deal*, Vol. 2, Boston: Houghton Mifflin, 1959, 522-526.

21. *Ibid.*, 528. See also Thomas H. Greer, *What Roosevelt Thought: The Social and Political Ideas of Franklin D. Roosevelt*, East Lansing: Michigan State University Press, 1958, 92-93; and James McGregor Burns, *Roosevelt: The Lion and the Fox*, New York: Harcourt, Brace & Co., 1956, 371-374.

22. Dr. Stanley Hornbeck, personal interview with the author, Washington, D.C., August 13, 1960.

23. Welles interview.

24. Hornbeck interview.

25. *The Memoirs of Cordell Hull*, Vol. I, New York: The Macmillan Company, 1948, 509-510.

26. Hornbeck interview.

27. Welles, Sumner, *Seven Decisions that Shaped History*, New York: Harper & Brothers, 1950, 12.

28. Ferrell, Robert H., *American Diplomacy in the Great Depression: Hoover-Stimson Foreign Policy, 1929-1933*, New Haven: Yale University Press, 1957, 151-153.

29. Langer and Gleason, *op. cit.*, 8-9.

30. Blum, John M., *From the Morgenthau Diaries*, Boston: Houghton Mifflin Company, 1959, 452.

31. Cole, Wayne S., "Senator Key Pittman and American Neutrality Policies, 1933-1940," *The Mississippi Valley Historical Review*, XLVI, March 1940, 647-649.

32. Welles, *op. cit.*, 8-9. Mr. Welles told the author that although the ideas behind the "Eight Pillars" were Hull's; they were actually written by George Fort Milton, an advisor to Hull.

33. Ambassador Grew to the Secretary of State, Tokyo, July 19, 1937, *ibid.*, 701-702.

34. The Japanese Embassy to the Department of State, August 13, 1937, *ibid.*, 787.

35. *The Secret Diary of Harold Ickes: The Inside Struggle, 1936-1939*, Vol. II, New York: Simon & Shuster, 1954, 186.

36. Entry of August 27, 1937, J. Pierrepont Moffat MS Diary, Houghton Library, Harvard University.

37. Ambassador Johnson to Secretary Hull, Nanking, August 18, 1937, *Foreign Relations*, 1937, III, 437-438.

38. Ambassador Grew to Secretary Hull, Tokyo, September 7, 1937, *ibid.*, 515-516.

39. President's Personal Files, 1 P Press Conferences, Volume 10, Franklin D. Roosevelt MSS.

40. Hull, *op. cit.*, 557.
41. Shepardson and Scroggs, *op. cit.*, 202–206.
42. Grew, Joseph C., *Turbulent Era*, Vol. II, Boston: Houghton Mifflin Company, 1952, 1135–1136. See also Memorandum by Dr. Stanley Hornbeck, Washington, September 17, 1937, *Foreign Relations*, 1937, III, 531–532.
43. Welles, *op. cit.*, 8–9.
44. McIntyre, Vice Admiral Ross T., *White House Physician*, New York: G.P. Putnam's Sons, 1946, 109.
45. Welles, *op. cit.*, 8–9.
46. Feiling, Keith, *Life of Neville Chamberlain*, London: MacMillan, 1946, 325.
47. Ickes, *op. cit.*, 213.
48. Borg, Dorothy, "Notes on Roosevelt's 'Quarantine Speech,'" *Political Science Quarterly*, LXXII, September 1957, 422. The original document is in the Roosevelt Papers, Official File 20, State Department, Box 6, FDRL, Hyde Park, New York.
49. Hull, *op. cit.*, 544.
50. Borg, *op. cit.*, 413–141. The drafts of the speech can be found in the President's Chicago Speech Folder in the Roosevelt Papers. The Davis drafts are dated September 18, four days before the President started on his trip. Copies of the drafts are also to be found in the Davis papers.
51. Franklin D. Roosevelt, Hyde Park, New York, December 20, 1937, letter to James Hilton, President's Personal File 5066, James Hilton Folder, Franklin D. Roosevelt MSS. This letter was very brief; Roosevelt did not elaborate on what he meant by "questions." However, the book represents an idealist's search for peace and as such would have been peculiarly appealing to someone of Roosevelt's nature.
52. Ickes, *op. cit.*, 222.
53. Rosenman, Samuel I., *Working with Roosevelt*, New York: Harper & Co., 1952, 164–165.
54. Franklin D. Roosevelt, aboard train, September 24, 1937, letter to Lord Tweedsmuir, Ottawa, Canada, President's Personal File 3396, Lord Tweedsmuir Folder, Franklin D. Roosevelt MSS.
55. Tully, Grace, *F.D.R., My Boss*, New York: Charles Scribner's Sons, 1949, 231.
56. The President's Chicago Speech Folder, Franklin D. Roosevelt MSS. This conforms to the final draft, which can be found in *Roosevelt's Foreign Policy, 1933–1941: Franklin D. Roosevelt's Unedited Speeches and Messages*, New York: Wilfred Funk, Inc. 1942, 129–132.
57. Quotation from Hilton, James, *Lost Horizon*, Publisher's Edition, New York: William Morrow & Co., 1957, 144. This was not the only time the President borrowed from *Lost Horizon*. In 1942, when asked by reporters where the Doolittle fliers who combed Tokyo were based, Roosevelt replied inscrutably, "Shangri-La."
58. Bishop Frank M. Sterrett, Bethlehem, Pennsylvania, September 18, 1937, letter to President Roosevelt, President's Personal File 2080, Bishop Sterrett Folder, Franklin D. Roosevelt MSS.
59. The President's Chicago Speech Folder, Franklin D. Roosevelt MSS.
60. Cardinal Mundelein, Chicago, Illinois, letter to the Most Reverend Amleto G. Cicognani, Apostolic Delegate, Washington, D.C., President's Personal Files 321, Cardinal Mundelein Folder, Franklin D. Roosevelt MSS.
61. Phillips, William, *Ventures in Diplomacy*, Boston: The Beacon Press: 1952, 206–207.
62. President's Personal Files 1P Press Conferences, Vol. 10, Franklin D. Roosevelt MSS.
63. Moffat's statement does not coincide with the recollection of Dr. Stanley Hornbeck, who told the author in an interview on August 13, 1960, that few of the men in Hull's office expressed any opinion when they got word of the speech.
64. *New York Times*, October 6, 1937. See also Welles, *op. cit.*, 63.
65. Raymond L. Buell, New York, October 20, 1937, Letter to James Roosevelt, Washington, D.C., President's Personal File 200B, Public Reaction Folder, Franklin D. Roosevelt MSS.
66. President's Personal File 200B, Public Reaction Folder, Franklin D. Roosevelt MSS.
67. Borg, Dorothy, *The United States and the Far Eastern Crisis of 1933–1938*, Cambridge: Harvard University Press, 1964, 395.
68. *New York Times*, October 13, 1937.
69. Ambassador Grew to Secretary Hull, Tokyo, October 7, 1937, *Foreign Relations*, III, 584–586.
70. Preface to diary of Joseph C. Grew. dated September 26–October 10, 1937, quoted in Joseph C. Grew, *Turbulent Era*, Vol. II, 1167–1168.

71. Entry of October 7, 1937, Joseph C. Grew MS diary, Houghton Library, Harvard University.
72. Chargé Gilbert to Secretary Hull, Berlin, October 7, 1937, 7/11:00/16 MS, National Archives.
73. Ambassador Dieckhoff to German Foreign Ministry, Washington, October 9, 1937, United States Department of State, Documents on German Foreign Policy, 1918-1945, Series D, I, Washington, D.C.: Government Printing Office, 1954, 634-635.
74. Ambassador Dieckhoff to German Foreign Ministry, Washington, October 15, 1937, *op. cit.*, 639-641.
75. Chargé Johnson to Secretary Hull, London, October 6, 1937, 711.00, Pres. Speech, October 5, 1937/2MS, National Archives.
76. Memorandum by the Under Secretary of State, Washington, October 12, 1937, *Foreign Relations*, 1937, III, 600-602.
77. Chargé Wilson to Secretary Hull, Paris, October 6, 1937, United States Department of State, Foreign Relations of the United States, Diplomatic Papers, 1937, I GENERAL, Washington, D.C.: Government Printing Office, 1954, 132-135.
78. Ambassador Johnson to Secretary Hull, Nanking, October 8, 1937, 711.00 Pres. Speech, October 5, 1937/24 MS National Archives.

Chapter X

1. *New York Times*, November 2, 1937.
2. Ambassador Bullitt to Secretary Hull, Paris, November 10, 1937, *Foreign Relations*, 1937, IV, 172-174.
3. Consul Everett to Secretary Hull, Geneva, August 30-31, 1937, *op. cit.*, 6-9. See also British Embassy to Department of State, Aide-Memoire, Washington, August 31, 1937.
4. Secretary Hull to Minister Harrison, Washington, September 11, 1937, *op. cit.*, 15-16.
5. Secretary Hull to Minister Harrison, Washington, September 24, 1937, *ibid.*, 32-34.
6. Minister Harrison to Secretary Hull, Geneva, October 5, 1937, *Foreign Relations, op. cit.*, 54-58. For the full text of these reports see *Foreign Relations*, JAPAN, 1931-1941, I, 384-394.
7. Minister Harrison to Secretary Hull, Geneva, October 6, 1937, 61.
8. Press release issued by the Department of State, Washington, D.C., October 6, 1937, United States Department of State, *Peace and War: United States Foreign Policy, 1931-1941*, Washington: Government Printing Office, 1943, 387-388.
9. Ambassador Grew to Secretary Hull, Tokyo, October 7, 1937, *Foreign Relations*, III, 585-586.
10. The British Embassy to the Department of State, Aide-Memoire, Washington, October 6, 1937, *Foreign Relations*, 1937, IV, THE FAR EAST, 64.
11. Entry of October 7, 1937, Moffat diary.
12. Department of State to the British Embassy, Memorandum of a Conversation between Mr. Mallett, British Chargé d'Affaires, and Mr. Wilson, Washington, October 7, 1937, *Foreign Relations, op. cit.*, 65-66.
13. Chargé Johnson to Secretary Hull, London, October 8, 1937, *Foreign Relations, op. cit.*, 69-70.
14. Chargé Johnson to Secretary Hull, London, October 15, 1937, *ibid.*, 79-80.
15. Memorandum by the Assistant Secretary of State (Wilson) of a trans-Atlantic telephone conversation with the Chargé in the United Kingdom (Johnson), Washington, October 15, 1937, *ibid.*, 81-82.
16. The British Embassy to the Department of State, Aide-Memoire, Washington, October 19, 1937, *ibid.*, 89-91.
17. The Department of State to the British Embassy, Memorandum of a conversation with Mr. Mallet, British Chargé d'Affaires, October 19, 1937, *Foreign Relations*, 1937, IV, 92.
18. Ambassador Grew to Secretary Hull, Tokyo, October 15, 1937, *ibid.*, 80.
19. Ambassador Grew to Secretary Hull, Tokyo, October 20, 1937, *ibid.*, 93-94.
20. Quoted from the Japanese Note to the Belgian Government, Ambassador Grew to Secretary Hull, Tokyo, *ibid.*, 112-113.
21. Memorandum of a telephone conversation between Norman Davis and Foreign Secretary Eden, October 13, 1937, File Box 4, Norman Davis MSS, Library of Congress.
22. Cordell Hull, Washington, October 18, 1937, letter to Norman Davis, Washington, D.C., File Box 4, *ibid.*
23. Memorandum of a conference between Norman Davis and President Roo-

Notes—Chapter X

sevelt, Hyde Park, New York, October 20, 1937, File Box 4, *ibid.*
24. *New York Times*, October 20, 1937.
25. Entry of October 28, 1937, Moffat diary. See also Ambassador Bullitt to Secretary Hull, Paris, October 23, 1937, Foreign Relations of the United States, Diplomatic Papers, 1937, III, "The Far East," 634–637.
26. Memorandum of a conversation between Ambassador at Large Davis and Dr. Wellington Koo, Paris, October 28, 1937, File Box 4, Norman Davis MSS.
27. *New York Times*, November 2, 1937.
28. Chairman of the American Delegation (Davis) to Secretary Hull, Brussels, November 2, 1937, *Foreign Relations*, 1937, IV, 145–147.
29. Friedman, Irving S., *British Relations with China: 1931–1939*, New York: Institute of Pacific Relations, 1940, 9.
30. Estimate of the Situation and Suggestion of Certain Possibilities by the Chairman of the American Delegation, Brussels, November 2, 1937, File Box 4, Norman Davis MSS
31. Ambassador Grew to Secretary Hull, Tokyo, October 30, 1937, *Foreign Relations*, 1937, IV, 124–125.
32. Ambassador Bingham to Secretary Hull, London, October 30, 1937, *ibid.*, 126–128.
33. Ambassador Grew to Secretary Hull, Tokyo, November 1, 1937, *ibid.*, 134–135.
34. *New York Times*, November 4, 1937.
35. United States Department of State, The Conference of Brussels, November 3–24, 1937, Convened in Virtue of Article 7 of the Nine Power Treaty of Washington of 1922, Washington: Government Printing Office, 1938, 31.
36. The Chairman of the American Delegation (Davis) to Secretary Hull and President Roosevelt, Brussels, November 6, 1937, File Box 4, Norman Davis MSS.
37. Pierrepont Moffat, Brussels, November 8, 1937, letter to George A. Gordon, the Hague, Moffat MSS.
38. Memorandum from the President to Under Secretary Welles, Washington, November 12, 1937, President's Secretary's Files, File 20, Franklin D. Roosevelt MSS.
39. U.S. Congress, Congressional Record, 75th Congress, 2nd Session, Vol. 82, Part 3, Washington: Government Printing Office, 1937, 158.
40. Memorandum of a Conversation with Mr. Malcolm MacDonald, Brussels, November 8, 1937, File Box 4, Norman Davis.
41. Memorandum of a Conversation with Mr. Maxim Litvinov, Brussels, November 8, 1937, *ibid.*
42. Entry of November 8, 1937, Moffat diary. See also Memorandum of a Conversation between Dr. Stanley Hornbeck and Mr. M. L. Aubert and Henrik de Kauffman, Brussels, November 7, 1937, File Box 4, Norman Davis MSS.
43. Acting Secretary of State Welles to Ambassador Bullitt, Washington, November 9, 1937, *Foreign Relations*, 1937, IV, THE FAR EAST, 170–171.
44. Ambassador Bullitt to Secretary Hull, Paris, November 8, 1937, *Foreign Relations*, 1937, III, 666–667.
45. Chairman of the American Delegation (Davis) to Secretary Hull, Brussels, November 10, 1937, *Foreign Relations*, 1937, IV, 175–177.
46. Secretary Hull to the Chairman of the American Delegation (Davis), Washington, November 12, 1937, *ibid.*, 180–181.
47. Entry of November 10, 1937, Moffat diary.
48. United States Department of State, The Conference at Brussels, November 3–24, 1937, Convened in Virtue of Article 7 of the Nine Power Treaty of Washington of 1922.
49. Chairman of the American Delegation (Davis) to Secretary Hull, Brussels, November 14, 1937, *Foreign Relations*, 1937, IV, 183–185.
50. Secretary Hull to the Chairman of the American Delegation (Davis), Washington, November 15, 1937, *ibid.*, 187–188.
51. Declaration adopted by the Conference at Brussels, November 15, 1937, United States Department of State, Peace and War: United States Foreign Policy, 1931–1941.
52. Entry of November 13, 1937, Moffat diary.
53. Ambassador Grew to Secretary Hull, Tokyo, November 16, 1937, *Foreign Relations*, 1937, IV, 189–193.
54. Secretary Hull to Ambassador Grew, Washington, November 16, 1937, *ibid.*, 196–197.
55. Memorandum by Assistant Secretary of State Wilson of a conversation with the Counselor of the Japanese Embassy, Mr. Suma, Washington, November 16, 1937, *ibid.*, 194–196.

56. Entry of November 18, 1937, Moffat diary.
57. Chairman of the American Delegation (Davis) to Secretary Hull, Brussels, November 17, 1937, *Foreign Relations, 1937*, IV, 200–202.
58. Secretary Hull to the Chairman of the American Delegation (Davis), Washington, November 17, 1937, *ibid.*, 203–204.
59. Secretary Hull to the Chairman of the American Delegation (Davis), Washington, November 16, 1937, *ibid.*, 197–198.
60. Entry of November 21, 1937, Moffat diary.
61. Memorandum of a conversation between Dr. Wellington Koo and Dr. Stanley Hornbeck, Brussels, November 19, 1937, File Box 4, Norman Davis MSS.
62. Secretary Hull to the Chairman of the American Delegation (Davis), Washington, November 17, 1937, *Foreign Relations, 1937*, IV, 205–210.
63. Declaration adopted by the Conference at Brussels, *Foreign Relations*, JAPAN, 1931-1941, I, 417.
64. The Conference at Brussels, 69.
65. *New York Times*, November 25, 1937.
66. Dr. Stanley Hornbeck, personal interview with the author, Washington, August 13, 1960.

Chapter XI

1. *Japan Weekly Chronicle*, November 25, 1937.
2. Morley, *op. cit.*, 277.
3. Crowley, *op. cit.*, 357.
4. Morley, *op. cit.*, 278.
5. The Second Secretary of Embassy in China (Atcheson) to the Secretary of State, Nanking, November 28, 1937, *Foreign Relations, op. cit.*, 726.
6. U.S. Military Intelligence Reports, Report No. 9616, Reel 10, November 27–December 20, 1937, Report of David D. Barrett, Major, Infantry, Assistant Military Attaché.
7. *New York Times*, December 6, 1937.
8. Bergamini, *op. cit.*, 20.
9. *Japan Times and Mail*, November 24, 1937.
10. The Consul General at Shanghai (Gauss) to the Secretary of State, Shanghai, December 1 and December 3, 1937, *Foreign Relations, op. cit.*, 949–950.
11. *New York Times*, December 14, 1937.
12. *Japan Times and Mail*, November 24, 1937.
13. Crowley, *op. cit.*, 360–362.
14. *Saionji-Harada Memoirs*, Chapter 258 (18 December 1937), 1970–1971.
15. Crowley, *op. cit.*, 361–365.
16. Timperly, H.J., ed., *Japanese Terror in China*, New York: Modern Age Books, Inc., 1938, 75–78.
17. *New York Times*, December 7, 1937.
18. Bergamini, *op. cit.*, 22–24.
19. *New York Times*, December 10, 1937.
20. *Japan Times and Mail*, December 8, 1937.
21. *New York Times*, December 12, 1937.
22. Okumiya, Matsatake, "How the *Panay* Was Sunk," United States Naval Institute Proceedings, Vol. 19, June 1953, 588–590.
23. Koginos, Manny T., *The Panay Incident: Prelude to War*, Lafayette IN: Purdue University Studies, 1967, 26–27.
24. The Consul General in Shanghai (Gauss) to the Secretary of State, Shanghai, December 17 1937, *Foreign Relations, op. cit.*, Report of George Atcheson, 505–506.
25. Okumiya, *op. cit.*, 590–598.
26. Heinrichs, *op. cit.*, 256.
27. Brice, *op. cit.*, 56–59.
28. Abend, *op. cit.*, 270–273.
29. Okumiya, *op. cit.*, 587–596.
30. The Chargé in the United Kingdom (Johnson) to the Secretary of State, London, December 13, 1937, *Foreign Relations, op. cit.*, 494–495.
31. Memorandum of the Secretary of State, Washington, December 14, 1937, *ibid.*, 499–500.
32. *Japan Weekly Chronicle*, December 23, 1937.
33. The Ambassador in Japan (Grew) to the Secretary of State, Tokyo, December 15, 1937, *Foreign Relations, op. cit.*, 502–503.
34. Heinrichs, *op. cit.*, 256–258.
35. Koginos, *op. cit.*, 72–73.
36. Bergamini, *op. cit.*, 31–32.
37. Honda, Katsuchi, *The Nanking Massacre: A Japanese Journalist Confronts Japan's National Shame*, New York: Armonk, an East Gate Book, 1999, 154–155.
38. Timperly, *op. cit.*, 19–22.
39. *Ibid.*, 27–40.
40. Bush, *op. cit.*, 185.
41. Bush, Lewis, *The Road to Imamura*, London: Robert Hale, Ltd., 1961, 119.
42. Honda, *op. cit.*, 195–196.

43. Lord, Russell, *The Knights of the Bushido, The Shocking History of Japanese War Atrocities*, New York: E. P. Dutton & Co., 1966, 43–45.
44. Drea, *Japan's Imperial Army, op. cit.*, 197.

Chapter XII

1. *Japan Weekly Chronicle*, December 16, 1937.
2. *Japan Times and Mail*, December 18, 1937.
3. Ambassador in China (Johnson) to the Secretary of State, Hankow, December 29, 1937, *Foreign Relations, op. cit.*, Report of the American Military Attaché (Stilwell), 843–844.
4. The President of the Chinese Executive Yuan (Chiang Kai-shek) to President Roosevelt, December 24, 1937, *ibid.*, 832–833.
5. Crowley, *op. cit.*, 366–370.
6. *New York Times*, January 12, 1938.
7. Crowley, *op. cit.*, 371–372.
8. Oka, *op. cit.*, 68–69; Crowley, *op. cit.*, 373–374.
9. Crowley, *op. cit.*, 374–375.
10. *New York Times*, January 16, 1938.
11. Oka, *op. cit.*, 70–71.
12. Crowley, *op. cit.*, 377.
13. Oka, *op. cit.*, 71.
14. *Ibid.*, 81–82.
15. The Ambassador in China (Johnson) to the Secretary of State, Hankow, February 3, 1938, *Foreign Relations*, IV, 1938, "The Far East," 64–65.
16. Coox, *op. cit.*, 305–306.

Bibliography

Official Papers

711.00 Pres. Speech, October 5, 1937/2.
711.00 Pres. Speech, October 5, 1937/24.
711.00/16.
793.94 Conference/223.
793.94 Conference/228.
793.94 Conference/293.
International Military Tribunal Far East, Exhibits.
Records of the U.S. Department of State Relating to the Internal Affairs of Japan, 1930–1938.
Report on American Public Opinion (Far East), January 3, 1943.
Report on British Public Opinion Following the Outbreak of the Undeclared War in China, September 22, 1942.
U.S. Military Intelligence Reports: China, 1941.

Private Papers

Bonnewell File, Papers of A.L. Zavilenski.
Davis, Norman, MSS, Library of Congress.
Grew, Joseph C., MSS, Houghton Library, Harvard University.
Ickes, Harold L., MSS, Library of Congress.
Moffat, J. Pierrepont, MS Diary, Houghton Library, Harvard University.
Roosevelt, Franklin D., MSS, Franklin D. Roosevelt Library, Hyde Park, New York.
Saionji-Harada Memoirs, Library of Congress.

Oral Interviews

Grew, Joseph C., personal interview. Manchester, Massachusetts, August 23, 1960, with the author.
Hornbeck, Stanley, personal interview. Washington, D.C., August 13, 1960, with the author.
Welles, Sumner, personal interview. Bar Harbor, Maine, August 24, 1960, with the author.

Official Documents

The Conference of Brussels, November 3–24, 1937. Convened in Virtue of Article 7 of the Nine-Power Treaty of Washington of 1922, Washington: Government Printing Office, 1938.

Congressional Record, 75th Congress, 1st Session.
_____, 75 Congress, 2nd Session.
Department of Commerce, Bureau of Foreign and Domestic Commerce: *Statistical Abstract of the United States, 1937.* Washington: Government Printing Office, 1938.
Documents on German Foreign Policy, 1918–1945, Series D. Washington: Government Printing Office, 1954, I.
Papers Relating to the Foreign Relations of the United States. Washington: Government Printing Office, 1954, 1937, III, IV, The Far East.
_____, Japan, 1931–1941. Washington, Government Printing Office, 1943, I.

Newspapers

Boston Herald
Chicago Tribune
The Christian Century
Detroit Free Press
Japan Times and Mail

Japan Weekly Chronicle
Los Angeles Times
New York Times
Philadelphia Record
St. Louis Globe Democrat

Periodicals

Borg, Dorothy, "Notes on Roosevelt's 'Quarantine Speech,'" *Political Science Quarterly*, LXXII, September 1957.
Cole, Wayne S. "Senator Key Pittman and American Neutrality Policies, 1933–1940," *The Mississippi Valley Historical Review*, XLVI, March 1940.
Coox, Alvin D., "Effects of Attrition on National War Effort: The Japanese Army Experience in China, 1937–1938," *Military Affairs*, XXXII, October 1938.
Donovan, John C., "Congressional Isolationists and the Roosevelt Foreign Policy," *World Politics*, III, January 1951.
Hirota, Koki, "Japan as Bulwark of Peace in the Far East," *The Japan Magazine*, XV, No. 2, March 1934.
Homan, Paul T., "Must It Be War with Japan?" *Political Science Quarterly*, LIII, June 1938.
Janeway, Eliot, "Japan's Partner: Japanese Dependence on the United States," *Harper's Magazine*, 177, June 1938.
Kublin, Hyman, "The Modern Army of Early Meiji Japan," *The Far Eastern Quarterly*, IX, 1949.
Lockwood, William W., "American-Japanese Trade: Its Structure and Significance," *The Annals of the Americal Academy of Policy and Social Science*, May 1941.
Neuman, William L., "Franklin D. Roosevelt and Japan, 1913–1933," *Pacific Historical Review*, XXII, May 1953.
Ogata, Taketori, "The Real Hirota," *Contemporary Japan*, II, No. 4, March 1934.
Okumiya, Masatake, "How the PANAY Was Sunk," *United States Naval Institute Proceedings*, Vol. 79, No. 6, June 1953.
Roosevelt, Franklin D., "Shall We Trust Japan?" *Asia*, July 1923.
Utley, Freda, "Japan Fears a Boycott," *The Nation*, 145, October 2, 1937.
Wickware, F.S., "What We Think About Foreign Affairs," *Harper's Magazine*, 179, September 1939.

Diaries and Memoirs

Abend, Hallett, *My Life in China, 1926–1941*, New York: Harcourt, Brace and Company, 1943.

Blum, John M., *From the Morgenthau Diaries*, Boston: Houghton Mifflin Company, 1959.
Bush, Lewis, *The Land of the Dragonfly*, London: Robert Hale, Ltd., 1952.
_____, *The Road to Imamura*, London: Robert Hale, Ltd., 1961.
Byas, Hugh, *Government By Assassination*, New York: Alfred A. Knopf, 1942.
Craigie, Sir Robert, *Behind the Japanese Mask*, London: Hutchinson and Company, Ltd., 1946.
Gibney, Frank, ed., translated by Beth Cary, *Senso: The Japanese Remember the Pacific War*, New York: M.E. Sharpe, 1995.
Grew, Joseph C., *TURBULENT Era, II*, Boston: Houghton Mifflin Company, 1952.
Hane, Mikiso, trans., *Emperor Hirohito and His Chief Aide-de-Camp; The Honjo Diary, 1933-1936*, Tokyo: The University of Tokyo Press, 1982.
Hull, Cordell, *The Memoirs of Cordell Hull*, New York: Macmillan Company, 1946.
Ickes, Harold L., *The Secret Diary of Harold L. Ickes: The Inside Struggle, 1937-1939*, New York: Simon & Schuster, 1954, II.
Phillips, William, *Ventures in Diplomacy*, Boston: The Beacon Press, 1952.
Piggott, F.S.G., *Broken Thread*, Aldershot: Gale and Polden, 1950.
Rosenman, Samuel J., *Working with Roosevelt*, New York: Harper and Company, 1952.
Sebald, William J., *With MacArthur in Japan:A Personal History of the Occupation*, New York: W.W. Norton, 1965.
Shigemitsu, Mamoru, *Japan and Her Destiny*, London: Hutchinson and Company, Ltd., 1958.
Tully, Grace, *F.D.R. My Boss*, New York: Scribner's, 1949.
Welles, Sumner, *Seven Decisions That Shaped History*, New York: Harper and Brothers, 1950.

Secondary Works

Adler, Selig, *The Isolationist Impulse: Its Twentieth Century Reaction*, New York: Abelard-Schuman, Ltd., 1957.
Allen, Louis, *Japan: The Years of Triumph*, New York: American Heritage Press, 1971.
Asado, Sadao, *From Mahan to Pearl Harbor: The Imperial Japanese Navy and the United States*, Annapolis: Naval Institute Press, 2006.
Bailey, Thomas A., *A Diplomatic History of the American People*, New York: Appleton-Century Crofts, Inc., 1958.
Bergamini, David, *Japan's Imperial Conspiracy*, New York: William Morrow and Company, Inc., 1971.
Bisson, T.A., *Japan in China*, New York: Macmillan Company, 1938.
Borg, Dorothy, *The United States and the Far Eastern Crisis of 1933-1938*, Cambridge: Harvard University Press, 1964.
Borg, Dorothy, and Okamoto, Shumpei, eds., *Pearl Harbor as History: Japanese-American Relations, 1933-1941*, New York: Columbia University Press, 1973.
Borton, Hugh, *Japan's Modern Century*, New York: The Ronald Press Company, 1970.
Brice, Martin, *The Royal Navy and the Sino-Japanese Conflict, 1937-1941*, London: Ian Allen, 1973.
Brown, Delmar, *Nationalism in Japan*, Berkeley: University of California Press, 1955.
Butow, Robert J.C., *Tojo and the Coming of the War*, Princeton: Princeton University Press, 1961.
Cameron, M.E., Mahoney, T.H.D., and Mc Reynolds, G.E., *China, Japan and the Powers: A History of the Modern Far East*, New York: The Ronald Press Company, 1960.
Close, Upton, *Behind the Face of Japan*, New York: D. Appleton Century, 1942.
Coble, Parks M., *Facing Japan: Chinese Politics and Japanese Imperialism, 1931-1937*, Cambridge: Harvard University Press, 1991.

Connors, Leslie, *The Emperor's Adviser: Saionji Kinmoshi and Prewar Japanese Politics*, London: Crom Helm Ltd., 1987.
Coox, Alvin D. and Conroy, Hilary, eds., *China and Japan: A Search for Peace Since World War I*, Santa Barbara: ABC-Clio, Inc., 1978.
Crowley, James B., *Japan's Quest for Autonomy, National Security and Foreign Policy, 1930-1938*, Princeton: Princeton University Press, 1966.
Davis, Kenneth S., *FDR, The Beginning of Destiny*, New York: G.P. Putnam's Sons, 1971.
Dorn, Frank, *The Sino-Japanese War, 1937-1941, from the Marco Polo Bridge to Pearl Harbor*, New York: Macmillan Company, 1974.
Drea, Edward J., *In the Service of the Emperor: Essays on the Imperial Japanese Army*, Lincoln: University of Nebraska Press, 1998.
_____, *Japan's Imperial Army: Its Rise and Fall*, Topeka: University Press of Kansas, 2009.
Ebon, Martin, *Lin Piao*, New York: Stein and Day, 1970.
Ellerman, Bruce, *Modern Chinese Warfare*, London: Rutledge, Taylor, France's Group, 2001.
Feiling, Keith, *Life of Neville Chamberlain*, London: Macmillan Company, 1946.
Ferrell, Robert H., *American Diplomacy in the Great Depression: Hoover-Stimson Foreign Policy, 1923-1933*, New Haven: Yale University Press, 1957.
Friedman, Irving S., *British Relations with China, 1931-1939*, New York: Institute for Pacific Relations, 1940.
Gow, Ian, *Military Intervention in Prewar Japanese Politics*, New York: Rutledge Curzon, 2004.
Gowen, Herbert, H., *An Outline History of Japan*, New York: D. Appleton and Company, 1947.
Hackett, Roger F., *Yamagata, Aritomo in the Rise of Modern Japan, 1838-1922*, Cambridge: Harvard University Press, 1972.
Hane, Mikiso, *Japan, a Historical Survey*, New York: Charles Scribner Sons, 1972.
_____, trans., *Emperor Hirohito and His Chief Aide-De-Camp, the Honjo Diary, 1933-1936*, Tokyo: The University of Tokyo Press, 1982.
Harcave, Sidney, *Russia: A History*, Chicago: J.B. Lippincott, 1956.
Harries, Meiron and Susie, *Soldiers of the Sun: The Rise and Fall of the Imperial Japanese Army*, New York: Random House, 1991.
Haruo, Tohmatsu and Willmott, H.P., *A Gathering Darkness: The Coming of the War in the Far East and the Pacific, 1921-1942*, Lanham: S.R. Books, 2004.
Heinrichs, Waldo H., Jr., *american Ambassador Joseph C. Grew and the Development of the United States Diplomatic Tradition*, Boston: Little, Brown and Company, 1966.
Honda, Katsuchi and Gibney, Frank., ed., *The Nanking Massacre, a Japanese Journalist Confronts Japan's National Shame*, New York: Armonk London: M.E. Sharpe, 1999.
Hoyt, Edwin J., *Japan's War: The Great Pacific Conflict*, New York: McGraw-Hill.
_____, *Yamamoto, the Man Who Planned Pearl Harbor*, New York: McGraw-Hill, 1990.
Huish, Marcus B., ed., *Fifty Years of New Japan*, Vol. I, London: Smith Elder and Company, 1970.
Ito, Massanori, and Pineau, Roger, *The End of the Imperial Japanese Navy*, New York: W.W. Norton, 1962.
James, David H., *The Rise and Fall of the Japanese Empire*, London: George Allen and Unwin, Ltd., 1951.
Johnstone, William C., *The United States and Japan's New Order*, New York: Oxford University Press, 1954.
Jones, F.C., *Japan's New Order in East Asia, Its Rise and Fall*, London: Oxford University Press, 1954.
Koginos, Manny T., *The Panay Incident: Prelude to War*, Lafayette, Indiana: Purdue University Press, 1954.

Bibliography 341

Langer, W.L. and Gibson, S.E., *The Challenge to Isolation, 1937–1940*, New York: Harper and Brothers, 1952.
Levi, Werner, *Modern China's Foreign Policy*, Minneapolis: University of Minnesota Press, 1953.
Li, Lincoln, *The Japanese Army in North China, 1931–1941: Problems of Political and Economic Control*, Tokyo: Oxford University Press, 1975.
Liang, Hsi-huey, *The Sino-German Connection, Alexander Von Falkenhausen Between China and Germany, 1900–1941*, Amsterdam: Van Gorcum, 1978.
Lone, Stewart, *Provincial Life and the Military in Imperial Japan*, New York: Rutledge, 2016.
Lord, Russell, *The Knights of the Bushido: The Shocking History of Japanese War Atrocities*, New York: E.P. Dutton and Company, 1958.
Lory, Hillis, *Japan's Military Masters: The Army in Japanese Life*, New York, The Viking Press, 1943.
Lu, David J., *From the Marco Polo Bridge to Pearl Harbor*, Washington, D.C.: Public Affairs Press, 1961.
Maki, John M., *Japanese Militarism, Its Cause and Cure*, New York: Alfred A. Knopf, 1942.
Mayo, Marlene J., ed., *The Emergence of Imperial Japan*, Lexington: D.C. Heath and Company, 1970.
McIntyre, Ross T., *White House Physician*, New York: G.P. Putnam's Sons, 1946.
Mitter, Rana, *A Bitter Revolution: China's Struggle with the Modern World*, New York: Oxford University Press, 2004.
Montgomery, Michael, *Imperialist Japan: The Yen to Dominate*, New York: St. Martin's Press, 1987.
Morley, James W., ed., *The China Quagmire, Japan's Expansion on the Asian Mainland, 1933–1941*, New York: Columbia University Press, 1983.
_____, ed., *Dilemmas of Growth in Prewar Japan*, Princeton: Princeton University Press, 1982.
Mosley, Leonard, *Hirohito, Emperor of Japan*, Englewood Cliffs, New Jersey: Prentice-Hall, Inc., 1956.
O'Connor, Richard, *Pacific Destiny: An Informal History of the U.S. in the Far East, 1776–1969*, Boston: Little Brown and Company, 1969.
Okamoto, Shumpei and Murray, Patricia, eds., *Konoe Fumimaro, a Political Biography*, Tokyo: Tokyo University Press, 1983.
Paine, S.C.M., *The Wars for Asia, 1911–1949*, New York: Cambridge University Press, 2012.
Payne, Robert, *Chiang Kai-Shek*, New York: Weybright and Talley, 1969.
Peattie, Mark, *Ishiwara Kanji and Japan's Confrontation with the West*, Princeton: Princeton University Press, 1975.
Presseisen, Ernst L., *Before Aggression: Europeans Prepare the Japanese Army*, Tucson, The University of Arizona Press, 1956.
_____, *Germany and Japan, a Study in Totalitarian Diplomacy*, New York: Howard Fertif, 1969.
Quigley, Harold S., and Turner, John E., *The New Japan: Government and Politics*, Minneapolis: The University of Minnesota Press, 1956.
Randau, Carl and Zugmit, Leanne, *The Setting Sun of Japan*, New York: Random House, 1943.
Range, Willard, *Franklin D. Roosevelt's World Order*, Athens: The University of Georgia Press, 1959.
Reardon, Jim, *Cracking the Zero Mystery: How the United States Learned to Beat Japan's Vaunted World War II Fighter Plane*, Harrisburg: Stackpole Books, 1990.
Rice, Edward, *Mao's Way*, Berkeley: The University of California Press, 1972.

Schlesinger, Arthur M., *The Age of Roosevelt: The Coming of the New Deal*, Vol. I, Boston: Houghton-Mifflin Company, 1959.
Shepardson, W.H. and Scroggs, W.O., *The United States in World Affairs, 1937*, New York: Harper and Brothers, 1938.
Shilong, Ben-Ami, *Revolt in Japan: The Young Officers and the February 26 Incident*, Princeton: The University of Princeton Press, 1974.
Shunsake, Tsurumi, *An Intellectual History of Wartime Japan, 1931–1945*, London: KPI, 1986.
Silberman, Bernard S. and Harootunian, H.D., eds., *Japan in Crisis: Essays on Taisho Democracy*, Princeton: Princeton University Press, 1974.
Storry. Richard A., *The Double Patriots: A Study of Japanese Nationalism*, Boston: Houghton-Mifflin Company, 1957.
_____, *A History of Modern Japan*, London: Cassel and Company, Ltd., 1960.
_____, *Japan and the Decline of the West in Asia*, London: The MacMillan Press, Ltd., 1979.
Timperly, H.J., ed., *Japanese Terror in China*, New York: Modern Age Books, Inc., 1938.
_____, compiled and edited, *Japanese Terror in China*, Freeport: Books for University Press, 1969.
Toynbee, Arnold J., *Survey of International Affairs, 1937*, London: Royal Institute of International Affairs, 1938.
Tuchman, Barbara, *Stilwell and the American Experience in China, 1911–1945*, New York: The MacMillan Company, 1970.
Van de Ven, Hans, *China at War: Triumph and Tragedy in the Emergence of the New China*, Cambridge: Harvard University Press, 2018.
Ward, Robert E. and Rustow, Danward E., eds., *Political Modernization in Japan and Turkey*, Princeton: Princeton University Press, 1964.
Wilson, Dick, *When Tigers Meet: The Story of the Sino-Japanese War, 1937–1945*, New York: The Viking Press, 1982.
Wray, Harry and Conroy, Hilary, eds., *Japan Examined: Perspectives of Modern Japanese History*, Honolulu: The University of Hawaii Press, 1983.
Yanaga, Chitose, *Japan Since Perry*, New York: McGraw-Hill Book Company, Inc., 1949.

Index

3rd Division (Japan) 153, 161
4th Marine Regiment (U.S.) 125, 153, 288
5th Division (Japan) 28, 207, 209
6th Division (Japan) 175
6th Marine Regiment (U.S.) 158
8th Route Army (China) 145, 209, 214
10th Army (Japan) 283
11th Division (Japan) 153, 161
11th Reserve Division (Japan) 176
12th Air Group (Japan) 296
13th Air Group (Japan) 296
14th Army Group (China) 204
14th Division (Japan) 206
16th Division (Japan) 177
18th Division (China) 175
20th Army Group (China) 204
23rd Infantry (Japan) 19
29th Army (China) 26, 129, 137, 204
36th Division (China) 160
66th Army (China) 175
87th Division (China) 152, 175
89th Division (China) 152, 202
109th Division (China) 175

Abend, Hallett (*New York Times* Far Eastern correspondent) 123, 155–158, 163, 176, 285, 287, 302
Adachi, Kerzon (Japanese Minister of Home Affairs) 79
Aichi Prefecture 28
Aizawa, Saburo (Japanese lieutenant colonel) 93–94, 96–97
Aldrovandi-Marescotti (Italian representative) 278; *see also* Brussels Conference
Aleutian Islands 54, 103, 300
Amau Statement 87
Amerasia 235
Anglo-Japanese Alliance of 1902 31–32, 40, 44, 51–53, 69
Anhwei Province 44
Anti–Comintern pact 216; *see also* Anti-Comintern Pact of 1936
Anti–Comintern Pact of 1936, 69, 101–102, 104
anti-Semitism, 196

Aoki (Japanese vice chief of Manchurian Bureau) 213, 303
Araki, Sadao (Japanese general) 60, 73–75, 79, 82, 83, 84, 85, 93, 96, 97, 100, 101, 107, 186
Army Ministry (Japanese 24–26, 34, 84, 127–129, 149, 208
Asahi 111, 139, 245, 257, 310, 312
Asaka, prince 294
Atcheson, George (U.S. Embassy second secretary) 293, 298, 299
Atlanta Constitution 244
Attlee, Clement (British prime minister) 227
Aubert (Norwegian delegate to Brussels Conference) 272–273
Augusta 159–160
Australia 40, 41, 47, 53, 230, 252, 265
Austria 14, 24, 27, 49, 223, 289
Azabu Regiment 82

Baba, Aichi (Japanese finance minister/minister of home affairs) 111
Bai Chonxi (Chinese general) 149
Baikal, Lake 32, 50
banzai 155, 165, 166, 170, 173, 182, 185, 208, 295, 311
Barrett, David D. (U.S. major/military attaché) 126, 285
Barry, William (U.S. Congressman [D-NY]) 268
Beaumont, John (brigadier general, commander, U.S. Marines in Shanghai) 288
Belgium 53, 75, 252, 255–256, 257, 261, 264, 265, 267; *see also* Brussels Conference
Berthaut, Henri (captain, French infantry officer) 24–25
Biddle, James (commodore) 7
Billingham, Anthony (*New York Times* reporter) 137–138, 163
Bingham, Robert (U.S. ambassador to Great Britain) 265
Black Currant Society 100
Black Dragon Society 73, 133
Black Ocean 29
Blomberg, von (general, German minister of defense) 101, 217
Blood Brotherhood League *see Ketsumeidan*

343

344 Index

Bohlen, Charles (U.S. secretary) 258; *see also* Brussels Conference
Bolivia 265, 277
Bolshevik/Bolshevism 49–51, 219, 246, 317; *see also* Bolshevik Revolution
Bolshevik Revolution 46, 48, 74
Borah, William (U.S. senator [R-ID]) 53, 224, 225, 231, 243
Boston Herald 244
Boxer Protocol 141, 142
Boxer Rebellion 31, 125
Britain 8, 10, 11, 14, 30, 31–32, 34, 40, 41, 43–45, 47, 48–54, 64, 69, 72, 82, 89, 90, 91, 93, 95, 99, 102–104, 107, 108, 113, 125, 137, 141, 142, 143, 144, 153, 156, 164, 166, 167, 171, 172, 173, 174, 179, 188, 189, 193, 195, 196, 214, 215, 216, 223, 226–228, 236–237, 241, 242, 246, 247, 249, 251, 252, 254–258, 260–269, 271–272, 274, 276–278, 280, 287, 288, 297, 299, 301, 303, 304, 307, 309
Britannia *see* Britain
Brussels Conference 4, 173, 216, 219, 247, 250–281, 288
Buell, Henry (president of Foreign Policy Association) 243
Buenos Aires Conference 231, 237
Bullitt, William (U.S. ambassador to France) 142–143, 260–261, 269
Bund 153, 172, 174
Bush, Lewis 309
bushido 5, 33, 161, 321
Butler, Smedley (U.S. Marine general) 125
Byas, Hugh (*New York Times* reporter) 182–183, 196–197, 211, 248–249

Cadogan, Alexander (British undersecretary of state) 303
Caldwell (U.S. consul general) 144
California 7, 184, 189, 221, 235, 262
Canada 53, 189, 239, 244, 253, 265, 272
Canton 44, 45, 47, 153, 282, 319
Capper, Arthur (U.S. senator [R-KS]) 231
Chahar Province 113–115, 200–202, 207, 213; *see also* Hopei-Chahar Political Council
Chamberlain, Neville (British prime minister) 227, 237, 280
Chang Hsueh-liang 66, 77, 78, 117
Chang Tso-lin 65–66, 198
Changchun 35, 76
Changsha 64, 153, 284, 313
Chapei 80, 153, 158, 165, 169, 172–173, 174
Chaplin, Charlie , 82
Chautemps, Camille (French premier) 247–248, 250, 260, 269
Chengtu 104, 120
Chennault, Claire (U.S. colonel) 159
Cherry Blossom Society 72–73, 75–76
Chiang Kai-shek 2–4, *64*, 64–66, 77–78, 87, 112–121, 123, 128, 130–135, 137, 139, 143–145, 149–150, 152, 154–156, 159, 161, 163, 164–168, 172–180, 199, 204, 207–210, 213, 215–220, 248, 263, 271, 280–282, 284, 287–292, 295, 312–317, 321
Chicago 163, 220, 227, 237–240, 242–244, 247, 250, 253–254, 260, 268, 274, 279, 281; *see also* "quarantine" speech
Chicago Tribune 244
Chin Te-chun (deputy commander, Chinese 29th Army) 129
Chinda (viscount/count) 47
Chinese Central News Agency 179
Chinshanwei 175
Choshu (clan) 9–13, 15–16, 31, 39, 43, 55, 60–61, 63, 74
Chu Teh 145
Chungking 153, 159, 178–179, 276, 284, 292
Chungshan Gate 296, 311
Clark, Champ (U.S. senator [D-MO]) 224
Clemenceau, Georges 48
Cleveland Plain Dealer 243
comfort bags 190–191, 193
Communism/Communist(s) 49, 57, 63, 74, 78, 80, 81, 87, 102, 113–114, 116–119, 124, 131, 145, 146, 149, 156, 174, 179, 180, 208–209, 214, 258, 315, 320
Connally, Tom (U.S. senator [D-TX]) 231
Control Faction 93, 100–101; *see also* Toseiha
Coolidge, Calvin (U.S. president) 222
Cossacks 50
Craigie, Sir Robert (British ambassador to Japan) 107, 164, 298
Czechs, Czechoslovaks 49, 50

Dagongbao 156
Daily Telegraph & Morning Post 268
daimyo 12, 16
Dan, Takum (Japanese baron) 83
Davis, Norman (U.S. diplomat) 230, 237–240, 254–255, 258–273, 275–280
Delbos, Yvon (French foreign minister) 142–143, 252, 264, 266–267, 269, 271–273, 277, 280
Denmark 265
Depression *see* Great Depression
Des Moines Register 243
Detroit 89, 140
Detroit Free Press 268
Dieckhoff (German ambassador) 246–247
Diet (Japanese legislature) 38, 39, 51, 55–57, 62–63, 69, 70, 75, 84–85, 87, 100, 105–107, 109, 130, 139, 191, 318–319
Diplomatische Korrespondenz 246
Dirksen, Herbert von (German ambassador) 218–219, 288, 291–292, 317
Disney, Walt 174
Doihara, Kenji (Japanese general) 73, 114–117, 206, 207
Dunn, James (U.S. State Department staff member) 238
Durdin, Tillman *New York Times* correspondent) 284
Dutch *see* Netherlands

Index

East Hopei Anti-Communist Autonomous Council *see* Hopei
East Hopei Autonomous Government *see* Hopei
Echo de Paris 268
Ecuador 252
Eden, Anthony (British foreign secretary) 179, 247, 250, 255, 258, 260, 262–267, 269, 271–273, 276, 280, 303
Eddy, Nelson 94
Edo 5, 8, 9, 10, 12, 14; *see also* Tokyo
Eichelberger, Clark (U.S. State Department assistant) 237
England *see* Britain
Ensminger, Charles (U.S. seaman) 299
Ethiopia 223, 227, 234, 235, 254, 271

Falkenhausen, Alexander von (German military advisor) 149–150, 217–219, 305
Farley, James 223
Feng Yuxiang (Chinese Northwest Army general) 149
Finland 168
"fireside chat" 244–245, 247; *see also* Roosevelt, Franklin D.
Fish, Hamilton (U.S. Congressman [R-NY]) 235, 268
Fitch, George (YMCA secretary in Nanking) 304, 307–308
Five Ministers Conference 84, 90–91, 103–105
Fleet Faction 69, 102
"Flying Tigers," 159
Foochow 153
Ford 75
Foreign Affairs 222
Formosa 21, 22, 29
Four Ministers Conference 146
Four Power Pacific Pact 51, 53
Fourteen Points 48; *see also* Wilson, Woodrow
France/French 8, 10, 14–16, 23–28, 30, 31, 33, 40, 45, 47, 48, 49, 50, 51, 54, 60, 64, 75, 108, 125, 142–143, 153, 166, 176, 177, 193, 223, 227, 247, 250, 251, 252, 255, 260, 261, 264, 265, 266, 267, 268, 269, 271, 274, 276, 277, 280
French Concession 153, 156, 158, 161–163, 166, 174, 176, 179, 180, 196
Fukuzawa, Yukichi 42
Fushimi, Hiroyasu (prince/Japanese admiral/chief of naval general staff) 69–70, 91–92, 314

Garner, John Nance (U.S. vice president) 232
Gauss (U.S. consul general) 167, 298
General Motors 75
Genro (elder statesmen) 40, 43–44, 46, 47, 51, 57, 58, 69, 70, 79, 83, 87, 94, 100, 102, 103, 106, 108–110, 133, 215, 314, 319; *see also* Saionji
Genyosha see Black Currant Society
George V (king) 52
Germany 13, 15, 19, 23–28, 30–31, 33, 40–43, 45, 47–49, 69, 75, 81, 89, 90, 101–103, 119, 125, 128, 134, 149, 152, 155, 157, 159, 177, 181, 206, 211, 215–219, 223, 232, 235, 237–238, 246–248, 252, 254–256, 261–263, 288, 291, 296, 305, 315, 316–317
Gibson (U.S. ambassador to Belgium) 261
Gifu Prefecture 28
Ginza 192
Goette, John 125
"Good Neighbor" policy 229, 242
Gordon, George (U.S. minister to the Hague) 267
Goshimpei 16
Goto, Fumio (Japanese prime minister) 96
Great Britain *see* Britain
Great Depression 61, 66, 227
Great Wall of China 29, 86, 100, 113, 126, 130, 200–202, 209, 210
Green Society 180
Grew, Joseph (U.S. ambassador to Japan) 94, **95**, 98–99, 111–112, 170–171, 215, 230, 232–234, 245–246, 257–258, 264–265, 273–274, 280, 301, 303–304
Grey, Sir Edward (British Foreign Secretary) 43–44, 48
Grutschreiber, Maj. baron 28
Guadalcanal 150, 301
Guam 54
Guangxi Clique 149
Gunka (Japanese martial songs) 192

Hainan 104, 272
Hamada, Kunimatsu 84, 106
Hamaguchi, Yuko (Japanese prime minister) 59, 66, 67–69, 71, 76
Hamilton, Maxwell (assistant chief, U.S. State Department Division of Foreign Affairs) 141–142
Hampshire 34
Hangchow 130, 175–176, 208
Hankow 3, 104, 125, 128, 153, 204–206, 209, 211, 217, 282, 284, 293, 294, 299, 313, 319; *see also* Peking-Hankow Railway
Hara, Takashi (Japanese general/prime minister) 46, 51, 71
hara-kiri 23, 37, 63, 83, 84, 106
Harada (Japanese baron) 103, 124, 132–133, 169, 198, 213, 214, 215, 289–290, 317, 319
Harding, Warren (U.S. president) 52
Harris, Morris (U.S. correspondent, Associated Press) 163–164
Harris, Townsend 9–10
Harrison, Leland (U.S. minister to Switzerland) 251–253
Haruna 151
Harunomiya, Yoshihito 37–38; *see also* Taisho
Hasegawa (Japanese admiral) 164, 298–302
Hashimoto, Gun (Japanese general) 128–129
Hashimoto, Kingoro (Japanese lieutenant colonel/colonel) 72, 73, 83, 297–298, 301–303, 311

Index

Hata, Ikuhito (Japanese general) 73, 208
Hatoyama, Ichiro (Japanese minister of education) 87
Hawaii 35, 36, 54, 103, 221
Hayashi, Senjuro (Japanese general/prime minister) 78, 84, 94, 106–107, 110, 121
Hearst newspapers/press 143, 166, 187, 242, 244, 258, 260, 262
heimen 13
Henry, Jules (French chargé d'affaires) 269
Higuchi, Kiichiro 72
Hilton, James (U.S. author) 238
Hiranuma, Kiichiro (Japanese baron) 69, 100, 315
Hirohito (Japanese emperor) 38, *39*, 52, 59, 79, 87, 91–92, 96, 109, 111, 146, 155, 171, 175, 178, 191, 196–198, 214, 314, 316, 317
Hiroshima 28
Hirota, Koki (Japanese prime minister/foreign minister) 85, *86*, 87, 98–100, 102, 103, 105–106, 109, 111, 113–115, 128, 132–133, 137, 147, 164, 191, 215, 218–219, 257, 265, 273–274, 284, 288, 290–292, 301, 303–304, 313–314, 316–317
Hitler, Adolf 69, 159, 165, 168, 217, 235, 252, 264
Hizen (clan) 12
Holland *see* Netherlands
Homma (Japanese general) 216
Hong Kong 7, 320
Hongkew 153, 157–158, 172, 180
Honjo, Shigeru (Japanese general) 86, 96
Hopei Province 113, 115–116, 117, 120, 121, 126–127, 130, 138, 146, 205–207, 209–211, 214, 217; *see also* Hopei-Chahar Political Council
Hopei-Chahar Political Council 116, 126–127, 129, 136, 140, 146, 213
Horigane (Japanese officer) 185
Horinouchi, Kensuke (Japanese vice minister of Foreign Affairs) 102
Hornbeck, Dr. J. Stanley (chief of U.S. State Department Division of Foreign Affairs) 141–142, 144, 229–230, 232–234, 242, 252, 258, 261–262, 269, 276, 280
Hotel de Pekin 137
House of Commons, British 179, 262
Hughes, Charles Evans (U.S. secretary of state) 53–54, 261
Hughes, J.J., Commander 298; *see also* Panay
Hughes, William M. (Australian prime minister) 47
Hull, Cordell (U.S. secretary of state) 142, 144, 159, 166, 229–234, 236–239, 242–243, 245, 251–255, 258–259, 261, 263–264, 267, 270–277, 280, 301, 303, 304
Hulsebus, Edgar (U.S. seaman) 299
Hyde Park 237–238, 240, 243, 248, 259; *see also* Roosevelt, Franklin D.
Hyuga 151

Ichang 153
Ichiang Gate 304

Ickes, Harold (U.S. secretary of the interior) 231–232, 236–238, 243
Iesada (shogun) 8
Ieyoshi (shogun) 8
Ijuin (baron) 47
Imai, Takeo (Japanese major) 124
Imamura, Hitoshi (Japanese lieutenant colonel) 78
Imperial Army 5, 14, 22, 67, 183, 184, 282
Imperial Guard 25, 26, 82, 96
Imperial Japanese Army 183
Imperial Palace 18, 95, 173, 207, 290, 295, 315
Imperial Rescript 18, 20, 37, 38, 80, 196
Imperial Way Group 73, 75, 87, 94, 100–101, 109
India 52, 153, 265, 321
Indo-China 260–261, 266, 269, 271, 274
Ing, Mr. 142
Inoue (Japanese admiral) 89, 118
Inoue, Junnosuke (Japanese finance minister) 62, 66, 78, 83
Inoue, Nissho 82
International Settlement 153, 155–156, 158, 160, 162–166, 169, 172, 174, 176, 179–180, 287
Inukai, Tsuyoshi (Japanese prime minister) 79–84
Ise 151
Ishii (Japanese viscount) 45, 48
Ishii Regiment *see* 3rd Division
Ishiwara, Kanji (Japanese colonel/general/ operations division chief) 73, 77, 94, 96, 105, 112, 118–122, 123–124, 127–129, 131–132, 135–136, 146, 201, 207–208, 216, 321
Ishiwara, Koichiro 123
Isobe, Asaichi 94–95, 97
Isolationism: American 143, 220, 222–224, 226, 233, 237, 240, 260, 264, 268; Japanese 5–6
Itagaki, Seishiro (Japanese Army chief of staff) 77–78, 80, 113, 201–202, 207
Itagaki, Taisuke 16, 73
Itagaki Division 214
Italy 45, 47, 48, 54, 81, 125, 153, 159, 181, 223, 227, 232, 234, 235, 237, 238, 240, 251, 254, 263, 264, 265, 266, 273, 277, 278, 299
Ito (prince) 31–32
Ito, Miyoji 69
Itsuki (Japanese battalion commander) 2
Iwakura, Tomoni 12
Iwasaki (Japanese baron) 62
Iyemochi (shogun) 10
Izumo 130, 151–152, 157, 299

Japan Advertiser 286
Japan Times and Mail 138, 169, 185–189, 191–194, 202, 213, 282, 287, 295
Japan Weekly Chronicle 185, 191–192, 196, 282–283, 310
Jehol Province 86–87, 99, 202
Johnson, Hiram (U.S. senator [R-CA]) 224, 226, 231, 260

Index 347

Johnson, Nelson T. (U.S. ambassador to China) 125, 141, 143, 157, 159, 166–167, 233, 293, 320–321
Jones, Helen 140
Jukong Road 169
Junyo 300–301

Kagoshima 10, 17, 22–23
Kalgan 200–202, 204, 209
kamikaze 185
Kanagawa, Treaty of 8
Kanin (Japanese prince/chief of general staff) 70, 127, 171, 316, 317
Kanko Maru 9
Kansu Province 204
Kao Tsung-wu (head of Chinese Foreign Ministry Asiatic Department) 146–147
Kasahara (Japanese captain) 185
Kato, Kanji (Japanese vice admiral; later admiral) 54, 68, 69–70, 89–93
Kato, Takaaki (Japanese baron) 40, 42–44, 48
Kato, Tomosaburo (Japanese admiral baron) 54, 68
Katsuki (Japanese general) 136–137
Katsura, Taro (Japanese general) 26, 31, 38–39
Kawabe, Torashiro (Japanese general/war guidance chief) 127–128
Kawagoe, Shigeru (Japanese ambassador to China) 146–147, 163
Kawakami (Japanese general) 26
Kawamoto (Japanese colonel) 66
Kawamoto, Suemori (Japanese lieutenant) 77
Kawashima (Japanese general) 96
Kazami, Akira (Japanese cabinet secretary) 132, 151, 291
kazoku 13
Kazuki, Kiyoshi (Japanese lieutenant general) 205
Keiki (shogun) 11, 13
Kellogg-Briand Pact of 1928 62, 233, 239, 246, 250, 253, 254; *see also* Pact of Paris of 1928
Kempei (Japanese military police) 73
Kempei-tai (Japanese secret police) 132, 177
Kenseito Party 31
Kerensky, Alexander 49
Ketsumeidan (Blood Brotherhood League) 82–83
Khalkin Gol (battle) 19
Khan, Genghis 3
Kiangnan 153
Kiangsu 130, 313
Kiangwan 153, 165, 172, 174
Kiaochow 30, 40, 54; *see also* Tsinan
Kido (Japanese marquis, secretary to Lord Keeper of the Privy Seal) 198, 289–290
Kishu (clan) 15
Kita, Ikki 37, 75, 97
Kita, Seiichi (Japanese major general) 212
Kiukang 153
Knatchbull-Hugessen, Sir Hughe (British ambassador) 164

Knutson (U.S. congressman) 269
Kobayashi (Japanese admiral) 91
Kobe 11, 46, 82, 132, 170, 171, 183, 185
Kodama (Japanese general) 26, 33–34
Kodo 74, 75, 100, 101; *see also* Imperial Way
Kodogikai see Kodo
Kodoha see Imperial Way; *Kodo*
Kokuhonsha (Country Foundation Association) 82, 100
Kokumin 286
Kolchak (admiral) 50
Komei (emperor) 11
Komoto, Daisaku 73
Konoe, Atsumaro 107; *see also* Konoe, Fumimaro
Konoe, Fumimaro (prince (Japanese prime minister) 100–101, *101*, 105, 107–111, 123, 130–134, 137, 145–146, 151–152, 154–155, 171, 191, 198, 214, 216, 284, 288–291, 296, 313–319
Konoe, Hidemaro (Japanese viscount) 187–188
Koo, Dr. Wellington (Chinese ambassador to France) 47, 142, 252, 260, 261, 266, 272, 276, 278–279
Köppen, Sgt. Karl 15
Korea 1, 21, 22, 29–34, 35, 42, 45, 67, 76, 78, 80, 107, 125, 129, 212, 221
Koyama, Kango 154
Kung, Dr. H.H. (Chinese Minister of Finance) 141, 235–236
Kuomintang 44, 47, 77, 115, 116, 118, 119, 120, 140, 144, 163, 179, 208, 209, 282, 319
Kure 150–151
Kuroki (Japanese general) 33, 34
Kurume Engineering Corps 185
Kurusu, Saburo (Japanese ambassador to Brussels) 274
Kusaka, Dr. (Central Laboratory of South Manchurian Railway Company) 192
Kwan 205
Kwangha Gate 295
Kwangteh 285
Kwantung Army 65–66, 77–79, 81, 83, 86–87, 96, 101, 104–105, 113–114, 118, 120, 122, 124, 126, 127, 129, 135, 142, 146, 201–202, 207, 210, 212–213, 216
Kyoto 4, 10, 12, 13
Kyoto Imperial University 87, 108
Kyushu, 10, 22

Labor Party, British 227
Ladybird 297, 301–302
LaFollette, Robert M., Jr. (U.S. senator [Pro-WI]) 225, 231
Langfang 136
Lansing, Robert (U.S. Secretary of State) 48, 49
Lansing-Ishii Agreement 45
Lathrop, Carol 141
League of Nations 4, 47, 48, 52, 78, 90, 142, 143, 222, 246, 248, 250–255, 257–258, 260, 262, 265, 268, 273–274, 278

348   Index

Leahy (U.S. admiral) 232
"Lend-Lease" policy 242
Lenin, Vladimir 49, 50
Li Hung-chang (viceroy) 29
Liaison Conference (Japanese Inner Cabinet and Supreme Command) 289–291, 314, 317
Liaotung Peninsula 29–30, 32, 35
Lienyunkiang 204
Lin Piao 214
Lindley, Ernest (U.S. journalist) 241–242, 248
Litvinov, Maxim (Soviet foreign minister) 261, 265, 269, 272, 276
Liuho 160, 165
Lloyd George, David (British prime minister) 48, 52, 53
London 21, 44, 48, 52–54, 56, 69, 75, 91–93, 102, 142–143, 164, 220, 247, 254–256, 258, 262, 264, 268, 276, 287, 303; *see also* Britain
London Naval Conference 21, 54, 68, 70, 89–90
London Naval Treaty of 1930 88, 90
Los Angeles Times 243, 260, 279
Lost Horizon 238–239; *see also* Hilton, James
Lotien 165
Ludendorff, Erich 27
Lukouchiao 3, 125, 129, 131
Lunghai Railway 130, 136, 204
Lushan 131
Lusitania 224, 301
Lytton Commission 81

MacDonald, Jeanette 94
MacDonald, Malcolm (British Secretary of State for Colonies) 269, 276–277
Machang 205
Magee, the Rev. John 293
Mainichi 46
Makino, Nobuaki (baron/viscount) 47, 76, 94
Manchester Guardian 247, 268
Manchukuo 79, 81, 98, 101, 103–104, 112–115, 118, 121, 127, 131, 135, 146, 202, 216, 219, 292, 315–316
Manchuria 2, 29–32, 43, 44, 65–66, 73, 75–81, 87, 90, 99, 100, 103, 107, 112, 113, 116, 117, 120, 126, 131, 135, 194–195, 206, 212, 217, 221, 246, 263
Manchurian Incident 90, 223; *see also* Manchuria
Mao Tse-tung 113, 117, 135, 179, 208–209, 214
Marco Polo Bridge 3, 122, 123–147
Marshall Islands 41, 47
Marston, John (U.S. Marine colonel) 125
Marx, Karl 50, 59, 63, 87
Marxism *see* Marx, Karl
Matsudaira (Japanese ambassador/Imperial household minister) 93, 215
Matsui, Iwane 47, 73, 129, 153–155, 164, 169, 171, 174, 177, 215, 283–284, 287–288, 292, 294–295, 301–302, 304, 310–311
Matsukata, Shiburo 3
Matsuo (Japanese colonel) 95

Matsuoka, Yosuke 81, 148, 212, 265
Mazaki, Jinsaburo 73–75, 93–94, 96–97, 124
McReynolds, Samuel (U.S. congressman [D-TN]) 269
Meckel, Klemens Jacob (German major) 23–28, 31, 33–34, 60, 134
Meian 297–298
Meiji (emperor) 1, 5, 11–13, 19, 21, 23, 25, 30, 37–38, 41, 43
Meiping 297–298, 304
Meisian 297–298
Mexico 265, 277
Mikasa 34–35, 69, 150
Ming dynasty 3, 292
Minseito (Democratic Party) 55, 56, 59, 62, 63, 66, 69, 83, 85, 107, 318
Mitchell, "Billy" (U.S. general) 88
Mitsubishi 46, 59, 62–63, 157, 312
Mitsui 46, 55, 59, 62, 67, 83
Miyazaki, Ryusuke 132
Moffat, J. Pierrepont (head of U.S. State Department of Western European Affairs) 230, 232–234, 242, 245, 252–255, 258–259, 262, 264–267, 269, 271–273, 276–277, 280
Mohl, Ottmar von 25
Moltke, Helmuth von (German chief of staff) 24
Mongolia 29, 43, 73, 86, 101, 112, 114, 120, 145, 146, 200, 202, 210, 216, 219, 292, 315
Moore, R. Walton 230, 232
Morgenthau, Henry (U.S. Secretary of the Treasury) 228, 230–231, 235, 243
Mori, Kaku (Japanese cabinet secretary) 79, 80
mori-shio (Japanese salt ceremony) 191
Morishima, Morito (Japanese diplomat) 78
Morison, Samuel E. (U.S. naval historian) 302
Movietone News, 187
Mukai, Toshiaki (Japanese lieutenant) *286*, 286
Mukden 2, 21, 33, 65, 76–78, 81, 87, 94, 114, 118, 123, 131, 194, 201
Mundelein (cardinal, archbishop of Chicago) 240
Murakami, Hyoe 82, 97
Muranaka, Koji 94–95, 97
Musashi 92–93
Mussolini, Benito 159, 223, 235, 248–249
Muto, Akiro (Japanese colonel) 122, 127–128
Mutsu, Munemitsu (Japanese foreign minister) 30
Mutsuhito (prince) 11, 37; *see also* Meiji (emperor)

Nagata, Tetuzan 73, 93
Nagato 34–35
Nakajima, Kesago (Japanese lieutenant general) 177, 294, 309–310
Nankai University 138
Nanking 3, 4, 64, 80, 105, 112, 114–116, 119–121, 124, 125, 127, 128, 130–134, 136–138, 140–143,

Index 349

145–147, 149, 152–153, 155, 157, 159, 161, 163, 164, 166–168, 174, 177–179, 181–182, 190, 196, 199, 205, 207, 216, 218–220, 276, 281, 282–312, 318, 319; *see also* Rape of Nanking
Nankow 200–203, 209–210
Nantao 156, 158
Nanyuan 137
Napoleon I 131, 203
Napoleon III 14–16
Nashimoto, Yukei 133–134
Nationalists, Chinese 64–66, 78, 87, 112–113, 115, 116, 117, 119–121, 127, 134, 135, 139, 141, 145, 146, 149, 151, 159, 178–179, 199, 209, 217, 260, 284, 286, 289, 290–291, 296, 308, 313–318, 320
Nemoto (Japanese lieutenant colonel) 73
Netherlands 6, 7, 8, 9, 11, 13, 40, 53, 102, 104, 227, 252, 255, 265, 277, 278
Neutrality Act of 1936 224, 233–236, 241
Neutrality Law of 1937 225–227, 259, 269–271
New Deal 189, 222, 225, 237, 242; *see also* Roosevelt, Franklin D.
New Hampshire 35
New York Times 123, 137, 155, 158, 160, 162, 163, 166–168, 171–173, 176, 182, 205, 210, 233, 240, 244, 245, 248, 268, 279, 284, 285, 320
New Zealand 41, 47, 221, 252, 265
Nichi Nichi 245, 312
Nicholas II (Russian czar) 30, 32, 49
Nimitz 35
Nimitz, Chester (U.S. admiral) 35, 185
Nine Power Treaty 4, 55, 143, 144, 173, 189, 216, 220, 228, 233, 241, 245, 247, 248, 249, 250–255, 257, 261, 265, 270, 271, 273, 275, 278, 279, 281, 318
Nishio, Toshizo (Japanese lieutenant general) 205
Nitsugu, Nishida (Japanese lieutenant) 97
Noda, Tsuyoshi (Japanese lieutenant) **286**, 286
Nogi, Maresuki 34, 37
Nomura (Japanese admiral) 215
North China Daily News 158
Norway/Norwegian 265, 272, 277
Nye, Gerald (U.S. senator [R-ND]) 223–225

Ocean-Ocean Society 73
Okada, Keisuke (Japanese admiral/prime minister) 70, 88, 91–92, 94–95
Okamoto, Kiyotami (Japanese colonel, Military Administration Section) 123–124
Okawa, Shumei 75
Okayama Prefecture 17
Okinawa , 7, 93, 294, 301
Okubo, Toshimishi 12
Okumiya, Masatake (Japanese lieutenant) 296–297, 299–300, 302
Okumo (Japanese prime minister) 45
Omura, Masujiro 13–16
One Evening Society 73
"Open Door" policy 45, 55, 141, 189, 222

Opium War 152–153
Osaka 17, 46, 192
Osaka Imperial University 191
Osaka *Mainichi* 46
Oshima, Hitoshi (Japanese general) 101, 218
Osumi, Mineo 90, 91
Otaka, Miota (member, Japanese Young Women's Association) 182
Ott, Eugen (general/German attaché) 218–219
Oyama, Iaawo (Japanese general) 24

Pact of Paris of 1928 80, 259, 318; *see also* Kellogg-Briand Pact
Panama Canal 92
Panay **293**, 293, 297–304
Pantheon Theater 169
Paoshan 153
Paoting 130, 139, 144, 146, 204–207, 209–211
Paotow 200
Paris Peace Conference 108
Patriotic Women's Society (Japan) 190
Paxton, J. Hall (second secretary to American legation in Nanking) 299
Peace Preservation Corps 129, 138, 320
Peace Preservation Law 57, 63
Peake, Charles (British press officer) 276
Pearl Harbor 90, 92, 151
Peiping 130, 138; *see also* Peking
Peiping Chronicle 124
Peking 3, 43–45, 47, 64–65, 79, 86, 87, 115, 116, 117, 122, 123–129, 131–132, 133, 136–142, 144, 145–146, 153, 200, 201, 203–207, 209, 210, 211–213, 295, 313, 318, 320
Peking-Hankow Railway 125, 128, 204–206, 209, 211
Pell, Robert (U.S. press officer) 258, 262; *see also* Brussels Conference
Pembroke 11
Pepper, Claude (U.S senator [D-FL]) 231
Perkins, Frances (U.S. secretary of labor) 228–229
Perry, Matthew (U.S. commodore) 7–8, 9
Perry, Oliver Hazard 9
Pershing, John J. (U.S. general), 99
Philadelphia Record 233, 260
Philippine Islands 54, 103, 156, 221, 222, 269
Phillips, William (U.S. ambassador to Italy) 230, 240
Phipps, Sir Eric (British ambassador to France) 143
Pittman, Key (U.S. senator, chairman, Foreign Relations Committee [D-NV]) 159, 231, 234
Poland 252
Polo, Marco 3
Port Arthur 29–35, 41, 43, 107
Portugal 6, 53, 265
Potemkin, Vladimir (Soviet official) 276, 277
President Hoover 166–167
Presseisen, Ernst 33
Price, Charles (colonel, commander, U.S. Marine 4th regiment) 288

350 Index

Privy Seal, Lord Keeper (Japanese imperial official) 58, 76, 88, 94, 106, 198, 214–215
Prussia 16, 23, 25–27, 33, 74, 149, 235, 289
Pu Yi, Henry (Manchukuo emperor) 79, 81, 140

"quarantine" speech 221, 227, 236–242, 244–248, 259, 266, 279; see also Chicago; Roosevelt, Franklin D.

Rape of Nanking 4, 138, 155, 177, 282–311; see also Nanking
Red Cross 140, 190, 293
Ribbentrop, Joachim von 101–102
Richardson Affair 10–11
Rising Sun flag 172–173, 177, 190, 200, 205, 208, 283
Robertson, Douglas (*New York Times* reporter) 205
ronin 6, 13, 200
Roosevelt, Franklin D. (U.S. president) 4, 141, 158, *160*, 166, 215, 220, 221–248, 250, 253–255, 258–260, 263, 266, 267, 268–270, 274, 279, 281, 301, 303, 313; see also New Deal
Roosevelt, Theodore (U.S. president) 35, 275, 279
Rosenman, Samuel, (U.S. presidential speechwriter) 238
Russia 6, 8, 15, 16, 26, 28, 30–35, 37, 40, 46, 49–50, 51, 60, 64, 65, 73, 74, 75, 88, 100, 101, 102, 118, 119, 122, 125, 135–136, 150, 153, 167, 168, 171, 174, 182, 206, 218, 223, 252, 256, 261, 266, 269, 280, 313
Russo-Japanese War 34, 65, 107, 148, 171, 192, 275

Saigo, Takamori 11, 16, 22–23
Saigo, Tsugimichi 15–16
St. Louis Globe-Democrat 244
Saionji, Kinmochi (prince) 38, *40*, 47, 58, 59, 69, 70, 76, 79, 83, 87–88, 94, 100, 102, 106–109, 111, 133, 134, 215, 289, 314, 319; see also Genro
Saito, Makato (Japanese admiral viscount/Lord Keeper of the Privy Seal) 81, 84, 85, 87, 88, 94
Sakai Brigade 126
Sakata, Yoshiro 72
Sakhalin 35, 51
Sakurakai see Cherry Blossom Society
samurai 5–6, 9–10, 12–14, 21–22, 29, 37, 38, 60, 72, 192, 321
San Francisco Chronicle 243–244
Sandi, Sandro (Italian journalist) 299
Satsuma (clan) 9–12, 13, 16, 21, 39
Satsuma Prefecture 22
Satsuma Rebellion 21, 23, 27
Scott, Winthrop R. (U.S. consul [Kobe]) 170–171, 183
Seeckt, Hans von (Reichswehr general) 27, 216–217

Seiyukai (Party of Friends of Democratic Government) 31, 39, 46, 55, 59, 62, 63, 76, 79, 84, 85, 106, 107, 291, 318
Shang Chen (Chinese general) 204
Shanghai 7, 64, 80, 104, 123, 129, 133, 139, 146–147, 148–154, 156–159, 161–180, 182, 185, 187, 189, 196, 199, 204, 205, 208, 216–220, 232, 263, 280–281, 282–283, 285, 287–288, 292, 294–296, 298, 299, 301, 304, 306, 310, 313
Shanhaikwan Pass 87
Shansi province 113, 149, 201, 204–205, 207 209–213
Shantung 29, 40, 43, 45, 47–48, 54, 64, 66, 113, 115, 145, 207, 214
Shensi province 113, 117, 145, 214
Shi Hwang-ti (Chinese emperor) 200
Shidehara, Kijuro (baron, Japanese foreign minister) 54, 55, 59, 61–63, 66, 76, 78–81
Shigemitsu, Mamoru (Japanese ambassador to China) 80, 98, *99*, 105, 110, 126
Shihkiachuang 204, 207, 209–212
Shimada (Japanese admiral/vice chief of Navy general staff) 146
Shimizu (Japanese captain) 1–2, 129
Shimomura, Sadamu (Japanese major general/chief of operations division) 208, 284
Shimonoseki 11, 40
Shimura (Japanese private) 1–3, 126
Shipstead, Henrik (U.S. senator [farm-labor-MN]) 231
Shiroyama 23
shizoku see samurai
Shizouka Prefecture 17
Shogun 5–11, 13–14
Showa ("enlightened peace") 59, 96, 97, 126, 198; *see also* Hirohito
Shunteh 211
Sian Incident 117, 120
Siberia 19, 46, 48–50, 61, 75, 100, 101, 112, 136
Sincere (department store) 163
Singapore 54, 103
Siyuan 137
Skeda, Ikuo (Japanese private) 184–185
Soejima, Taneomi 1
Soochow 177, 283, 286, 292
Soochow Creek 156, 158, 162, 174, 176
Soong, Meiling 64
Soong, T.V. 64, 163
South Africa 265
Soviet Union 50, 64, 74, 77, 81, 93, 99, 100–104, 112, 117–119, 122, 124, 131, 135, 136, 152, 168, 174, 207, 216, 217, 254, 256, 258, 261, 265, 266, 267, 269, 276, 289, 316, 317; *see also* Russia
Spaak, Paul Henri (Belgian foreign minister) 261, 264, 265
Spain 6, 223
Staff College (Japanese Army) 19, 24, 25, 28, 34
Stalingrad 155
Standard Oil 297–299, 304

Index   351

State Department, U.S. 141, 143, 225, 227–231, 233–234, 237–238, 244, 246–248, 254, 256–260, 262, 268, 272, 275, 279, 281
Sterrett, Frank W. (Episcopal bishop) 238–239
Stilwell, Joseph (U.S. colonel) 125–126, 130–131, 199–200, 202–204, 312
Stimson, Henry (U.S. secretary of state) 80, 230, 235
Suchow 130
Suetsugu, Nobumasa (Japanese admiral) 68–70, 88–89, 91–93, 290–291, 315
Sugamo Prison 98, 110, 115, 155, 201
Sugiyama, Hajime (Japanese field marshal/minister of war) 60, *61*, 110, 111, 122, 128, 129, 132, 133, 152, 153, 173, 191, 214, 291, 295, 317
Suiyuan Province 113, 120, 122, 124, 137, 146, 200, 210
Suma, Mr. (Japanese counselor in Washington) 274–275
Sumitomo 46, 62
Sun Yat-sen 2, 44, 63, 64, 292, 311
Sung Che-yuan (Chinese general) 115–116, 126, 129, 136–137, 139
Suzuki, Kantaro (Japanese grand chamberlain baron) 94
Suzuki Brigade 126
Sweden 75, 252, 265, 273
Szechuan Province 104

Tachang 172, 174
Tada, Hayao (Japanese general/vice chief of general staff) 116, 178, 207, 283–284, 289–291, 314, 316–318, 321
Tadashi (Japanese major) 78
Tai, Lake, 285
Taisho, emperor 37–38, 41, 59; *see also* Harunomiya
Taiwan 29, 67, 175; *see also* Formosa
Taiyuan 204, 205, 207, 209, 211–213, 304
Takahashi, Korekiyo (Japanese finance minister) 59, 85, 94
Takahashi, Sankichi (Japanese admiral/vice chief of Navy staff) 69
Takahashi, Tan (Japanese general staff lieutenant) 187
Takarabe (Japanese admiral/Navy minister) 66, 68
Takigawa, Yukitori (Kyoto Imperial University law professor) 87
Taku, Mikami (Japanese lieutenant) 82
Tanaka, Giichi (Japanese prime minister) 57, 63–66, 76
Tanaka, Shinichi (Japanese colonel) 127, 128
Tanaka, Sueo (Japanese Embassy attaché) 308
Tang Shing Chih (Chinese general) 284, 294
Tangku 29, 144
Tangku Truce Agreement 87, 99, 113–114
Tatekawa, Yoshitsugu (Japanese major general) 73
Tatung 212, 213

Teh (prince) 216, 292
Terauchi, Hisaichi (Japanese Army general) 84–85, 105–106, 205–207, 210, 215
Terauchi, Juichi (Japanese Minister of War) 97
Terauchi, Masatake (Japanese Minister of War) 44, 46, 51, 100, 106
Third Fleet, Japanese 104, 300, 302
Third International 102
Third Neutrality Law 225
Third Reich 288
thousand-stitch girdles/belts 139, 182, 190
Tientsin 3, 29, 65, 86, 87, 115, 116, 124–127, 129, 130, 133, 136, 138, 142, 144, 145, 146, 203, 205, 207, 212, 213; *see also* Peking
Togo, Heihachiro (Japanese admiral) 34–36, 150
Toibana, Kurio (Japanese lieutenant commander/air operations officer) 298–300
Tojo, Hideki (Japanese general/chief of staff/vice minister of war) 73, 93, 124, 155, 202, 319
Tokugawa (clan) 5, 9, 11, 13
Tokugawa, Ieyasu (shogun) 5
Tokyo 5, 12, 13, 14, 17, 22, 25, 27, 30, 32, 33, 34, 38, 39, 40, 43, 53, 65, 71, 72, 76, 77, 78, 81, 82, 86, 93, 94, 95, 96, 101, 105, 112, 114, 115, 116, 123, 124, 127, 129, 132, 136, 137, 139, 140, 142, 145, 148, 151, 153, 161, 167, 169, 172, 174, 177, 178, 181, 182, 184, 190, 191, 192, 195, 200, 202, 207, 212, 213, 214, 215, 216, 218, 220, 233, 248, 258, 265, 267, 274, 280, 281, 283, 288, 295, 298, 301, 302, 303, 304, 312, 313, 320, 321; *see also* Edo
Tokyo Bay 7–8, 197
Tokyo High School 180
Tokyo Imperial University 98
Tokyo Stock Exchange 190
Tonkin Gulf 104
Tosa (clan) 9, 12, 16
Toseiha 74, 75, 93, 100; *see also* Control Faction
Toshihara, Tokaji (Japanese private) 165–166
Toyama 24
Toyama, Mitsuru 79, 133
Trans-Siberian Railway 31, 32, 49–50
Trautmann (German ambassador to China) 219–220, 288
Tsinan 54, 64, 66, 204, 207, 214
Tsingtao 40–41, 64, 129, 152, 204, 207, 319
Tsung-wu, Kao (head of Asiatic Department, Chinese foreign ministry) 146–147
Tsushima 34, 36, 69, 150
Tully, Grace (presidential secretary) 239–240
Tungchow 137–138
Tungshan 213
Tweedsmuir, Lord (governor general of Canada) 238
Twenty-One Demands 42–45, 99

Ueda, Kenkichi (Japanese general) 202, 216; *see also* Kwantung Army

352 Index

Uehara (Japanese general) 38
Ugaki, Issei (general, Japanese war minister) 60, 61, 66, 72, 74, 76, 81, 96, 106
Umezu, Yoshijiro (Japanese vice chief minister of war) 78, 97, 122, 132, 216

Vandenberg, Arthur (U.S. senator [R-MI]) 224, 231
Van Zeeland (Belgian prime minister) 255
Versailles Treaty 48, 216–217, 235
Victoria, Queen 10
Vladivostok 32, 34, 49, 50
Volunteers Act 60

Wachi Regiment see 11th Division
Wagner, Robert F. (U.S. senator [D-NY]) 231
Wakatsuki, Reijiro (Japanese prime minister) 59, 68, 78, 79, 83
Wake Island 54
Wallace, Henry 243
Wan Fulin (Chinese general) 206
Wang, C.T. (Chinese ambassador to the U.S.) 141, 144, 251
Wang Ching-wei (Chinese chairman of the Central Political Council) 149, 295, 319, 391
Wang Chung-hui (Chinese representative to the Permanent Court of International Justice/foreign minister) 114, 157
Wanping 2, 126, 129, 136
War Academy, German 23, 27, 31, see also Meckel
Warner, Gordon 184
Washington 260
Washington Conference of 1922 4, 21, 52, 54, 62, 68, 141, 222, 261
Washington Naval Treaty 90–92, 142
Washington Post 233
Wei Li-huang (Chinese general) 204
Weiheiwei 29
Weimar Republic 217
Welles, Sumner (U.S. under secretary of state) 222, 229–232, 235–238, 243, 247, 255, 268, 279
Wheeler, Burton K. (U.S. senator) 225
Whitehall 256; see also Britain
Wichita 235
Wiegand, Carl van (U.S. reporter) 262; see also Hearst newspapers
Wilson, Hugh (American chargé/assistant secretary of state) 247, 274–275, 308
Wilson, Woodrow (U.S. president) 21, 47–48, 50, 52, 53, 221, 223, 228, 236, 240, 246, 251, 301
Wing On (department store) 163
Wong, H.S. "Newsreel" 187
Woosung 160, 167, 180

Woosung Creek 165, 172
World War I 21, 52, 59, 60, 88, 108, 154, 172, 193, 194, 217, 222, 223, 224
World War II 17, 18, 35, 57, 64, 65, 88, 95, 101, 105, 125, 131, 139, 165, 167, 168, 175, 178, 183–184, 185, 197, 215, 310
Wuhu 153, 296, 301–302
Wusih 284–286

Xia Shujin 305–306

Yalu River 30, 32, 33
Yamagata, Aritomo (prince) 15–16, 31, 43–44, 51, 55, 58–60, 63, 68, 75
Yamamoto, Gombei (Japanese admiral) 39
Yamamoto, Isoroku (Japanese admiral) 88–90, 93, 118, 304
Yamashita, Tomoyuki 73
Yamato 92–93
Yamato spirit 19, 74, 89, 185
Yan Xishan see Yen Hsi-shan
Yanagawa, Heisuke (Japanese general/vice minister of war) 175–177, 283, 294
Yangtze River 139, 150, 152–153, 160, 165, 167, 175, 177, 178, 282, 285, 292–294, 296–299, 301–302, 304, 310, 312
Yangtze Valley 43, 218, 320
Yangtzepoo 157, 172
Yarnell, Harry E. (admiral, commander, U.S. Asiatic Fleet) 157, 158, 162, 298, 301
Yasuda 46
Yasukuni Shrine 161, 295
Yen Hsi-shan (Yan Xishan) 120, 149, 209–210
Yenan 135, 179, 208
Yenmen Pass 210
Yin Ju-keng 116
Yokohama 10, 12, 14, 15, 34, 52
Yokosuka 14, 34–35, 69
Yonai, Mitsumasa (Japanese admiral/Navy minister) 111, 128, 151–152, 191, 291, 300, 317
Yorktown 34, 150
Yoshida, Shigeru (Japanese ambassador to Great Britain) 102, 265
Yoshizawa, Kenkichi (Japanese foreign minister) 80
Yoshizawa, Seijuro (director of American Affairs Bureau, Japanese Foreign Office) 274
Young Officers, Imperial League of 60, 73, 94, 96–97, 185
Yuan Shih-kai (Chinese president) 43–44
Yuasa, Kuruhei (Japanese baron) 106, 215
Yungting River 1, 3, 127, 129, 139, 203–204

Zaibatsu (money groups) 46, 62, 63, 67, 74, 83
Zhukov (general) 19

www.ingramcontent.com/pod-product-compliance
Lightning Source LLC
Chambersburg PA
CBHW021340300426
44114CB00012B/1019